LATENCY

L A T E N C Y

Charles Sarnoff, M.D.

JASON ARONSON INC.
Northvale, New Jersey
London

To Allison and Jon,
only threads in the warp of
humankind, and yet to me
bigger than it all: their
role in the eternal puzzle.

CONTENTS

Preface   IX

Acknowledgments   XIII

Chapter 1   *INTRODUCTION*   3

Chapter 2   *THE STRUCTURE OF LATENCY*   13
        Freud and Latency • Current Concepts of Latency •
        Clinical Findings

Chapter 3   *SEXUAL DEVELOPMENT DURING
              THE LATENCY AGE*   37
        Motor and Fantasy Components of Masturbatory
        Activity: Infancy to Latency • Masturbatory
        Activity in Latency Age Girls • Masturbatory Activity in
        Latency Age Boys • Masturbatory Content During the
        State of Latency • Late Latency-Early Adolescence • Sexual
        Intercourse During the Latency Years • Prepubertal Fantasy
        Activity • The Impact of the First Menstrual Period • The
        Meaning of the First Ejaculation

Chapter 4   *COGNITIVE DEVELOPMENT*   85
        The Cognitive Organizing Periods of Latency • The First
        Cognitive Organizing Period • The Second Cognitive
        Organizing Period • The Third Cognitive Organizing
        Period • Cognition and Superego Development

Chapter 5   *THE WORK OF LATENCY*   147
Latency at Work • The Influence of Latency on Character •
The Influence of Latency on Society

Chapter 6   *PSYCHOTHERAPEUTIC STRATEGIES FOR*
               CLINICAL PROBLEMS OF
               LATENCY AGE CHILDREN   183
Specific Strategies • Strategies Utilizing the Potential of
the Structure of Latency • Working with Parents •
Modification of the Technique of Psychotherapy Required
by the Latency State • Ego and Latency Phase Cognitive
Growth • Starting Psychotherapy with a Child in
the Latency State • Problems of Motivation in Psychotherapy
in the Latency State • Terminating Psychotherapy with
a Child in the Latency State

Chapter 7   *SPECIAL TECHNICAL PROBLEMS OF*
               LATENCY AGE PSYCHOTHERAPY   263
Working with Slips of the Tongue • The Analysis and
Interpretation of Dreams • Differential Diagnosis of
Nocturnal Phenomena Occurring During Sleep in
Childhood • The Fetishes and Transitional Objects
of Childhood

Chapter 8   *PROJECTION AND PARANOIA*   299
Benign Persecutory States During the Latency Period •
Persecutory States of Pathological Significance During
the Latency Period • The Vicissitudes of Projection •
Manifestations of Projection During the Latency State •
Summary and Guidelines for Differential Diagnosis

Appendix A   *THE ONTOGENESIS OF*
               THE SYSTEM CONSCIOUSNESS   335

Appendix B   *THE ORIGINS OF LATENCY*
               IN PREHISTORY   343

Appendix C   *PATHOLOGICAL CONDITIONS*
               IN LATENCY   381

PREFACE

Now we know.

The period of "Latency" is rich in drives and developmental events.

It was not always thus.

In the psychoanalytic view of child development, the years six to twelve have traditionally been a quiet corner. The name *Latency*, which has been used to identify it, implies and reinforces this view. Indeed, even today, if one were to look at the latency years from the prospect of the psychotherapeutic-free associations of patients in analysis, there would appear to be confirmation of the idea that little happens during these years. Memories from these years make little contribution to the spontaneous psychotherapeutic work and associations of adults.

The concept of latency as a wasteland is seemingly confirmed by work with adults. This wasteland concept becomes bewilderingly inaccurate when applied by those who work with children directly. The latency years contain a roiling cauldron of developmental events, from which emerge adolescence and adult life. Experience during the latency years influences fantasy and the distortions of adult life. Latency-age reparative mastery works through prelatency fantasy and clears the way for normality in adult life. Conclusions derived from child observation and child therapy tear a "Tarnhelm" (the magic cap of invisibility) from the events of the latency years and reveal "Latency" as a fundamental and important period in human development. As well, latency holds the spectres of future troubles to be confronted and overcome.

Bringing "Latency" reality to the forefront and setting aside misconceptions derived from the concept of "Latency as silent years" has been a slow and unheralded development in the evolution of psychoanalysis and child development. One of the elements in this process was the codification of the experience of one analytically trained child psychiatrist. Thirteen years ago it was published in this book. Before that, attempts to find an audience for clinical reports of extensive drive manifestations in latency-age children were stifled by criticisms that discounted the reports as impossible. The drives of latency-age children were thought to be too weak to produce such derivatives. The first paper was turned down by three journals before the *Psychoanalytic Quarterly* published it as a lead article. The article drew lecture invitations. Occasional lectures evolved into a yearly lecture series in the child development course at the Columbia University Psychoanalytic Clinic for Training and Research. Then came this book. Interested clinicians asked questions and invited me to lecture on topics of their choice. The new lectures organized themselves around topics related to normal and pathological development and treatment during the latency years. These lectures were expanded to become the published book *Psychotherapeutic Strategies During the Latency Years*. A natural outgrowth of the conceptualization of "Latency" as a potent time filled with energy and seminal events was the organization of observations into a theory that would encompass the period of transition between "Latency" and adolescence. Such an undertaking produced a developmental psychology with new details and insights to replace a theory that saw late latency-early adolescence as a momentary fracture between two phases. Late latency-early adolescence has become a phase in its own right with its own development, pathology, and psychotherapeutic treatment strategies. These observations were published in *Psychotherapeutic Strategies in Late Latency through Early Adolescence*.

In recent years, few writers or leaders have devoted themselves to a focus on the topic of "Latency." It has not become a platform for leadership. The most intense responses to its message have come from child therapists and clinical supervisors, who have consistently bought and recommended this book through many printings, and whose interest has generated this new edition. "Latency" as a fundamental developmental period with derivatives in adolescence and adult life has flourished only on its merits. It is likely, therefore, that it will continue to grow when I no longer speak for it. This is only just, for it is the slow but certain outcome of truth's career.

CAS
Great Neck, N. Y.
August 1989

ACKNOWLEDGMENTS

I have been particularly helped and encouraged in this work by Dr. Isadore Bernstein, Dr. Rhoda Lorand, and Dr. Otto Sperling. I should also like to thank my wife Carole for help in proofreading and Mrs. Deborah Tax for typing. Seminars form invaluable opportunities for the clarification of concepts. I am indebted to the following colleagues for their help as this work evolved over the past fifteen years: Dr. Marion Hart, Dr. Leni Estampador, Dr. Fred Henderson, and Dr. George Landberg.

In addition, the cultural and anthropological aspects of this book have been strengthened by my participation in the Interdisciplinary Colloquium in Anthropology and Psychoanalysis of the American Psychoanalytic Association. Each member of the group has helped me to correct and to revise ideas. Foremost among these have been Dr. L. Bryce Boyer, Professor Joseph Campbell, Professor Arthur Hippler, and Professor Robert Murphy.

The preliminary work on this book was a labor of many years. Here and there within the text are specific reflections of this effort, contained in adaptations and revisions of brief sections of material published in scholarly journals during these years. I should like, at this point, especially to express my gratitude to the editors of the *Psychoanalytic Quarterly*, the *International Journal of Psycho-Analysis*, and the *Journal of the American Academy of Child Psychiatry* for granting permission for extended adaptations of material which appeared in their journals for use in this book: pages 14 to 36 from Sarnoff (1971a); pages 72 to 82 from Hart and Sarnoff (1971); pages 94 to 103 from Sarnoff (1970); and pages 312 to 327 from Sarnoff (1972b).

Charles Sarnoff, M.D.

Chapter 1

INTRODUCTION

Therapist: Is it really so tough being eight years old?
Child: How would you like to be half the size of
everybody else and not have a dime to
your name?

Long before I first set foot on the psychiatric scene, the term *latency* had fallen into a state of disuse. Few could countenance the idea of a totally subdued childhood in the face of clear clinical evidence of hyperactivity in children and the everyday testimony that literally shrieked of childhood's excitement from schoolyards, parks, and playgrounds. By chance, I myself had entered child psychiatry in the company of some who still believed firmly that latency children were quiet and that the drives diminished in latency to almost nonexistence. What they believed, they saw, and I, wishing to find a place among them, was ready to agree and to see as they saw. My attempts to carry through this intention were short-lived. The very first latency age youngster to whom I was assigned as a therapist tore the theory to shreds and cast it to the winds. This, for me at least, put an end forever to any imagery that could conceive of adolescence in terms of a fire in spring which followed hard upon the dormant winter days of latency. Whatever adult form that patient may have taken now, I hardly can guess. He would be twenty-five or twenty-six years old. When I met him, he was almost seven. He was blond and his eyes were blue. A sweet spring afternoon called one's thoughts only fleetingly from the clinic. The thought of an hour talking to a "latency child" was not an unpleasant prospect. What it was, was an idle dream.

He hadn't read the books I'd read. He could have written this one. His first words contained a command that I carry him piggyback. I suggested a game and went to get some equipment. Before I could get to the storeroom, someone noticed smoke. I rushed back to the therapy room to protect the child from burning, only to discover that it was he who had set fire to the furniture.

I hardly fared better with my second latency child. She was sad-looking and quiet. In the therapy room after I told her she could choose her own activities and do as she wished there, she asked, "Can I even jump out the window?" I asked, somewhat startled, "Where did you get that from?" She answered, "The lady who talks in my ear."

My third latency child was quiet in the sessions. He was so quiet and bereft of achievement that the working differential diagnosis required that mental deficiency be ruled out. He was eight years of age and had recently begun to rub his wrists together when in situations which were stimulating. He also misbehaved at home and in the classroom. I asked him why he rubbed his wrists. He told me that if he did not, his "tushie itched." I obtained toy shields and swords and engaged him in swordplay. His hands were full. His excitement and tension mounted. He tried to rub his wrists together but the straps of the shield prevented this. He dropped the sword and began to rub his anus. He then took a pencil and drew an amorphous cylindrical shape. "What is it?" asked I. "Smoke," said he. He then began to chant, while staring at his drawing:

> From the land beyond beyond,
> From the world that knows no fear,
> I bid thee, genie, now appear!

My early experiences in working with latency age children gave me little to support the concept of latency as a state of diminished drive activity. States of extreme excitement, psychotic states, and anally fixated fantasy-dominated states were readily apparent. Where was the quiet, the calm, the pliability, and the educability that marked the latency age child and led to the belief that drives were diminished in the latency age period? Those who had developed and taught the concept of latency were brilliant clinicians and skilled in the construction of theories. There must have been something that they had seen that typified the behavior of children six to twelve years of age which justified their conclusions. If I wanted to be a good child psychiatrist, I had to search it down and know what it consists of and what produces it. Since the state of functioning during late childhood had produced a theory which had been related to latency age children in general, it was logical to conclude that it was a normal state. Apparently, the child guidance clinic was no place to look for it. Equally apparent was the parallel conclusion that states of psychopathology in latency age children reflected a failure to achieve or maintain this state of latency. Beyond the clinic, in placid homes and in schools, latency age children who had achieved a state of latency were to be found. By and large their lives are characterized by a calm. They have no apparent sexual outlets, the amount of masturbation being markedly reduced in relation to similar activities in prelatency and adolescent children. Their energies are discharged in sports, intense horseplay and teasing, work and fantasy of many forms. More often than not, the fantasy is played out in games such as cops and robbers or hide and seek.

The typical latency age boy is mostly well behaved, patterning himself as best as he can after his father. He understands guilt and does his best to behave in a manner that will win the approval of adults even when they are not present. He develops strong and lasting friendships, but always with boys. Girls, though related to in passing, must be avoided when boy pals are around. He throws himself without cynicism or second thought into group activities which are microcosms of what he knows best of adult life. When playing baseball, the score, the plays, and the outcome are real and important. Sandlot play becomes the World Series. He is an inveterate collector. Anything that has a distinctive form or color and is small enough to fit in his pocket or is subject to categorization becomes his domain. Cards with pictures of favorite athletes, coins, stamps, pennies, shells, and stones are lined up on shelves or glued to boards.

The typical latency age girl is a good little girl. She is sweet and cuddly, lovely to hold and to behold. She is mother's helper and daddy's friend. She follows her mother about joining in the chores and learning household skills as well as any activity the parents place before her. She forms close, if impermanent ties with groups of girls, and these groups tend to be larger than those with which boys are involved. Activities such as Girl Scout meetings are taken quite seriously. Ballet lessons become the basis for belief that stardom and a life's career in dance are only a matter of growing up. Boys can be treated as friends briefly, but the appearance of girl friends on the scene results in the immediate fall from grace of newly

found male friends. Alliances among girls are less stable than those between latency age boys. There are fights, breakups, and makeups in unending series. Parents find it is best not to criticize an enemy for fear she
will be a best friend tomorrow. Close groups of girls are often organized
into short-lived clubs whose sole purpose, as far as I have ever been able to
find out, is the exclusion of a classmate or friend who has offended one of
their number.

Both girls and boys of latency age find a ready escape from painful situations and disappointments by entering a world of fantasy which is believed in as firmly as the baseball games and ballet lessons just described.
A period of arduous difficulty and chaotic interaction with parents comes
to an end when the child can combat the humiliation that he feels by entering a dream world in which wrongs are righted and his image of himself
is restored to a reassuring sense of improved self-worth. The metamorphosis is so complete that some children leave themselves notes upon
retiring to remind them in the morning of their anger at their parents.
Barrie, in *Peter Pan*, attributed this cleansing of bad thoughts from the
minds of sleeping children to the activities of diligent mothers who
searched about in their children's thoughts and removed the unpleasant
ones. The resulting maintenance of childhood calm in the face of stresses
appears to be the core of the process that returns the latency age child to
an emotional equilibrium and has resulted in the surface impression that
sources of emotional difficulty are latent during this period. Apparently a
well-structured universal process is involved in the maintenance of this
stability. There is not a decline in drive energy; rather, a personality
process is activated. The land of fantasy and dreams provides the locale
and a key to the process. I could find no alternative to the conclusion that
even in this Arcadia, there is an ego.

The process was brought into focus for me in stunning fashion. The
father of a patient called and asked for an appointment to see me. His son
was a rebellious late latency child who often fought with his father at the
dinner table. The father came with advice to give me, rather than in search
of information. He advised me to augment my techniques with foolproof
advice to parents aimed at bringing wayward youngsters into line. I listened eagerly for some good advice. "Beat them," said the father, "That's
what I do. When he doesn't behave at the table, I beat him. He runs away
bawling, but is back in a few minutes as quiet and well-behaved as you
could want." I could not convince the father of the error of his ways. He

was sure of his technique because the results were so good. In the next session with the boy, I asked him about it. He confided that it worked well. "At first I'm angry. I run upstairs saying, I could kill him, I could kill him. I throw myself on the bed and shout it into the pillow. Then it's all gone. I feel okay. I go back downstairs. I eat. Everything is calm. You should tell the other parents about it." He had been doodling as he talked. I asked him to explain what appeared to be a map. "It's the banks near here," said he, "I'm planning a robbery." He unfolded a fantasy of robbing banks, his parents, and his neighbors. The reaction to the beating by his father had been dissipated through the medium of fantasy. Real objects are not sought for the discharge of drives during latency as they are during early childhood and adolescence. Fantasy becomes the channel for discharge. When real objects are involved they serve only as armatures upon which form derived from fantasy is projected. When a latency age child is stressed, this pattern of pathways for discharge is activated and the drives and fantasies involved in the response to the stress are dissipated through fantasy. I soon found that such dissipation of stress responses was not the only process that was resolved through this pattern of pathways for discharge. The normal excitements, seen for instance in prelatency children, which had been discharged through masturbation, contact with objects, and the evocation of memories of past experiences of gratification, are denied expression for long periods by teachers and parents in latency age children. Words and culture myths are provided for use for discharge of energies. In this way drives are harnessed to the process of acquiring the traditions of culture.

I came to call this pattern of pathways for discharge, which operates when other pathways are forbidden, the *structure of latency*. When this process is active, available, and effective, the latency age child is in a *state of latency*. It is the potential for achieving this state that defines the years six to twelve as the latency age.

Armed with the information that such an ego structure is the keystone of the latency state, I was able to study the behavior of latency age children from the standpoint of the ego. Latency states are not homogeneous throughout the six years of the latency period. There are characteristics at different ages which can be related to cognitive maturation and social pressure. Because of the flexibility of the ego at this age, the characteristic calm of latency can easily give way to excited destructive behavior and overt sexual play. This breakthrough phenomenon can be seen in a number of situations with great frequency and is probably the source of the tendency to question the entire concept of latency in the minds of professionals and lay public alike. The most common break in the latency pattern is the socially approved recess period. The children are given time to let off steam and to run and play. The effect is like the Saturnalia of ancient Rome. Permissiveness helps to release tension and reinforces the ability of the child to conform in situations in which conformity is demanded, as occurs in the classroom.

A frequent challenge to the concept of latency is based on this excited behavior of children at recess in schools. Clearly latency is a result of a variable state of the defenses and not the unchanging product of a diminution of drives. "Latency," not always seen from six to twelve, is often present from 9:00 to 11:30 A.M. A child whose behavior in his sessions was usually well modulated and controlled came in one day with no ability to sit still. He jumped up and down, played with a ball in an excited fashion and seemed on the brink of breaking furniture. When I asked him why he was so excited, he replied that the teacher had not given them recess and that he had had no chance to let off steam till he got to my office.

A common indicator of a break in the latency state is the appearance of projection. The use of projection that is inherent in latency fantasy becomes the most noticeable characteristic of latency age function when the child is exposed to an accusation of responsibility for a wrong. A boy of six and a half years rode his bike past some people who were proudly displaying pails of clams that they had dug up from a nearby saltwater inlet. His control was not good and he sideswiped one of the pails, spilling the clams all over the walk. When reproached, he insisted that his sister, who was half a block away, had pushed him. He was subject to episodes of depression which followed wrongdoing. During these times he heard the voice of a man inside his head criticizing him. Another situation in which the breakthrough of drives occurs in latency relates to the diminution in ego strength that accompanies sensory deprivation. Exposure to darkness tends to propagate the use of projection. An eight-year-old boy sat terrified at the sight of a monster that sat near the foot of his bed. He called to his parents, who turned on the light. The four-legged demon turned out to be a table with clothes on it. A ten-year-old girl became nauseated whenever she was put to bed. This caused her to seek out her parents and to try to crawl into their bed. Investigations revealed that she feared a kidnapper and attacker whom, she placed in the closet when it was dark.

As the investigation of the varying strengths and circumstances of occurrence of the latency state progressed, it became apparent that the state itself was not universal. Certain children were not capable of it. Indeed, there were youngsters who had failed to enter latency. Typically, these youngsters were intensely stimulated by parental cruelty, nudity, or seduction. Their capacity to form symbols was minimal, as was their awareness of the definition of guilt. They were overexcited and hyperactive, with little in the way of attention span or ability to delay. One such six-year-old boy continuously disrupted his classes, talked out of turn, drew pictures with sexual reference on the blackboard, and could recall nothing of stories seen on television save the excitements, fights, and explosions depicted. Story contents were unknown to him. "What is your favorite program on TV?" asked I. "Popeye," said he. "Tell me about it. Tell me your favorite Popeye story," I said. He answered by telling me about how Popeye punched the big guy and the fight followed.

Some children can enter latency showing calm, pliability, and educability but cannot retain the state under stress. Thus, a child with good behavior in school can become anxious, excited, and disruptive in the less structured environment at home. One such child went into acute anxiety states days in advance of school activities that she feared. She showed no evidence of discomfort in school. She showed discomfort only at home, discomforting her parents as well. Her capacity to use symbols spontaneously was poorly developed. She was therefore unable to form fantasies as alternative pathways for discharge.

Other children, who are able to enter into a state of latency through an excellent capacity to symbolize and form fantasies that contain plans to undo humiliations, are still apt to become involved in excited misbehavior. This does not negate the concept that fantasy is a discharge pathway during the latency age period. Every organ of the body and every structure of the mind which has a use can be found to have states of misuse. The latter processes underlie pathology. Such outcomes in the structure of latency are multiple. If stresses are great enough the fantasy that had been used to lower instinctual pressure may itself become the template for an assault on the world. The boy whose beatings at the hands of his father led him to fantasies of theft crowned a period of such beatings with an actual robbery. No matter how complex the fantasies, should reality bow to meet them unbidden, the child will cease to strive. His development stops. In later years such children enter the adult world unprepared. While I was chief of psychiatry in a community mental health center in the Brownsville poverty area in Brooklyn, I was called to interview a ten-year-old boy who failed to apply himself in school though he was bright and well organized enough to succeed. I went to his school to see him. He was a sturdy, good-looking youngster with a single gold ring in his right ear. His fantasy was to be a "street dude." To him this meant patterning himself after older youths he had seen who he claimed lived off the streets stealing pocket-books from old ladies and "selling." At the age of ten he could live like a grownup. More specifically, he could live like one of the grownups he admired. Reading, school, education held no promise for him that could equal the short circuit to manhood provided by acting on his dreams. There were members of his community who cheered him on. Data in his school record confirmed that he was actually involved in the thefts he described.

The eventual outcome of the use of fantasy to undo humiliation in latency is the shift in the symbolic content of the fantasies to signifiers whose identity and nature are realistic and among the cherished culture elements of a useful and creative society. When this transition has occurred we no longer say that the child has fantasies. Instead we say that he deals with stress through mobilization of good future planning. The calm, the pliability, and the educability of the latency period coupled with the frustrating dichotomy between transient fantasy and the unreachable nature of reality fulfillments make fertile ground for preparations for tomorrow. Through written and spoken words, the traditions and elements of society are transmitted during latency. Skills in the media for the transmission of these elements are vital to adult success. In the construction of fantasies, fantastic elements are replaced by social realities as the result of the work of latency. An understanding of the nature of society and its demands on the individual is conveyed from one generation to the next. Latency apparently serves culture as an arterial conduit conveying the "lifeblood of master spirits" through the generations. What follows is a study of the events and importance of latency, both as an age and a state, wherein may be found the portal to manhood and to mankind.

Chapter 2

THE STRUCTURE OF LATENCY

To H.C., six years old

Oh thou! whose fancies from afar are brought;
Who of thy words dost make a mock apparel,
And fittest to unutterable thought
The breeze-like motion and the self-born carol. . . .

—William Wordsworth

Since its introduction in 1905 the term *latency* has been used ambiguously. Understanding of the concept is obscured by confusion surrounding the use of the word. There are a number of definitions of latency, the most common of which follow:

1. The time period from six to twelve years of age. Here age is taken as the sole criterion.

2. A psychic phase whose time of onset and content are physiologically determined. Clinically this phase is characterized by a well-behaved, pliable, and educable child. A change in the defensive organization of the ego is not implicated; rather, modifications in the behavior of the child are attributed to a change in the drives at a preordained time—a biological lessening of drive activities.

3. A period of static defenses during which a reorganization of the ego defenses results in a stable condition in which the child becomes well-behaved, pliable, and educable. Hereditary, historical, and phylogenetic factors are implicated.

4. A period of dynamic defenses when the child experiences a complex reorganization of the defensive structure of the ego. The state of good be-

havior, pliability, and educability is maintained only as a result of an equilibrium between defenses and drives. This state is possible because of the evolution and ontogenesis of mechanisms of defense that can produce it. However, it is not obligatory and is facultatively present at the discretion of the culture in which the individual lives.

Disparate as these definitions are, the word itself is rarely used with identifying qualifications. Yet a clear usage for "latency" can be achieved if modifying phrases are added which sharpen meaning. "Latency age period" and "state of latency" are examples. My purpose in this book is to explain these concepts of latency and their usefulness in understanding growth, development, and psychopathology in the years six to twelve. But first some historical review may be useful.

Freud and Latency

In 1908 in "Character and Anal Erotism," Freud fixed the timing of latency to that period of life with which we now associate it: "the period of 'sexual latency'—i.e., from the completion of the fifth year to the first manifestations of puberty (round about the eleventh year) . . ." (p. 171).

The concept of latency as the product of a "biological lessening of drive activities" is mentioned directly by Freud only once. In his 1926 paper "The Question of Lay Analysis," he says: "During [the period of latency] sexuality normally advances no further; on the contrary, the sexual urges diminish in strength . . ." (p. 210). The drive diminution theory emphasizes the role of biology, heredity, and the id while lessening the role of the ego. Thus latency becomes a preordained and physiologically determined obligatory stage in human development. The great influence of the drive diminution theory probably relates to the fact that it was really Freud's final statement on the subject. Though his last thoughts on latency were published in *Moses and Monotheism* (1939) and *An Outline of Psychoanalysis* (1940), there was little in these works that could be used to support a contradiction of the drive diminution theory.

The concept of latency as an organization of ego defenses, both static and dynamic, was explored in depth by Freud before 1926.

The forerunner of an idea of a mechanism of defense in latency is contained in a letter to Fliess dated May 30, 1896 (to be found in *The Origins of Psychoanalysis*, 1950). Freud mentions two periods, "A and B [as] the transitional periods during which repression usually takes place" (p. 163). ". . . Morality and aversion to sexuality . . . in A and B, provide the motives of defense for obsessional neurosis and hysteria . . ." (p. 165).

In "Three Essays on the Theory of Sexuality" (1905) the concept of defense in latency is presented. "It is during this period of total or only partial latency that are built up the mental forces which are later to impede the course of the sexual instinct . . ." (p. 177). What are these mental forces? Freud points toward suppression as the mechanism responsible for latency. "[The] germs of sexual impulses are already present in the newborn child and . . . these continue to develop for a time, but are then overtaken by a progressive process of suppression. . . . Nothing is known for certain concerning the regularity and periodicity of this oscillating course of development" (p. 176).

What is the origin of this "oscillating course of development"? Freud tells us that the ego structure in latency develops from phylogenetic and physiological-hereditary bases. ". . . [The] period of total or only partial latency . . . is organically determined and fixed by heredity . . ." (p. 177). The strength of the drives is seen as sustained; ". . . the activity of those impulses [infantile sexual impulses] does not cease even during this period of latency, though their energy is diverted, wholly or in great part, from their sexual use and directed to other ends [that is, sublimation and reaction-formation]" (p. 178). "From time to time a fragmentary manifestation of sexuality which has evaded sublimation may break through; or some sexual activity may persist through the whole duration of the latency period until the sexual instinct emerges with greater intensity at puberty" (p. 179). One of the factors that can effect this breakthrough is seduction: ". . . external influences of seduction are capable of provoking interruptions of the latency period or even its cessation, and in this connection the sexual instinct of children proves in fact to be polymorphously perverse . . ." (p. 234). Clearly, at this point (1905) latency was seen as a situation in which the strength of the defenses dammed up the drives. At any time, the defenses might be shattered and the ever-present undiminished impact of the drives revealed. Here we find the beginning of the concept of latency as dynamic defense.

Latency as dynamic defense is further developed by Freud in "Character and Anal Erotism" (1908). "During the period of life which may be called the period of 'sexual latency' . . . reaction-formations, or counterforces, such as shame, disgust and morality, are created in the mind. They are actually formed at the expense of the excitations proceeding from the erogenic zones . . ." (p. 171). The question of whether latency produces defenses or whether defenses produce latency is not clearly delineated at this point. A relationship to defense is seen as of primary importance and the drives are seen as transmuted qualitatively but not changed quantitatively.

In "Formulations on the Two Principles of Mental Functioning" (1911) Freud introduced fantasy formation as an adaptive regressive defense related to latency: "The long period of latency, which delays sexual development until puberty . . ., [results in a situation in which] . . ., the sexual instinct . . . remains far longer under the dominance of the pleasure principle. . . . In consequence of these conditions, a closer connection arises . . . between the sexual instinct and fantasy . . ." (p. 222). Satisfaction in reality is withheld from the drives, and fantasies develop for the alternative discharge of the drives. A predominance of the fantasy-forming function of the ego in the presence of immature reality testing is one of the key elements in the ego structure in latency.

In *Introductory Lectures on Psychoanalysis* (1915), Freud said: "From about the sixth to the eighth year of life onwards, we can observe a halt and retrogression in sexual development, which, in cases where it is most propitious culturally, deserves to be called a period of latency. The latency period may also be absent: it need not bring with it any interruption of sexual activity and sexual interests along the whole line" (p. 326). Here we find the implication that latency is a cultural matter.

In *Group Psychology and the Analysis of the Ego* (1921), defenses are described as factors producing latency. Freud states: ". . . the Oedipus complex, succumbs . . . from the beginning of the period of latency onwards to a wave of repression" (p. 138).

In "Two Encyclopaedia Articles" (1922), Freud referred to the role of latency in the transmission of ethics. "Towards the end of the fifth year [the] early period of sexual life normally comes to an end. It is succeeded by a period of more or less complete *latency*, during which ethical restraints are built up, to act as defenses against the desires of the Oedipus complex" (p. 246).

By 1922, development of the concept of latency had reached the point at which a purely psychological theory of latency as a manifestation of ego function might have been formulated. However, in 1923 Freud's writings on latency again began to turn toward hereditary, biological, and physiological factors, first mentioned in "Three Essays on the Theory of Sexuality" (1905). In *The Ego and the Id* (1923) he speaks of the biological and historical factors in the child's lengthy dependence and ". . . of his Oedipus complex, the repression of which we have shown to be connected with the interruption of libidinal development by the latency period and so with the diphasic onset of man's sexual life" (p. 35).

In *A Short Account of Psycho-Analysis* (1924), Freud again describes latency in terms of defense. He says, ". . . sexual life reaches a first climax in the third to fifth years of life, and then, after a period of inhibition, sets in again at puberty" (p. 208).

In 1923, the time he was writing *A Short Account*, Freud's concept of latency contained two divergent points of view which might be considered contradictory. One was the sociological-psychological theory in which the defenses of the ego respond to psychological needs under the pressure of social demands; the other, the theory that latency is produced by a phylogenetic historical-physiological hereditary complex. In the latter, latency is a state in which defenses are brought to bear on the drives as part of a developmental step whose timing is determined by heredity. In 1924 Freud's works contained both points of view.

In "The Dissolution of the Oedipus Complex," published in 1924, he indicates that the passing of the Oedipus complex and the onset of latency are defensive responses to fear of castration. There is a clear statement of the role of defenses (sublimation) in the onset of latency. "The libidinal trends belonging to the Oedipus complex are in part desexualized and sublimated. . . . The whole process has, on the one hand, preserved the genital organ . . . and on the other, has paralyzed it—has removed its function. This process ushers in the latency period, which now interrupts the child's sexual development" (p. 177). Elsewhere in the paper he describes the passing of the Oedipus complex with the appearance of latency as the "next preordained phase of development" (p. 174). In one paper, then, latency as a preordained phase is juxtaposed to latency as a phase which is ushered in by the ego mechanisms of desexualization and sublimation of libidinal trends. The two points of view seem irreconcilable. Freud, of course, recognized the dichotomy and stated that "the justice of both these views cannot be disputed" (p. 174).

Freud finally resolved this problem in 1924, in *An Autobiographical Study*. Repression initiates latency. Reaction-formations are produced during latency. The ego that produces latency is, in turn, a product of phylogenesis. Freud states: "For the most remarkable feature of the sexual life of man is its *diphasic* onset, its onset in two waves, with an interval between them. It reaches a first climax in the fourth or fifth year of a child's life. But thereafter this early efflorescence of sexuality passes off; the sexual impulses which have shown such liveliness are overcome by repression, and a *period of latency* follows, which lasts until puberty and during which the *reaction-formations* of morality, shame, and disgust are built up" (p. 37). In a footnote added in 1935 he said: "The period of latency is a physiological phenomenon. It can, however, only give rise to a complete interruption of sexual life in cultural organizations which have made the suppression of infantile sexuality a part of their system" (p. 37, n.).

At some time in the phylogenesis of man, mutation and selection provided the ego function that would permit and support latency as we know it. This much is the hereditary and physiological sine qua non of latency. In those individuals who live in a society that demands a latency period, and whose parents conform to the society's demands, these ego functions produce latency.

Physiological views of latency, then, have their roots in the physiological and hereditary factors described by Freud. The concept of latency as a state characterized by social determinants also has roots in the views of latency expressed by Freud in *An Autobiographical Study* (1925). Here Freud describes factors that trigger structures of the ego to produce predictable patterns of behavior, which may not be fixed throughout the entire period.

In "Inhibitions, Symptoms and Anxiety" (1926a), Freud gave an even more detailed picture of his concept of the ego functions related to the production of latency in man. The concept of retrogression mentioned in *Introductory Lectures on Psychoanalysis* (1916-1917) is elaborated into the concept that regression is active in the establishment of latency. He says: "The genital organization of the libido turns out to be feeble and insufficiently resistant, so that when the ego begins its defensive efforts the first thing it succeeds in doing is to throw back the genital organization (of the phallic phase), in whole or in part, to the earlier sadistic-anal level. This fact of regression is decisive for all that follows" (1926, p. 113). Here regression is described as one of the defenses. "We can most clearly recognize that the motive force of defense is the castration complex and that what is being fended off are the trends of the Oedipus complex. We are at present dealing with the beginning of the latency period . . ." (p. 114).

Current Concepts of Latency

The theory of the primary diminution of drive activity in latency is mentioned by Anna Freud in *Normality and Pathology in Childhood: Assessments of Development* (1965). She speaks of "the post-oedipal lessening of drive urgency and the transference of the libido from the parental figures . . ." (p. 66). Later she states: "Extreme castration fear, death fears and wishes, together with the defenses against them, which dominate the scene at the height of the phallic-oedipal phase, and which create the well-known inhibitions, masculine overcompensations, passive and regressive modes of the period . . . disappear as if by magic as soon as the child takes the first steps into the latency period . . . as an immediate reaction to the *biologically determined lessening of drive activity*" (p. 163; italics mine). "The drop in pressure from the drives at this time corresponds to the high level of social response during latency" (p. 179). In a panel discussion on latency at a meeting of the American Psychoanalytic Association in 1956, Maurice Friend speculated that "there may be a biological diminution in the libidinal drive, in addition to repression, which then allows the aggressive energy to predominate" (1957, p. 528). In a panel discussion on child analysis in 1951 (published in *The Psychoanalytic Study of the Child*), Berta Bornstein divided latency into two phases (five-and-a-half to eight, and eight to ten). One of the characteristics of the later period is that "sexual demands have become less exerting . . ." (p. 281).

The theory that the origins of latency lie in the defenses that make up a part of the ego was also put forth in the panel discussion and in Mrs. Bornstein's paper. She described "surging impulses" and said that "temporary regression to pregenitality is adopted by the ego. . . ." She notes further that new defenses against the pregenital impulses must be evolved by the child, reaction-formations being one defense (p. 280). These concepts relate to those delineated in *Inhibitions, Symptoms and Anxiety* (1926). Throughout the recent literature mention is made of a sustained masturbatory temptation in latency which must be continuously defended against. One can well conclude that the existence of this temptation attests to the sustained strength of the drives during the onset of latency. Nor is a diminution of the urgency of drives reflected in any lessening of the defenses that are maintained to balance their force (e.g., reaction-formation).

Clinical Findings

The theory of latency as defense is supported by clinical findings, as the following observations, based primarily on psychoanalysis of latency age children will show. I have also occasionally referred to children seen in diagnostic situations and in psychotherapy.

CASE 1

When a child moves from prelatency into latency during a psychoanalysis, one can observe a shift from acting out of pregenital, genital, and oedipal wishes with members of the immediate family to a situation in which excited feelings with the family are felt only momentarily. These are dealt with through a complex of defenses resulting in the appearance of fantasies or fantasy-oriented actions which at one and the same time conceal and reveal the true attitudes and reactions of the child. These fantasies require little energy and free the rest of the child's energies for useful work.

A little girl was brought to analysis at age six because of failure to progress to reading readiness in the first grade, lack of spontaneity, regressed behavior, and uncontrolled masturbation. As an infant she was picked up continually; she was weaned at twenty-eight months. She walked at twelve months and talked at sixteen months. She had been toilet trained at three after a stormy and scream-filled period of pressure from her mother. Bladder training had been delayed until this age because of a constriction of the urethra which required sounding. Concurrent with a separation of several months from her parents, which took place after toilet training had been completed, there was regression in bladder control.

At the start of treatment the child would come into the playroom without her mother, but would soon want to return to her in the waiting room. After about three weeks she began to have episodes of encopresis on the way to, and during, the sessions. Because of these episodes it was necessary for the mother to clean her. Just preceding the onset of the encopresis the mother had stopped washing and cleaning the child's perineum after she had gone to the bathroom. It can be assumed the resulting diminution in stimulation was a factor in a concomitant cessation of the child's open masturbation.

I repeatedly told the patient that she wished to remain a baby and not grow up. At times she herself said this spontaneously. I pointed out to her the role of the encopresis in helping her to remain a little baby who is taken care of by mother and that if she were successful, she wouldn't learn or get to be a mommy herself. The encopretic episodes soon gave way to periods during which she would insist upon straightening up my office. During this activity she talked about how the maid would scream if she could see how messy things were. With this change of behavior, she began to report fantasies and was able to begin the first steps in reading. She had entered the latency stage. A return to perineal cleansing and stimulation by the father after toileting evoked a resurgence of oedipal feelings. When the mother reproved the father, the child ordered the mother out of the room saying, "Go away and leave us alone. I like it." Thus the drives were available to the child in full strength in spite of the onset of latency.

This case illustrates the association between anal regression, reaction-formations, and the freeing of energy for useful work that occurs with the onset of latency, as well as the sustained availability of drive strength during the latency time period.

CASE 2

Perhaps the most telling clinical observation to contradict the theory that in latency "sexual urges diminish in strength" (Freud, 1926, p. 210) is the fact that sexual intercourse is possible during latency. It occurs in children who have been seduced into genital sexual activity.

A nine-year-old girl, who lived in a foster home, was seen once a week in psychotherapy because of periods of excitement and forgetfulness whenever the family was preparing to visit the foster mother's aunt. At other times she was alert and calm and did average work in school. The child had little to say about the episodes of excitement and confusion. Matters were somewhat clarified when the child's social worker received a report from the foster mother that during a visit to the aunt, the child had as usual retired with her thirteen-year-old foster cousin to his room to play. When the foster mother found that she had to leave earlier than expected, she went to the room to get the girl and found the two children "mating." This behavior was prohibited on subsequent visits and the child's episodes of excitement and forgetfulness stopped.

The child explained to me that she had first been introduced to sexual intercourse by her brother when she was six and he was seven. At the time, they lived with their mother in a two-room apartment with curtains but no doors between the rooms. The children, peeking through the curtains, were able to observe the mother having intercourse with a series of men each day. Eventually they imitated what they saw. The brother had initially been placed in a cottage setting with other boys, but frequent attempts to seduce these boys into anal intercourse led to his placement in a foster home at the age of eight. There were unsubstantiated reports from his school that he was accepting money from older boys for his passive participation in anal intercourse.

In these children urgency of the sexual drive was not diminished. Hence the changes that occur in latency cannot be explained in terms of a diminution in drive energies, but rather through a shift in the way they are discharged. The drives in latency may be stirred into activity at any time by seduction or sympathetic stimulation. The regression that occurs in the face of oedipal stresses results in the replacement of phallic drives with anal-sadistic drives, which are then defended against by the appearance of the mechanisms of defense that typify the character of the latency child. These are sublimation, reaction-formation, fantasy, regression, and repression.

These latency defenses permit the child to direct his energies toward co-operative behavior and learning. What happens when a situation in real life threatens to bring the sadomasochistic drives out into the open? What happens when the life situations reawaken the phallic oedipal wishes? In some children, as in Case 2, there is a deterioration of the latency defenses. Normally, there is a protective set of mechanisms within the structure of the ego (the structure of latency) that comes into action and preserves the latency. When a latency child has thoughts, excitements, and fantasies about a parent with whom he is directly involved, drives may be stimulated and threaten the stability of the latency adjustment. Examples of this situation may be seen in the case of a cruelly punishing father who provokes aggressive or murderous feelings in his son, or in the case of a seductive parent who stimulates fear of retaliation from the parent of the same sex. The content of the stimulating situation is repressed quickly and replaced with substitute mental events, including highly detailed fantasies. These substitute mental events take such forms as fantasies of carefully planned robberies, fears of being attacked or kidnapped, romantic thoughts of marriage, and sexual relations that are abruptly interrupted by a punishing intruder. The needs of the moment are satisfied through the medium of fantasy. The feelings toward the primary objects or their substitutes are safely displaced onto symbols.

CASE 3

An eight-year-old boy was brought to analysis because he talked back to his parents, failed to learn at school, had a diminished attention span, fidgeted, stole, had few friends, was the butt of jokes and beatings by other boys, and was a clown in class. Further, his parents feared he would become a homosexual. When first seen he was unable to pay attention to any activity for longer than three minutes. Although he tried to be co-operative, he was repeatedly overwhelmed by his feelings and frequently teased and attempted to provoke the interviewer by either verbal or active threats to destroy objects in the room. This behavior continued to occur frequently during the analytic sessions. More commonly, however, he would engage in the playing out of his fantasies, and invariably the stories that he played out could be related to events of the day with which he could not deal directly.

When it was discovered that the patient had stolen or failed to do his homework, his father scolded and beat him. The boy reported feelings of intense humiliation and anger. He would run from the room swearing vengeance, and in his own room his mind would be filled with fantasies of killing his father. After a few moments his mind would go blank. He could then return to his father and be friendly. This is not an uncommon reaction in children after beating. However, later he would dwell on fantasies of greatness and schemes for robbing. He worked out the street plan near my office and evolved a design for a bank robbery. One scheme involved the entry of men into a house in which a great deal of money was hidden in a safe. After the owner of the house was forced to open the safe, the gang prepared to kill him. They were stopped by the police, who fought and killed the robbers. This was acted out with gusto, the patient playing all the parts. At one time, when punishments had raised his aggressive drives to new heights, he actually broke into the house of a neighbor and stole some coins. When the lights of the neighbor's car indicated that they were returning, the patient left the house, buried some of the coins, and then reentered the house and hid, waiting to be captured and punished.

During one session, when he was describing a particularly strong interchange with his father, he "ran out of things to say" and decided to make up a story. He went from the playroom into my office and announced that the desk was a castle. He told the story of poor peasants who were being mistreated by a king and who were arming themselves for revolt under their leader, Marshall (the patient's middle name). They stormed the castle and took the king captive. The multitude cried, "Kill him, Marshall, kill the king." Marshall went up to the king with sword drawn. He raised his arm to kill. At that moment, the patient turned to me and said, "I'm thirsty. I'll be right back after I get a drink of water." He returned but could remember nothing of the fantasy of killing the king. It had been subjected to repression. The symbol for the father in the context of killing had lost its mask and had acquired a valence for attracting affect. The story could not continue under these circumstances. It had failed in its function.

In reflecting on the relationship of punishment, feelings of humiliation, and the creation of these fantasies, the youngster once remarked, "I get angry. I run away and think of killing them and saying to myself, I hate them. I hate them. But then I forget it and before you know it, I'm making up these stories to take out my feelings." When he was sixteen, he reflected on the story of the peasant killing the king in association to the following dream fragment.

> I'm in this hotel. I walk into a room. There is a woman there undressing. She has large breasts like my sister. She smiles. Then her husband comes into the room. He asks what I'm doing there. I say that I was pushed down the staircase and fell into the room. He looks like he's going to hit me. I don't know whether to fight or run.

His association to this dream was, "I can't get even with my father any more by making up stories of killing the king. I've got to find another way to handle my problems." Fantasies were ineffective as a discharge of his parricidal wishes.

From the three cases described above we can discern three separate clinical pathological states that are encountered in relation to latency: failure to enter latency, a regressive deterioration of the structure of latency, and regression to prelatency behavior.

Failure to enter latency is illustrated in Case 1. It resulted from a maturational defect in an ego function. The child lacked the capacity to form symbols, which impaired her capacity to form fantasies. Thus hobbled, she could not vent the drives stirred up by parental seductions and remained in a state of constant excitation. There was no energy to devote to learning. Parental stimulation together with the ego defect destroyed her "latency" in its beginnings.

Case 3 illustrates regressive deterioration of the structure of latency. All components of the structure of latency, especially fantasy formation, were present and operable. Latency-age fantasy formation provides for drive discharge while preserving pliability, educability, and socially acceptable behavior. As long as this child could discharge aggression toward his father through fantasies without impairing the ability to learn, he appeared to be a "normal latency child." When his aggression reached large proportions, he became anxious and distractible. He ceased to daydream but instead acted out his fantasy of being a robber by entering the house of a neighbor and stealing. Petty pilfering in department stores is sometimes related to similar dynamics. When fantasies are constantly being acted out, neurotic delinquency as a pattern of maladjustment results (see Anna Freud, 1949). Such behavior in latency presages the possibility of delinquency in adolescence.

If regressive deterioration of the structure of latency becomes chronic, the child becomes so involved in his fantasies that he has no energy for useful work. There is a regression to prelatency behavior. Parents often participate in the acting out of pregenital fantasies. In these situations the latency state disappears and the child experiences difficulty in peer relationship, impulse control, and learning.

It should be noted that the latency phase is characterized by an instability which is manifested by shifts between normal latency and the three states mentioned above. There is no intimation of serious pathology when one of these shifts occurs unless the shift becomes characteristic, chronic, and results in behavior that interferes with the progress and growth of the child. The potential stability of the state of latency in a child is defined in terms of the strength of the ego structures related to the production of latency.

When a conflict or feeling which occurs during the latency time period cannot be experienced consciously by a child because of strong fears and intense feelings, the conflict cannot be dealt with on a realistic level. The ideas are repressed and represented in consciousness in the form of distorted fantasy. The repression serves as a two-edged sword for the child. It holds his reactions in check so that there can develop a period of calm when learning can take place. On the other hand, as a result of repression, pregenital and oedipal conflicts are not resolved. In adult life, the presence of wishes and conflicts more appropriate to childhood will cause emotional difficulties.

Except in those situations in which the drives are too strongly stimulated and acting out of fantasy occurs, fantasies serve to reduce tension and to help the child resolve otherwise unresolvable conflicts. I have designated the configuration of defenses in the latency ego that provides the stabilizing discharge by way of fantasy "the structure of latency." This new term is introduced for heuristic purposes in the belief that naming it will delineate its form and draw attention to the phenomenon.

Freud (1911) first pointed out that in latency "a closer connection arises ... between ... instinct and fantasy ..." (p. 222). I have attempted to expand this concept. In latency more than in any other psychological period of development, fantasy is linked to the drives as a derivative and a sole outlet. In adolescence and beyond, fantasy detracts from the solution of emotional problems through relationship with the real world and object seeking. Only in the creative artist is it seen as acceptable in the form of sublimation. In latency, fantasy gives vent to the drives and permits the child to live in peace with the parental figures.

This can be illustrated by further material from Case 1. The child, as a result of analytic work, had developed reaction-formations and some capacity to learn. She was confronted by a frustration which stirred murderous feelings toward her mother with accompanying oedipal feelings toward her father. A description of a fantasy in statu nascendi of this six-year-old girl follows.

A friend had spent the afternoon with her. In the evening the mother took the friend home. When the mother returned she found her child in a rage. She pulled at her hair, wrenched the cloth of her dress, and said, "I want someone to sleep with at night." She had wanted her friend to stay. Her mother explained to her that sleepover dates are for more grown-up girls in their teens, and added that grown-up means being able to study, use books, read, and be promoted. She told the child that she would not be promoted if she did not work. The child became silent and prepared for bed. Before going to sleep she told her mother the first detailed fantasy that she had ever reported.

> There was a little girl. She was naughty. Her mother told her she would punish her by not letting her go to school. She went to school to tell the teacher. The girl followed her. When they got home, the girl fired down the house. The mother was killed. When the father came home he saw the house fired down and he asked the girl what happened. He didn't punish her because she told the truth. They moved to another house. A stepmother came, but she didn't stay long. Then the girl and the father moved away to a new house where they lived together.

In this fantasy we see the characteristic shift from the primary object to a substitute. The child is represented by a little girl. All the major people in the child's life are represented, and yet the child does not recognize herself. The anger at the frustrating mother in reality was stifled. It appeared in the content of a story told at bedtime. The real mother hears the story but the anger is not directed at her. Rather, she is to be entertained by her child's inventiveness. The consuming flames that "fire down" the house and kill the mother in the story represent the anger transmuted into a symbolic story element.

Such fantasies are the normal products of the structure of latency that help the child deal with unbearable wishes in relation to the parental figures. In prelatency the wishes are expressed directly. In adolescence, substitute objects can be sought or the wishes can be obscured by regression. In latency, these wishes normally find expression in fantasies and their derivative, play.

A prime example of such a fantasy is the well-known "plumber" fantasy of Little Hans (Freud, 1909), an attempt to resolve his oedipal conflict during latency. Hans had fear of castration. He produced the fantasy: " 'The plumber came; and first he took away my behind with a pair of pincers, and then gave me another, and then the same with my widdler' " (p. 98). Hans's father interpreted to him that the replacement organs were bigger than those removed. Hans agreed. Freud commented, "With [this] fantasy the anxiety which arose from his castration complex was also overcome, and his painful expectations were given a happier turn" (p. 100). Through the use of the structure of latency, Hans set aside his conflicts and anxieties. His improvement may be explained on the basis that he was helped less through gaining insight than through a shift of his defenses from those that produce phobias to those that produce the state of latency.

It must be kept in mind that a technical procedure in child analysis derives from the fact of the normality of these fantasies in latency. It would have been inadvisable to return the child described in Case 1 to the original situation of anger at the mother. In this child, insight was overly present and was a source of anxiety that sapped the capacity to function and to learn. It is important to encourage the development and maintenance of the latency state ego in children on the borderline of latency. On the other hand, neurotic children who are well able to enter the state of latency can benefit from the interpretation of their fantasies. This is illustrated by the following clinical example.

CASE 4

A ten-year-old girl insisted on playing out a game in the session. She did her best to dislodge some clay that she had driven into a corner. She told of the difficulty of removing it and spoke of the great value it had because it had been in the "cave" so long. When asked about constipation problems, she spoke of her parents' concern with her constipation and of long wrangles with her grandmother about drinking prune juice. She got more attention when she was constipated. But her symptom was a mixed blessing, for she paid for her pleasure in retention with gas pains, stomach aches, and painful bowel movements. She was able to question her behavior, understand her motivation, and gain relief from her constipation. For this neurotic child, the interpretation of her fantasy opened a mine of information which she had formerly withheld. In such children, the interpretation of fantasy results in an understanding of their relationship with their parents and the nature of their fantasies. On the other hand, in the "borderline" latency child such interpretations leave the child defenseless, with massive aggression stirred up as a means of dealing with the anxiety which the latency fantasy had formerly quelled.

The mechanisms and techniques of fantasy formation in latency are characteristic of the period. If we define the ego as the group of functions that regulate the relationship between id, superego, and the world of reality, we would have to say that the ego of the latency child is different from that of the adult in content, conformation, and the degree of intensity with which certain mechanisms of defense are used. This can best be illustrated by describing the mechanisms of defense in latency.

The child of five is struggling to cope with unresolved conflicts over instinctual urges. He cannot fulfill his oedipal wishes, for he cannot kill his father; nor can he have intercourse with his mother. But his sexual urges in relation to his parents have an exciting quality. Of course they are not viewed by the child in the same light that similar feelings are viewed by a healthy adult. To the five-year-old the world of excitement and gratification is frightening and overwhelming. Like the explorer whose leap into the unknown jungle is edged with fright, the child views the step into genitality as a thing of wonder and of fear. Society provides neither gratification nor explanation of this unknown realm. The child's attempts to solve the riddle or to experience this new world are met with frustration, threats of castration, and fear of loss of love, and he responds by repressing his drives.

When perceptual awareness is withdrawn from the area of oedipality and genitality, attention cathexis may be shifted to such real activities as athletics. There can also be regression to prior stages of development when earlier drives and conflicts, now safely negotiated, were experienced. The child may return to the sadomasochistic, smearing fantasies of the anal stage. This is one reason that parental aggression so stimulates these children: during latency they are more attuned to aggression than to oedipal sexuality even though genital sexuality is the underlying problem that is defended against by the regression to anality.

Since the child is older and has further developed his techniques for dealing with his anal drive energies, clinically he looks quite different from when he was first involved in these urges. He represses them and sublimates them. He develops obsessive-compulsive defenses, such as counting, obsessional thoughts, and the collecting of stamps, coins, and rocks. Reaction-formations are developed and strengthened so that we see an industrious child who is aware of reality. Clinically, at this point the child is in the latency state. Should oedipal or sexual situations arise, or aggression-stimulating situations threaten to undermine the defenses against aggression, fantasy formation can be used to quiet the stirrings that would otherwise shatter the mental equilibrium of latency. At first, the situation is remembered with full force, then it is repressed. The remembered situation—for instance, unexpected nudity in the home, seduction by an adult, sustained and unjust punishment—is fragmented. Only parts of a situation are represented in any one latency fantasy. The fragments are displaced onto symbolic representations that are then elaborated and synthesized into a series of coherent conscious fantasies. These fantasies discharge the drives and protect the mental equilibrium of the latency state.

The primary mechanisms of defense which characterize the ego structure that institutes and maintains the latency state may be summarized as follows. (1) In dealing with oedipality and genitality: regression to anal-sadistic drive organization, reality cathexis, repression; (2) in dealing with the regression to anal-sadistic drives: sublimation, obsessive-compulsive defenses (doing and undoing), reaction-formations, repressions; (3) in dealing with breakthroughs of the anal, genital, and oedipal conflicts once the latency state has been established: repression, fragmentation, displacement, symbol formation, synthesis and secondary elaboration, fantasy formation. It is this third group that I designate the "structure of latency."

The development of latency is strongly influenced by the environment. There are primitive societies and subcultures in which latency is not encouraged and sexual activity is encouraged. Malinowski (1962) described such a society:

... among the Trobriand Islanders 'Sexual Freedom' is considerable. It begins very early, children already taking a greal deal of interest in certain pursuits and amusement which come as near sexuality as their unripe age allows. This is by no means regarded as improper or immoral, is known and tolerated by the elders, and abetted by games and customary arrangements. Later on, after boys and girls have reached maturity, their freedom remains the same . . ." (p. 5).

Here there is no latency as we know it. Since there is no biological obligation to enter latency in human beings, a parent in our culture, through his or her behavior toward the child, may lead him to manifest some infantile drive. The most common example of this is the parent who stimulates the child's aggression. The result varies. The consequence may be stable latency with occasional temper tantrums or a fully disorganized child with no capacity to delay any need gratification. The disorganized child may appear psychotic because of the degree of disorganization. Such children rarely hallucinate, and when hallucinations do occur they are of the superego type. Should the condition continue untreated, the child in some instances will mature and even settle down. However, he will never become all that he is capable of being since so much important basic learning time has been usurped by the excitement of an interrupted latency. The child who continues to be stimulated by the parent aggressively and sexually turns intensely to fantasy formation, as in Case 3, in order to deal with the overwhelming excitement that stirs within him. Direct gratification of body needs short-circuits the achievements that the interposition of delay provides. There is interference with the ego functions required in learning skills. Frequently this is at the root of learning and reading disorders.

A clinical situation which is the mirror image of the one just described is that of latency-age children who enter physiological puberty (idiopathic isosexual puberty). These children can produce a state of latency in spite of premature pubescence. Parental and social influences, as well as phase-specific psychological development, are sometimes used to explain the fact that psychological stages develop independently of the flow of hormones (see p. 129, and Krim, 1962). This observation is further illustrated in adolescence by girls with Turner's syndrome (Hampson et al., 1955). In these children there is no puberty in the early teens because of gonadal dysgenesis. But under the influence of parental expectations, they become interested in clothes and boys and experience all the trials and tribulations of adolescence. In idiopathic isosexual puberty, in Turner's syndrome, and in the onset of latency, cultural factors outweigh the biological ones in determining the manifest behavior of the child in latency and adolescence.

From the standpoint of culture, latency is necessary for the formation of civilization. Latency provides the period of time in which children can learn the complicated skills needed in the society (see Chapter 5). The child learns to accommodate himself to the world. Sexual gratification is delayed during a period when there can be no genital gratification, and oedipal feelings are allayed so that the child can live in peace with those people who love him. This is vital at a time when it is necessary to have someone care for him because of his economic dependence, his need to learn social skills, attitudes, and manners of living. The child can remain within the family and continue to be an accepted part of the family, and still accept the authority of the parents. It is a period when the child consolidates his image of himself in relation to the world.

In modern usage, latency has been divided into two phases: from six to eight years (the early phase) and from eight to twelve years (the later phase). The early phase is marked by the child's preoccupation with himself. There is an inhibition of masturbatory activity. Fantasies contain amorphous monsters. The superego is strict and brutal. Real objects are denied to the child as drive outlets. In the early phase, fantasy is the primary means of adjusting to emotional stresses and becomes a defense. The child uses reality only to disengage himself from untenable and unfulfillable drives and fantasies. Cathexis of reality, for instance, in school or sports, serves as a guarantee of the secondarily autonomous functions of the ego (Rapaport, 1958).

The later phase is marked by an increasing availability of the outside world as the source of objects through which fantasies can be gratified. Masturbatory activity becomes less proscribed. Fantasies contain figures that resemble people: monsters and ghosts change into witches and robbers. In effect the child's thoughts and fantasies begin to dwell upon gratifications with objects that resemble human forms. He can accept his oedipal urges a little more, and so can represent the parents with symbols that are a little less disguised. There is an overall diminution of the strictness of the superego. As a result of maturation, the child becomes more aware of the world, his place in it, and his relationship to the future.

This second phase of latency is thus characterized by a move toward cognition which is well grounded in reality. As a result there are more realistic creatures in the fantasies. As cognitive function and reality testing improve, the mechanisms of defense that support latency, especially fantasy formation, become less tenable and the structure of latency weakens. By the time the child is eleven or twelve, he usually forsakes fantasy as a means for drive discharge and begins to integrate reality, using fantasies for planning. He is forced to view the parents as sexual objects and develops new techniques to deal with his incestuous feelings. But infantile drives, once dealt with through repression and fantasy formation, gradually reassert themselves because of the growing strength of reality testing. Latency wavers as puberty and parental encouragement of teen-age interests become manifest. The structure of latency crumbles, and the child is thrown into the chaos of adolescence.

One might well ask if fantasy is given up completely at the end of latency. The answer is obviously no. Fantasy merely ceases to be the preferred means for expressing the drives. More mature object relations with the real world are developed in its stead. There are of course exceptions. In neurotics the persistence of fantasy is manifested in the development of symptoms. Freud (1911) tells us that the artist has persistence of fantasy and is able "to mould his fantasies into truths of a new kind, which are valued by men as precious reflections of reality. Thus in a certain fashion he actually becomes the hero . . . [and] favorite he desires to be, without following the long roundabout path of making real alterations in the external world" (p. 224). For the average person, skills at weaving fantasy to cope with drive needs and experiences of humiliation are harnessed to that area of ego operations which can be called future planning. Reality elements replace psychoanalytic symbols, and plans for tomorrow replace fantasies of the moment.

From the point of view of development, late latency is a period of transition. During this time, the structure of the ego which is typical for latency is transformed. Instincts are withdrawn from fantasy and are articulated with real situations and real objects. Since we are dealing with an exposition and elaboration of Freud's (1911) concept that in latency a closer connection arises between instinct and fantasy (p. 222), it would be useful to pursue what lies behind the dissolution of the closer connection. In prelatency, the child had been buoyed by a sense of omnipotence and a feeling of indestructibility. The introduction of castration fear, fear of loss of love, and the incest barrier made fantasies which involved the parent in sexual and aggressive contexts unbearable. The poor reality testing and cognitive function of the child permitted the use of repression, fragmentation, displacement, symbol formation, and synthesis of symbols into story patterns to be used for the production of fantasies which could serve as safe objects for drive discharge. In this way the drives are discharged without danger to loved ones. In youngsters in the state of latency, situations which relate to or stir up the core fantasies of prelatency are resolved through the formation of such seemingly unrelated conscious fantasies.

The configuration of ego functions that produce this activity becomes an important part of the structure of latency. Formation of benign fantasy in this context provides the buffer which permits the continuation of the total ego structure in latency. Failure or default of these mechanisms can result from excessive stimulation of sexual or aggressive drives. School regression and aggressive outbursts in latency children are explained by this phenomenon. In the absence of these stimuli, the child may continue endlessly to use fantasy for vicarious problem solving and thus guard against the incursions of drives which demand objects. However, latency is not endless, and at the age of seven and one-half to eight years, improvement in reality testing and cognitive function begins to impair the child's use of fantasy for solving problems. Not only is there marked improvement in cognitive function but there is maturation of the capacity to appreciate cause and effect relationships between objects which are concretely present (see p. 116 and Piaget on concrete operational thinking in Woodward, 1965, pp. 74-75). There is also greater objectivity, and reality objects become less assimilated to the subject's wishes. By the age of twelve, this process reaches its height. The magical power of words can no longer be used to cause changes in the relationships between real things and real people. Cause and effect relationships are recognized. The structure of latency crumbles and reality becomes the obligate outlet for the discharge of the drives. The stage is set for the turmoil of adolescence. The demands of the world and prelatency fantasies must now be faced and resolved.

Clinical data support the concept that the latency state is a socially guided configuration of ego structures. During the latency time period, drive strengths are sustained. In the state of latency, fantasy formation is a means of vicarious problem solving. Through fantasy, conflicts may be played out in thought rather than reality. This spares the individual a conflict with the real objects in the environment and diminishes the impact of drives to the extent that maturation and sublimation are facilitated. In this way the relative stability and the diminution of drive pressures, typical for the latency time period, come into being. In later latency, when maturational improvement in reality testing gradually minimizes the defensive effectiveness of manifest fantasy formation, there is a gradual shift to the use of more reality-oriented defenses. This sets the stage for adolescence.

Note

1. In Freud's writings references to these mechanisms of defense in latency may be found in the following works, identified by dates (the papers are listed in the Bibliography):

Sublimation (1905, 1924)
Reaction-Formation (1905, 1923)
Fantasy (1911)
Regression (1916-17, 1926)
Repression (1921, 1923)

Chapter 3

SEXUAL DEVELOPMENT DURING THE LATENCY AGE

*You should not take a fellow eight years old
And make him swear to never kiss the girls*

—Robert Browning

As we have seen, clinical observations clearly support the concept of latency as an organization of ego mechanisms used to cope with sexual and aggressive drives. Sexual drive intensity is so marked during the latency age period that a complex organization of defenses must be maintained for its control. Sexual drive derivatives are everywhere in evidence. As Malinowski (1962) indicates, in societies which encourage overt sexuality during the latency years sexual play is given rein to express the sexual drives. In societies that restrict sexuality in latency, diminished sexual drive pressure is an illusion. It derives from observations of the covert and devious manifestations through which the sexual drive evades prohibition during the latency years. This is the result of social suppression of overt masturbation, but only in part. Other factors producing less easily recognized forms of sexual expression relate to: the latency age tendency to move from reality objects to fantasy objects and introjects; the availability of fantasy as an outlet for the sexual drive during the latency years; and the essentially immature nature of the physical sexual apparatus during the latency age period. In regard to the last point, it is important to note that from birth to thirteen or fourteen years of age, sexual and aggressive drives are the only human drives not associated with a mature functioning physical apparatus. There is little possibility for drive discharge involving an object. Much of the psychological development of childhood, including the state of latency, consists of developmentally determined attempts at resolution of this problem.

What follows is a review of these resolutions as found at different ages and stages of development.

Motor and Fantasy Components of Masturbatory Activity: Infancy to Latency

The relationship between the motor aspects of masturbatory activity and masturbation fantasy is not always close. Lampl-De Groot (1950) has pointed out that "both components may join in following the same path or they may be separated. Whenever this separation occurs psychoanalysis can always demonstrate that in the unconscious they belong together (p. 156)."

The varying configurations of these components in relation to one another, considered in the context of a developmental framework, is an important factor to be considered in understanding the resolution of the expression of the sexual drive during the latency period. In the developmental relationship between motor masturbatory activity and fantasy, fantasy activity appears to be a relatively late development. In the early phases of individual human experience, during the first months of life, motor masturbatory components are primary. They consist of manipulation of body parts with concomitant libidinal gratification. This was considered by Freud (1905) to occur at the mother's breast: "The child's lips . . . behave like an erotogenic zone, and no doubt stimulation by the warm flow of milk is the cause of the pleasurable sensation" (p. 181). No fantasy is postulated to occur at this point. This early sexual manifestation had an organ for expression, but no object. Freud described such a process as autoerotic. In this activity the sexual drive is discharged through the use of a nonsexual body function (eating) carried out by a nonsexual body organ (the mouth). Manipulations of parts of the body, the skin, and the mucous membrane during later years represent attempts to recreate this experience with one's own body used for drive gratification.

Spitz (1949), in his study of autoerotic activities of children during the first year of life, places no emphasis on the fantasies of the children. Rather he found that rocking, fecal play, and genital masturbation "represent stages of object relations" (p. 118). The first two activities can be identified with gratification in the form of a regression to the self. This can be considered a narcissistic source of gratification from the standpoint of comforting of self. Genital masturbation before the age of one is considered to be a sign of normal object relations and is considered to be a "subordinate activity of minor importance" (p. 119).

Piaget (see Woodward, 1965), in his description of perceptual motor growth during the early years of childhood, provides information that is of value in appreciating the psychological organization of masturbatory activity during the first year of life. It should be noted that Piaget does not conceptualize the development of the relationship between the child and the world and between the child and his own body in terms of libidinal and aggressive drive theory. Rather, he theorizes in terms of unfolding cognitive maturation interacting with environmental influences. His observations, however, are germane to the material with which we are dealing. There are linking references to psychoanalytic theory in his writings. According to Piaget's observations, during the first month of life there is a "stage of reflex schemata" during which children exercise their reflexes independently of each other.

Examples of the reflexes exercised in the stage of reflex schemata during the first month of life are grasping, touching, rubbing, and sucking. During the period of one to four and one-half months there is a stage in which the reflexes which were exercised in the first month undergo reciprocal assimilation. This refers to a coordination of individual reflex schemata into patterns of schemata. Permanent associations of reflex patterns are acquired at this time. This development is called a primary circular reaction. One such primary circular reaction is the "reciprocal assimilation between grasping and sucking" (p. 62). The sexual drive energies initially linked with the sucking reflex, as described in Freud's autoerotic concept, find gratification through both grasping and sucking as the result of the coordination of these reflexes. When sucking is withdrawn at weaning, the other part of the reciprocal assimilation, rubbing with the hand, continues as an available schema through which sexual energies are discharged onto objects. This explains why it is that activities such as hair twirling and rubbing fingers over velvet-fringed blankets also serve for the expression of oral drives. Through the coordination of reflexes, pathways for displacement are established. Thus, with the withdrawal of the bottle or the nipple, the search for comfort can take forms other than closeness to mother as a differentiated object.

Masturbatory activities in the first year of life also involve the genitals. Levine (1951) reported on his observation of masturbatory activities in children at this stage. He described infants playing first with the ear and then at six months shifting attention to the genitals.

During the first months of life, autoerotic activity serves as a medium for drive discharge and comfort derived from the self. There is no alternative to this state of affairs until the second half of the first year of life when self-object differentiation begins. Then sources of pleasurable sensations are resolved into two spheres. There is the sphere of two-point sensations, consisting of feelings emanating from the sensing organ (mouth) and the part of the child's own body with which he comes into contact (thumb). There is the sphere of single sensation consisting of feelings emanating from the sensing organ (mouth) in contact with an object (breast) which is external to the child (that is, non-I). Self object differentiation first becomes apparent to the child through the awareness that two-point sensation is missing with non-I objects. These sensations are less intense. In addition, they are not under the total control of the child as are two-point sensations. From the beginning of self-object differentiation there is a continual shift between the two spheres of sensation available for libidinal gratification. No fantasy or other, verbal content accompanies this shifting. Masturbatory activity is motor activity alone under the domination of the above described coordinated patterning of reflex behavior, through which certain activities such as sucking and rubbing had become definitively linked (reciprocally assimilated) and interchangeable as pathways for sexual drive discharge.

From the onset of early object differentiation, during the second half of the first year of life until eighteen months, drive gratification is achieved through such activities as rhythmic touching, sucking, and rubbing of soft parts of the body. This alternates with cuddling, snuggling, and warm interactions with differentiated parental figures. The latter leads to a consistent object tie with an animate responding object. Subsequent losses of this object may be followed by a regression. This can result in seeking a part of self (thumb-sucking, rocking), a body product (fecal play), or some external thing (for instance a doll—an object to be handled) as libidinal object. With the first stages of the maturation of symbols, concept formation, and speech, these substitute objects are secondarily interpreted by the child as undifferentiated, concrete, conscious representations of the lost object. At this point primitive concrete conceptualizations accompany actions bent toward libidinal discharge. These are the primordia of masturbatory fantasies. They are tightly integrated with motor activity.

During the second half of the second year of life, fantasy activity becomes more complex. Masturbatory fantasy participates in this maturation. Symbolic play and physiognomic thinking enrich the fantasy life. Piaget (1945) describes the appearance of symbolic play during the fifteen to eighteen-month period. Signifying elements (words and things) no longer are considered to be concrete representations of that which they signify. Play objects are free to retain their identity while representing something else in play. A toy block may now be placed upon another toy block during play and the complex made to represent a child sitting on the toilet. In effect, at this point, words and objects may be used as metaphorical symbols to represent what they are not.

In 1940, Werner described a similar observation on the maturational shift in cognition that occurs in the second year of life. He described as "physiognomic thinking" the interpretation of things as " 'animate,' even though actually lifeless" (p. 69). He noted, using data from Buhler (p. 79) that this form of thinking dominates the play of a child at the two-year level. It is then that the child becomes involved in "the physiognomic transformation of material [pretending that a block is a train, etc.]" (p. 79). The child can now pretend while seeking physical outlets for his drives. The circumstances of sexual gratification can be represented in the brain conceptually and can be expressed verbally. An object or a word can have a dual meaning; it can signify itself concretely or something else abstractly. Inanimate things can be thought to have life. Symbolic thinking in the metaphorical sense becomes possible and words formerly used only for naming may be harnessed so that they represent and express drives through displacement. The child adds fantasy formation to the skills used in the discharge of sexual drive. Symbol formation, with its potential for giving dual meaning to words and objects, is capable of distorting the meaning of any object to the point that it becomes a potential sexual object. There is utilization of schemata coordinated in the first years of life as pathways for the discharge of libidinal drive. It is likely that it is this point in development that Winnicott (1953) had in mind when he stated that "at some theoretical point early in the development of every human individual, an infant . . . is capable of conceiving of the idea of something which would meet the growing need which arises out of instinctual tension" (p. 239). This act of conceiving he called "primary creativity" (p. 239). The role of primary creativity in the creation of masturbatory fantasy is the distortion of the psychic image of reality to fit preestablished pathways which have been used for the gratification of drives. This is a function which is basic to the distortion of reality in the service of drive gratification. It is therefore basic to the development of masturbation fantasies.

The contents of masturbation fantasies are the products of the trans-mutation of objects and the world into instruments for the expression of drive energies. After this step during the second year of life, ideas and objects can be distorted through the malleability of their mental images to fit designs which serve for sexual gratification. These distorting skills pro-vide the mechanism through which sexual drives find expression in ideas.

The distorted use of a word or object for drive satisfaction has a precur-sor during the first year of life. This is the use of thumb-sucking for re-evoking the pleasure felt while sucking at the breast. Freud (1905) recog-nized this infantile behavior to be a sexual manifestation. He, like Winni-cott, traced the distortion involved to the anaclitic relationship of sexual gratification to the physiological function of nursing. He recognized that objects and functions could be distorted to serve libidinal needs. Piaget (1945) actively related his thoughts in this area (the conceptual distortion of new perceptions by the influence of past experiences) to Freudian con-cepts. He illustrated his view with the example of "a child who has been weaned for a long time [finding] pleasure in pretending that he is a baby again and is being suckled." He refers to the explanation of "the Freud-ians . . . [who] reply that the child is still clinging to the memory of the mother's breast. . . ." States Piaget, "there is probably something to be said for this idea, since the schema of sucking the breast is for so long of primary importance to the child" (p. 175). Piaget thus places within the context of his theory and terminology concepts which are expressed in psychoanalytic terminology as the translation of autoerotic experiences into relationship with objects. To an impressive degree, Piaget conveys to us his observation that schemata and modifications of schemata which have occurred early in life influence the way that new objects are dealt with. He calls this process imitation. With the exception of the concept of drives, the theoretical constructs upon which the modern psychoanalytic explanation of the influence of prior learned patterns on future behavior is based find a parallel in Piaget's work. This is well exemplified in the following quote: "While the child imitates an absent model that he evokes through the image, the situation again involves a substitute object or signifier, an evoked object [the model] and the imitative image of the model" (p. 282). Note that the word "imitative" here connotes the influence of past patterns during the act of conceiving of the idea of something, which in turn will influence the interpretation of a newly perceived object.

From the observations and theoretical conclusions of Piaget and Werner, one could postulate that during the second half of the second year of life, fantasy content containing conscious metaphorical symbolic representations can be available as a masturbatory component. Actually there are no reported observations of this phenomenon in the literature until the first half of the third year of life. Substitute objects are seen to take part in symbolic play activity, but there are no reports of verbalization of the erotic fantasies with which they are associated. During the first half of the third year of life, masturbation and such autoerotic activities as thumb-sucking therefore still retain roles as comforters and means for drawing a kind of mothering from one's own body.

Genital masturbation begins in the child's first year according to Spitz (1949) and Levine (1951). Genital masturbation and rocking are sometimes accompanied by excitement rather than comfort. Levine noted that children who rock do so with "great vigor and even tension" (p. 119), while children up to "thirty months of age indulge in genital play with a certain degree of satisfaction but without any apparent emotional excitement or increased stimulation" (p. 119). A small group is referred to who have excitement from genital stimulation. Galenson (1972) reports seeing excitement far more frequently. Such genital masturbation with excitement can often be achieved, accompanied by fantasies, at the age of three. These first-reported masturbation fantasies are similar in content to the activities played out in earlier forms of masturbation. Kris (1951) described such fantasies in the following way: "masturbation fantasies of boys during the phallic phase . . . have in common the sexual aim to be touched and handled by the mother" (p. 101).

By the first half of the third year of life an additional cognitive step provides for an enrichment of the fantasy that accompanies masturbation.
Prior to this, fantasies consisted of conscious wish and metaphor. After
this, latent fantasy elements can be expressed through psychoanalytic
symbols. Psychoanalytic symbols, or in Piaget's terminology "secondary
symbolism," have been defined by Jones (1916) in the following terms:

> In most uses of the word, a symbol is a manifest expression for an
> idea that is more or less hidden, secret, or kept in reserve. Most
> typically of all, the person employing the symbol is not even conscious
> of what it actually represents. . . . Symbols [are] made spontaneously
> . . . and in the broad sense of the word, unconsciously. The stricter the
> sense in which this is used, the truer is the statement (p. 90). . . . Only
> what is repressed is symbolized. Only what is repressed needs to be
> symbolized. This conclusion is the touchstone of the psychoanalytic
> theory of symbolism (p. 116).

Briefly stated, in the formation of such a symbol, the link between the signifier and the signified has been repressed.

I have seen evidence that psychoanalytic symbols capable of use for the
formation of neurotic distortion in fantasy appear early in the first half of
the third year of life (see Sarnoff, 1970). This age would seem to be the
earliest that fantasies accompanying masturbation could be used for
gratification while masking meaning, as opposed to use of fantasy based
on conscious simile or metaphor. This may serve as an explanation for the
fact that overt masturbatory fantasy activity does not become prominent
until about eight months after it is theoretically possible. Fantasy content
can be expressed in verbal rather than action or organ experiences once its
full meaning can be cushioned by symbolization associated with repression. As we will see, this form of symbolization is not universally present in
prelatency. However, the richness newly imparted to fantasy by these skills
makes fantasy more attractive for masturbatory use.

Werner (1940) observed a parallel shift in cognitive skills at three to four
years of age. He noted that play containing "make believe" or "fantastic
situations" became dominant, displacing play activity based on a physiognomic thinking pattern (p. 79). The type of symbolization inherent in
physiognomic thinking is similar to the symbolic play of children of
eighteen months described by Piaget: such symbolic play itself recedes
during the first half of the third year of life as the result of the development of the capacity for psychoanalytic symbolism (true symbols) which,

in turn, underlies the capacity for the creation of make believe or fantastic situations.

Masturbation fantasies, according to Eidelberg's (1945) principle, "represent not a pure satisfaction of an infantile wish but a compromise between an infantile wish of the id and a defense against it by the ego and the superego" (p. 131). Through the developmental timing explicated above, it should be possible to apply this principle to manifest masturbation fantasies during the first half of the third year of life. Indeed this seems evident. However, this organization of defenses is not fully achieved until five or six years of age, at which time repression becomes strong enough to support unshakable psychoanalytic symbols. From the third year of life until the time that children enter the state of latency, their ability to express oedipal fantasies in a very direct and conscious form remains a common observation. Overt and thinly masked oedipal fantasies are available as masturbation fantasies during this period of relatively weak repression and psychoanalytic symbol formation. Overt sadistic and oedipal content in masturbation fantasies during the phallic phase is attested to by Blanchard (1952). She also described in the phallic stage of development "masturbation fantasies of both boys and girls . . . concerned with the acquisition of a big penis." This was typical for boys, but also occurred in little girls in cases where the parents' wish for a boy was known to the girl (p. 29). "Children masturbate with sadistic, destructive fantasies about brothers and sisters, as well as about parents," notes Blanchard. "Fantasies so often are concerned with injuring, torturing or killing people whom they love, as well as hate" (p. 30).

Lampl-De Groot (1950) asserted without direct reference to the development phase involved that "it is absolutely certain that children of both sexes develop the most active aggressive games and fantasies with the anal gratification; one could say with anal masturbation or masturbation of the introitus or of the labia."

Kris (1951) has pointed out an important aspect of the development of masturbation fantasies. In speaking of fantasies beyond the phallic phase, he notes that "the later development of . . . masturbation fantasies [consists of] condensation [of wishes] with other wishes and the defenses against them" (p. 101). Essentially, highly symbolized masturbation fantasies of prelatency and beyond are condensations and distortions of the conditions for sexual gratifications experienced in early childhood. In prelatency, motor masturbatory activities and masturbation fantasies usually occur simultaneously. At the point that a child reaches the latency period, repression and psychoanalytic symbol formation are strengthened to a marked degree. Unconsciously peers and objects in the environment can be transmuted through the capacity for fantasy into "things" to be used for the discharge of drive energies. Primary creativity becomes a more active process with these mechanisms at its disposal. Repression, displacement, and symbolization produce condensations and distortions of the early childhood conditions for sexual gratification. As a result sexual energies, which are discharged in play and fantasy, are masked to the degree that their sexual origin is not detectable. The organization of defenses which produces these distortions, aimed at preserving the calm of latency, is called the structure of latency.

In latency period children, drive discharge can take the form of overt masturbation or fantasy play. In the next three sections I will discuss these activities in some detail; but because of the difference between boys and girls in regard to masturbation in the latency period, a section is devoted to each. The third section examines the continuing development of motor and fantasy components involved in discharge of drive energies during the state of latency.

Masturbatory Activity in Latency Age Girls

In describing masturbatory activity in latency age girls, we can establish a continuum of activities serving for the discharge of sexual drives. At one extreme, there is highly symbolic fantasy play which couples symbolized fantasy and whole body movements in the service of drive discharge. At the other extreme there is manual manipulation of the clitoris and labia, rarely with vaginal penetration, accompanied by directly represented sadomasochistic fantasies. The former represents the functioning of a youngster who utilizes the ego structure of a child in the state of latency. The latter represents the functioning of a child whose drive energies and ego organization are involved in direct expression of sexual drives. We should note that the less symbolized fantasies contain sadomasochistic elements in keeping with the expected level of the libidinal drive regression of the latency age period.

Clower (1974) and Bernstein (1974) have described girls whose masturbation proceeded to heights of sensation followed by relaxation. In one case—my own clinical experience—this was traced by the child back to the eighth year of life (Sarnoff, 1972b). A sister who observed the masturbation described much motor activity at the height of the excitement. In Bernstein's case, sadomasochistic fantasies accompanied the masturbatory activity. Blanchard (1952) described such sadomasochistic fantasies during latency age masturbation, commenting that "it is not strange that children usually are anxious and guilty about masturbating, in view of the fact that the fantasies so often are concerned with injuring or killing people whom they love as well as hate" (p. 31). It could be stated as a dictum of the latency age in both sexes that the aggressive drive in latency is served through mastery of the environment, learning, and sports, and sadomasochistic regression expressed in nail-biting, self-injury, and masturbation fantasies.

Fraiberg (1972) has described the cessation of genital masturbation in two girls early in the period of latency. She attributed this to a flight from "explosive discharge that has the characteristics of orgasm, even if it may not be identical with orgasm" (p. 474). Both Fraiberg and Bernstein (1974) reported that accompanying this flight from sensation, there appeared a genital anaesthesia. This is an example of blocking of the use of masturbation as an outlet for sexual drives in latency. Such proto-orgastic sensations are apparently possible for some girls. I have reported the case of a girl who became aware of the possibility of such strong sensations when she observed her sister masturbating. When she tried to produce these feelings in herself, she found that she was capable of only slight arousal when she stimulated her clitoris and a calming sensation when she stroked her labia. With the onset of puberty, orgastic sensations became possible for her (see Sarnoff, 1972b).

Apparently a physiological potential for the use of the genitals for achieving sexual pleasure, though minimal, is usually present in latency age girls. It is variable in extent as well as character. Sensations range from orgastic responses and sensations of excitement to soothing sensations. Whatever the case, it is a rare girl who continues masturbation as a primary sexual outlet throughout the latency age period. Usually there is a cessation of masturbation by the age of six or seven. There is some softening of social and superego restrictions on masturbation at about eight and one-half years. There is another increase in masturbation that occurs with the appearance of orgastic potential. This usually occurs with puberty.

Kinsey et al. (1953), reporting on retrospective interviews with adult women, found that 14 percent of all women interviewed reported having orgasms before puberty. Before 3 years, 0.3 percent reported orgasm, 2 percent by 5 years, 4 percent by 7 years, 9 percent by 11 years, and 14 percent by 13 years, after which most women became capable of orgasm.

The latency age girl and boy both experience the exciting sensations from stimulating those highly sensitive areas derived from the embryological phallic protuberance (glans in the boy, clitoris in the girl) and can usually identify it. One girl asked spontaneously, "What is that button in the front of my sissy that I like to touch?" Unlike the boy, however, the rest of her genitalia are often a mystery to the girl. Though the clitoris is known, girls have great difficulty in identifying the origins of sensations from other anatomical structures in the perineal area. This relates in large part to the primarily tactile aspect of the girl's contact with her genitals, as opposed to the tactile visual contact a boy has with his genitals. A girl would have great difficulty in drawing a map of her genital sensations. This has resulted in a failure even to the present time to ascertain whether latency age girls have vaginal excitements and sensations during masturbation and other sexually exciting activities. The current tendency is to believe that such sensations do exist and are utilized for pleasure by the children who have in some way been drawn to the discovery of the vagina through either exploration or stimulation from infections. Because of the protected position of their genitalia, girls are less often subjected to genital contact with others or objects. Spontaneous erections are not constantly present to remind them of their sexuality. Since girls do not experience these casual seductions as often or strongly as boys, restrictive organizations of ego defenses in relation to drives are less a factor in the latency contribution to the superego than are social pressures. Girls therefore enter adolescence with a less well internalized set of inhibitions. They remain in a position of being influenced by group shame, as adolescence approaches, more than by guilt (see Kaplan, 1974). Adolescent sexual behavior is molded by the inhibiting factors which had been operative in the latency age period.

The intensity of orgastic sensation can result in a flight from sensation through the inhibition of masturbation. Concomitant genital anaesthesia has been reported. An affect of disgust results in inhibition of genital manipulation and is usually the result of associating the genitals with ex-cretion. This is part of the little girl's use of the cloacal theory in under-standing her genitals and contributes to one of the reaction-formations used in establishing the state of latency. Parental attitudes conveyed through constant admonitions to stop masturbation have a strong influ-ence in limiting masturbation as well as communicating general social disapproval of masturbation to girls. Kaplan (1974) has pointed out that latency age girls are more aware of the attitudes of others and are more sensitive to shame than are boys. Parents convey an ego ideal that excludes masturbation for girls. Shame and limitation of proscribed activities occur when the needs of the child tend to draw her away from the dictates of the ego ideal. As Blanchard (1952) has pointed out, guilt over associated sado-masochistic, parricidal, fratricidal, and torture-laden fantasy content turns the child from masturbation. There are physiological limitations in the failure to be able to achieve gratification. This limits the usefulness of masturbation as an instrument of sexual discharge.

As a result of the factors just described, overt masturbation usually ceases during the latency period. Sexual drive energies are discharged through other pathways. These include three primary areas. First, there is regression to the oral phase with overeating, thumb-sucking, and transi-tional phenomena. Second, there is the activation of the state of latency (see Chapter 2). Latency age children usually function with a regressed sadomasochistic drive organization. To cope with this situation, reaction-formations and obsessional defenses combine to convert the latent sado-masochistic fantasies and drive energies into a manifest state of calm, educability, and pliability. States of heightened sexual drive with intensi-fied needs for discharge find outlet in displacement of the intended mas-turbatory activity into movement that is expressed through the whole body. The latent sadomasochistic and oedipal fantasy content is converted into manifest fantasies which are so highly symbolized that they mask the guilt-laden original contents while giving vent to the drives. This pattern of response is the average expectable response for a child who has achieved a state of latency. Third, there is masked masturbation. This refers to direct stimulation of the genitals done in such a way that the original masturba-tory intent of the activity is hidden from the child. In effect, the act of masturbation continues. The child, a bit unaware of what she is doing, achieves physical pleasure without experiencing shame or guilt. Such activities as sustained rubbing of the vulva and/or anus with large amounts of toilet paper in the service of hygiene, rapid opening and closing of the legs, swinging of the legs, horseback riding, and sliding down ropes are examples of masked masturbation in girls.

Masturbatory Activity in Latency Age Boys

Boys and girls reveal great similarity in the dynamics and vicissitudes of masturbation during the latency years. The primary areas of difference relate to the presence of erections, the physical differences between the genitals of the two sexes, the external exposed position of the penis, and, as Bornstein (1953) has pointed out, the more frequent appearance of "limited orgastic experience" in boys (p. 70). The combination of these differences tends to increase the possibility of encountering stimuli that will seduce the child toward direct masturbatory activity. As a result genital masturbation can be observed more frequently with boys than with girls throughout the latency period.

Lampl-De Groot (1950) has described her impressions that there are quantitative differences between boys and girls in the degree of "suppression of masturbation during latency and perhaps puberty also," (p. 172) indicating that girls more often relinquish masturbation during the latency period (p. 105).

As in the case of girls, masturbatory activity in latency age boys can be categorized in terms of a continuum of activities serving for discharge of sexual drives. At one extreme, there is highly symbolic fantasy play which couples symbolized fantasy and whole body movements in the service of drive discharge. At the other extreme there is manual manipulation of the penis and frequently of the scrotum and anus accompanied by directly represented fantasies of penetration and sadomasochistic fantasies. The

former activity involving symbolized fantasy play represents the functioning of a youngster who utilizes the ego structure of a child in the state of
latency. The latter represents the functioning of a child whose drive energies and ego organization permit more direct expression of sexual drives.
Note that the fantasies contain sadomasochistic elements in keeping with
expected libidinal regressions of the latency age period. In boys as well as
girls, the sadistic content of the fantasies contribute to a sense of guilt in
relation to masturbation. There is a potential for the production of orgastic sensations in boys as a result of stimulation of the glans and shaft of the
penis. Before the onset of puberty, most boys are satisfied if they achieve a
pleasurable sensation. The child stimulates himself, enjoying the experience of excitement till satiated. With the onset of puberty and the intensification of the sexual feelings that accompany it, there develops a feeling
of frustration and a sense that the level of excitement is not enough. Ejaculation with orgasm is required. At that point behavioral phenomena
identifiable as the derivatives of a search for orgasm become apparent.
Under this pressure the late latency-early adolescent boy is seen to act out
thinly masked masturbation fantasies. During early latency, most children
can be satisfied with achieving a state of mild sustained excitement.
Because of the frequent occurrence of erections, especially morning erections and erections associated with REM sleep and urinary urgency, and
the ease with which the externally available penis can be casually exposed
to friction, there are a multitude of factors which stimulate the child and
initiate masturbatory activity involving the penis. Scrotal masturbation,
which occurs with less frequency than penile masturbation, is not subject
to such influences. The sensations associated with scrotal masturbation in
boys, though imbued with an undercurrent of excitation, are primarily experienced as soothing. The visual accessibility of the male genitals results
in very specific localization by boys of areas associated with erotic responses. Boys can practically draw identifying maps, including sensations
related to their scrota. The tip and shaft of the penis are described as the
source of greatest pleasure.

Kinsey et al. (1948) concluded from data collected from a number of
preadolescent populations that over half of the boys in an uninhibited society could achieve adult-form orgasms before the age of latency and that
all could achieve such orgasms three to five years before entering adolescence. Ejaculation does not occur until puberty and adolescence. Most
latency age boys in our culture do not take advantage of this physiological

potential for discharge because of strong psychological and social inhibitions. There are boys with strong orgastic responses who limit the degree and intensity of their excitements by aborting their masturbatory activities short of the most intense feelings, or who produce anaesthesias to ablate the potential for strong feelings. In effect, these reactions produce the equivalent of a physiological limitation of the potential that masturbation has for providing relief of sexual tensions.

Another factor that turns the boy away from overt masturbation is the guilt over the sadomasochistic, parricidal fratricidal, and torture-laden content of the fantasies that accompany masturbation in latency age children. This has been pointed out by Blanchard (1953) with a multitude of illustrations. She described one youngster who fantasied that he was urinating in his mother's rectum (p. 27). If one keeps in mind that fantasies sometimes enter consciousness unbidden, this illustration will suffice to explain why it is that children will avoid masturbation. Children have little control over the nature of the fantasy that appears. They begin to masturbate and the fantasy develops, as does a dream, in the course of the development of the excitement. One way to avoid such unbidden fantasy is to avoid masturbation.

Parental attitudes conveyed to the child by constant admonitions to stop masturbating have a strong influence in limiting this activity as well as communicating general social disapproval for masturbation and for sexuality in children in general. Threats of castration take the form of direct admonitions—"If you keep doing that, it will fall off—and of more subtle threats such as the warning that one will experience softening of the brain or insanity if masturbation continues. Through these messages of prohibition, parents establish an ego ideal that excludes masturbation as an activity for boys. Shame and guilt are stirred whenever these activities are stimulated. This stimulation happens more often with boys because of the more exposed nature of their genitals, and the concomitant increased possibility of contact with stimuli from the environment. The boy is therefore forced into greater efforts at practicing control over sexual urges. In those boys who have succumbed to social demands that masturbation be controlled in latency, there is produced an intense, internalized set of prohibitions and cultural inhibitions in adolescence. Thus, those who have entered the state of latency bring strong controls over sexual urges into their initial contacts with the increased sexual drives of adolescence. This continuation of strong restrictions on sexuality beyond latency explains the ascetic adjustments so commonly seen in early adolescence in both sexes.

During latency, social restrictions and personal inhibitions are in constant conflict with sexually stimulating experiences. Because of the exposed position of the penis and the associated ease with which stimuli seducing toward masturbation occurs, some direct phallic stimulation usually is sustained throughout the latency time period in the form of occasional conscious masturbation. In youngsters with a good structure of latency, much of this stimulation is discharged through fantasy formation. Other youngsters mobilize aggression when sexually stimulated and physically attack peers. At times, actual sexual contact with others are made.

Conflict over masturbation is an elementary factor in the psychology of latency. At about eight years of age, social and superego restrictions lessen for some, decreasing the amount of anxiety generated by the urge to discharge sexual tension through masturbation. As a result of factors resulting in the entanglement of masturbation with guilt, shame, and social opprobrium, there develop in the latency age child, patterns of ego mechanisms for the discharge of the sexual drive through alternative pathways. These include three primary areas. First, overeating, thumb-sucking, and transitional phenomena may occur—a regression to the oral phase. Second, there is the activation of the state of latency. States of heightened sexual drive with intensified needs for discharge find outlet in the transfer of the masturbatory activity to movement expressed through the whole body in a conversion of the latent sadomasochistic and oedipal fantasy content into manifest fantasies which are so highly symbolized that they mask the guilt-laden original contents while giving vent to the drives. The fantasies are expressed in the motor sphere through the whole body activity and latency play. This pattern of response is the average expectable response for the child who has achieved a state of latency. Third, there is masked masturbation. This refers to direct stimulation of the genitals, done in such a way that the original masturbatory intent of the activity is hidden from the child. In effect, the act of masturbation continues. The child, unaware of what is being done, achieves physical pleasure without experiencing conscious shame or guilt. The more exposed position of the male genitals provides a host of possibilities. Rubbing against the sheets and rocking against the bed, wrestling with other boys, are but a few of the multiple variations available to an imaginative stripling.

Masturbatory Content During the State of Latency

In our examination of masturbation in girls and in boys during the latency age period we repeatedly find situations in which overt masturbatory activity undergoes inhibition as a result of such factors as shame reactions to parental disapproval, fear reactions to intensified feelings, and guilt reactions to the content of the fantasies associated with the masturbation. As Bornstein (1951) points out, masturbation as an outlet diminishes under the sway of the strict superego, which finds expression in the struggle of the child against masturbation. Masturbation unquestionably diminishes markedly during latency, producing an illusion of diminished sexual activity. Kinsey (1948) could only estimate orgastic potential in boys because of the influence of an inhibited society on the sexuality of the latency period child (p. 178).

But sexual drives remain strong through the latency period; indeed during the breaks in the latency state, overt sexuality including masturbation appears. We must, then, ask what becomes of the sexual urges while the child is in the state of latency. How are these strong sexual drives expressed? Friedlaender (1942) suggests an answer. "The physical expression of the sexual urge, masturbation, after much struggle, becomes entirely or partially repressed, masturbatory fantasies undergoing further change and finding outlets in daydreams" (p. 136). Under the pressure of masturbatory inhibitions, fantasy components and the motor components undergo a transformation. The motor components are transformed from direct motor stimulation of the genitals to an expression of drive activity utilizing movement of the entire body. Such discharge utilizing muscles and movements of the body takes three forms.

Disorganized jumping is one outlet. At times, masturbatory inhibitions force the child into a regression to primitive use of the whole body for the expression of drives, such as occurred early in the first year of life. When it happens in the latency period it illustrates the strength and persistence of drives during latency. An example of this kind of activity is revealed in the following incident: An eight-year-old boy walked up to his father and placed his hand on his head, measuring his height against his father's back. He commented on how much he was growing. The father was delighted by this and went onto his knees in front of his youngster and then bowed his head further until his head was an inch or so below the top of his son's head. He then moved his hand to the point on the son's forehead that the top of his head reached in his kneeling position and stated, "Before very long you'll be this much taller than I." A flood of affect associated with oedipal feelings engulfed the child. He showed an unrestrainable excitement. He began to jump up and down and to flip over head first onto the floor many times. His parents eventually had to stop him from doing this because of fear that he would hurt his neck. Such activity is sometimes seen in play-therapy sessions. When it occurs, an interpretation that did not take into account the degree of ego distance from which the child was viewing the material being discussed is a likely cause.

A second form of motor discharge is organized athletic activities. Schools schedule recess and gym periods to permit youngsters to let off steam in this way. This is illustrated by the activities of a nine-year-old boy who usually came into the office and behaved in a quiet manner. He usually talked about his problems, augmenting his presentation with drawings and play which disclosed fantasies he could not otherwise convey. One day he came in, in what appeared to be a highly excited state, moving around the room quickly, jumping on and off the table, and using a ball in an excited manner which presaged further loss of control in the session. I asked him what he thought had resulted in this change in his behavior. His response was that the teachers had neglected gym and recess that day. He was suffering severely from a state of excitement produced by failure of the school to provide physical activities as a pathway for discharge during the school day. Throughout latency and on into adolescence, this form of discharge of energies is sought out by youngsters.

A third form involves organized total body movement in play, alone or with peers, which can be used for acting out the fantasy products of the structure of latency. Through this type of activity, discharge of drives becomes possible without interfering with the state of latency. Drives are played out in manifest fantasies which are distortions of latent masturbatory fantasies. This is illustrated by the case of a child with a potential for latency state functioning who, following a situation which had stirred oedipal feelings, acted out in an analytic session the following fantasy. He became a peasant leader who was ordered by his followers to kill the king. He did so by jumping on my desk brandishing a toy sword. This case was more fully described in Chapter 2.

In the present chapter, we have traced a striking phenomenon: the developmental relationship between motor activity and fantasy activity as they serve sexual drive discharge. At first, drives find expression through purely motor acts such as nursing. When nursing is blocked, displacement to reflex schemata coordinated with nursing occurs. This produces rubbing of genitals and of soft soothing objects, such as blankets. Soon whole body activities such as rocking and cuddling with a real object are sought as sources of comfort. Then, after eighteen months, with the development of the capacity to conceptualize verbally, words are added to the resources of the drives. Fantasies begin to develop which contain a description of the motor activities which are the necessary conditions for discharge of the drives. Fantasy and motor activity become, at this point, inseparably linked. Words and fantasy undergo a maturation of their own which provides expanded potentials for use for the expression of drives. Language and symbols develop. The child can now use words to conceive of things to be used for the discharge of drives. Therefore drive discharges can be separated from the immediate physical activities through which they have been channeled in the first years of life, and new activities and objects can be found. In addition, through psychoanalytic symbol formation, the fantasies and objects which now constitute the latent potential pattern for discharge of drives can be masked to the point that they become unrecognizable. Thus even forbidden wishes can be gratified. The psychological potential is now present for the establishment of the state of latency. Typically, children at this point of development involve themselves in genital stimulation accompanied by fantasy. From the time that fantasy evolves till the latency stage begins, a close tie exists between the two. With the beginning of the latency stage, multiple prohibitions are brought to bear on overt masturbation, and internal prohibitions block the fantasies. Fantasy and physical stimulation, under these pressures, part company for the duration of the state of latency as a result of transformations that alter their forms to a degree that makes coordination incongruous. Only in the energetic playing out of fantasies is the old relationship approximated.

We have already dealt above with the vicissitudes of the motor component of masturbation. We have now to turn to the workings of the transmutation of fantasy. The fantasy itself is repressed and then fragmented. The fragments are symbolized and organized into a series of manifest fantasies which are so different in appearance and characteristics from the symbols and content elements of the original fantasy that they are essentially unrecognizable and without valence for attracting affect. Thus, anxiety, which would have interfered with achieving libidinal discharge, is avoided, and the child can play out the transformed fantasy. Fantasy activities can exist independent of motor activity. We observe this phenomenon when a child listens to or reads a story and interprets pictures in accord with the content of his own modified manifest fantasies. It also becomes apparent when the child tells what he has been thinking while sitting still. Friedlaender (1942) has pointed out that latency books mirror conflicts of the latency child.

In the latency state child, fantasy activity undergoes a transformation through masking of meanings and through distortions which produce manifest fantasies whose relationship to latent fantasy is not detectable. Motor activity, as noted above, follows a parallel course. Motor activity involved in drive discharge, such as direct masturbatory stimulation involving genitalia and erotogenic zones, is inhibited. Motor activity is displaced into whole body activities which may or may not be correlated with fantasy activities. And so, the link between fantasy and masturbation is broken during the latency state. Either motor activity or fantasy activity can serve as a vehicle for the relief of tension and the discharge of drives during the latency state. Extensive use of fantasy and fantasy play is available to the child as an independent pathway for the masked discharge of drives.

Since, during the latency age period, the child often goes in and out of the state of latency, within the course of a day he may experience the appearance of masturbation and fantasy as a unified activity such as typifies prelatency masturbation in alternation with the inhibition of masturbatory acts and fantasies, and the appearance in play and fear of their derivatives.

In summary, during the state of latency, there is a dissociation between masturbatory fantasy and masturbatory activity. The association between the two becomes facultative. In any given situation, the meaning of each, separately and together, is modified beyond the point that its original masturbatory intent can be recognized.

Late Latency-Early Adolescence

Late latency-early adolescence is a term sometimes used to denote the period during which thoughts of fantasy objects become less important during masturbation than thoughts of objects in reality. It can begin as early as eight and a half and end after puberty. As I have pointed out elsewhere (Sarnoff, 1971), there is rapprochement of fantasy and masturbation during late latency. The outside world is increasingly available as the source of objects through which fantasies can be gratified. Masturbatory activity becomes less proscribed. Concrete operational thinking, which is characterized by an increase in the reality orientation of the child, interferes with the use of fantasy as a means of discharge of sexual drive. The child is forced into a search for objects in reality. The cessation of fantasy play as an outlet ushers in a resurgence of direct masturbatory activity accompanied by fantasy. In late latency-early adolescence, there is a reexperiencing of the simultaneous occurrence of masturbatory activity and masturbation fantasy that characterized ages three to five.

A. Reich (1951) states that ". . . in puberty, there may be a return from the pregenital activity of fantasy back to genital masturbation. But these apparently genital activities are frequently found to be still accompanied by unconscious pregenital fantasies" (p. 88). During this period there is normally a shift in the objects sought for instinctual-drive gratification (see also Sarnoff, 1973a). Objects in fantasy are replaced by objects in reality. Parents are replaced by peers. The waxing of the drives produced by the hormonal changes of puberty, coupled with the late latency disenchantment with fantasy as a mode of instinctual discharge, force this change. A surge of turmoil accompanies it. If adult object relations, which are the blossoms of this tide, are to exist free of the taint of earlier, indeed infantile, object ties, a definitive series of steps must be negotiated. This series of steps, as will be detailed below, has a uniform thrust and direction in the lives of all who issue from the arduous defile of adolescence with normal object relations.

Pathology occurs when there are strong impediments which interfere with progress along this series of steps. Foremost among the elements which impede the forward thrust is the increase in narcissism which characterizes early adolescence. Narcissistic investments of fantasy during object seeking imbue the new object with the characteristics of the old and, in so doing, halt the process of early adolescent realistic object seeking in mid-course.

The goal of the latency state in relation to the libidinal drives is that of a successful holding action. Late latency-early adolescence is characterized by a continuous shift between this holding action and a behavioral pattern which is oriented toward a distant goal. The shifting is often marked, with therapists noting in each session whether the patient is in a state of latency and wants to play or wants to discuss the problems of growing up and its associated fears and trials. The future and its tasks and responsibilities are the concern of the late latency-early adolescent period. The child is concerned with extricating himself from the admonitions of parents and dependence on them. There is a sharp increase in this age range in the capacity for increasingly intense orgastic responses to sexual stimulation. Normally youngsters respond to this situation by a realignment of masturbatory fantasy and the act of masturbation. This reunion of masturbation and fantasy during late latency-early adolescence serves an important purpose. In this way, the maturing organism learns to test, experience, bear, and finally to enjoy the welling sensations that constitute orgasm before establishing ties with an object in reality. Laufer (1968) emphasizes the role of conscious early adolescent masturbation fantasies as a tool used by the developing person to experience in "trial action . . . adult sexual behavior" (p. 115).

The shift from the state of drive expression through coupled masturbation and fantasy to the state of drive expression manifested in a realistic relationship with a real object is accomplished with difficulty. There is a surge of narcissism that occurs with puberty that militates toward the selection of objects and life patterns which relate to the content of the masturbation fantasy, detracting from the cathexis of reality. There is danger that the fantasy content will lead to a distortion of reality situations sought by the child. This situation can give rise to neurotic interactions with partners and lovers in adult life. Alternatively, the establishment of contact with a real object may be interfered with as a result of a developmental fixation characterized in the following way. There is a coupling of poorly symbolized masturbatory fantasy with involvement of the whole body in playing out the fantasy. Only slightly distorted latent fantasies are played out. If unresolved, this fixation of ego functions provides the child with the groundwork for perversions without partners in later life.

This intense state of narcissism occurring in adolescence was known to Freud (1914), who explained it as an intensification related to the bodily changes of adolescence. He related this in girls to the maturing of the female sexual organs; the onset of puberty brings about an intensification of the original narcissism, a situation unfavorable to the development of a true object choice (p. 88). In boys heightened narcissism may be detected in body building activities and preoccupation with appearance. Pumpian-Mindlin (1965) has described a state of "omnipotence" which he attributes to late adolescence. This state resembles the narcissistic cathexis of masturbation fantasies that I have observed beginning with preadolescence. He describes the "resolution of omnipotentiality . . . as [resulting from] . . . 'acting out' of the omnipotential fantasies in reality, thereby submitting them to testing. Gradually, as they are tested against reality, the diffuse omnipotential energies are channelized to modify the omnipotential fantasies in accord with the demands of reality" (p. 9). This description resembles strongly one of the pathways which shall be described below by which masturbation fantasies are decathected and set aside.

The relationship between masturbation fantasies and adolescent behavior has been described by Anna Freud (1949), A. Reich (1951), and P. Blos (1963). Anna Freud recognized that "masturbation fantasies are acted out in dealings with the external world" (p. 203), while Reich stated that "behavior patterns are derivatives of masturbation fantasies" (p. 92). Blos placed these concepts in the area of object relations: "we recognize in acting out, an autoerotic use of the outside world which is always available for momentary or immediate gratification" (p. 123). "The acting out individual . . . turns to the outer world as a tension relieving part object" (p. 123). "The adolescent process proceeds from a progressive decathexis of primary love objects, through a phase of increasing narcissism and autoerotism to heterosexual object finding" (p. 125).

There is as a result of the confluence of intense narcissism and the return to masturbation associated with prelatency fantasy content during early adolescence, a strong recathexis of prelatency fantasy which intrudes into the early adolescent's attempts to find peer objects in reality to replace the parents. Often the object is seen in the guise of the parents.

Freud (1914) spoke of three types of possible paths leading to the choice of an object within the context of narcissism. Where narcissism dominates, there are described two paths. On the first path, choice of objects is based upon characteristics of the subject; this Freud calls "the narcissistic type" (p. 90). On the second path, choice of object is based upon characteristics of those who cared for the child and the succession of substitutes who take their place; this is called the "anaclitic or attachment type" (p. 90). The third type of path in the choice of the object involves the search for an object in reality. This is the path taken by those "who have renounced part of their own narcissism and are in search of object love" (p. 89). It is the shift from the narcissistic and anaclitic grouping of pathways to the pathway of object love that characterizes the successful negotiation of the "search for reality." Narcissism as used here is derived from Freud's writings during the period in which the libido theory predominated. It consists of the durable concept that there are patterns of object choice which are guided by the characteristics of the subject or of those who have tended him during the formative years. The motive force that perpetuates these patterns is libido extended in cathexes, which are invested in the subject (self). The seeking of an object that conforms to patterns derived from the nature of the subject and his early caretakers, in the context of the subject's fantasies, is a manifestation of narcissism.

Two papers have been devoted, in large part, to the shift of cathexis from parents as primary objects to peers. Though neither deals specifically with masturbation fantasies and the narcissism of late latency-early adolescence, each contains information of value for us. Katan (1937) refers to the displacement of instinctual desires from the incestuous objects onto other new objects during adolescence as a normal nonreversible phenomenon called "removal" (pp. 42, 43).

The need to move to the new object in reality is related to the fact that fantasies about the original objects involve anxiety-producing incestuous thoughts. Katan noted that it was possible that the removal would not be complete. "Naturally, the adolescent does not always succeed completely and immediately in this process of removal. His first love objects frequently show traits of the incest object" (p. 44). Some remain fixed to this type of object relationship, while others experience a series of relationships (sometimes with the same person) in which gradually the object relationships veer toward reality and away from narcissistically cathected incestuous contents of the masturbation fantasies.

In a 1972 article I described one of the pathways by which fantasies can be used to establish a bridge to new objects. A person who is fearful of new relationships among peers may project fantasy elements onto them which are manifestly fear provoking; but the covert use of such fantasy elements provides a means whereby the fearful person can enter into a relationship in which there is control through familiarity with a situation. The unknown is too much feared. The projection of a familiar and partly mastered fear provides a bridge by which the new object is clothed in motives of "an old friend." Once this bridge has been established, it is possible for Pumpian-Mindlin's concept of the "resolution of omnipotentiality" (described above) to be activated to modify the influence of incestuous fantasies. If this partial removal of omnipotential fantasies does not go on to full removal, then a masochistic life pattern of object relationships with a strong and clearly apparent narcissistic component develops.

In dealing with studies of object relations and object seeking, the concept of the object alone is a pale point with which to start. Objects do not exist outside a context of wishes and conditions. Former caretakers are not sought in isolation. Rather, the way one was cared for serves as the touchstone in selection. This is the reason that so often in the psychoanalytic literature terms such as the *oedipal mother* appear rather than *mother* in isolation. It is the context of the fantasies in which the early self and objects appear that the adolescent attempts to reproduce during the narcissistic phase of his search for reality. The attempt at reproduction undergoes modification, like that which occurs during the translation of latent content into the manifest form of the dream. Thus behavior and object choice characteristics derived from the fantasy-clothed contexts of childhood are modified and truncated representations of the originals. The realistic aspects of the object choices require this modification and distortion. A representation of the original fantasy-clothed contexts which dominate object seeking activities may be seen with a minimal degree of distortion in the manifest content of the masturbation fantasies of children in late latency-early adolescence. Studies of changes in masturbation fantasies and concurrent changes that happen in the object-seeking activities of the subject can give a clear indication of the progress that the child has achieved in overcoming his narcissism.

The degree to which there is lack of concordance of masturbation fantasy and behavior patterns is an indicator of the extent to which the subject can ignore fantasy and cathect reality, as well as the degree to which he pursues a path that is free of narcissistic domination in his object choice.

If, in the course of change, the masturbation fantasy and the behavior patterns remain similar, but both give evidence of modification in the direction of the search for an object in reality, a stable adjustment and a most successful resolution of the search for reality is indicated. Motor and fantasy components involving masturbatory content during late latency-early adolescence normally pursue a course of events intermediate between latency fantasy play and adolescent masturbation. During the state of latency the content of the masturbatory fantasy is divorced from the act of masturbation and is expressed in fantasy play. There follows a transitional situation in which a relatively undisguised masturbation fantasy is acted out as in play, accompanied by physical manipulation of the body. The child becomes physically involved with the acting out of the fantasy. In effect, these are latency play states in which the fantasy is relatively undistorted by the action of the symbolizing function. The degree to which the symbolizing function of the ego is too weak to deal with the increasing drives of early puberty is expressed in the degree to which it functions poorly. This phase is often observed and its manifestations are well known. It can take the form of fantasies of a lover, who is talked about by a young girl as though he were real. At times the girl will send herself letters signed by the imaginary lover. This condition is sometimes referred to as pseudo-logia fantastica. The intermediate fantasy of late latency can take the form of fantasies about the appearance of the adult human body. Boys and girls seek out magazines with nude pictures to study. A period of peeping tomism often marks the transitional time. It is not unusual during this period for mothers to discover that some of their underwear is missing, only to discover that it is in the room of their late latency-early adolescent son. Cross dressing is common during this period. With the onset of full puberty, these activities should cease and masturbation should take on the characteristic of masturbatory manipulation of the genitals while lying still with the entire fantasy experienced mentally. As will be discussed later, the onset of puberty is accompanied by the transition to the adolescent form of masturbation. The changeover does not always occur completely at this time. The strength with which the individual cathects the fantasies with narcissistic energies determines whether or not the transition is complete.

The following clinical examples illustrate this behavior.

E.P. was seen when he was sixteen and one-half years old. His chief complaint was that he chose as dating partners girls who were in his estimation far below his station. He was made uncomfortable by this situation. Careful questioning revealed that he had very high marks, as did the girls he dated. What caused the girls to be devalued in his eyes was the characteristic for which he selected them: full and voluptuous figures.

He was the son of divorced parents. His mother had obtained a divorce when she learned that the father teased, beat, and tortured the child for no apparent reason whenever he was left alone with the boy. The patient remembered these incidents as occurring as early as two years of age.

When he reached age eleven, he began to develop erections every time he saw himself or another boy without a shirt on. In fact, he could produce an erection in himself simply by standing in front of a mirror with his shirt off. He could deal with the erection by making cuts into the skin of his back with a knife. The appearance and flow of blood was accompanied by a release of feelings similar to orgasm. When he achieved physiological ejaculation and orgasm readiness, he found that it was possible for him to masturbate successfully with a fantasy about a girl. He reported no cruelty in fantasy to be present. He manipulated his genitals with the fantasy content being wholly mental. Use of the knife and cutting were rarely "acted out" at this time. When he began dating at the age of sixteen, the girls with whom he became involved had, in common, characteristics which, in his interpretation, demeaned him and caused him to be embarrassed in public.

In this clinical vignette, the following elements can be seen. A masochistic masturbatory fantasy appears at about eleven years of age. In this fantasy we can see a reliving of passive, masochistic submission to the father who had tortured him as an infant. The fantasy is acted out as in latency play. With the start of genital masturbation and ejaculation, a healthier masturbation fantasy content appears. In the healthier fantasy, the father (homosexual object) is replaced by a nonincestuous heterosexual object. The latent content behind the original fantasy, however, retains its potential to influence. This becomes apparent when maturation and social pressures force a shift to a reinstatement of the disassociation of narcissistic fantasy and genital masturbation. Narcissistic fantasy shapes object seeking. Drives begin to seek gratification with peer partners in reality through patterns based on these fantasies. The resulting relationships contain elements derived from earlier latent and manifest fantasies. There is a heterosexual object and there is discomfort for the patient.

The effectiveness of the impact of social and reality demands upon this patient's fantasies reflects the degree to which he is able to free his instinctual energies from narcissism and other inner forces, and respond to the imposition of reality stresses.

It is not unusual to find apparently deviant masturbation fantasies appearing concurrently with more mature ones. I have not seen in early adolescents gradual changes in masturbation fantasies toward more mature forms, but rather the concurrent appearance of new forms and the lessening in frequency of use of the old contents, with a gradual decathexis of the old contents until they cease to appear.

R.L.K. was referred for treatment for poor school grades. During therapy sessions, while he was eleven years old, he excused himself and went into the bathroom that was attached to my playroom. He did this repeatedly. I became aware of what was going on when, one day, he came out of the bathroom with traces of blue eyeshadow on his lids. When I asked him about this, he informed me that he had obtained the eye shadow from his mother by stealth. When asked if my office were the only place in which he carried out such activities, he told me that he usually put on makeup when his parents went out. He would dress in an older girl cousin's clothes and pretend that a date was coming to pick him up. The exciting part of the fantasy had to do with the fantasied arrival of the date who forced the boy-girl to have sexual intercourse with him. When he began to masturbate using phallic stimulation and could reach orgasm and ejaculation, the fantasy content reflected that of the dating fantasy with little change. He masturbated, fantasying that he was having intercourse with a man. If he tried to think about having intercourse with girls, he was unable to become excited.

Let us think about these two cases for a moment. In both youngsters presented, there occurred a form of masturbation during the period preceding the first ejaculation which has not been singled out for attention in the psychoanalytic literature—a relatively undisguised masturbation fantasy is acted out in play. This activity combines the play discharge of latency with pubertally intensified sexual excitement and content derived from the prelatency fantasy life. With the appearance of fluid discharge (ejaculation) as an end point in masturbation, there was a shift to masturbation while lying relatively still with the entire fantasy experienced mentally. That this course of events occurred in both patients is unquestioned. I am under the impression that these are not unique findings but are exaggerated forms of a commonly occurring stage in late latency-early adolescent development, such as peeping at neighbors or pseudologia fantastica.

Although these phenomena occur in girls, they rarely occur while the child is alone. Usually the girl becomes involved in peeping or pseudologia fantastica in the company of others. I have not yet seen a girl who reported complicated play rituals such as those described by the boys. In any event, the more striking examples of this phenomenon occur preponderantly in the experience of boys. It is equally rare to see a female carry this form of behavior into adult life. A male who continues to use the ego structures that provide for such sexual gratification through fantasy-dominated activity (that is, latency play mechanisms with minimal displacement during symbol formation) in middle and late adolescence and adulthood would exhibit behavior indistinguishable from exhibitionism, frotteurism, auto-strangulation, transvestitism, and others of the sexual perversions without partners, which make up the limited sex lives of some males but are rarely seen in females. This vicissitude in male development could explain the rarity of such perversions in females.

The occurrence of pre-ejaculatory masturbatory fantasy play has been reported by Werner and Levin (1967):

> Between the ages of 8 and 12 the giant fantasy was replaced by day-dreams of wrestling with his older brother, as he had actually done on several occasions. He was always defeated by his brother, both in fantasy and in reality, and he experienced strong sexual excitement in both. With the onset of puberty there was a further change in his fantasies, which were now accompanied by genital stimulation. He pictured himself struggling with a stronger girl who overwhelmed him physically, handling his genitals and bringing about orgasm. As he passed from adolescence into maturity, the fantasy was again modified. He now saw himself as an active seducer of a woman (p. 322).

We can observe a common pattern in the above. Prior to the onset of ejaculation the following characteristics accompany expressions of the masturbation fantasy: The latent fantasy is thinly masked. The object is of the same sex. The subject is represented in the passive mode. In two cases he is the recipient of sadism. The fantasy is played out in action, and there are physical feelings of sexual excitement in keeping with what Bornstein (1953) has referred to as "limited orgastic feeling" (p. 70).

Following the onset of ejaculation, the following characteristics accompany expression of masturbation fantasy. The latent fantasy undergoes distortion and is more masked; the object changes sex; the subject may be represented in the active mode. The fantasy is experienced in thought, and physical manipulation of the penis produces physical feelings of sexual excitement which culminate in ejaculation.

In normal adolescent development, the use of masturbation is reinstated as an outlet for drives expressed through fantasies. What exists beyond early adolescence for this relationship and its components? Ideally, both masturbation and the expression of the drives through fantasy will be extinguished and replaced by an object in reality and adult sexuality. Often the use of fantasy to enhance the effects of physical stimulation accompanies sexual intercourse. It can serve as a means to an end throughout life. Should the persistent fantasies threaten and as a result require repression, neurotic outcomes may occur. Some have been described by Arlow (1953), and by Spiegel (1951). According to Spiegel, "the conflict may be solved in specifically neurotic ways, as for instance by the dissociation of the masturbatory activity from the fantasies, a solution which is frequently found in obsessive compulsive types" (p. 386). "Often," Spiegel continues, "the masturbatory fantasies are completely repressed, but may manifest themselves in hysterical conversion symptoms, especially in female adolescents" (p. 387).

On the other hand, Anna Freud (1949) has this to say about the relationship between such inhibition of masturbatory fantasy and character formation: "As a result, the masturbatory-fantasy is deprived of all bodily outlet, the libidinal and aggressive energy attached to it is completely blocked and dammed up, and eventually is displaced with full force from the realm of the sex-life into the realm of ego-activities. Masturbation-fantasies are then acted out in dealings with the external world, which become, thereby, sexualized, distorted, and maladjusted" (p. 203).

In latency, then, there is a discharge of drive energies through fantasy and play with little overt masturbatory component. With puberty, there is a marked increase in narcissistic libido, with drive discharge through masturbation with fantasies. Early in this phase, there may occur phenomena which contain elements both of latency play and masturbatory excitement. In these states, youngsters act out their incestuous masturbation fantasies with little distortion. This is followed in turn by a masturbatory behavioral state in which the child remains in one place and withdraws his body from total participation in the fantasy. Action is limited, usually to physical manipulation of the genitals. The fantasy is experienced only mentally and ejaculation and/or orgasm, rather than acting out of the fantasy, gives gratification. This union of fantasy and mastur-bation is short-lived.

When the possibility of sexual intercourse with real objects appears, the masturbation fantasy is then applied to the real objects as a result of the heightened narcissism. Often the fantasies, which are familiar and have been experienced and mastered in the past, can be used as a bridge to new and unknown objects. Once the real objects are cathected, it becomes possible to replace fantasy with reality, in those whose narcissistic upsurge is sufficiently light to permit the setting aside of fears. In these people, re-moval of the drive-discharge wishes from incestuous objects is accom-plished spontaneously.

Sexual Intercourse During the Latency Years

The most convincing evidence that the state of latency is the product of a reorganization of the ego rather than the result of a biologically pre-determined diminution in drive pressure is presented by those latency age youngsters who regularly seek sexual intercourse for the relief of drive pressures. In chapter 4, I discuss the case of a latency age girl who ap-proached sexual intercourse with interest and excitement. She had a sus-tained relationship with a constant partner. Those who are familiar with comparative anthropology studies of primitive societies are not surprised by such cases. Malinowski (1962) reported such sexual freedom in the Trobriand Islanders. Kinsey (1953) lists a number of other societies in which this occurs. It should be kept in mind that such behavior is the ex-ception in primitive societies (see discussion of Latency in Primitive Socie-ties in Appendix B). However, its presence is an indicator of the true state of drives during latency, and provides an insight into the nature of what things would be if the ego of latency were not so moved in the direction of drive inhibition.

Boys are capable of erection throughout the latency years. Kinsey (1948) reported that erection and intromission had been reported during the boyhood of 22 percent of all the males that they interviewed. Orgastic sensations were frequent in this circumstance. Ejaculation was rare, usually first occurring with the onset of puberty. Latency age coitus usually was introduced to the little boy by an older girl. Although such behavior is considered abnormal only from the standpoint of cultural relativism, there is a problem for the child in our culture in that the youngster who devotes himself to these pursuits is apt to neglect important developmental activities, such as education, to his detriment (see Sarnoff, 1971c). In Kinsey's study, only a small percentage of college-bound youngsters had experienced coitus during latency. For those who were involved, there were few episodes reported. On the other hand, for those who were not going to finish grammar school, the percentage of participants in coitus was large. The number of different episodes and partners for this group was also greater.

Kinsey (1953) reported that of all the women interviewed, 48 percent recalled some sort of preadolescent sex play. The investigators felt that the actual statistics were somewhat higher, but were aware of the capacity of individuals to forget latency age experiences. Seventeen percent of all the women who reported any form of heterosexual play had some form of coitus. Retrospective reporting made it difficult to determine if actual penetration had occurred. Often the sex play took place with peer partners and it was not clear whether more than juxtaposition of the genitals had been achieved. In twenty-nine cases the preadolescent girls were reported to have had contacts with older boys or adult men. In these cases complete genital union was reported (p. 113). Of all who reported any form of sex play during the latency years 61 percent reported that it happened in one year, 35 percent reported that it happened over a period of two years, and 9 percent reported sexual activity spanning five years.

Prepubertal Fantasy Activity

A persistent theme denotes the difference between early- to midlatency, and the late latency period that encompasses prepuberty. The earlier periods deal with stopgap measures and glances backward. Late latency deals with preparations and expectations for the future. Nowhere is this more evident than in the area of the fantasies of latency. Early latency fantasies deal with oedipal fantasies or the products of regressions from oedipality. Oral fantasies and anal-sadomasochistic fantasies dominate the symbolic life of the midlatency child. For the prepubertal child, the themes have more to do with preoccupation with future planning, reality objects, passivity, freedom from parental domination, preoccupation with the mature physique they are moving toward, and the mysteries of sexuality. Certain themes are more the province of girls than boys, but there is rarely a fantasy that is the exclusive province of one sex. The mental task of one often is found to be the labor of the other with little change. However, for the sake of organizational clarity, in the rest of this section I will discuss boys and girls separately.

In boys, Blos (1957) has pointed out that "castration anxiety in relation to the phallic mother is not only a universal occurrence of male preadolescence, but can be considered as its central theme. . . . Before a successful turn towards masculinity is effected, the employment of the homosexual defense against castration anxiety represents the typical stage of male preadolescence" (p. 50). There is a great deal of concern with body size and the size of the penis; self-defense and fantasies of power and karate chops fill the minds of the children. Underlying this there is often the fear that one is not truly male or will not be able to compete effectively against older males. Positions of passivity are especially feared. In order to escape the feeling of being subjugated, the child will overreact: fighting, ranting, or even running from situations of passivity.

In girls, Blos (1957) has described prepubertal experiences dominated by a "massive repression of pregenitality" (p. 51). "In normal female development the phase of preadolescent drive organization is dominated by a defense against the preoedipal mother" (p. 54). The defense against the preoedipal mother takes the form of an attempt to free oneself from the mother-child relationship in which the child was not considered to be sufficiently skilled to function on her own, independent of the mother. "Mother! Let me do it myself!" becomes the battle cry of these days. Often the best-intentioned mother will find herself attacked by a daughter who insists that any attempt to help is a signal of an attempt on the part of the parent to enslave the child. The child's attempts to shift the superego contents that are identified with the parent into the background and to replace them with a peer group's conscience is often a product of the child's rebellion against what may or may not be an imagined subjugated position vis-a-vis the parent.

Perhaps the most dramatic fantasies of the prepubertal girl are those held in expectation of puberty. Since puberty in boys is not associated wtih a sudden and decisive moment that heralds the beginning of the next stage in life, there is less expectation and dread. For boys it comes on gradually and there is time to absorb and work it through. Usually this is the case; for exceptions see discussion of the impact of the first ejaculation below. For girls many of their pubertal preoccupations are involved with expectation of the moment of onset and its counterparts. There is a strong sexual preoccupation in girls during prepuberty. Most prepubertal girls know the basic facts of reproduction; their interests in sexuality are concerned with how sexual intercourse feels. They do not fantasy so much about having sexual relations as they do about how they will look when they mature. Unable to accept the delay attendant upon seeing what they will look like, they choose to look at pictures of nude women to achieve mastery and settle their fears. The stories told by friends about periods cause the children to fear the experience. Uncertainty about the exact time of onset of the period and curiosity about how it will feel contribute to awakening in the child fears of being overwhelmed by the physical events of development. The child likens this to fear and shame related to toilet training and control of body products. How is it controlled? is a frequent question a frightened child asks herself about menstruation. Still another fantasy in expectation of menarche that dominates the child's response has to do with unresolved conflicts about sexual identity. If there is a hidden fantasy of being a boy, it is stirred awake by the approach of the most incontrovertible physical statement of femininity possible.

B.L. had been in analysis for four years at the time of the clinical vignette here reported. Her presenting complaints had been multiple. The most important of these was a preoccupation with neatness. This was so severe that she spent all of her time throwing away her papers and redoing the first letters of her assignment. This left her without time to learn first-grade work. As this complaint was dealt with in analysis, there appeared in the analysis strong anger and resentment toward her brother. She revealed (Sarnoff, 1969, p. 94), in fantasies and even in slips of the tongue, that she had castrated feelings and castrating wishes. The following vignette occurred when she was ten years, nine months old.

B.L. announced that she was going to attend a movie about menstruation at school. She spontaneously suggested that there would be no need for us to discuss this since she knew all about sex and menstruation because her mother had taught her a lot. Although I mentioned the movie to her before the showing she continued to avoid discussion saying that she really knew it all. After seeing the film, she retained her claim that she understood all and that "fortunately, that I am comfortable with." She was concerned that some boys had teased some of the girls, saying that the movie was about something that begins with a "p" (period), but passed this off with the comment that the boys were silly. About a week after the showing of the movie, she had a dream through which the reactions stirred up by the movie and the associated lecture were brought into the analysis. She began the session with the dream, which follows.

In the dream, I turned to my mother and said: "Mommy, I understand the movie, but I'm still scared. I worry about what it is going to feel like." My mother said, "I know a lady who has a machine that can make you menstruate. Then, when you know what it feels like, she can turn it off and you can wait for it to start naturally." Mother took me to this place. Me and my mother were walking down to that room down the long hall. There were bats, goblins, snakes, and witches. Mother said, "Don't worry about this, I've been through this before."

The witch called out, "Don't listen to her." The monsters followed us. I dreamed I was walking into this room with my mother. In the room there were like a lot of computers—machines and everything. There were things flashing. My school nurse was in it. She was standing by a bed. She was the one who showed us the menstruation movie. There was this menstruation machine that makes you menstruate to see how it feels. Mother said, "She just wants to know how it feels." Then I went and lied down on the bed in there and it starts flashing [Figure 1]. Then I start menstruating. The nurse said, "It won't gush like a faucet. It will drip slowly." That's what the nurse told one of the girls at the movie. Then I stopped gushing. My vagina turned into a faucet and started dripping very slowly. Here's how it changed [She

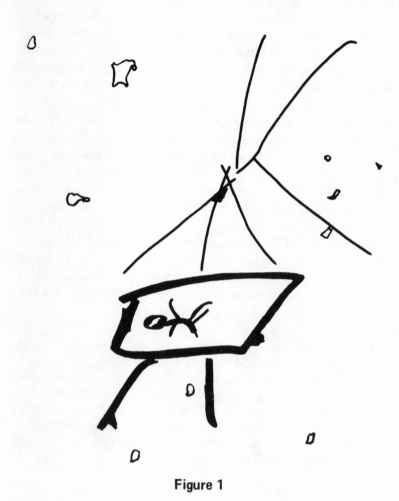

Figure 1

drew pictures]. Here is my vagina with a normal crack and peeing siss [Figure 2A]. Here it is bleeding. There is no more crack [2B]. Then it gets thinner [2C]. Then two pieces come out and make it look bent [2D]. Then the pieces move up and make the faucet controls [2E]. You know something, it looks like a penis [2F].

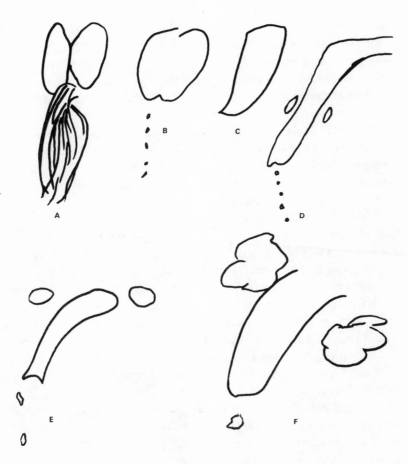

Figure 2

The dream had a definite effect on the analysis. She was able to speak more freely of her penis envy and to see its relationship to her depression and the overt anger she showed toward her brother. There is here a striking example of the unconscious meaning of the impending menarche. It reawakens bisexual fantasies. As such, as we will see, it stirs up aggression and confusion in the child.

The Impact of the First Menstrual Period

There are three basic aspects to the impact of menarche. There is the expectation of menarche and its effect on the psychology of the late latency-early adolescent child. There is the effect of menarche itself, with its realistic statement of womanhood, which identifies the child with the adult sexual potentials and which either squelches or intensifies conflict in relation to bisexual body image fantasies. There is the impact of menarche on the reactions of others in the child's environment. This last may be highly personal responses or highly traditionalized rituals. Such rituals are primarily characteristics of primitive cultures, but remnants of these rituals remain in the myths and fables of succeeding generations and cultures.

During the period of expectation of menarche, which starts as soon as the little girl first hears about and develops a concept of menstruation, there lies in wait in a corner of each little girl's mind, ready to spring to the center stage, a preoccupation with periods. There are hidden fantasies that somewhere within oneself there is a bit of a boy, perhaps even a penis, ready to grow. These are bisexual fantasies left over from the confusions of the prelatency period. Boys have similar fantasies, and of course, they are mirror images of the girls'.

This upsurge of pregenital bisexual conflicts and fantasies produces periods of identity diffusion and emotional disequilibrium in the girl. This period of expectation has been extensively studied by Blos (1962), Deutsch (1944), Fenichel (1945), Anna Freud (1936, 1965), Kestenberg (1961, 1967), and Hart and Sarnoff (1971). All consider the bisexual phase of late latency-early adolescence to be a normal reaction to the expectation of menarche. The illusory penis is seen as a psychic reality maintained in order to protect the little girl against narcissistic depletion. Menarche is anticipated by children in terms of fantasies experienced in earlier years. Thus, there is fear of oral deprivation derived from the thought that once one reaches womanhood, one is one step closer to being on one's own. There are revulsion feelings at the thought of messiness, and fear that the process cannot be controlled occurs. This mobilizes defenses in the direction of controlling everyone in the immediate environment as a way of working through the passivity involved in the expectation of an uncontrolled flow of blood. Concern with body changes and slight body injury is a manifestation of the preoccupation with the castration, in fantasy, that is expected with the coming of an event whose reality relegates the thought of possessing a penis to limbo.

Almost universally this is a time of inner turmoil, resulting from a combination of the psychological factors described above and internal sensations derived from the bodily changes of puberty. Kestenberg (1961) has described how "spurts of intense but poorly defined sensations flow into each other," as a result of the increasing flow of hormones which bring on the bodily changes that presage the onset of menarche. Girls can become so preoccupied with the nipping in of the waist, which is one of the first signs of puberty, that they develop obsessional symptoms and refuse to go to school. Confusion of body image which occurs at this time can interfere with the child's capacity for abstract thinking (Keiser, 1958), resulting in impaired mathematical progress and difficulties in spatial relations, chart and map reading. Kestenberg (1961) recognized that confusion of body image and sexual identification produces vague and clouded thought processes in conflict areas and beyond. It is imperative that psychotherapists work through these areas in youngsters who present with this symptomatology. Social pressures can intensify the problems (Kestenberg, 1967), sometimes evoking relatively dormant bisexual fantasies. Educational activities such as sex education movies can mobilize bisexual fantasies. The child, previously described, who dreamed that she grew a faucet to control her menstruation, with the associations that the faucet in the dream looked like a penis, illustrates this. Other factors involved in stirring up conflicts around pregenital bisexual fantasies in the premenarche child are parental conversations and the maturation of friends. The influx of bisexual fantasies stirred by these inputs concentrates the fantasy life of the individual around sexuality. Kestenberg (1961) has viewed this circumstance from a potentially positive aspect. For some children, this organization of fantasy provides the child with an opportunity to work through and even resolve earlier conflicts. These might not otherwise have been reached.

Menarche itself, when it appears, makes a realistic statement of womanhood. With the first menstruation an unambiguous reality event intrudes on the confusion. Menstruation defines the sexual role and identity.

Kestenberg (1961, 1967) and Blos (1962) describe the first menstruation as the necessary organizer which, for the young girl, serves to crystallize and define body boundaries. To the extent that there is confusion about identity and body image, this clarification is paralleled by a consolidation of the feminine role and clearer thinking. To the extent that the girl finds a feminine role unacceptable, the menarche, with its finality of meaning, intensifies and organizes fantasies related to feelings of castration and impaired self-esteem. These fantasy systems are in turn responded to by a panoply of defenses producing disparate symptomatology.

Helene Deutsch (1944) described the first menstruation as traumatic no matter what prior instructions are given. J. Kestenberg (1961, 1967, 1968), emphasizing its positive aspects as an organizer, calls it "a turning point in the acceptance of femininity." Peter Blos (1962) contrasts the preadolescent and adolescent girl—vagueness and ambiguity giving way to clearness of perception following menarche. The complexities of the reproductive apparatus of the human female are hidden within the body. In the male, the organs are outside to see. The prepubertal girl is told that there is something within her which is as fancy on the inside as that which is fancy on the outside for the boy. The nondemonstrable nature of the female internal sexual apparatus permits the child much leeway in fantasy. The illusory penis fantasy is a case in point. Menstruation provides a concrete proof of the existence of a complex system of organs deep in the body. Hart and Sarnoff (1971) described children who bemoaned their inability to define their body image—to know what was inside. The first menstruation provided proof of femininity. Penis fantasies were unsubstantiated. What was most striking was that following menarche there was a change in their acceptance of themselves as feminine, and they emerged with a better defined body image. Thinking was clearer; they dealt more directly with genital conflicts, oedipal strivings, and their own realistic future roles as wives and mothers.

Menarche does not always bring with it the resolution of conflicts. In those who cannot accept a setting aside of bisexual and penis fantasies, the first menstruation intensifies the problem. This aspect of the impact of the menarche relates to childhood experiences, feminine identifications, and to the mother's acceptance of the girl's role as a woman. Kestenberg (1961) described a direct correlation between emotional disturbance and proneness to view menarche as a threat. The genital conflict and castration complex come to the fore and stir up intense emotions—anger, depression, feelings of inferiority, guilt over increased masturbatory urges. If the cloacal theory is strongly cathected, then the child must deal with feelings of shame and disgust (Bonaparte, 1949; Deutsch, 1944). The child must resolve guilt mobilized by increased aggressive and sexual drives.

Kestenberg (1961) emphasized the role of menstruation in enabling the girl to differentiate fantasy from reality. Feminine tendencies are mobilized and hopefully master the genital trauma. There is intensification of sexual excitement, fantasies of defloration and rape. Wishes and fears related to pregnancy and childbirth appear. Many menstrual cycles occur before fuller "reintegration" (Kestenberg, 1967) can be achieved as the young adolescent emerges from the disequilibrium and diffusion of prepuberty.

At the menarche, there is reorganization of the ego around a more clearly defined body image. Reactions to menarche are based on unconscious fantasies, educational experiences, and the nature of feminine identifications.

Menarche has clear impact on the people around the child, producing a gamut of reactions both personal and ritualized. Even before menstruation begins, attitudes of the parents shape the nature of what will be told to the child.

Helene Deutsch (1944) described frequent neglect on the part of mothers in giving prior instructions on menstruation, although other aspects of reproduction were dealt with. This is an additional indication of how emotionally charged the subject is for individuals and societies. It is not unusual for fathers to feel estranged from their daughters during the time of menarche or to, as one man described it, "take her out for the evening on a date." Often the reactions of people around her add to the child's difficulties. People in the immediate surroundings respond with characteristic behavior which reflects not only their concern for the child, but for themselves. Today these self-oriented responses are not as easily recognized. They are present, however, in the special movies and educational activities explaining menarche and in the withdrawal of some fathers from closeness to their daughters at this time.

Fortunately, reports of the behavior of peoples from less sophisticated times are still available to us. In these cultures magic predominated over intellect and logic as we know them. The unconscious motives for the behavior surrounding menarche are clearly manifest. Frazer (1922) and Scheinfeld (1944) have written of these reactions in primitive man. In general, all menstruating women were treated as though they were dangerous. They were not permitted to touch growing things and that which they had touched must be discarded. They were secluded and were considered to be unclean. "Amongst the Bribri Indians of Costa Rica—the only plates she may use for food are banana leaves, which when she had done with them, she throws away. . . . If anyone drank from the same cup after her, he would surely die" (Frazer, 1922, p. 241). In addition to these responses to menses (seclusion, fear of danger, attitude of uncleanliness), menarche was responded to with a number of irrational demands upon the child. These were prolonged seclusion, hanging high, exclusion from contact with the sun, heaven, and earth, and denial of permission for the child to scratch herself. "In New Ireland, girls are confined for four or five years in small cages, being kept in the dark and not allowed to set foot on the ground." "Among the Zulus," Frazer continues, "when the first signs of puberty show themselves . . . [the girl] runs to the river and hides herself among the reeds for the day, so as not to be seen by men. She covers her head . . . so that the sun may not shine on it and shrivel her up into a . . . skeleton. . . . After dark, she returns home and is secluded in a hut for some time" (p. 690). "When symptoms of puberty appeared on a girl for the first time, the Guaranis of Southern Brazil . . . used to sew her up in a hammock, leaving only a small opening in it to allow her to breathe" (p. 696). "In similar circumstances, the Chiriguanos of Southeastern Bolivia hoisted the girl in her hammock to the roof where she stayed for a month: the second month, the hammock was let half way down from the roof; and in the third month, old women, armed with sticks, entered the hut . . . saying they were hunting the snakes that had wounded the girl" (p. 690). Among the Vancouver Island Indians (Nootka), the child may not touch her hair with her hands, but is allowed to scratch her head with a comb or a piece of bone provided for that purpose. To scratch the body is forbidden, as it is believed that every scratch would leave a scar. Murphy and Murphy (1974) describe menarche customs among the Mundurucu of Brazil: "When a girl has her first menses, she is prohibited from bathing for three days, as a certain kind of bird may drink the blood, causing the girl to turn yellow and die. She is also sent to fetch firewood, and to do it speedily, for now she . . . is a woman and must become strong" (p. 176).

Even the ancient Romans held such beliefs. According to Frazer they believed that "the touch of a menstruous woman turned wine to vinegar, blighted crops, killed seedlings, blasted gardens, brought down the fruit from the trees, dimmed mirrors, blunted razors, rusted iron and [especially at the waning of the moon] killed bees" (p. 702).

Frazer believed that "the object of secluding women at menstruation is to neutralize the dangerous influences which are supposed to emanate from them at such times. . . . The danger is believed to be especially great at the first menstruation. To repress this force within the limits necessary for the safety of all concerned is the object of the taboos in question" (p. 702). He noted a "deeply engrained dread which primitive man universally entertains of menstruous blood. He fears it at all times but especially on its first appearance; hence the restrictions under which women lie at their first menstruation are usually more stringent than those which they have to observe at any subsequent recurrence of the mysterious flow" (p. 698). In the light of the multiple implications of menarche described above, this does not appear to be a sufficient explanation for the intense response to the first menstruation of primitive peoples. In culturally more advanced peoples, myths, legends and folk tales contain a transmuted form of these customs of primitive man. From the contexts in which symbols of primitive menarche customs appear, it should be possible to gain further insight into their meaning. As an example, there is Danae, who was confined by her father, out of fear that he would be killed by her son, in a *tower high above the earth*. This was meant to prevent her impregnation. However, she was impregnated by Zeus who came to her as a *shower of golden light*.

There are reflections of these universal primitive customs in fairy tales and legends. In Snow White, whose maturing caused her stepmother envy, poisoning by the stepmother resulted in a period of prolonged sleep (withdrawal) in a glass-covered casket *held off the ground*, from which she awakened only when her future husband appeared.

Sleeping Beauty gives us a parallel to the strange custom which forbade girls to scratch themselves. Princess Aurora was also told *not to scratch herself*. She did cause blood to flow from a scratch on a pubertal birthday. She was immediately isolated from the world and slept *in a tower* for a hundred years until the coming of her lover. Rapunzel had to let down her hair because of the *height of the tower* in which she was kept, to prevent her from meeting potential mates. The contexts in which we find symbolic elements which are derived from the menarche customs of primitive peoples relate to delay of sexuality and sexual contact. The maturing child in Snow White was pushed into seclusion. This was the result of the reaction of an adult, the queen, to her growing maturity. The maturing child in Sleeping Beauty slept in seclusion in a high tower for many years after a scratch and a flow of blood.

From these tales we can conclude that fear of menarche derives from fear and uneasiness at the presence of attractiveness, sexuality, and reproductive potential in young girls, with their implications for incest. Isolating the girls is like returning a bun to the oven or a negative to the developer until it is done. This is a forerunner in cultural evolution of the social attitudes that result in stilted sex education at puberty and a denial of the id and the unconscious resulting in social planning and theories which disregard the drives.

In addition to the organizing impact of menarche, there is also an aggressive response in the girl who may see the first menses as a manifestation of weakness, messiness, and loss of control. It is a phenomenon that stirs up castrated feelings and penis envy. These feelings are similar to the reactions described by Freud (1918) in "The Taboo of Virginity." A good deal of the reaction of adults to menarche is also in the nature of a response to the confusion and anger of the child approaching and experiencing menarche.

The Meaning of the First Ejaculation

For the boy, the phenomenon comparable to menarche as a herald of maturity is the first ejaculation. From studies of primitive customs, the psychoanalytic literature, and books devoted to myths, symbols, and rituals, it appears that the only individuals who care much about this phenomenon are pubescent boys. Even for them, it is a matter of passing interest. The phenomenon does not even have a name.

In the experience of psychoanalysts working with pubescent boys, the first ejaculation does have an impact on the maturing personality. The end of a long developmental path has been reached. The sexual drive no longer need seek substitute means for finding expression. There is now an apparatus for this. Erection, orgasm, and ejaculation provide the child with a mature organ and a means for articulating the drives with an object in reality. Since there has always been in strong evidence a complex apparatus identifying the sexual identity of the boy, the act of ejaculation has little to add on this score. As noted above, changes in the masturbatory fantasy sometimes become evident after the first ejaculation. Any tendency to act out poorly symbolized fantasies diminishes. Exceptions to this are found in highly narcissistic individuals who develop perversions without partners; for example, transvestites or exhibitionists. It is striking that in these individuals, ejaculatory inhibitions occur. The ability to ejaculate carries the import of an ability to communicate, procreate, and involve oneself in reality. Erections have always been present, so they cannot be used by a pubescent youngster as a sign of sexual maturity and a readiness for object-directed sexuality.

The heightened narcissism of early male adolescence can be in part explained as a pubertal increase in drive energies in the absence of an available physical mechanism (ejaculation) for the expression of the sexual drive toward objects. As a result, latency style fantasy play continues to be overcathected. With the onset of the first ejaculation, a discharge pathway involving reality becomes available. At that point fantasies are opened to reality influences. The actual act of the first ejaculation is not as important as the circumstance in which it occurs. Menarche comes as a surprise. Its context is not the product of the action or the wish of the girl. Indeed, it cannot be blamed on her in any way. By way of contrast, the first ejaculation always occurs in a situation of sexual excitement and within a context which can become a source of pride or concern to the child involved. In a youngster whose prepubertal fantasy life was rich in bisexual and homosexual fantasy activity, the occurrence of the first ejaculation in a heterosexual context can be very supportive and positive. If the context of the first ejaculation was of a homosexual nature, the effect on the child can be devastating. His first contact with sexual reality confirms his fear that he is homosexual. This is made more meaningful if taken in the light of the observation of Coren (1967): "When a reality event occurs which mirrors the internal conflict of a child, specifically the repressed id impulse, the psychological trauma is very great, particularly to the reality testing apparatus, and necessitates a rapid shift in defense mechanisms which often fails" (p. 356). The fantasy at the time of the first ejaculation seems to be the clue to its impact. As Freud (1919) stated, ". . . in the main [guilt] is to be connected not with the act of masturbation but with the fantasy which . . . lies at its root" (p. 195). Jacobson (1964) has described this aspect of the first ejaculation: "the boy's first ejaculations commonly . . . evoke guilt conflicts of such intensity that frequently the pleasure of becoming a man is overshadowed or smothered by long-lasting fears of this step" (p. 102).

In summary, the first ejaculation, like the menarche, is an organizing experience that serves as an increased contact with reality and the object world. It is one of the maturational pressures that impels the individual toward a dissociation of masturbatory fantasy from masturbatory activities and an increased articulation of the drives with objects in the surround. Should the fantasies accompanying the first ejaculation be comfortable for the child, either because they or sexuality are acceptable to him, the maturational step is taken in stride. In those with severe bisexual conflicts, a first ejaculation in a heterosexual context is a reassuring experience. As with the girl, it helps the boy to define his identity. If the child is anxious about bisexual fantasy, and the first ejaculation occurs in a homosexual context, the child will experience an intensification of the disorganization and confusion that accompanied the bisexual conflicts of prepuberty. There is evidence that children who are conflicted about ejaculation, usually on the basis of severe castration anxiety, may fail to achieve a consistent shift from narcissistic, poorly symbolized sexual fantasies, associated with latency style acting out of the fantasies, to articulation of drives with reality objects. These individuals, when in the state of regression that is associated with this inhibition, manifest perversions without partners.

Latency, like crystal held to the light, has facets unsuspected till it is viewed from another angle. This entire chapter has been devoted to the sexual aspects of latency. Now, we shift our angle of vision and begin again with the prelatency child, exploring the ontogenesis of cognition and its role in the development of the state of latency.

Chapter 4

COGNITIVE DEVELOPMENT

A wanderer is man from his birth.
He was born in a ship
On the breast of the river of Time;
Brimming with wonder and joy
He spreads out his arms to the light,
Rivets his gaze on the banks of the stream,
As what he sees is, so have his thoughts been.

—Matthew Arnold

The Cognitive Organizing Periods
of Latency

The age of latency and the state of latency are usually clinically distinguished on the basis of behavioral findings. The age of latency is a state of being, a mere time period (six to twelve years). The state of latency is a functional organization, its surface appearance characterized by the behavior of a child who is calm, pliable, and educable. These criteria, though accurate, provide inadequate guidelines for clinical diagnosis and the organization of therapeutic strategies. Better guidelines result from an understanding of the antecedents and developmental timetables of the cognitive elements that contribute to establishing the characteristic behavioral manifestations of the state of latency.

As we will see, there are definitive cognitive organizing periods involved: the onset of the state of latency, maturation during the state of latency, and the passing of the state of latency. Each cognitive organizing period denotes a time sequence during which specific cognitive skills mature and develop. Clinically they are characterized by manifestations of the immature skills. The periods come to an end when the developing skills, having reached a high level of effectiveness, coordinate to produce a demonstrable alteration in the general behavior of the age group.

The first such period occurs in prelatency. Before the onset of the state of latency its strength has been determined by the adequacy of the development of the symbolizing function, repression, verbal-conceptual memory organization, and behavioral constancy. Strength in these cognitive areas is acquired gradually. As early as four years of age, maturation and development in these areas can achieve a level of refinement which allows for states of calm, pliability, and educability. Ordinarily this level of development is reached at about six to seven years of age. Clinically, the passage into the latency state is first marked by the appearance of clear ability to differentiate fantasy events from reality. Dreams are clearly known to be dreams and not things that happened while sleeping. Fantasy events are viewed from an "as if" standpoint. Second, human figure drawings develop a clear differentiation and separation of the head and the body in latency age children (Figures 3 and 4). A definitive neck appears. The theory behind this is that there is established at this time intellectualization and superego, which intensifies the separation of the mind and the body. I have found this sign to be of use, but not necessarily definitive. Latency age youngsters who draw primitive, neckless head-in-body human figures should be evaluated for sudden and intense brief periods of severe regressive behavior (see chapter 6). Third, is a modification in the nature of the superego motivating affects. This is manifested in an awareness of guilt and the use of it in guiding ethical decision-making (see discussion of superego development at end of this chapter). Fourth, there is suppression of masturbation, accompanied by calm, pliability, and educability. Fifth, children become more dependable. They can be relied upon to behave with appropriate variations in different circumstances and variations.

The second cognitive organizing period encompasses the age period seven and one-half to eight and one-half years. Cognitive areas which mature during this time period are: concrete operational thinking, abstract conceptual memory organization, the shift in fantasy content from thoughts about fantasy objects to thoughts about reality objects, and reorganization of superego contents in the direction of ethical individuation of the child's own motives from motivational contents derived from parental demands.

The maturation of these cognitive skills becomes manifest clinically at about eight and one-half years of age. This is approximately the age at which most clinicians divide the state of latency into early latency and late

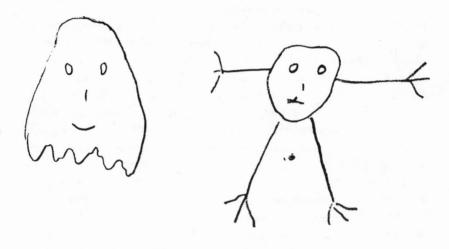

Figures without necks (4 and 5 year olds)

Figures with necks (8 year olds)

latency (see Bornstein, 1951). Clinically, we see the following in the cognitive domain of late latency:

First, we see conflict with parents over freedom of movement and a tendency to use peers as criteria for behavior. Second, there is reappearance of masturbation with an apparent greater leniency of society in regard to superego demands. This undoubtedly relates to greater recognition of the improved judgment and motor skills of the child, which permit greater social leniency with safety. It is remarkable that this age carries greater freedom for children in all societies, even those which do not have a state of latency for boys as we know it in our society (see Latency in Primitive Societies, in Appendix B). In many primitive societies boys from eight to puberty intensify the degree of separation from their mothers and join a kingdom of boys in a "neverland" set in an area beyond the boundaries of the village.

Third, there is a change in the nature of the night fears of children from fears of monsters and amorphous demon figures to humanoid pursuers such as witches, robbers, and kidnappers. This is one of the products of the cognitive shift in fantasy elements from thoughts about fantasy objects to thoughts about reality objects. It is the midlatency step in the developmental series that takes the child, who, in the course of his development, seeks things to be used for the discharge of drives, from no objects through part objects, inanimate objects, fantasy objects, objects in fantasy, fantasies about real objects, to objects free of fantasy.

Fourth, there is a marked intensification in certain youngsters of obsessive compulsive symptoms and persecutory fantasies. Transient symptoms of this nature are frequent. The symptomatology is often related to the control of affects associated with wishes to do things forbidden by the parents. The affect reflects guilt over rebellion. Sustained intensification of these symptoms occurs in youngsters with strong unremitting internalized prohibitions. The strength of the internalized prohibitions on the act reflect the intensity of parental admonition, defensive recoil from the strength of excitements associated with the act, and the degree to which disagreeable elements in the latent fantasy associated with the act cannot be masked in converting the latent urge into the manifest act.

Psychosomatic affect equivalents and affect symbols such as vomiting, headaches, and hives often appear or intensify at this age. The content of persecutory fantasies of this period reflect the change from thoughts about fantasy objects to thoughts about real objects. The persecutors are more and more based on humanoid forms.

The third cognitive organizing period encompasses the age period ten to thirteen years. The cognitive areas of development during these years are involved in achieving a shift to reality knowledge of the world and the ability to find an object in reality for the expression of the drives. The developmental events related to cognition that appear during this time period are the preadolescent vicissitudes of projection, changes in body image associated with prepubertal body changes, object-oriented changes in the intensity and direction of object relatedness, and intensification of narcissistic investment of the libido in fantasy structures. (The content of the fantasies changes to reality objects, but fantasy remains an important factor.)

The maturation of these cognitive skills sets the stage for adolescence. From the standpoint of latency these skills preside at its dissolution. As such, their maturation does not result in a phase of latency, but rather in the phase of early adolescence. The clinical characteristics of these developing phenomena color the nature of late latency.

Clinically the presence of the third cognitive organizing period is first manifested in a decline in the use of the structure of latency. Fantasy becomes less tenable as an outlet for the drives as reality testing interferes with its use. During this period therapists can note a shift back and forth of the therapeutic setting between playroom and consultation room as the children shift their cognitive organization from fantasy for discharge to words for communication.

Second, parents become less the center of attention in the object seeking related to the discharge of drives. As the child moves toward adolescence, parents and even therapists lose their value as sticking places for transference. The loved peer becomes primary. This process is called removal.

Third, there are preoccupations with the body changes that accompany prepuberty. Pinching in at the waist in girls and hair growth and voice changes in boys initiate a turning inward of attention and a heightening of narcissism. These experiences intensify conflicts and fantasies in regard to bisexuality. In girls with intense bisexual conflicts there appear at times interferences with cognition, especially those skills related to science, cartography, and mathematics. This reflects an interference with abstract thinking (see Hart and Sarnoff, 1971).

Fourth, as a result of heightened narcissistic cathexis of fantasy and increased narcissism, there is often an interference in the ongoing process of shifting to real objects for the discharge of drives. Only slightly distorted sexual fantasies are played out with the motor characteristics of latency state play. Fantasy structures become entangled in the psychic representations of objects in reality. Fantasy images involving early caretakers become the guidelines for selecting or interpreting the behavior patterns that define the objects who are attractive to the early adolescent. This interferes with object removal.

The First Cognitive Organizing Period

The state of latency does not spring full-grown from the heads of six year olds. The concatenation of cognitive skills required to bring it into action develops throughout the years that precede it. When social demands can be internalized to guide behavior, when guilt is there to enforce the demands, and mechanisms of restraint and the structure of latency are there to serve as the ego mechanisms that make enforcement possible, then there will be calm, pliability, and educability during suitable times and in suitable situations. To establish the groundwork for this response, four basic cognitive skills mature and develop during the prelatency years:

1. The capacity to symbolize. Once symbols are available for use in discharging energies which have been deflected from meaningful objects, periods of calm can be maintained.

2. The capacity for repression. Repression adapts symbolization for use as a mechanism of defense. Once the connection between a signifier (symbol) and that which is symbolized can be repressed, the signifier can serve as an object for the discharge of drives, bypassing and protecting the latent object which had been signified.

3. The achievement of a highly developed verbal conceptual memory organization. This interferes with more primitive forms of memory (eidetic and affecto-motor), resulting in an infantile amnesia and a requirement that memory and memory-based interpretations of the environment and new situations be patterned after socially dictated schemata.

4. Behavioral constancy. The socially dictated schemata for interpreting perceptual situations has a counterpart in the motor area in the form of socially dictated schemata or patterns (syntaxes) of behavior. Behavioral constancy refers to the mental ability to retain the patterns of behavior and to apply them in appropriate and varying situations to the extent expected by the society. These patterns dictate positive actions as well as the inhibition of socially inappropriate drive-dominated patterns. Inhibition can be maintained, producing socially approved behavior, when repression can adapt symbol formation in the service of discharge of the drives through the formation of fantasies for discharge. This process is called the structure of latency (see chapter 2).

When the four functions have reached the level of maturity that permits them to act upon each other to the degree that socially approved behavior can be consistently produced, the full-grown state of latency is ready to make its appearance.

Now that we have briefly defined the cognitive components of the latency state and described their interactions, we turn to a more detailed consideration of the ontogenesis of each.

DEVELOPMENT OF THE SYMBOLIZING FUNCTION

If man is to function as a unit accepted into the protective bosom of a society, channels for the discharge of drive energies must be available. Physiological outlets are available for adults but are not universally available. Psychoanalytic symbol formation constitutes a primary pathway for drive discharge in the state of latency, allowing for indirect drive discharge if the internalized demands of society block the direct discharge of drives. The adjective *psychoanalytic* is important here. It carries the connotation that there is repression of the abstract connection between that which is signified and the signifier, which we call the symbol. When we speak of a symbol in ordinary terms, we mean representing an original idea or feeling by something else. The mind which is capable of doing this can perceive the signifying object for what it is and in terms of a second meaning. Thus the signifier can be seen to represent itself concretely as well as something else. With the development of repression, the second meaning attributed to the signifier is lost to conscious awareness. At that point the signifier becomes a psychoanalytic symbol. Through its hidden meaning it can serve as an object, albeit occult, for the discharge of drives. If the affects that had been associated with the hidden meaning are not equally excluded from consciousness, the symbol formed will be on the level of those which participate in the formation of a phobia. Psychoanalytic symbols participate in the formation of the fantasies of latency; they are the backbone of the structure of latency. Inherent in this symbol formation, however, is the capacity to regress to the production of symbols which, though masking meaning, convey unpleasant affect. This is an explanation for the fragile defensive quality of latency fantasy. It easily slips over into night fears. (See chapter 8.)

During latency, symbols are not used alone. They are grouped into fantasies whose relationship to the latent fantasies for drive discharge is to hide their meaning while they represent them. During the first cognitive organizing period, which occurs in prelatency, the evidences of representation occur before eight months. At this time there is evidence that can be detected by an observer. The inner experience expressed in these representations are not verbal memories or events. They are feelings. There are no conceptual or verbal elements—just feelings. Visual images, affects, ideas without words, such as you will find if you try to go from one language to another, occupy the mind of the eight-month-old. Such elements exist from the time the child has the capacity for recognition recall. However, we can only know of this when there is some evidence which impinges on the world, such as a planned action that will produce an effect from the environment, or a word phrase that represents a concept. Such actions or words are the earliest forms of representations and the beginnings of representational symbolism. Passive experiences come first, as in the crying child who quiets on hearing the sound of his mother's footsteps, or the child who delights at six months at the repeated experience of touching his father's teeth. Then come verbal signifiers. At first the child can recognize verbal signifiers and can point to people and parts of the body when they are named. They passively use the symbols of others. This skill is paradigmatic of the ability to conform to the schemata and social patterns encountered during acculturation. The words, so learned, become the basis for speech and the means for representation (active symbolization) of thought content. This skill exemplifies the ability to adapt schemata to one's own use in the creative symbolizations that produce fantasies for discharge during latency.

The development of the capacity to produce spontaneous representations of thought contents is illustrated in the following clinical vignette.

The parents of a small child eight months of age had an intercommunication system in their apartment which permitted them to hear what was happening in their child's room. The child had been taught that if she would say "Mommy" her mother would come. At least her parents had tried to teach her this. She could recognize the word. She had difficulty finding the word when she needed it. One morning she awakened and she started to scream *Wa Wa*. Then she stopped and said, *Upup, ah-ah, um-wa, ee-ee, ma ma, ur-u*. She stopped and then returned to *ma ma*. She repeated the word with obvious delight. She had found what she was looking for, the consensually accepted verbal signifier of the thought concept she wished to represent.

The experience of this child represents the first spontaneously produced verbal symbol, a vocal signifier which is not an integrated organic part of the expressed inner content. Though words may be used in this way, objects in the child's environment continue to be used in play only as concrete objects (i.e., without distortion). At fifteen months, they begin to take on the characteristics of words; namely, they are themselves and at the same time can take on a second meaning. The harnessing of the dual representation potential of object in the service of the purposes of the ego does not occur until the first half of the third year of life, when a relatively weak form of repression comes into action.

At times, the manifestations of this newly established ego apparatus are quite striking. Hitherto unmanifested symptoms and behavior are mobilized to express conflicts and fantasies in new ways. These newly acquired ego skills provide the means for more sophisticated ways of expressing conflict. The following case illustrates this sudden appearance of phobic symptoms during the first half of the third year of life.

Jan, age twenty-seven months, was brought to my office because of bad dreams and a fear of seaweed. Her birth was uneventful. At nine months she had been suddenly weaned from the bottle, which was replaced by the cup along with a great deal of attention from the mother. There was no difficulty. The child was wanted and loved by parents and grandparents who gave her much attention. The mother interfered with thumb-sucking and removed any substitute object that the child might take to bed. She replaced these with attention and communication. The child developed into a highly verbal youngster who spoke full sentences at twenty-four months. She was without thumb-sucking and had no substitute objects. Toilet training was started at twenty-two months. From twenty-two months on, the child would awaken repeatedly on a given night, crying and afraid, but unable to explain. She could not describe any dream nor any thoughts to her mother. She was trained day and night for bowel and bladder by twenty-five months.

Daytime fears first appeared at twenty-six months with complaints about, and fear of, children who wore Batman masks. The mother dealt with this by buying the child a mask and desensitizing the child. At twenty-seven months concern about separation from the mother intensified. She refused to stay with a baby-sitter whom she knew. The parents had to remain with her until she went to sleep. The following weekend she did not want to stay with her grandmother as baby-sitter. The parents left her crying. Intense fear of separation from the mother was manifest. The parents and the child went to visit the grandmother the following weekend. On Friday she seemed happy and unafraid. She went to the beach and enjoyed playing in the sand and water. However, she remained highly sensitive to separation from her mother and refused the attentions of her grandmother while at the grandmother's house.

On the next evening, still with the parents at her grandmother's house, she was afraid when her mother went out. She asked if her mother would come back. The following night she awakened and said she was afraid of a toy rubber mouse in her room. The next day the family went to the beach. At first the child played in the sand. Then she went down to the water's edge with her father, who protected her from the undertow. She enjoyed facing the water while holding onto her father's legs. As they walked away from the water she insisted on being carried to avoid touching the "green stuff" on the beach.

The next day she went to the beach with her mother. She played well in the sand. Her mother led her to the water's edge. Suddenly she reached for her mother in terror and insisted on being held out of the water. Seaweed at the water's edge seemed to have drawn her attention. "Carry me," she said. "Why?" asked the mother. "What's that?" she asked. "Just seaweed," said her mother, "like spinach, like lettuce, like grass." She picked up the seaweed and showed it to the child. The child recoiled in terror. She insisted on being carried across the sand and on leaving the beach. She would not touch the sand or water. Her parents provided her with a small plastic wading pool at the grandmother's house. The child enjoyed it until some grass got carried into the water on her feet. She then refused to use the pool.

That evening she and her parents slept at the home of the grandparents. (Two months before, at twenty-five months, the parents brought the child to the grandmother and left her there without difficulty for two nights.) The parents went out that evening to dinner. The child was prepared for this. She had been told the parents were coming back. That night she awoke from sleep several times crying hysterically.

She had awakened thus on occasion from the time that she was twenty-two months old. This time there were new features to her behavior. She was kicking her feet in the air, using the motions she had used to get her feet out of the water that afternoon. For the first time she could tell what had awakened her. She said that she was taking her feet out of the water away from the green stuff. She could not say what she was afraid of. While sitting on her mother's lap, she urinated.

The next day, the distraught parents brought the child to my office. With the mother present I asked the child about her dreams. Highly verbal and still very much impressed by the dream, she told me that she was trying to take her feet out of the water, away from the seaweed. "I'm afraid of seaweed." Her pronunciation of the last word was not clear and I repeated the slurred word with a questioning tone. She looked at me with some disbelief and said in a tone of voice that implied that she was talking about something important, that everyone must be acquainted with "the *green* stuff." I asked, "What are you afraid of with seaweed?" Her body was wracked with hysterical sobbing. I asked, "What are you afraid it will do?" She cried more. "Are you afraid it will hurt you?" "No," she said. "I'm afraid it will hurt Mommy."

To myself I thought that seaweed does not have hostile affects but that little girls do. I asked the child if she were the seaweed. "Yes," she answered. "Are you ever angry at Mommy?" "Yes," said she. "When she goes away." The child had projected her own hostility onto the seaweed. I went on to explain that children do feel anger when mommies go away and that children have a right to feel angry and that it is good to be able to tell mother and that she can be sure if she tells mother, mother will not be angry at her.

I suggested to the mother that she encourage the child to discuss her feelings with her. The idea behind this was to reopen the conflict to the resolving effects of maturation and development rather than leave the dependency needs and separation anxieties fixated and bound by a symptom. Following this interview the child was able to swim with the help of the mother, who reminded her that seaweed was only seaweed. She could also sleep without interruptions. A month later the family went on a short vacation during which the child was often left with a baby-sitter. She began to blink repeatedly. Seaweed no longer bothered her. The parents, recognizing that the child's separation conflicts had been reawakened, decided to devote more time to the child. The blinking then dropped off and soon ceased.

What had happened between the twenty-fifth and twenty-eighth month of age was a shift in the way that she expressed her conflict over her mother leaving her. The conflict was the same before and after the development of the phobia, but at first she directly expressed her feelings of anxiety, fears, and thinly masked hostility. Later she developed the phobia: her frightening aggressive feelings toward her mother were projected onto a symbol, seaweed; the anxiety over her own aggressive feelings was displaced to a fear of the seaweed.

Could it be that the child had experienced a change in her symptom picture, not to more severe pathology, as the mother had thought, but to a higher level of ego function which includes the ability to form and use symbols modified by repression? In order to answer this question we need to know when the capacity to form such symbols first appears. The child suddenly looked sicker. The mother became frightened. Yet the child may have made a step forward. Her phobia may have represented the development of the capacity to form psychoanalytic (repression modified) symbols. Such symbols are the basis of culture and civilization as well as neurotic symptoms.

The meaning of the word *symbol* varies among experts and among the various disciplines devoted to the study of human thinking. Usually people are really talking of metaphors when they speak of symbols. In psychoanalysis, *symbol* has a specific meaning that has been best defined by Ernest Jones (1916). According to Jones a symbol is formed when there has been repression of the connection between a representation and that which is represented:

> In most uses of the word, a symbol is a manifest expression for an idea that is more or less hidden, secret, or kept in reserve. Most typically of all, the person employing the symbol is not even conscious of what it actually represents. . . . Symbols [are] made spontaneously . . .

and, in the broad sense of the word, unconsciously. The stricter the sense in which this is used, the truer is the statement (p. 90). Only what is repressed is symbolized. Only what is repressed needs to be symbolized. This conclusion is the touchstone of the psychoanalytic theory of symbolism (p. 116).

In pursuing this study, the word *symbol* will be used only for mental phenomena that fulfill these criteria. By this I mean that when the word symbol is used in this book to describe a mental event, it implies psychoanalytic symbols like those which are brought into the service of neurotic symptom formation, rather than symbolic metaphors.

For a mental event such as a symbol to occur, there must be an advanced level of cognitive organization. Memory, image retention, spontaneous recall, language skills must have been achieved. The addition of some form of repression is required for psychoanalytic symbol formation. A large number of developmental steps must be successfully negotiated before symbols, as defined by Jones, can be formed.

The most extensive direct study of the development of such symbols in childhood is that of Piaget (1951). He describes a number of preliminary steps in the development of the capacity to form symbols. He based his conclusions on direct observation of the nature of a child's relationship to the objects with which he plays. The observations that draw our interest begin after the development of thought, memory, and the use of words. This is well established by one year. At this time, one can observe a syncretic ritual response to objects. One sees only the capacity to deal with objects in a patterned manner that adds nothing to the object. At this stage the object concretely represents itself to the child and nothing more. Blocks are piled on blocks as blocks. Seaweed is seaweed.

At fifteen months Piaget saw the first examples in children of the ability to bring ideas from their own experiences unrelated to the object into the treatment of the object. They could verbalize this. For them the object had come to represent something besides its concrete presence (for example, a child punishes a doll for being naughty). The connection between the object and what it represents remains conscious. Piaget calls this type of activity symbolic play. It is well exemplified by the child who places one block upon another and describes this as "a child sitting on the toilet." An object (seaweed) can have two meanings. The child is aware of it. This fits the common definition of symbol.

Piaget records a step beyond the level of symbolic play. The second meaning of the object is repressed. The association between signifier and signified is not available to consciousness. Piaget calls this "secondary symbolism." He defines it in the same way as defined by Jones (1916). Piaget describes the development of secondary symbolism during the period from two to four years. In reviewing his direct observations of children at these ages (1951, p. 177 and following), I could find few symbols, in Jones's sense, before the age of three. Piaget points out that at two, the child seems to be aware *in part* of the linkage between the symbols and the thing represented, but some of the link has been lost. Therefore according to his observations it seems that the personality structure necessary for the formation of psychoanalytic symbols can exist at twenty-four months. At this time affects as well as contents may be expressed.

From a study of published case reports of treatment of young children, it may be possible to get a close estimate of the age range when children first become capable of using psychoanalytic symbols. The earliest reported treatment of a phobia in the psychoanalytic literature is in Max Wulff's "A Phobia in a Child of Eighteen Months" (1928). In this paper there is no report of a true symbol nor of a true phobia. The eighteen-month-old girl showed signs of anxiety early one evening, crying, "Mamma, don't give Linchen away." She clung to her mother and clearly showed signs of uneasiness and anxiety. This happened several days in succession. Then she began having anxiety attacks both day and night. Her anxiety increased whenever anyone knocked on the door. She had fears of the dark window, church bells, and the sound of passing motors but no exaggerated fears in relation to a neutral object. These fears are examples of the phobic avoidance and anxiety reactions commonly seen in children at this age in response to general perceptions which stimulate drives and affects. The interposition of displacement and symbolization does not occur. They are not phobias. Wulff himself commented that the phobias he described could best be called "incipient," and that in this case he was dealing with symptoms of anxiety rather than phobia. In his analysis of the case, Wulff found that the child has become anxious and afraid of rejection when she failed to achieve toilet training at the rate her parents demanded.

The absence of symbols and neurotic symptoms is of interest to us. We see in the signs of this one-and-a-half-year-old a parallel to the first stage of little Jan's illness. There were the physiological signs of anxiety. The capacity to manifest emotional disturbance through symbol formation and phobia was not seen. As in all the cases, the child was highly verbal, related well, and had no unusual growth or developmental pattern abnormality.

Further information comes from a paper by Editha Sterba (1949), "Analysis of Psychogenic Constipation in a Two-Year-Old Child." At sixteen and a half months, the child, a boy, showed anxiety when his mother talked to a stranger. He would not go to sleep alone, awoke screaming during the night, stood up in bed, and when his mother came, clung to her and looked anxiously around the room. He cried whenever his mother began to leave during the day. The origin of this difficulty was traced to the deflection of his nurse's interest from him when she met a man in the park. When the boy was twenty months old, the parents became aware of the fact that the child held back his stool. This symptom had begun earlier, but had been concealed by his nurse. During one four-month period constipation became so severe that all bowel movements were assisted by an adult. He was taken for treatment at twenty-six and a half months. The therapist noticed his interest and play with little wooden balls in the playroom. She said, "I can do something much better with the ballies." She loaded the sleeve of her blouse with them and let them fall into the box. He wanted to do the same; but after loading up, he became pale, thoughtful, and silent and said, "I don't want to take the ballies out." He kept them in his sleeve for a half hour. He asked the therapist to take them out. This incident at twenty-six and a half months illustrates the transition between symbolic play and a true symbol formation. The child dealt with the balls as though they were something else. We cannot tell if the connection was conscious.

Wulff's case illustrates the nature of nonpsychotic disorders of early childhood before the development of the capacity to develop symbols. The children develop anxiety, sleep disturbance, and somatic symptoms. These are children with no evidences of the ego functions that produce the state of latency. Sterba's case also illustrates such prepsychoanalytic symbolic emotional reactions (anxiety, somatic symptoms). In addition there is evidence of the onset of the activity of the symbolizing functions of the ego, at twenty-six months.

Melitta Sperling (1952) reported the case of a girl who began treatment at twenty-three months. The chief complaints at first were attacks of paroxysmal tachycardia for which no organic cause could be found. The child would grunt and assume a crouched position. At twenty-six months, following the birth of a brother, a sleep disturbance appeared. Nightly she would wake up in fear and scream, "A doggy (a kitty or a fish) is biting my finger." The child carried these fears into the daytime. She avoided feeding her doll because she was afraid the doll would bite her finger and swallow it. Sperling interpreted to the child that she was the one who wanted to bite and swallow something of which she was afraid. This brought to the fore the child's jealousy of her baby brother.

In Sperling's case we see the phenomena seen in Jan. First there is the typical emotional response before symbol formation (anxiety and somatic symptoms), then the appearance of the phobia along with the development of the symbolizing function.

We find in the works of Piaget a close study of the stages in the development of symbols. Three steps in this development can be seen: first, from zero to fifteen months, the child deals with objects without distortion (syncretic ritual response); second, from fifteen to twenty-four months, the child can deal knowingly with objects in a manner that imparts meanings foreign to the intrinsic qualities (symbolic play); and third, at twenty-four months the child can unknowingly use objects in a manner that imparts meaning foreign to the intrinsic qualities of the object. Through this capacity the child can express otherwise threatening and frightening feelings and thoughts (symbol formation).

Step one (zero to fifteen months) represents a time when there is no capacity to form symbols from objects.

Step two represents the time of the development of metaphorical symbols. This takes place at fifteen months. Such metaphor formation is possible as the result of the prior maturation and interaction of precursor capacities which are four in number: (1) The capacity to perceive similarities on the basis of few and superficial cues. This is necessary for the mind to be able to establish mental linkages and perceive abstract relationship between objects. (2) The capacity for displacement. Displacement occurs along the line of the linkages made possible by the perception of similarities. These linkages are the earliest precursors of symbols. They are unstable and facultative at first. They do not provide consistent and reliable pathways for instinctual drive discharge. (3) The capacity to delay is vital. Only with the establishment of the capacity to delay is time provided for the objects of instinctual drives to be modified along the lines of displacement. (4) A need, such as the need to protect self or primary object from aggressive urges, is necessary as the motivation for displacement.

When these four factors are present, the budding personality is ready to establish metaphorical symbols. They take the form of mental linkages which are constant and obligatory such as mother-nurse, penis-bird, father-king. Motivated by defense of the body ego and primary objects, displacements are obliged to seek such fixed pathways for discharge. I call these obligatory fixed pathways for displaced discharge of drive energies "symbolic linkages." From the standpoint of adaptation and object relations, the establishment of an obligatory pathway for discharge serves to preserve the body ego and primary objects. Through these symbolic linkages, substitute objects for drive discharge are made available. Symbolic linkages are the basis of conscious substitute representations such as the double entendre, metaphors, and similes—"Thy two breasts are like two young roes that are twins. . . ." Symbolic linkages (metaphors) are the psychoanalytic analogues of the symbolic play of Piaget.

Step three represents the time of true psychoanalytic symbol formation. Piaget calls this secondary symbolization, and places its onset at twenty-four months. Two new factors contribute to the metamorphosis that transmutes a metaphor into a true psychoanalytic symbol. First, repression is necessary. By repression, I refer to the fact that the link to the primary object is made unavailable to consciousness. Second, reality testing is necessary. It supports the intellectualization necessary to maintain the conscious denial of the relationship between symbol and primary object. For instance a tower and a phallus can be equated on the basis of superficial similarity; and one can symbolize the other. Anxiety is avoided through the repression of this similarity. This is further enhanced by the reality-supported rationalization that they are not at all alike since there is such a realistic difference in size. Thus reality testing supports psychoanalytic symbol formation.

Psychoanalytic symbol formation can be characterized as the unconscious use of a metaphor as a pathway for the displacement of drive energies from the body or primary object to the word representation of a mentally linked object in the environment. The symbolizing function effects the discharge of drive energies in such a way that more meaningful object representation is spared.

Psychoanalytic symbols are available for use as a means of dealing with conflicts at least as early as the first half of the third year of life. Earlier onsets have been reported without documentation. A more exact timing will require further and more extensive clinical studies and investigations.

Variations in the timing depend upon individual variations in children. The course of nonpsychotic human psychopathology in early childhood appears to be marked by a transition from diffuse representations of anxiety to the development of neurotic symptoms during the first half of the third year of life. The same mechanisms can be used for the formation of highly symbolized defense-oriented fantasies.

REPRESSION

The mechanism of repression transforms metaphorical symbols into psychoanalytic symbols. Psychoanalytic symbols are necessary for the maintenance of the state of latency. Repression must therefore be included among the skills upon which the establishment of latency is dependent. Most of our codified knowledge of the ontogenesis of repression in childhood is derived from the reconstructions based on Freud's work with adults. As such, there is only a shadowy timetable. As previously noted, Piaget (1951) in his studies of symbol formation, reported the observation of the workings of repression in the formation of secondary symbols as early as twenty-four months (p. 174, observation 96). In this regard he described "games . . . in which the affective tendencies which give rise to them are to some extent *outside the child's consciousness*" (174; italics mine). The timing of the beginning of the ontogenesis of repression apparently can be set at twenty-four months with some surety. The timing of subsequent developments presented below are based on clinical estimates. More widely based research is needed to establish a more accurate timetable. Clinically, as established through the appearance of phobic symptoms, repression is operative at twenty-six months. There appears to be a major activation of repression with the passing of the Oedipus complex (Freud, 1924) and the appearance of the infantile amnesia at six years of age. By the infantile amnesia is meant what appears to be a massive forgetting of prelatency events. The amnesia is seen clinically during the analysis of adults. During the course of a successful analysis, a good deal of the infantile amnesia is lifted.

Clinically, in children, repression associated with symptom formation is relatively weak at first. This is most characteristic of prelatency repression. The ease with which little Jan was able to respond to the interpretation of the meaning of her symbol-determined symptoms is typical of the way children can perceive and confirm the unconscious meaning of such symptoms when an interpretation is made. The intensity of the repression of the awareness of the connection between the symbol and what is represented increases with age. By the time children are four or five years old, they ordinarily do not respond affirmatively to such interpretations. However, it is not unusual for an occasional child to respond affirmatively and with confirmatory material as late as nine years of age. This is especially so in youngsters with psychosomatic symptoms and compulsions.

The series of clinical observations described above are difficult to reconcile with a theory based on a single type of mechanism of repression. For this reason, repression is best defined as an exclusion of content or affect from conscious awareness as the result of a number of processes.

Freud (1915d) observed that "repression is not a defensive mechanism which is present from the beginning . . ." (p. 148). The fact that repression may be detected first in Piaget's observations at twenty-four months confirms this. Freud (1915d) spoke of a series of processes involved in producing repression. He called the initial mechanism at work primal repression "which consists in the psychical (ideational) representative of the instinct being denied entrance into the conscious" (p. 148). He elaborated on the process that produced exclusion from consciousness at this stage by describing "anticathexis [as] the sole mechanism of primal repression" (1915e, p. 181). Essentially what is meant by this is that the attention of the child is riveted on some element in reality. This may occur at any time that a concept or affect becomes troublesome. Usually something symbolically linked to the concept or affect becomes the target of attention. Thus little Jan was reminded of her anger at her mother by the green stuff (seaweed) and could take her mind off the anger by concentrating her attention and affects on it. The child had been dressed in green during a particularly trying separation from her mother. At that time, a baby-sitter had begun calling her a little green leprechaun. Thus the metaphorical link behind the symbol was established. Since she still knew of her anger, calling her attention back to it was possible, as is the case with primal repression.

The process of anticathexis involved in primal repression is apparently responsible for the ease of undoing repression in childhood. This type of repression is involved in a great deal of the unconscious symbolization that takes place in children's play and dreams. Freud (1915d) pointed out that there is a stronger form of repression—repression proper—which is produced at a later age. This form of repression is hard to interpret away, becomes more prevalent with age, and is the form that people who work with adults usually have in mind when they say *repression* without a modifying adjective. Before we proceed to a discussion of repression proper, we turn to Piaget's understanding of the process that produces repression. He worked with children primarily. Although his definition of the mechanism of repression is identical with Freud's, his understanding of the process that produces it is somewhat different from Freud's explanation. Even so, Piaget's conclusions have a marked similarity to the mechanisms that Freud ascribed to primal repression. Piaget (1951) states, "The origin of the unconscious symbol is to be found in the suppression of consciousness of the ego by complete absorption in, and identification with, the external world . . ." (p. 199).

This concept certainly is not congruent with Freud's (1915d) view of the factors involved in exclusion of elements from consciousness in repression proper. In repression proper, ideas originating elsewhere which have become associated with that which has been primarily repressed are affected and "experience the same fate as what was primarily repressed" (p. 148). That which is repressed continues to establish connections and put out derivatives. Only the connection with consciousness is broken. "If these derivatives have become sufficiently far removed from the repressed representative, whether owing to the adoption of distortions or by reason of the number of intermediate links inserted, they have free access to the conscious" (p. 149). The derivatives so distorted are the psychoanalytic symbols of which I have spoken. The ability to establish links is the capacity to form metaphorical symbols. The repression of the abstract link between the signifier and the signified is accomplished through the displacement of representations of what is unconscious to signifiers so removed from the original that meaning is masked. In repression proper, the meaning of the signified element is not easily reached through interpretation. The signifier (i.e., symbol) cathected with the anticathexis is so far displaced that it is closer to reality than to that which is signified. In addition, Freud (1915e) postulated that not only was attention directed away from the repressed element but the ability to pay attention to it and to draw it into consciousness was lost.

"In the case of repression proper there is in addition withdrawal of the Pcs cathexis. It is very possible that it is precisely the cathexis which is withdrawn from the idea that is used for anticathexis" (p. 181). In effect, the words that could be used for conscious recall of the thing signified are no longer held in the preconscious area of the mind. Such repression proper is probably involved in the hard-to-break repressions that appear strongly at five and constitute the basis for symptom and dream symbols that are hard to analyze. The operation of repression proper strengthens psychoanalytic symbolism to the point that the symbol formation of the structure of latency can produce fantasies in support of the state of latency. The maturation of psychoanalytic symbols and the strength of the structure of latency depend on the maturation of repression proper.

The repression associated with the infantile amnesia, which occurs with the onset of the latency years, has a multitude of mechanisms for producing exclusion from conscious awareness. Primal repression and repression proper are undoubtedly operative. In addition, there is an exclusion from consciousness which occurs for past events, memories, and thinking. Thus there is a great deal that is unavailable to consciousness because its primitive roots and diffuse style of recall are incomprehensible to the more mature mind. This contribution to the infantile amnesia will be further pursued in the next section.

DEVELOPMENT OF THE VERBAL CONCEPTUAL
MEMORY ORGANIZATION

Before an individual can appreciate and acquire the complex and subtle variations of superego content that are required during the latency age for appropriate independent functioning in the many environments outside the home, he must have developed syntaxes and verbal skills of comparable subtlety and complexity. Once these skills develop, the fantasies and actions of prelatency whose memory is couched in a more primitive cognitive style of recall can find scant opportunity or media for expression. As a result, these experiences are unavailable to consciousness and become a part of the infantile amnesia. The relationship of this transition, during the maturation of the cognitive organization of memory, to the onset of latency is a phenomenon that has been independently discovered by psychoanalysts a number of times. The process of maturation has best been described by Piaget (1951).

The shift from hallucinatory perceptual thought (images) to abstract speech signs was described by Ferenczi (1911):

Apart from the fact that it takes some time to learn to speak, it seems that speech-signs replacing images, i.e. words, retain for a considerable time a certain tendency to regression, which we can picture to ourselves in a gradually diminishing degree until the capacity is attained for "abstract" imagination and thought, that is almost completely free from hallucinatory perceptual elements (p. 139).

This paragraph prepares one for his cognitive explanation for the beginning of the latency period proper.

It is the suppression of these sexual fantasies and actions, manifested in the weakened form of speech, that really connotes the beginning of the latency period proper, that period in which "the mental counterforces against infantile sexuality, namely, disgust, shame, and morality, are formed," and the child's interest is turned in the direction of social activities (desire for knowledge). . . . At [this] time . . . speech . . . is so strongly invested with affects, [it] is still characterized by a high degree of regressive tendency and by a vivid "mimicry of imagery." . . . Suppressed verbal material must in consequence of the latency period (i.e. the deflection of attention), remain at this more primitive developmental stage, while the rest of the vocabulary gradually becomes, for the greater part, divested of its hallucinatory and motor character by progressive exercising and training, and is rendered through this economy suitable for higher thought activity (p. 145).

Piaget (1951) presented a similar explanation for the infantile amnesia:

There are no memories of early childhood for the excellent reason that at that stage there was no evocative mechanism capable of organizing them. Recognition memory in no way implies a capacity for evocation, which presupposes mental images, interiorized language, and the beginnings of conceptual intelligence. The memory of the two or three-year-old child is still a medley of made-up stories and exact but chaotic reconstructions, organized memory developing only with the progress of intelligence as a whole (p. 187). [The] ". . . transposition of active recognition into representative evocation presupposes the complete organization of interiorized intelligence . . ." (p. 188).

The richest and most elegant presentation of the relationship of latency and the infantile amnesia to the maturational cognitive drift from affecto-motor memory to the mental-verbal appreciation of the world is that of Schachtel (1949). He describes the shift in memory schemata that is de-scribed by Ferenczi and Piaget. In addition he shows how this shift serves for the continuation and preservation of society, since in the process "cul-turally unacceptable or unusable experiences and the memory thereof [are left] to starvation by the expedient of providing no linguistic, conceptual, and memory schemata for them and by channeling later experience into the experience schemata of the culture" (p. 47). An extensive study of this process is the topic of chapter 5. The exclusion from consciousness that befalls prelatency experience with the development of a new style of cogni-tion for evaluative memory (spontaneous recall) is similar in form to the mechanisms that produce primal repression.

The setting aside of ways of remembering which include feelings and evocations of mood in favor of subtle language-oriented memory skills sharpens and increases the capacity of the child to acquire knowledge of expected behavior in disparate situations. This sets the stage for the aug-mentation of the superego imagoes derived from introjected parental fig-ures which guide personal adjustment within the family, by imagoes de-rived from verbally subtle rules and regulations which guide the conduct of life in groups. The experiences that gave rise to the content of the parental introjects are lost to memory in the cognitive shift to verbal memory content. Transference in psychoanalysis brings the influences of the introjected parental imagoes into the treatment situation. Supportive psychotherapy deals with the superego contents acquired in latency. The capacity for sustained recall of verbally subtle contributions to superego content based on early latency age experiences, including guidelines for appropriate latency state behavior, makes consistent good behavior possible. Such behavior constancy is the topic of the next section.

BEHAVIORAL CONSTANCY

Socially approved behavior can be maintained in the presence of stimu-lating inputs through the action of the symbolizing function. Through the production of symbol-laden fantasies for discharge (the structure of latency) the latency age child establishes a safety valve to deal with heightened drives. The guidelines for socially approved behavior are acquired and retained through verbal memory skills which mature between four and seven years of age. The presence of a safety valve and guidelines are not sufficient to maintain proper behavior. Also required are motivations to retain concepts of proper behavior and to use them. When these factors all work together, there is behavioral constancy, and the state of latency can begin. The motivating factors that activate the required behavior patterns and establish constancy are affects such as shame and guilt, fear and acceptance. One can recognize the achievement of behavioral constancy by the attainment of the child of differential patterns of behavior in specific situations. Another characteristic relates to the maturation of guilt as one of the superego-motivating affects. In prelatency, shame in response to what others think or will think is the primary motivating affect. Internalization of this negative response and repression of the source of disapproval results in the motivating affect of guilt. Freud (1924) has pointed out that with the passing of the Oedipus complex and the introjection of parental imagoes, the internalized affect of guilt begins to dominate the superego. This occurs with latency.

Piaget has done sustained observation of the development of skills related to behavioral constancy in children. Flavell (1963), in quoting Piaget's study on the development of moral judgment in the child, notes that in the development of moral judgment, the development of the capacity for "behavioral conformity to the rules" can be divided into four stages: Stage 1 is from zero to three years of age, during which the child uses objects as free-play materials without applying social rules for using the play materials in any culturally determined pattern or style. This stage Piaget refers to as the "stage of motor rules." The second stage, from three to five years of age reflects the use by the child of behavioral patterns that he has seen in others, which is primarily an assimilation of what he sees to private schemata. The third stage, from seven to eight years on, reveals the ability of the child to play in a manner that truly reflects social influences. The child can retain and follow rules. This lasts until the child is eleven or twelve. In the fourth stage, from eleven or twelve on, the child shows the ability to follow social rules as understood and agreed upon by all the members of a society. Apparently Piaget's temporal sequence (i.e., social awareness at age seven) is at odds with the observation made by psychoanalysis of the onset of guilt at about six years of age. Flavell points out that "similar studies carried out in populations of children different from [those studied by Piaget] would likely yield different developmental patterns . . ." (p. 291). It has been my observation in viewing Piaget's developmental stages that when a motivating affect such as guilt becomes involved, transitions from one stage to the next may occur at earlier periods and ages.

Piaget's more general theoretical study of the development of moral judgment in the child (1932) does not contain references to formal age guidelines. It is therefore easier to work with in applying his theory to populations of children different from those with which he worked. In it childhood morality is divided into two types: an earlier morality of restraint which is dominated by an absolute acceptance of higher law, apparently containing black and white and no shades of gray, with no motivation considered in the decision to act on the part of the child. The second form of morality is described as the morality of cooperation. This deals with moralities acquired from a "sharing of perspectives" (p. 296). Motivations are involved in choosing a course of action.

Morality of cooperation is "formed out of . . . reciprocal relationships among status peers and based on mutual rather than unilateral respect. With a growing understanding of the role of motives in the actions of self and others and of the social implications of antisocial behavior, the child [sees] . . . moral action as an autonomous good" (p. 296).

This division of morality into an earlier absolute adherence to moral rules and a later approach to morality in which motive, decision, and choice between activities judged in terms of learned concepts of good and evil are dominant is correlative with the preguilt and postguilt patterns of moral development as delineated by the Freudian school. There is an earlier period during which a child responds to group pressure, with the affect of shame controlling him and forcing him to adhere to rules out of a fear of loss of the love of the people around him. There is a later decision-making period during which there is an internal response related to guilt. In this circumstance the individual has internalized imagoes of what is expected and what is acceptable behavior. Even without the presence of an individual or group privy to the contents of the conflict, the individual is guided to choose to do what is right. What is right is defined in terms of that which would help to avoid guilt.

Internal decision and privacy is the key to the inherent weakness of latency age morality. Privacy and the availability of alternatives provide the potential for cheating and a lack of fair play. Private decisions carried out with a note of uncertainty are a common latency age experience. Actions based on decisions derived from alternatives give rise to guilt, especially in regard to masturbatory activities.

The term *morality of cooperation* implies communication within a social group. This could be taken to mean that external influences similar to that seen in the morality of restraint are at work. This suggests that the child chooses to avoid an action because it could be considered wrong in the manner of a social absolute. The concept of cooperation is best understood from the standpoint that the child cooperates out of choice. Under the morality of restraint there is no awareness on the part of the child that he has a right to choose to do anything. There is only correct behavior and incorrect behavior coupled with the expectation of shame in the face of dealing with external superego figures who are real people. Shame at the hands of others decides. When the rules have been set by those outside, and their contents refreshed by sustained contact, breaks in behavior occur away from structured settings. In the morality of cooperation, communication with others relates to their role as providers of the imagoes for good behavior which are internalized as they are acquired.

There is a relationship between the Piagetian concept of "sharing of perspectives" and the concept of passive mastery. Sharing of perspectives is accomplished through the acquisition of moral culture elements as a result of passive participation in the myths of the society. This process provides the individual with guidelines for behavior. Following the cognitive steps that make the acquisition of behavior constancy possible, the idea of what is appropriate can be internalized. At the point that this occurs, motivation, the influence of guilt, and the question of choice come into play in deciding whether to act in accord with social rules. Once the rules have been internalized, the structure and guidelines come from within. Solitary activities which breach the rules, such as bedtime masturbation, become a source of guilt.

This can be seen to occur in children in the early latency age (about six years of age). Internalization of rules is paralleled by changes in the intrinsic characteristics of the latency age child's superego. There is a shift from externally based superego contents in the form of crowds and parents to judgment from within. There is a shift from behavior selected in terms of feelings of shame to behavior controlled by a sense of guilt. There is a shift from the absolute unalterable behavior of the young child to the experience of deciding between behavioral alternatives. There is a shift from the surety of externally guided decisions, unquestioningly made, to the doubt attendant upon ethical decision making.

Since the latency age child must decide between alternatives, he becomes appreciative of stories in which equally complex and ethic-laden decisions must be made. These children experience making choices which require subtleties. There is a parallel move from the black-and-white, often sadomasochistic tales enjoyed by the prelatency child to the capacity to appreciate tales of individuals with complex personalities, who respond to complex situations.

The responses made within stories with ethical content are universally recognized as the appropriate ones within the cultures in which they are told. For this reason certain types of stories are described as not for children. In these stories socially unacceptable alternatives have been chosen by the heroes. Through exposure to stories containing universally accepted choices on an ethical level, examples are set for the child which will help him in the details of identification with the society.

The types of stories having appeal to the prelatency and to the latency child are of interest to us. There are, for instance, two versions of Hansel and Gretel. The version of the story that appeals to prelatency children is built about protagonists who have uncomplicated character traits. They make automatic decisions in the ethical sphere. The version of the story that appeals to the latency child is built around characters whose ethical decisions are a result of choice and reflection. There are changes of point of view, and intimations of the influence of a sense of guilt. The Hansel and Gretel story tells of two children who are set loose in the woods and who find their way to the home of a witch who raises them for eating. Eventually the children save themselves from this wicked person by putting her into the fire in place of themselves. As the story is usually told, the children are members of a family made up of two parents and two children. In versions for prelatency children the parents consist of a stepmother and the real father. The stepmother is all evil and insists that the children be sent from the home. The stepmother loses the children in the woods while the father is gone. The characteristics of absolute evil are represented in this typical mythical stepmother. The father, upon returning, discovers that the children are gone. He goes in search of them as a good father should. There is no doubt in his mind that he wants the children.

In the version of the story appreciated by the latency age child, both parents are the real parents of the children. There is no stepmother. They are beset by hunger and choose to lose the children in the woods because they cannot afford to take care of them. The decision is a difficult one for the parents who eventually change their minds and go into the forest to search for the children to bring them back. They realize their responsibility to their children.

The second story shows a situation in which the parents must make a very difficult decision, in which judgment and a sense of guilt are involved. When a wrong decision is made it is considered and later reversed.

The latency child is continually beset with sinister concerns about moral judgments and ethics and is continually pursuing an internal battle. These conflicts usually relate to masturbatory urges and hostile feelings toward parents. These first experiences with the important internal psychological functions which relate judgment and the superego to society are intense. They are dominated by a preoccupation with ethics and guilt in making decisions. A child becomes fascinated by similar decisions made by a character in a story. The character's decisions influence the internalized concepts of proper behavior for the child in related situations.

Elkind (1974) has commented on the capacity for social functioning that matures during early latency. He relates this to an advance in conceptual thinking described by Piaget in children at ages six to seven. At this age children begin to be able to solve problems in their heads rather than having to use trial and error. Maze solutions in a child entering into the period of concrete operations are reached through mental experiments rather than through experiments in which one moves objects through the maze to see whether they will go through or not. At this time, the selection of appropriate social behavior can be achieved through mental activity which utilizes internalized mental representations of appropriate behavior which relate to a given situation.

Elkind (1974) considers the basic unit of such memory elements to be a "frame" which he defines as "a set of rules, expectations and understandings that underlie behavior [required in] transient but repetitive situations." A form of conservation exists in the child's inner construct of the social world which is parallel to the conservation of quantity that contributes at this age to the child's concept of the physical world. Within this theory there is a direct communication of adult expectancies through precept and example. The communication occurs in different situations as a child comes upon them in the presence of parents and of peers. Frames are acquired directly in a manner similar to that seen in social control through shame (see Appendix B).

The concepts of introjection and guilt covered elsewhere in this chapter are not considered in this essentially behavioral interpretation of the acquisition through education of internalized social schemata. The material is quoted because of the support that it gives for the occurrence of a developmental change in cognition that contributes to the behavioral control of the state of latency with the onset of the latency age period. Conservation of internally maintained behavioral patterns is attributed to the latency age child. It is important to keep in mind that the internal imagoes of behavior are acquired through a process more complex than simple learning. Distortion of social and parental admonition is described above in stage 2 and early stage 3 of Piaget's concept of the development of moral judgment in the child. There are prior private rituals of play, in connection with which the child interprets what he sees in terms of personal schemas. This provides the basis for personalized organizations of social rules.

Elkind's concept of conservation of behavior patterns, or "frames," describes a cognitive skill necessary for the retention of the products of the projection-introjection process that produces the internalized imagoes upon which control of behavior is based. The projection-introjection process explains the variability of acquired social rules and the intensity with which guilt is felt. The projection of hostility onto parental figures intensifies fear of punishment and the associated sense of guilt. Cognitive maturation of the capacity to maintain imagoes of appropriate social behavior serves as support of the state of latency. The child in the early latency age undergoes the following process. Automatic response to parental demands gives way to experimental decisions made mentally in accord with a permanent armamentarium of internalized parental and social demands which have been acquired through a process of learning, projection, introjection, and epigenetic acquisitions through passive mastery. There occurs a conservation of these moral concepts. The child develops an ability to recognize similarities of social rules in superficially different but intrinsically similar social situations. The child who has learned to behave in school can recognize the need to behave in a concert hall when he sees others sitting and listening as they did in school, although the total activity is different. Conversely, the same child can recognize the combination of children and balloons as permission to behave in the style which is expected at parties or school recess.

With the maturation and integration of the functions that evolve during the first cognitive organizing period of latency, the cast has been gathered for the beginning of the phase of latency. The superego-motivating affect —guilt—is ready to motivate superego contents acquired as the result of a maturation in the cognitive organization of memory. Mechanisms of restraint are ready to hold in check the sadomasochistic drive organization that results from regression in the face of oedipal stresses. The mechanisms of restraint are one contribution of the ego to the implementation of superego demands. Another is the structure of latency which, combining symbolization and repression, provides fantasies for alternate pathways for the discharge of drives so that the mechanisms of restraint will not be overloaded. Latency begins.

The Second Cognitive Organizing Period

The dividing line between early and late latency falls in the eighth year of life, the division based upon changes in manifest behavior which are noted in all societies including those whose management of the latency years differs from our own. The changes in manifest behavior reflect better physical coordination, improved reality testing, greater dependability and reliability and the beginnings of involvement with nonincestuous figures as the objects for drive gratification. The move toward independence that begins at this time produces conflicts with parents and an enhancement of the influence of peer pressure. In addition there is some weakening of the symbolizing power of the structure of latency as manifested in the shift to more humanlike figures in persecutory fantasies.

Four cognitive skills mature and develop during the years seven and one-half to eight and one-half that produce the shift to late latency:

1. Concrete operational thinking. This is a term used by Piaget to describe cognitive improvement in reality testing.

2. Abstract conceptual memory organization. This is a skill which relates to the ability to recall on an abstract rather than a rote level.

3. A shift in fantasy contents from thoughts about fantasy objects to thoughts about reality objects.

4. Reorganization of superego contents in the direction of ethical individuation of the child's own motives and away from motivational contents derived from parental demands.

CONCRETE OPERATIONAL THINKING

A child's understanding and interpretation of the world follows a distinct developmental line according to Piaget (see Woodward, 1965). He divides this process into four stages. The first, lasting from birth to about eighteen months is called the "sensorimotor stage." It is characterized by responses limited to objects that are present and can be seen by the child. As a result, the child's behavior reflects the attitude that the world centers on his activities. The second stage lasts from eighteen months to seven years. It is called the "preoperational stage." The stage is subdivided into the symbolic and intuitive phases. During the preoperational stage the interpretation of the world is dominated by the personalization of perceptions and memories. This is based on a freedom to "manipulate words and mental images as representations of absent objects" (Woodward, p. 60). Distortion and incorrect conclusions are produced at will to fulfill the needs of the child. The creative freedom produced by this cognitive orientation supports the rich use of symbols and fantasies as a means of drive discharge during the latency state. A diminution in this potential impairs symbolization and weakens the structure of latency.

The third stage, lasting from seven to eleven years, is called the stage of concrete operations. At this point the child can reach correct conclusions about objects that are concretely available to him.

The stage of abstract operations, the fourth stage, begins at eleven years of age and remains through maturity. In this stage the child can deal with the possible and the abstract. This is the basis for the development of scientific thinking as well as the adaptation of the fantasy function of the latency structure for use in future planning in adolescence.

Concrete operational thinking is characterized by an improvement in adaptation to complex aspects of reality. Since there is greater objectivity, there is less tendency to misunderstand events on the basis of highly charged fantasy contexts. This limits the amount of stimulation of drive energies by the environment. Understanding of reality situations is increased, providing an opportunity to solve problems on a realistic basis, and this reduces the need for fantasy. Less freedom in the interpretation of objects results in a limitation of the nature of signifiers selected for use as psychoanalytic symbols. In persecutory fantasies, the pursuers become more human. The child appears to be more reality oriented, more dependable, and is less apt to distort that which he has seen.

ABSTRACT CONCEPTUAL MEMORY ORGANIZATION

There is a further shift in emphasis in the nature of the memory processes during the second cognitive organizing period of latency. Nonverbal memory and verbal conceptual memory give way to abstract conceptual memory in dealing with neutral topics and rote learning. Nonverbal memory consists of the retrospective apprehension and recall of experiences through the retention and evocation of physical nonverbal aspects of the subject's own responses to new events. Subjective restricting influences resulting from the limited potential of this system of recall limit the effectiveness of this system of memory for events. Descriptions of perceptions and experiences for each individual, though valid and consistent for the individual, cannot be exactly repeated or validated in the sensory experience of another individual. Therefore this system of recall cannot support a learning process which aims at a sharing of congruent concepts within a group of individuals. The exclusive presence of such a system of recall would permit the transmission of syntaxes of motor skills but would provide no mechanism for the development and transmission of culture based on the verbal, symbolic, and mythic transmission of culturally approved motor techniques and ethics.

Verbal conceptual memory consists of retrospective apprehension and recall of experiences. Recall of memory is achieved through words derived from social sources. As such they may partially mask intrinsic characteristics of the phenomenon under study. The source of the words and symbols used for the interpretation of new events is the social language group in which the individual gains membership through the acquisition of its verbal patterns. To a large extent these verbal patterns place restrictions on the freedom with which one may interpret new stimuli. This is the source of the limitation in poetic verbal creativity that befalls the child as he passes into latency. The limit on freedom of interpretation is compensated for by the development of a consistent, group-validated interpretation of events. This in turn supports the development of learning of complex motor patterns (syntaxes) through verbal means.

In contrast, abstract conceptual memory consists of the retrospective apprehension and recall of experiences through memory elements which represent the intrinsic characteristics of the phenomenon. An awareness of an intrinsic reality beyond the words used to describe events opens the way to scientific inquiry and creative interpretations of the world which are grounded in reality.

There is not a sharp shift from nonverbal learning to verbal and abstract learning during this second cognitive organizing period. There is, nevertheless, a marked intensification of the latter two at the expense of the former at this time.

Theories of child development usually divide the ontogenesis of the recording and recall aspects of memory and learning into three stages. First-stage learning occurs as the result of the acquisition of nonconceptual reflex patterns of response. Second-stage learning occurs as the result of the acquisition of the ability to evoke recall of learned patterns in the form of affects, perceptions, and bodily postures associated with the initial learning experience. Third-stage learning occurs with acquisition of the ability to evoke recall of learned patterns in the form of verbal signifiers such as words and related symbols. In the third stage abstract representations are possible. The transition from affecto-motor hallucinatory memory to verbal memory has been emphasized in the works of Ferenczi, Piaget, and Schachtel (see above) in relation to the infantile amnesia which is an important phenomenon of early latency. At that time, verbal and symbolic styles of memory place earlier forms of memory and the contents they represent into shadow. This is the product of the increased effectiveness of the newer technique. This change is associated with sufficient strengthening of symbolization to produce a structure of latency that will support calm, pliability, and educability by about age six. Memory at this age involves the recall of earlier emotional experiences through socially dictated verbal schemata for naming rather than the acquisition of abstract concepts representative of the intrinsic substance of things and events. The latter skill as a memory function matures between six and eight years of age.

Switzer (1963) has illustrated this experimentally by studying the performance of normal children learning two types of task: one which involves knowledge acquired through physical experience, and one which involves knowledge acquired through mental apprehension of an abstraction. Learning through physical experience, though reported through the use of words, is emphasized in an activity she calls the place task. In this exercise children are asked to remember the order in which a series of illuminated boxes are turned on. Children seeking to remember the order use pointing of the fingers as a memory aid. Recall is best done by remembering in terms of one's own body, and describing what is recalled with words.

Abstract conceptual memory is emphasized in an activity she calls the naming task. In this exercise, children are asked to remember the order in which a series of variously colored illuminated boxes are turned on. They experience color, a characteristic of light which cannot be recorded through body movement. In order to recall this, skill is required in developing a concise verbal means for recalling the order in which the lights were turned on. The entire process of apprehension and recall must be mental.

Three groups of normal children, consisting of six-year-olds, eight-year-olds and ten-year-olds were given these tests. The six-year-olds made comparatively fewer errors on the place task (position) than on the name task (color names). The eight-year-olds and twelve-year-olds made fewer errors on the name task.

The importance of this finding on the surface is that a child with a learning disorder has to be evaluated from the standpoint of the type of learning required for the particular skill being taught. Athletics and most of school learning before the age of seven and a half require affecto-motor (apprehension through physical experience) and simple verbal conceptive memory skills. The more highly regarded academic skills beyond this age require abstract conceptual memory. From the standpoint of latency there are other implications. In describing the children who were tested, Switzer differentiated three groups: the young, the hyperactive, and the inhibited. The young were six-year-olds. The hyperactive had a tendency to act, poor verbal abstract ability, and poor school performance. The inhibited sat still, preferred quiet pursuits, and "generally show rich fantasy" (p. 661).

Of the three groups, not a single young or hyperactive child attempted an abstract conceptual approach in remembering the order in which the illuminated boxes were lit. Inhibited and older children used techniques in dealing with the colored illuminated boxes that showed that for them names are more meaningful. Although the use of fantasy demonstrates the existence of potential for conceptual thinking in dealing with conflict situations in prelatency and early latency children, abstract conceptual memory applied to rote tasks does not become available until the second cognitive organizing period of latency. The pliability and calm of the latency state that support educability can appear at five or six as the result of the ego mechanisms of restraint and the structure of latency. Educability apparently requires additional factors—high social regard for education and maturation of skills in abstract conceptual learning.

THE SHIFT IN FANTASY CONTENTS

The shift from inner-oriented perceptions to reality-oriented perceptions as the source of fantasy content for the gratification of drives is a nearly universal phenomenon during the second cognitive organizing period of latency. Even in childhood schizophrenia (see chapter 8) there are changes in symptomatology which reflect the effect of this maturational shift. As in the case of abstract conceptual memory, this shift appears to be a continuation of a developmental line which started with verbal conceptual memory. The capacity to learn in terms of verbal signifiers which have shared social roots and culturally validatable implications is the major cognitive step involved in fixing and codifying the shift of human attention from personalized fantastic responses to socially oriented goals.

The most common clinical manifestation of this trend is the age-bound changes in the content of the fear-fantasy imagery of the latency age child. Anthony (1959) in a review of the literature on this subject has described the imagery of the fear fantasies of children from five to eight years of age as fantastic. Uncomfortable dreams consist of "ghosts, witches, giants, animals and suffocating" (p. 25). From the age of nine till twelve, the imagery of fear fantasies is social. Dreams consist of school friends and pets. This is one of the characteristic defining differences in cognition between the early and late latency periods. Underpinning this shift is a change in the symbolizing function in which the selection of signifiers to be used as symbols is based upon less fantastic and more socially oriented images and concepts. Symbols used in fantasies have less the characteristics of memory elements evoked through affectively distorted percepts and more the characteristics of shared social experiences. In those for whom such fantasy is unavailable, personalized affecto-motor and action-oriented responses constitute reactions to situations of stress. Such reactions can be disruptive. The role of fantasies in adjustment shifts, with the transition from early to late latency, from the role of discharge pathway for drives toward a role as a medium of social communication. The discharge capacity remains, but is less easily detected. In the construction of a manifest fantasy, the shift to socially dominated verbal signifiers and symbolic components increases its communicative function. Storytelling skills become more facile. This step indicates the ultimate maturation of psychoanalytic symbols.

Although psychoanalytic symbol formation could be said to have begun at twenty-six months, dependability in such symbols awaits further development. Psychoanalytic symbols pursue a developmental line that is independent of that of metaphorical symbols. The successful development of psychoanalytic symbols is contingent on the maturation of mechanisms of repression. Primal repression, during the first half of the third year of life, harnesses symbolism to the requirements of the adaptational functions of the ego. Repression proper, which is attendant upon the onset of latency, is involved in the production of more fixed and durable symbols. With the shift in emphasis in the selection of signifiers from fantastic to socially dictated, reality oriented signifiers, a final step in the ontogenesis of psychoanalytic symbols takes place. The dual role of the signifier as both symbol and as a common cultural element provides added potential for concealment of its purpose. A prime clinical manifestation of this shift occurs during the transition from the early to the late latency period. There is a change in the nature of the typical signifier selected to be a symbol in fear fantasies. There is a shift to more reality-oriented representations. An eight-year-old child who feared school because of dinosaurs chewing outside her window (see chapter 8) developed a persecutory fear involving her mother when she was ten. Change in the symbolizing function occurs. Symbolizations in which repression takes place share in this change. Fear fantasies and persecutory fantasies of children going from the early to the late latency period shift from fears of amorphous creatures with vague dangerous designs on the child to fear of figures with human qualities who will rape, kill, rob, or kidnap. (An extensive study of this material including the relationship of those persecutory fantasies to prepubertal schizophrenia appears in chapter 8).

REORGANIZATION OF SUPEREGO CONTENTS:
ETHICAL INDIVIDUATION

Toward the end of the second cognitive organizing period of latency, there is a shift in the source of adjustment patterns from a fantasy orientation based on affects and parental introjects to a reality orientation influenced by peers and experience. This sets the stage for the major internal conflict situation of the late latency period—the clash between internalized parentally approved patterns of behavior and potentials for behavior opened by newly developed vistas on reality. On the one hand, the child's behavior is guided by superego contents derived from introjected imagoes of early objects and experiences. In this process internalized past experiences and the influence of parents serve as the bastions about which behavior and young ethics are organized. On the other hand, new wishes begin to motivate the child. Desires at odds with parental ethical guidelines increasingly tempt him. Increased capacity to appreciate reality, including the behavior patterns of peer groups, proves the cognitive developmental basis for this step. To most youngsters, new vistas provide inputs which appear to change prohibitions on freedom of behavior. More activities and objects are potentially available for the expression of drives. In youngsters in whom internal prohibitions are shallow and in those who have the ability to defy parents, newly experienced reality assumes a strong role in influencing the ethical decisions that determine behavior. This process of ethical individuation is reinforced by expectation of society that the child will take on more responsibility, larger size, and better coordination. This results in alterations in that which society finds to be acceptable behavior in these youngsters. Usually this results in greater freedom of movement for the child. This general softening of superego demands is often accompanied by a resumption of masturbatory activity (usually clandestine).

In some youngsters who are not capable of relinquishing strict parental introjects, greater social permissiveness is confounded by the persistence of intense prohibitions. This is especially so in aggression-inhibited passive youngsters. They grow to maturity unable to defy the ethical patterns of their parents. The original internal prohibitions of early childhood maintain suzieranty over the motor behavior and most of the thoughts of the child. The inability to tear oneself away from parentally imposed patterns, especially those having to do with the inhibition of defiant aggression, establishes a vicious cycle. Internal prohibitions stand fast in the face of the force of reality influences. The entire process of the shift to current reality influences in the determination of ethical behavior is delayed by the presence of an inertia which is an intrinsic characteristic of the process. This relates to the nature of the memory organizations used for the retention of the contents of the superego. Whereas most of the newly acquired guidelines for behavior are acquired and retained in latency through the subtleties of verbal communication involved in contemporary experiences, internal prohibitions manifested in latency are derived from prelatency experiences utilizing the cognitive memory system that dominates that period. Specifically, retention and recall utilize the affecto-motor hallucinatory memory organization (see above). They feel and know, where no words guide. Cathexis of reality and words leads to a deemphasis of these earlier patterns (introjects) during the early latency period. However, they are not obliterated. Logic does not influence these feelings, which bid strongly for the control of behavior.

Reality influences and introjects both lay claim to control of ethical decisions and thus an interface for conflict may be established. In the group of youngsters who remain locked to parental ethics, the introjects are dominant and reality cathexes have little impact. Conflict is not manifest. In those who attach to the peer group easily, word and reality cathexes dominate and the potential for conflict is resolved. But for those who can form new wishes on the basis of new experience, and who at the same time are subjected to strong reinforcements of the influence of internalized introjects, the potential for internal conflict is great. The actualization of these potential conflicts occurs either when there is pressure to conform to open standards or when there is parental pressure to conform to "safe" old patterns of behavior. The former situation is exemplified by the child who was encouraged to steal by her friends but returned the item to the shelf. The latter is illustrated by the ongoing reinforcements of internal prohibitions that are produced by the presence of a phobic mother who must restrict a child's activities (see chapter 6). At the times that potential conflicts are actualized by seductive situations in reality, periods of strong affect develop. To complicate matters, symptomatic resolutions are produced by the personality of the child in response to these affects. Fear and punishment fantasies develop. These fuel and intensify nocturnal anxieties. For instance, the child who was induced to steal by peers and then returned the stolen items experienced fear of robbers at night and had anxiety dreams about being kidnapped and held for ransom following the episode.

In severe cases, somatic symptoms (hives, headache, vomiting), persecutory fantasies, and obsessive compulsive symptoms develop. Obsessive-compulsive symptoms, usually transient, are the most common of these manifestations. Obsessional defenses, almost universally present (see Silverman, 1972, p. 375) as part of the mechanisms of restraint that maintain latency, are mobilized in support of the psychic equilibrium. The intensification of obsessional symptomatology in children in late latency is explained by the coupling of ubiquitous obsessive-compulsive defenses during the latency period and the stresses of ethical individuation.

The reality situation most apt to peak the intensity of this coupling and thus to evoke obsessional symptoms are those which offer tempting new activities or in which there is a vying with another for the right to perform a coveted task. The latter contains a key to the intrinsic nature of the conflict involved in ethical individuation. There is a vying for control of the behavior of the child between representations of the parent and new-found wishes of the child. Some examples follow.

A nine-year-old girl was confronted by an art teacher who hit her hand with a ruler when she did not perform adequately. The girl wanted to drop the course. Parental admonitions had always been aimed at completing any project that was started. They insisted that the child remain in the class. The child developed a counting ritual consisting of categories of three units out of items in the classroom. Anger was found to be associated with the desire to withdraw from the course. Doubting and conflict associated with having a wish that contradicted the parents' demands produced guilt and the counting ritual.

A boy of eleven conceived of a paper construction depicting a house during a play-therapy session. The therapist, who was a gifted craftsman, worked with the child on the construction. At one point, the therapist became so affectively involved in a piece of the handwork that he lost sight of his therapeutic role. He beat the child to the task in which the child had as intense an interest. A vying for power had occurred. The child was crowded out. The therapist reported that as his attention was withdrawn from the task and returned to the patient, he could observe that the child was involved in a compulsive ritual—touching the desk and then his shoulder in a rhythmic pattern a score of times.

Situations which induce sexual fantasies provide fertile ground for the intensification of the conflicts of late latency. Oedipal fantasies are particularly important. The passing of the Oedipus complex is not a true dissolution but is rather a product of repression proper. Concurrent with this repression there occurs an inhibition of expressions of sexuality which have their roots in the affecto-motor experiences of early childhood. Internal controls trace their origins to the repression of the Oedipus complex and to inhibitions of urges to recreate infantile experiences. The increases in sexual drive pressures and social permissiveness which are identified with late latency sensitize a child so that phase-appropriate sexual fantasies are more easily stimulated by passing events. Though the structure of latency deals effectively with many fantasies, the amount of potential guilt associated with the appearance of overt sexual fantasy in late latency relates to the strength of the conflict between the related latent sexual fantasies and immutable internal prohibitions. Obsessional symptoms are often a manifestation of the conflicting affects that relate to concurrent sexual wishes and inhibitions. For instance, an eleven-year-old boy developed an obsessional touching ritual while waiting to see a neighbor girl undress by her unshaded window.

Since most of these symptoms are transient, it appears that they represent a period of working through. In this period the introjects are processed in such a way that the strictness with which their admonitions are followed is lessened. Often these take the form of replacement by peer group ethics that conform to wishes derived from contact with reality.

The processing of strict parental introjects produces superego contents which place less emphasis on obtaining parental approval. Social gains and long-range rewards become the orienting principle in the superego content produced during late latency. These are early steps in the loosening of the sexual inhibitions. The attendant loosening of superego demands is an early step in the object seeking that will result in object removal.

The Third Cognitive Organizing Period

This period is concurrent with the latter part of late latency. The time period encompasses nine to twelve years of age. Its maturation produces the cognitive organization of early adolescence. The shift from early latency to late latency entails a modification of the organization of fantasy so that fantastic objects are replaced by realistic objects in fantasy. The shift from late latency to adolescence entails a modification of the organization of the drive discharge mechanisms of the ego from the seeking of realistic objects in fantasy to seeking objects which are accurately perceived in reality.

The cognitive maturation of early latency (the second cognitive organizing period) prepares for a heightened awareness and exploration of reality. The cognitive maturation of late latency prepares for the utilization of reality.

From the standpoint of latency, this third cognitive organizing period is important because of the ongoing effect of the development of its components on late latency. The ultimate effect of its maturation is a problem of adolescence and outside the sphere of this book. However, the ongoing effects of its maturation are quite marked, and are the primary subject matter of a number of other chapters. Below, we will discuss developing cognitive processes that color late latency.

THE PREADOLESCENT VICISSITUDES OF PROJECTION

The mechanism of projection is a compound of simple component defenses. In some cases it is possible for component defenses to be changed without modifying the essential nature of the complex defense of which it is a part. Thus projection associated with repression and symbol formation gives way to projection associated with denial and the attribution of motives to real figures as a component of the third cognitive organizing period of latency. As a result of this, fantastic interpretations of reality can be checked against reality itself instead of symbols. In addition, repression, displacement, and symbolizations of affects and motives become less involved in the discharge of drives and more involved with communicative measures. There is a shift from defensive projection to sublimative projection. Through the projection of the ego idea, the superego is opened to influences from the peer group and the environment. The vicissitudes of projection are dealt with extensively in chapter 8.

CHANGES IN BODY IMAGE

The massive changes in body conformation that occur during prepuberty produce states of doubt and confusion; children wonder what and who they are. Latent bisexual fantasies and fears are stirred when youngsters experience growth patterns which they consider to be aberrant. It is common for young boys to develop breast buds, which are a growth of tissue under the nipple, during prepuberty. This becomes a source of great concern, for the boy interprets this as a sign of femininity. It is actually a part of male growth. The child's interpretation reflects his own doubts. Impairment of abstract thinking, which blocks an appreciation of the intrinsic meaning of puberty for sexual identification, may occur in prepubertal girls with strong conflicts in regard to sexual identity.

The increasing changes in body configuration that mark this period produce a situation of self-awareness similar to that experienced during the first year of life. At that time, there was a cognitive inconsistency. Memory skills progressed and regressed under the influence of illness, parental rejection, and maturation. The infant finds in his body each morning a new discovery, since some of what had been known of it can be lost with regressions in memory skills. This is certainly the epitome of an uncertain sense of self and doubtfulness in relation to identity. The same situation prevails in prepuberty. Changes in the sense of self and form occur. Whereas in early childhood fluidity of self-image was paralleled by fluidity in cognitive structures, in prepuberty fluidity of self-image is based on true fluidity of body form. The fluidity of self-image in prepuberty and early adolescence produces a distorted sense of self, coupling awkwardness and uncertainty. This provides a poor base from which to move into adolescent social competition. Often doubt and self-rejection derived from this become the source of the rejecting thoughts that late latency-early adolescent children project and attribute to peers. This circumstance can produce behavior patterns of fear and withdrawal in social situations in otherwise well-functioning youngsters.

CHANGES IN THE INTENSITY AND DIRECTION OF
OBJECT RELATEDNESS

The period of preadolescence is marked by a noticeable increase in drive energies. Erections become more frequent. Bodily changes portend the beginnings of maturity. Sexual fantasies become more intense and more overt. Fantasy contents begin to relate to planning around the search for objects in reality to be used for the discharge of drives. In content, the earliest of these fantasies entail looking, seeing, and fulfilling one's curiosity about the form and appearance of the mature male and female. Money (1972) has stated that "one of the essential aspects of puberty is that the visual image takes on a new importance with regard to erotic affection . . ." (p. 265). This is a step in the ongoing shift in seeking things to be used for the discharge of drives.

In going from early to late latency, there is a shift from thoughts about fantasy objects to thoughts about reality objects. During late latency-early adolescence the emphasis on reality objects becomes more intense. Eventually fantasy as object gives way to reality as object. The latter characterizes adolescence. What is striking is that this shift to reality objects in fantasy is a characteristic of all children at the threshold of late latency, be they normal, neurotic, or schizophrenic. There are variations in the capacity to go beyond this so as to seek for objects in reality for drive discharge. The examples of such variations are people with the ego impairments of schizophrenia and certain hypogonadotropic males.

Let us begin with the ego impairments of schizophrenia as they relate to thought processes. In the child who is developing normally, improvement of the appreciation of reality is contingent upon a shift in the emphasis of the cognition used in memory from affecto-motor hallucinatory memory to a memory organization based on verbal conceptual elements. Early in this transition, words often retain the affect they represented. This is a transitional step in the deaffectivization of words (see Ferenczi, 1911, p. 139 and 145; quoted and discussed in this book, pp. 106-108). The fantastic objects that populate early latency have more in common with primitive emotionally charged words than with affectively neutral words. Words with a less charged tone representing neutral reality objects are introduced as fantasy objects with the onset of late latency. Reality based objects populate the discharge and planning fantasies of this period. Essentially fantasy is still used for discharge and words are used as objects.

The process of maturation in relation to this use of words as objects has two directions in which it can develop. It can develop normally. This is characterized by finding objects in reality to use in place of neutrally toned words as fantasy objects. This is only a step away from involvement with objects in reality. Or it can pursue a pathological development. This occurs if, instead of replacing fantasy objects with real objects, the process of deaffectivization of words is emphasized. Instead of reality being strengthened, as a source of objects to be used for the discharge of drives, fantasies without affect are cathected at the expense of reality. It is at this point that flattened affect, thinking disorders, and delusional thinking can be used consistently in diagnosing schizophrenia. At age eleven, manifestations of schizophrenia indistinguishable from the adult form first appear (see chapter 6). The preference for words over people is a manifestation of ongoing poor relatedness. It is often detectable at a very early age. The use of fantasy as object in latency can create differential diagnostic problems. These problems are reduced once the child enters adolescence.

Among two hundred cases of delayed puberty, Money (1972) observed, during a follow-up period of as long as twenty years, that there were groups of "hypogonadotropic males [who] have great difficulty in falling in love" (p. 265). An example is Kallman's Syndrome (anosmia or hyposmia with gonadotropin deficiency). The administration of corrective hormones may initiate puberty. Social development of the child so treated may not be concurrently resolved. Maturation of physique and behavior appear to have different responses to corrective hormones. Money postulates a higher center that controls both deficiencies in hormone and "deficiency also with regard to sexual behavior, erotic behavior and falling in love" (p. 265). There is a hint here of an as yet unsubstantiated physiological brain mechanism and center. Activation of this center would control the secretions that govern the puberty. Independently it could control the normal physiological underpinnings of cognitive development. Variations in the degree of closeness to reality that characterize the contents of the fantasies of the late latency child could be explained in this way.

INTENSIFICATION OF NARCISSISTIC INVESTMENT IN FANTASY

The shift of drive objects from objects in fantasy to objects in reality characterizes a healthy development in object relations. It is countered by an increase in narcissism during late latency. This imbues the substance of the child, including his fantasies, with a quality of importance transcending the importance of reality. The confusing changes in the body image in prepuberty draw the child's attention to himself and heighten his need to see himself as important. Improved cognitive apprehension of reality intensifies the latter reaction. The more one sees oneself realistically as a small piece of a big world instead of its center, the more will such narcissism be mobilized. The presence of heightened narcissism in early adolescence interferes wtih the finding of objects in reality for the discharge of drives. As noted above, the first step in the move from early latency to late latency is accomplished by the introduction of reality objects into fantasy thoughts. The next step should be the seeking of real objects in reality. This step is interfered with by the upsurge of narcissism. Narcissistic cathexis of fantasy results in the intrusion of fantasy thoughts into the child's involvement with reality objects. Such intrusions on reality interfere with object removal. At times the narcissism serves a useful purpose. Often fantasies and their affects are more familiar and comfortable than contact with new reality situations. Dreams of great achievement produce willingness to undertake truly difficult tasks. Fantasies provide an orientation through which to relate to reality objects during the time that the reality objects are becoming familiar. Narcissistic invasion of reality situations with fantasies can serve a useful purpose, for they can give reality a chance to impress and win frightened fledglings on the brink of life.

Cognition and Superego Development

The cognitive organizing periods of latency contribute to the formation of the state of latency and adolescence. Many of the functions evolved during these periods contribute lasting modifications of the elements that make up the adult superego.

The superego may be studied from the standpoint of a number of elements: (1) the source of the conceptual contents of the superego, (2) the nature of the affects which arise in response to awareness of the degree to which behavior conforms to conceptual contents, (3) the dominant affects associated with a particular ontogenetic period of superego development, (4) the development of the cognitive skills that are necessary for the acquisition of conceptual contents, and (5) the nature of the effectors of the superego. These last are defined as those functions of the ego having to do with the implementation of superego demands.

In this section the sequential stages of superego development will be explored in relation to these elements to the extent that they are pertinent to the stage involved. The latency age will be the main focus. Other developmental stages are included to provide background for understanding superego formation associated with the latency age, as well as to emphasize that the onset of the state of latency is not the sole progenitor of the superego.

The development of the superego is a sustained process encompassing the first three decades of life. Cognitive maturation, psychosexual development, and social expectations contribute to superego changes throughout this period. The popular concept of the superego—that the superego forms only at age six with the internalization of parental imagoes that accompanies the passing of the Oedipus complex and is enforced through the negative influences of the affect of guilt—is far too limited. We present the view here that the superego is a product of a multitude of influences.

The conceptual contents of the superego begin to be acquired as early as six to eighteen months. At that age, they are primarily related to restrictions placed on a child's motility. At the age at which a child first walks he has motility which can result in damage to property or to himself. The first controls placed on children relate to the management of aggression and curiosity manifested in motor activities. A child who is capable of walking and touching poorly comprehended objects has great potential for destructiveness. In dealing with this, parents may say "No, no!" as the child reaches to touch a fragile glass item, perhaps to break it. In doing so, the parent contributes inhibition of impulse to the content of the superego on a primitive conceptual level. On the motor level effector mechanisms are called upon. These are control mechanisms of the early ego which, to enforce the earliest superego contents, impose impulse control, motor restraints, and inhibitions. The child learns to inhibit impulse in the motor sphere. Initially this takes place through conscious recall of the memory of the words, "No, no!" which are verbalized by the child as he approaches the proscribed tempting and fragile item. At times the child hits his own hand. The control that is achieved occurs within the context of an object relationship. The memory of the proscription is early evidence of internalization of the parent-child interaction. The child's verbalizations recreate the role of the parent through the parent's own words. Hitting of self recreates parental use of pain and punishment in achieving control.

The pattern of discomfort intensifying enforcement of admonitions derived from an object relationship is paradigmatic of superego functioning at all ages and levels of development. There are characteristic differences in this pattern which occur in relation to the variables of age and development and to the extent to which the elements which comprise the patterns are internalized and are unconscious. In very early childhood, internalized feeling reactions are expressed in actualizations such as hitting oneself. The associated affects are depression and elation (glee). The latter is particularly important because it is so often overlooked.

Henderson (1974) has noted the deemphasis in psychoanalytic superego theory of a positive affect encouraging conforming behavior. Hoffman (1970) has called for a delineation of the positive motivating aspects of conscience with emphasis on previous experiences that contributed to its development, recommending a "search for structures that form the basis for a positive morality" (p. 335). A study of the early development of the motivating affects of the superego reveals the basis of a positive morality.

Before the onset of the influence of the affects of guilt and shame in motivating ego functions to enforcement of superego demands, there were other affects. Foremost among these were depression and elation. The human personality is guided in a course aimed at fulfilling the ego ideal by the impact of these affects. Avoidance of depression influences behavior in the same way that avoidance of guilt or shame does. Depressed affects appear in situations in which an individual falls short of the ego ideal. Elation appears at times when behavior fulfills the ego ideal. Elation, good moods, and happiness evoke pleasure sensations akin to the pleasurable feelings of unity which occur in the experience of closeness to the mother. Depression relates to fear of loss of love. The concept of depression and elation as superego motivating affects has roots in Freud's theory that fear of loss of love propels a child into "latency," producing better-controlled behavior. If fear of loss of love encourages good behavior, the obverse is certainly true. Love itself sustains it. In effect, there is an internalized affect, elation, with a paradigm in maternal reward, which influences the implementation of superego demands and which provides a major positive motivation to achieve in latency. In the early years, when ego ideal contents are in the process of being established, they are sparse and weak. The superego motivating affects associated with them are equally weak but become more forceful during the prelatency years when the ego ideal becomes richer in content and other areas of ego function which are propelled by positive motivation expand and strengthen. Among these are achievement involved in the mastery of the syntaxes of movement required for motor skills and the sense of achievement that accompanies the acquisition of ethical conceptual superego contents as a result of passive mastery of drives using culturally approved myths.

As described above, the beginnings of motor impulse control are introduced during the period of the onset of motility. It is at its height from nine to eighteen months of age. Organ function control is usually added soon after. The first area of focus in organ function control is regulation of emunctory function through sphincter control. The exact timing of onset of this activity relates to the age chosen by the parents to introduce toilet training. The period eighteen to twenty-eight months is usual. Sphincter control is not enforced through the words "No, no" plus threat of physical discomfort derived from hitting or restraint alone. A new element is introduced into the superego motivating affects. There is a condensation and internalization of the affect memories associated with negative emotional responses, and this is instrumental in the production of shame. Pleasing the mother results in pleasurable sensations, failure to please through sphincter control results in pain, punishment, and a sense of humiliation. The evocation of these sensations during later confrontations with the parents is shame.

The need to control sphincter function when parents are not present parallels the need to avoid the evocation of the uncomfortable affects associated with failure in the presence of the parents. Shame can motivate through displacement of the parental reaction onto others or into mentally experienced expectations (that is, psychic representations of the parent). This uncomfortable affect, shame, is a memory component derived from sensations of humiliation, pain, and depression undergone during previously experienced punishment situations. Shame is an internalized affect whose memory accompanied by the concept of the shame returns to consciousness during periods of transgression. This infantile experience can be reawakened in later life in mob and group situations to set aside internalized superego demands and to enforce group superego contents. Small group (i.e., that is, primitive) societies utilize the affect of shame as their primary means of enforcing social conformity (see chapter 5, p. 175).

Ferenczi (1925) first described this early form of superego organization consisting of internalized parental demands (sphincter control), ego functions (inhibition and delay) which effect these demands, and enforcement of superego content through the recall of parental reactions. These include recreating physical punishment, as in hitting oneself, and the affect of shame. Shame itself consists of a reexperiencing of internalized patterns of sensations which evoke prior humiliations and pain associated with related impulses and activities. Ferenczi referred to this as "sphincter morality" (p. 267).

During the toilet training period, the child is exposed to pressure from his parents to identify with patterns of control that they themselves have achieved in regulating anal and urethral excretory functions. Ferenczi (1925) notes:

> . . . anal and urethral identification with the parents . . . appears to build up in the child's mind a sort of physiological forerunner of the ego-ideal or super-ego. Not only in the sense that the child constantly compares his achievements in these directions with the capacities of his parents, but in that a severe sphincter-morality is set up which can only be contravened at the cost of bitter self-reproaches and punishment by conscience. It is by no means improbable that this, as yet semi-physiological, morality forms the essential groundwork of later purely mental morality. . . . (p. 267)

This passage is of importance in understanding the early stages of the superego. It is remarkable, also, because it reflects Ferenczi's early appreciation for one of the basic cognitive differences between the prelatency and latency stages. Ferenczi refers to a "semi-physiological" nature in experience identifiable with prelatency. The "purely mental" potential of psychic functioning is a characteristic of the latency time period. This is reflected in the change in the superego that normally occurs at the beginning of the state of latency.

Sphincter morality is a step in an ongoing developmental series which contributes to the social individuation of the child. The initial step in this developmental series was self-object differentiation. This introduced the concept of others. Subsequently the development of object constancy permitted the child to exist alone in the face of the knowledge that there are others. Sphincter morality implies the capacity to initiate behavior based on demands of others made prior to the time of action. Enforcement takes place in the absence of others, but with the others in mind. The child learns to function independently of the parent in emunctory functions. He controls his bowels and his bladder and avoids the shame of having lost control. No one else has to be there. This functional level is achieved by the child under the pressure of the expectation of shame, a psychic response representing the parent, from whom sphincter morality is learned. From three to five years of age a child's behavior is dominated by the characteristics of sphincter morality. During this period there is a concurrent gradual development of a capacity for remembering on a verbal conceptual level. As a result, a number of specific verbal admonitions can be added to the requirement for sphincter control. The child learns whether he should touch his genitals; whether he should walk in the snow or walk on the sidewalk; whether he should cross the street by himself. These admonitions have to do with motor activities. Moral judgments are not at issue, nor is choice. The originators of the ideas are close at hand and acquiescence is required, enforced by punishment and shame.

Parental admonitions are communicated through precept and example at this age. Conceptual superego contents are also acquired directly through education. Another source of superego content is introjection of the characteristics of loved objects that accompany repeated separations. Since at this age the child is capable of symbolic distortions and the projection of aggression, he often distorts the information communicated to him. It is then retained with modifications in content and in the intensity of affect. Such distorted parental admonitions represent the parent to the child, and the child relates to an absent parent through obeying these admonitions. He obeys the distorted and remembered parent. Right or wrong does not govern what's to be done. Good behavior comes from acquiescence to the distortion-enhanced will of the authority.

This primitive form of superego is far from the superego of latency. The latter represents a more advanced step in social individuation. The motivating affect which characterizes the latency superego is guilt. It is an affect which can enforce verbal superego content in the absence of a psychic representation of the parent. The typical shift from what Ferenczi (1911) called "hallucinatory perceptual elements" (p. 139) to the abstract verbal thought organization of the latency state contributes to the development of the superego of latency.

At six years, the age of latency commences. This is not a mere numerical convention. Specific cognitive maturational events provide the child with the potential for transforming cultural demands into an organized, relatively immutable set of internally available memory elements to be used by the child in the regulation of drive and impulse and the organization of social behavior. As described on p. 108, there is developed at this age the moral equivalent of object constancy, "behavioral constancy." Subtle ethical controls on social behavior begin to replace affect-motivated inhibition of motor activity when verbal conceptual modes begin to dominate the memory functions that carry acquired superego content into the future. The child is apparently cognitively capable at six of retaining complex ethical concepts and is capable of appreciating and differentiating the situations in which they apply. With the development of object constancy, an image of the departed object could be retained. With the development of behavior constancy at the beginning of the age of latency, concepts of behavior with a degree of subtlety not previously possible can be retained in the absence of the object (the source of the admonitions). Maturation of verbal memory and abstract thinking permit the retention and ensuing transmission into the child's future life of subtle shadings of meaning that were not possible within the old cognitive context of affecto-motor hallucinatory memory modes.

Flavell (1963), in his summary of Piaget's *The Moral Judgment of the Child*, calls attention to theoretical concepts related to this maturational step at the onset of the latency age. In broad general outline, Piaget has described an earlier "morality of restraint" and a later developing "morality of cooperation." The morality of restraint is dominated by an absolute acceptance of higher law. What is handed down by the parent is to be responded to absolutely. All is black and white. There are no shades of grey, and no motivation other than the desire to obey is brought into action. The later developing morality of cooperation contains subtleties, considers motivations, and implies that decisions to act require choices on the part of the child.

The morality of cooperation assumes motivation in the decisions of a person under the pressure of superego contents and affects. This means that the individual recognizes that he may choose the way he is going to act in relation to the dictates of the superego. In the words of Hoffman (1970), "the child at this age gives up his moral absolutism and recognizes a possible diversity of views of right and wrong" (p. 255). These quotes related to the work of Piaget reveal that the cognitive shift that accompanies the onset of the age of latency is not a new concept, but is one that has attracted the attention of mental health scientists for decades.

Sphincter morality and parental admonitions have to do with the morality of restraint. During the early years of the latency age, the child places diminished emphasis on behavior consciously aimed at pleasing the parent. Actions are taken because they feel right or because failure to follow the accepted pattern will result in guilt. Awareness of diversity of views and the awareness of motivation in selecting a course of action introduce the potential for ethical considerations in evaluation of one's own decisions and the evaluation of the decisions of others. Ethical decisions encountered in the lives of others and in the activities of characters in the histories, myths, folk tales, and current events with which the child comes into contact have far-reaching effects in shaping the ethical characteristics added to the ego ideal during latency.

The essential characteristic of the cognitive shift that accompanies the first years of the latency age period entails an augmented capacity to work at a distance, both physical and temporal, in resolving tasks. In the physical sphere, puzzle tasks which had required actual tracking can be solved through the use of abstract thought processes. There is a shift from perceptual motor activity in problem solving to the primary use of trial action in the form of thought. A five-year-old solves a maze by running his fingers through it. A six-year-old shows trial action. He doesn't move his fingers; he uses mental problem-solving techniques representing the object in the maze and the maze itself by mental images. He moves from physical techniques for solving problems to solving problems in his head.

In the temporal sphere, the children conceive of and prepare for problems involving situations removed in time. A shift from physical reexperiencing as a manifestation of the memory function of recall to increased reliance on recall through abstract signifiers such as words and verbally based concepts also occurs. Words become of primary importance for solving problems. A verbal catalog of solutions begins to be accumulated. Much more subtle and much more complex problems can be solved through the use of the virtual library of potential responses which are acquired during this period.

There occurs a period of curiosity and concept hunger which supports the educability of the latency state. There is a need for stories, legends, myths, and other verbal schemata to be used as patterned outlets for the drives, whose prior outlets had been through the evocation of sensations and experiences related to prior gratifications. As these patterned outlets are acquired, associated ethical concepts augment the content of the ego ideal. The influence of society skews these contents to match its needs and to insure conformity and proper fit for the individual in the society of the mass.

A shift to the use of words and related phenomena dominates the mental life of the latency age child. Formerly insoluble problems can be resolved in fantasy. With the aid of repression and masking symbols, which have been available and in use to a small degree since at least the first half of the third year of life, solutions in fantasy can be so covert that the child is not even aware of the process. This process is involved in the resolution of an important prelatency conflict, the Oedipus complex.

This resolution results in much content being added to the ego ideal. The Oedipus complex is rich in feelings and affecto-motor memories. In the prelatency child, intense sexual feelings for the parent of the opposite sex are paralleled by intense feelings of hostility and fear toward the parent of the same sex. In order to live at peace with the parents, the child eventually must repress these wishes and replace them with fantasy contents that are more congenial, or at least better able to be handled with the defense mechanisms at hand. An extensive exposition of the defenses involved may be found in chapter 2.

With the passing of the Oedipus complex the child gives up the old oedipal parental objects and goes on to a different kind of relationship to parental objects. The mother who was to have been the sexual partner and the father who was to have been killed continue to be important in the child's unconscious life, but cease to be important in the child's conscious life. Interactions on a fantasy level provide some outlet during periods of frustration. In conscious life this results in a more comfortable relationship with the parents. In effect, the oedipal parents are lost.

In the early latency child the loss of an object is responded to by introjection. This is a basic reaction. It is part of the tissue response of humanity. The characteristics of the lost object become a part of the identity of the child. Patterns of ego response are transmitted as well as admonitions which contribute to the content of the ego ideal. As a result of this internalization of parent and parental demands, the child no longer need say, "My mother or father says this should be done," but rather, "It is within my mind that it should be done. It is within *my* mind that this is right or that is wrong. If I do not do it this way it isn't that someone else will punish me. The punishment will be within myself." Even the punishment has been internalized. The cognitive shift to abstraction and the tendency to relate to objects on a psychic level rather than on a reality level which typifies the latency age are in evidence here.

A new motivating affect is introduced during the early latency years. It is the affect of guilt. Prior experiences of pain and humiliation are evoked in situations in which demands based on ego ideal contents have been transgressed. This is not unlike the origin of the affect of shame which has its beginnings in the prelatency years. The difference lies in the fact that shame occurs in the presence of others or in the expectation of the presence of others, while guilt occurs in the absence of a conscious psychic representation of the object. In relation to the affect of guilt, the punisher is in the self. The punisher so contained is derived from the internalized imago of the parent, which has become a part of the ego ideal and is included in the self-image of the latency age child. Guilt takes its place alongside shame and fear of depression as a negative motivating affect in the enforcement of superego contents. Clinical states containing depression with guilt have their origin in the early latency period. This is usually a manifestation of a conflict with oedipal roots. The basic cognitive developmental principle underlying the appearance of guilt in the early latency years relates to the shift from unsymbolized parental objects to symbolized objects in fantasy, coupled with repression of the latent fantasy content. The trend is away from conscious awareness of the true object of the drives with the retention of affect associated with the object. Positive motivating superego affects do not undergo a similar change. Since the basis of the positive motivating superego affects is reward and love from the object, the development of a motivating affect free of an object would result in a discouraging diminution in reward. This is unlikely to develop as a positive motivating force in the early latency years, which is a period of object deprivation. During the early latency years the cognitive potential to deal with conflicts through verbal representation and symbolization is taken advantage of to effect a resolution of the oedipal conflict. There is an abandonment of recognizable psychic representations of objects. Symbols and distortions which hide the meaning of an object can be substituted. As a result the conscious mind experiences a deprivation in the form of a lost object. Introjection and the acquisition of characteristics of the lost objects augment the ego ideal.

Concurrently, object hunger is intensified. Under this circumstance, a positive motivating superego affect which continues to require a conscious object for its evocation makes a unique contribution to control of behavior and acculturation. The child in search of objects can find approval through obeying parents and teachers and accepting myths and other culture elements which provide an entree and acceptance into the social group. Approval of the teacher encourages pliability, calm, and educability.

The gradual transition of punitive superego affects from diffuse discomforts, humiliation, and shame sensations in the presence of an object or the expectation of the reactions of objects to a sense of discomfort in the face of one's own estimate of right and wrong is a clinically observable phenomenon. Children of six can recognize the word *guilt* and offer a definition. The development of guilt can be traced by questioning children in the early latency years. If the child is asked, "Do you know what guilt means?" and the child says, "Yes," the next question to be asked is, "What does it mean?" If the child says, "That means that if your mommy tells you not to do something you shouldn't do it," the negative motivating affect is not guilt. If the answer is, "If you do something wrong, you feel everything's okay till they catch you," an intermediate level of internalization in which the object is still necessary has been reached. The comments, "If you feel you shouldn't do something and then you don't do it" or "You think of something and you feel funny so you don't do it," is concordant in nature with mature guilt.

During the early latency period the major contributor to mature superego (ego ideal) contents is the internalization of parental admonitions and demands which occurs in response to the passing of the Oedipus complex. Descriptions of the origin of the superego emphasize this phase. There are other important portals of entry for superego contents (ego ideal). This is especially so for the accretions of the late (eight to twelve) latency years. Most prominent is formal learning such as occurs in schools. The child is taught that he lives in a given country. He is taught that he should be loyal, thrifty, and brave. This is learned quickly, almost by rote. It can be as easily unlearned.

The most important mechanisms for the acquisition of information for inclusion in the superego demands are coupled projection and introjection. This pattern of coupled defenses has its origins in the separation-individuation period of early childhood. At that time, the child learns that there is a difference between himself and the world outside. There is a self and there is an object world. As the child establishes the difference between himself and the object world he begins to become aware of the content and the nature of the object world, especially the nature of the mother.

He introjects, when the mother goes away, certain partial images of the mother. This is the origin of partial introjects and part-objects. If the mother has been a person onto whom hostility has been projected, she will be incorporated as hostile and punishing. The child may then distort his view of himself into a person who is hostile and overly aggressive. Projection of interpretations onto the world, followed by adjustments and corrections of the interpretation based on the impact of reality, followed in turn by introjections based on the resulting experience, which change one's view of oneself and the pattern of behavior which is expected of one, is the paradigm of the process of coupled projection and introjection that is repeated constantly over the years. As a result of this coupled mechanism the mutual influence of memory and environment shapes the expectations of the superego.

The child approaches the world through his projections. They are partially corrected under the influence of reality. From teachers and children and stories that he hears, little pictures of the world are provided for incorporation in his own world view. His view of himself, of what his superego is expected to demand of him, and his interpretation of the world are thus altered. The child at first, in achieving this alteration of the content of the superego (ego ideal), projects an image based upon earlier projections and introjections. Maternal admonitions to behave, which have become self-expectations, are projected onto the school situation. In turn, the teacher's behavior influences the child and contributes to modifications of the child's expectation of himself. The teacher, other children, and other people in the society take on and continue the role that the mother had been serving in conveying superego content to the child.

Elements which modify superego content are multiple: parents, teachers, pastoral guides, and other children are quite important. Also of great importance because of the shift to greater use of verbal psychic contents, both as a means of problem solving and as the object of drives, are the ethical contexts of stories and tales told during latency. The degree to which reality contacts can alter projections and superego expectations is governed by the tenacity with which the child holds to prior beliefs with which he is identified. The more intensely a child cathects his introjects with narcissistic libidinal energies, the less easily will misapprehensions contained in projections of them be modified by reality experiences. As a result apprehensions of self and expectations of self will be less easily changed. Projections resulting in distortions of reality will be less easily shaken. Such introjects hold the interest of the child, producing patholog-ical patterns (see chapter 6). Even in normal children narcissistic involve-ment can lead to an overvaluation of new knowledge at the expense of future knowledge.

For instance, a girl of nine was sent to religious school. She was taught to regard the world in the way of her people. Other children who attended a school of a different denomination learned another point of view. In dis-cussions with these other children the nine-year-old says to them, "You're all wrong." The information, though newly learned, is dealt with as though it were the only truth. Once an ethical or mythical concept has been internalized it becomes part of oneself and is subject to the effect of one's own personal narcissism. Thus imbued with narcissistic cathexis, it is defended as would be a part of one's own body, or a member of the fam-ily. Contrary information, acquired later, is rejected as untrue. That which is introjected becomes part of oneself. It becomes literally part of one's identification. Abstract concepts such as patriotism become internalized and become identified with the person. Cooperation between individuals becomes a matter of group identification. In moving from the obligatory fealty of the morality of restraint to the autonomous state of the morality of cooperation, the child is provided with the option to select motivations, ethical orientations, and personal identifications. Yet only in the smaller private part of his life is this process permitted to dominate the selection of additional content for the ego ideal. Social pressure and other forms of group influence introduce group-approved dogmatisms. The reward of group acceptance and the threat of shame push the individual toward characteristic myths, general cultural beliefs, and culturally accepted be-havior.

Two men who have much in common can come to stand face to face in anger—all because of the kind of interpretations of their world that were introduced in latency and cathected narcissistically. One of the techniques used by a society in introducing concepts to its people is the manipulation of the mechanism of passive mastery. In passive mastery, drives which for-merly had been expressed through perceptual motor resolutions, hallucinatory modes, affective memories, and direct fantasy representations are repressed, and represented in the form of symbol-laden fantasies. Stories are made up by the child and told by the child. Stories are heard and told to the child by others. Cognitively the child has shifted his capacity for problem solving to the use of words. Society demands this of the child. There is a great sweeping in of verbal memory content at about this time.

As the child begins passively to participate in the myths of his culture and to recognize ethical crises akin to those he is experiencing in the adventures of the protagonists with whom he identifies, he finds within those stories elements which are familiar and comfortable for him, or which provide him with responses that he can use in his own problem solving tasks. In addition the stories can be used to express drives that formerly had been expressed through the evocation of the contents of the affecto-motor memory area.

The child is able to express his drives through fantasies, identification with characters, internalization and introjection of certain of the components related to that character. He becomes himself like that character.

Those children who enter into the state of latency develop additional ego organizations which serve as the mediators of superego demands as they relate to the interaction of the id and reality. Following the regression to anal-sadistic drive organization that accompanies the passing of the Oedipus complex, the superego admonition to be calm, pliable, and educable is enforced by the restraining defenses of latency. These are sublimation, obsessive-compulsive defenses (doing and undoing), reaction formations, and repression. Once the latency state has been established through the restraining defenses of latency, a special defense organization is required in dealing with breakthroughs of oedipal conflicts resulting from environmental overstimulation. If overstimulation were responded to by intensification of the regression to the anal-sadistic drive organization, there would result an overwhelming of the restraining defenses of latency, accompanied by unbridled aggressive behavior. The superego demand for calm and pliability is served through a special group of defenses. This group is designated in this book as the "ego structure of latency." The group consists of repression, fragmentation, displacement, symbol formation, synthesis and secondary elaboration, and fantasy formation. The concerted action of this group converts the hypercathected oedipal fantasy into a distorted manifest fantasy that can be used for the discharge of the associated heightened drives in a covert and essentially protecting manner.

As the child passes into late latency, more and more potential activities are permitted him. Masturbatory prohibition becomes less. The child is permitted to cross the street by himself. He is given some control over his own money. The superego's demands (ego ideal) begin to soften. The child turns from fantasy toward real objects as the latency years begin to come to an end. The pressure of the sexual drives accompanying the approaching puberty adds to the stress. Parents who had found the children compliant begin to sense signs of defiance, as the children begin to object to the passivity that they experience in relation to the parents. The aggressive drive increases and is projected onto the parents, and the feeling of passivity intensifies. The child begins to break away from the parent. Narcissistic mortification at a passive position in relation to the parents results in a break with internalized imagoes identified with the parents. Contacts with peer groups are established. Projections of parental expectations onto the groups open the way to modifications of concepts. With the ensuing internalizations of these concepts, modifications take place in superego expectations (ego ideal). Thus during late latency-early adolescence important reorganizations of superego contents take place. Two sets of superego contents are established, those derived from introjection of parental imagoes, and those learned from the influence on projections of contact with the peer group. The child may alternate between them depending upon circumstances.

The organization of the content derived from the peer group has a more primitive quality than the organization of the parental introjects. The group-derived content has an organization similar to the shame-driven primitive superego organization of prelatency. The children are less concerned with right, wrong, and guilt. They are more concerned with shame feelings, group approval, and what others will think. Such an immature superego organization tends to be fragile and changeable. The late-latency superego organization tends to persist and dominate behavior until about twenty-six years of age. At that age people begin to divest themselves of the alternatives and begin again to manifest guilt and identifications with the original internalized parental views.

Notes

1. See also Sarnoff (1970), pp. 550-562.

2. This timing is derived from clinical data provided by reports of observations by Piaget (1951, p. 96, obs. 64a; p. 173, obs. 95).

3. Occasionally amorphous, nonsocially validated, and nonverbal symbolic elements such as shadow, fire, flood, and monsters appear in dream and fantasy contexts that convey the affects of fear and dread. Such affect-porous symbols reflect a regressive alteration in the symbolizing function (see Sarnoff, 1972a).

Chapter 5

THE WORK OF LATENCY

A good book is the precious life blood of a master spirit, embalmed and treasured up on purpose to a life beyond life.

—John Milton

The period of latency is a life phase, one of whose characteristics is a product. As in the phases of separation-individuation, early childhood, and adolescence, there are in latency tasks to be completed, and personality skills to be developed or acquired. These shape later stages. Failure to negotiate these tasks successfully is reflected in disordered psychic adjustment in later life. An impairment of latency can result in aberrant personality functioning in the later developmental stages subjuncted to latency.

The concept of "products of the work of latency" is not universally recognized. In part this is due to a tendency in the psychoanalytic literature to view the period of latency as congruent with a biological diminution of drive energies. This has resulted in a deemphasis of ego development during the latency period. Concomitantly, the direct and epigenetic results of related dynamic processes have attracted little attention. The dynamic aspects of latency should not be ignored. Latency is a personality organization which should be viewed as the resultant of a multitude of phenomena. The development and effectiveness of these phenomena during the latency time period are preliminary stages in the formation of socially adaptive adolescent and adult personality structures.

Fries (1959) has highlighted the fact that though many have written about latency in passing, few have concentrated their attentions upon it. Among those who have, a few have illuminated the theory that the latency state makes a developmental contribution to the socially integrated adolescent and adult personality. According to this theory, the latency state is a necessary phase contributing to the social adjustment necessary for successful negotiation of life stresses in later phases. It is not merely a chance and transient defensive configuration of the ego.

Foremost among the few was Freud (1924), who ascribed great importance to the influence of the "inhibitions of the latency period" on early adolescence (p. 27).

Campbell (1959) emphasized the role of the latency years in the transmission of culture when he stated, "It is during the years between six and twelve that youngsters in our culture . . . develop their personal skills and interests, moral judgments, and notions of status" (p. 78).

Schachtel (1949) emphasizes this important aspect of latency:

> No greater change in the needs of man occurs than that which takes place between early childhood and adulthood. Into this change have gone all the decisive formative influences of culture transmitted by the parents, laying the fundament of the transformation into the grown up "useful" member of society from the little heathen. (p. 8)

The influence of society on the events of latency is further emphasized by deMause (1974):

> . . . because psychic structure must always be passed from generation to generation through the narrow funnel of childhood, a society's child rearing practices are not just one item in a list of cultural traits. They are the very conditions for the transmission and development of all other cultural elements. (p. 505)

Boyer and Boyer (1970) in their study of the culture of the Apaches of the Mescalero Indian Reservation, describe the declining appearance over a period of years of organized cultural tradition and an inability to take on or develop new patterns. This resulted in "social anomie and personal insecurity and lack of productivity" (p. 1) in a group whose early child-rearing practices remained stable, while there occurred a deterioration in the social organization for the latency age child characteristic of the culture. (In this regard, see Appendix B, section titled Latency in Primitive Societies.)

In keeping with this, Pittell (1973) has found severe emotional trauma during the latency period which interfered with the achievement of latency calm in histories of many individuals who had subsequently deteriorated during the habitual use of marijuana and other hallucinogens while in adolescence. In point of fact, Pittell (1971) states: "It is not inconceivable that the psychodelic cult is made up of those who have been robbed of this essential part of childhood . . ." (p. 658). The adolescent and adult adjustment of these individuals could be described by Boyer and Boyer's phrase "social anomie and personal insecurity and lack of productivity." In a similar vein Eissler (1949) reported childhood situations among delinquents in which frank dishonesty was perpetrated on the children by parents. "The events [which are] reported by the delinquent and confirmed by others usually fall into the latency period" (p. 16). Eissler found this to occur with surprising frequency (p. 15).

Jordan and Prugh (1971), in their study of psychosis during the early latency period, concluded that "It seems clear that the importance of specific early school-age tasks and the difficulties in coping with them are comparable to those of any other developmental period. Early latency entails separation-individuation problems that are qualitatively unique but comparable in magnitude to those of the preschool period and adolescence" (p. 328). Cohen (1971) describes a category of rapists who are characterized developmentally by "an absence of the latency period" (p. 323).

Kris (1956) "linked the appearance of the integrated family-romance fantasy to latency . . ." (p. 668). This integrated fantasy becomes the basis for much adolescent and adult fantasy, action and character. Levy (1971) expressed a view related to that of Kris when he asked, "Does what occurs in latency distort not only the future life of the youngster but also his conscious and unconscious constructions about his past life? To what extent are these reconstructed distortions what we hear about and experience in the transference?" (p. 329).

Latency may be related to evolutionary development in that the state of latency is possible because of the evolution and ontogenesis of mechanisms of defense that can produce it. The evolution of culture and its transmission may be intimately related to the evolution of the ego functions that make latency possible (see Appendix B). As in other skills that have evolved in the animal kingdom, modification of an organ can result in a new function. One need only think of the development of prehensile skills in the elephant at the end of its elongated nose to find an example. The development of a new function can, in turn, provide for a new behavior pattern characteristic of a species. The evolutionary modification of the ego which produced the skills required to form the state of latency made possible periods of behavior characterized by pliability, calm, and the ability to cooperate in learning complex methods of communication, including written signs. This assured a conduit for the transmission of knowledge not only from man to man as speech and example had done, but across generations. Men who acquire these means of communication support their group's capacity to sustain knowledge and to transmit it. The transmission of the elements of culture is the work of the state of latency in sedentary societies.

When this work was improved by the introduction of writing, the "precious life blood of master spirits" could achieve a more assured journey through time. Oft-told tales could achieve a stabilized content. Once pictorial or written notation became possible, culture became capable of an existence of its own in a "life beyond the life" of a single individual. The transmission of culture elements to generations removed in time is intimately tied to the evolutionary advantage provided by the development of the phenomenon of latency.

The purpose of this chapter will be to explore the influence of the tasks and achievements of the state of latency on later phases as well as on the transmission of culture within and beyond the limits of single lifetimes.

Latency at Work

If latency is viewed merely as an absence of drive or as a configuration of defenses used like a tinker's dam to settle an instinctual crisis and then be cast aside, there would be no meaning to the state of latency beyond that ascribed to any ego vicissitude of the moment. There is clear evidence to the contrary. In at least two areas, the psychic events of the state of latency produce influences on adolescence and adulthood.

First, within the milieu of calm, pliability, and educability that is provided by latency, there are acquired the skills (particularly reading) through which our culture is absorbed. The more rich and complex the skills obtained, the more rich and complex will be the quality of the culture that can be transmitted. Primarily, these skills relate to the fantasizing (mythopoetic) and symbolizing functions. Latency as a psychological state is the result of a defensive configuration of the ego, an aspect of which is the utilization of fantasy as a means of discharging drive energies. Over and above the ability of these functions to provide discharge pathways for the drives during latency in the form of highly symbolized fantasies, these skills remain available to influence the characteristics of adolescence and adulthood. They provide the functions that create and support imagination, neurotic symptom formation, future planning, and creative planning. In addition, they make possible passive participation in the myths, traditions, and contexts that guide one in identification with a culture. Without latency states, well-organized cultural and moral norms would be hard to enforce. Societies harness latency states. Through the latency state, cultural control of large groups of people becomes possible. The acquisition of skills in individuals, which can be taken advantage of by keepers of tradition to shepherd them into flocks which travel well-worn roads, becomes a valuable element in the process of the transmission of culture. The work of latency is, in part, the production of these receptive mechanisms. Through them the individual is enabled to acquire and then, for the span of his mature years, to participate in the myths of his culture, those time-transcending master spirits which organize and guide the mass.

There occurs in latency a phase-specific organization of ego defenses aimed at the control of anal-sadistic drives, regression to which has been described by Bornstein (1951) as a characteristic of latency. Among the defenses involved are sublimation, obsessive-compulsive activities, reaction-formations, and repression. They produce the psychological state characterized by calm, pliability and educability. We could generalize that this state is the most characteristic aspect of latency. Understanding the production of this psychological state is basic to an understanding of latency, and it is worthwhile at this point to review its origins.

The latency state develops in the following way: latency age children regress from attempts to resolve oedipal conflicts to an involvement in the expression of anal-sadistic conflicts. Once a child has thus defensively regressed, he finds a situation that differs from the original anal phase. There are new ego mechanisms of defense to use which provide for the interposition of modifications of aggression. This helps the child to adapt to a world that expects pliability, calm, and the ability to acquire knowledge. In a latency age child who is capable of entering the state of latency the above-mentioned defenses (reaction formation, obsessional defensive activities—collecting of stamps, shells, coins and stones, doing and undoing —cleanliness, symbolization and sublimation) are available to keep in check otherwise disruptive drive derivatives. The latency age child is too small physically to express his aggressive drives effectively in reality. Latency age children are, with few exceptions, maturationally incapable of achieving orgasm and ejaculation. Those with orgastic capabilities are limited by social pressures or internal inhibitions. Children of the age period are therefore unable to express sexual drives effectively. In the absence of a primary organ and physiological apparatus for discharge, regressions and defenses guide the child to outlets compatible with socially approved guidelines.

Of course outbursts of rebellion and breakdowns in discipline may appear as expressions of revolt and the breakdown of adjustment. This behavior is doomed to bring the child frustration. There is no way out and no victory in reality for this biologically celibate soldier-dwarf. All that is possible is surrender and an attempt to please the masters, by learning well what there is to be learned. From the standpoint of the future, the pattern of defense, developed to hold drives in check, becomes the basis for some of the ego styles of adolescence. A template is formed in latency which guides the permissible expression of drives during puberty. There are further parallels to these latency patterns of ego organization in adolescence and adult life in the form of organizations of ego defenses which implement superego demands in controlling the drives. A number of these ego organizations are direct continuations of defensive configurations established in latency state children. The myths and mores acquired through the mechanisms described before (symbolization and mythopoesis) in concert with the mechanisms here described go far toward carrying through society's demands. There is thus thenceforth, as a byproduct of the formation of the latency ego, a deformation of the possible derivatives and expressions of the drives during adolescence and adult life.

In order that these defenses may continue undisturbed, a safeguard is provided to preserve their function in the face of seductions and traumas.

The child with a normal symbolizing function organizes what I have referred to as the "structure of latency". Through this special organization of the ego, the child quells the humiliation of trauma and demonstrated impotence through dismantling the memories of the traumatic event or seduction, and actively reorganizes and synthesizes them into highly symbolized and displaced stories. Through these, a latency child can discharge drives without resorting to anal-sadistic drive organization. He gains comfort or revenge without threatening the situation in which he wishes to function well (e.g., school) or interfering with his emotional equilibrium or adjustment. The mechanisms involved actively produce fantasies and symbols to be used for discharge, in which the hero can be covertly identified with the child's own self. Myths characteristic of the culture provide ready-made heroes for fantasies. Through such myths, the mechanisms of the structure of latency are adapted to passive identification with tales and legends characteristic of the child's social group. Ethical patterns conveyed by the legends are incorporated into the superego contents. The structure of latency persists beyond latency in the form of this psychological mechanism. Through it books, plays, and works of art can be enjoyed. Through it the individual has a mechanism for acquiring imagoes for cultural patterns of function and belief to guide his life, his mores, his opinions, and his social reactions for a lifetime. The use of the fantasies of others for the discharge of drives in latency is called passive mastery.

The rest of this chapter will deal with two areas of the latency state more extensively. First we will examine the influence of latency on character, involving the adolescent and adult character patterns which evolve with latency. Second we will consider the influence of latency on society, that is, the mutual influences of latency and society. Here we will deal with the implications for culture and society of the skills acquired in the area of symbolization and mythopoesis.

The Influence of Latency on Character

Freud (1925) and Roheim (1943) delineated the influence of latency on character and the superego. According to Freud, the reaction-formations of morality, shame, and disgust are built up during the period of latency. "In the sexual life of puberty, there is a struggle between the urges of the early years and the inhibitions of the latency period" (p. 37). In 1926 Freud had described as the product of the latency period the establishment of characteristic patterns of ego mechanisms in support of superego demands. These organized patterns shape the subject's responses in puberty by providing the template upon which the characteristic fantasy and behavior patterns of the individual will be based. This molding of the ego to suit cultural dictates becomes the basis of individual neurosis and character as well as of characteristic responses and personality patterns of the culture. Freud (1926a) describes the beginning of the latency period as "a period which is characterized by the dissolution of the Oedipus complex, the creation or consolidation of the superego and the erection of the ethical and aesthetic barriers in the ego" (p. 114). "In consequence of the erotic trends being disguised in this way and owing to the powerful reaction-formation in the ego (established in latency) the struggle against sexuality will henceforth be carried under the banner of ethical principles" (p. 116). These ethical principles may be considered to be "normal traits of character which develop during the latency period" (p. 157). "Fear of the superego . . . is appropriate to . . . the latency period" (p. 142). Freud (1926a) has stated that "[in latency] the majority of the instinctual demands of this infantile sexuality are created by the ego as dangers and fended off as such, so that the later sexual impulses of puberty which in the natural course of things would be ego syntonic, run the risk of succumbing to the attraction of their infantile prototypes and following them into repression" (p. 155).

Clearly these passages speak for the origins of many of the ethically dominated responses found in adolescence and adulthood as being in ego organization arising during the latency time period. Furthermore, it is made clear that these response patterns (repression, powerful reaction-formations and the development of ethical principles as traits of character) are developed to cope with latency age drives, which have been described above as having no immediate and direct outlet save a regressed and un-disciplined fury. Reich (1931) illustrated these principles in a clinical paper written early in his career. An adult patient presented with haughti-ness and a lordly bearing. These character traits could be traced back to his latency. "Dreaminess and self-constraint concealing active sadistic fantasies characterized him as a boy. He developed a 'lord fantasy,' [that he was secretly descended from the British Nobility]." In adolescence, the patient avoided masturbation, for "A dignified person does not do such things" (p. 224). In a passage that we could use as a conclusion here, Reich points out that "an intra-psychic situation in childhood is, as it were, re-corded by means of characterological attitudes of the ego" (p. 229).

In becoming established as lasting patterns of defense, the mechanisms of defense mobilized to deal with the infantile sadomasochistic urges of the latency child transcend the limits of the latency time period. In this way they contribute to the superego responses of puberty and to adult characterological responses.

This contribution to character and superego development derived from the onset of the state of latency was described by Freud (1924) as having a dynamic origin. Under the impetus of fear of castration or fear of loss of love, the child experiences a turning from oedipal strivings. As a result, "object-cathexes are given up and replaced by identifications." The authority . . . of the parents is introjected into the ego. . . ." The ego is se-cured from "the return of the libidinal object cathexis. . . . This process ushers in the latency period, which now interrupts the child's sexual de-velopment" (p. 177).

In the "Ego and the Id" (1923) and the "Dissolution of the Oedipus Complex" (1924) Freud talks of the acquisition of prohibitory content by the superego with the onset of latency, i.e., "the nucleus of the superego . . . takes over the severity of the father and perpetuates his prohibition against incest . . ." (p. 177). The establishment of these introjects are a product of dynamic forces. The tools for the implementation of prohibi-tory demands are those ego mechanisms which are developed as an essen-tial part of the state of latency. They include those mechanisms which in setting the pattern for the control of sadomasochistic regressions establish the characterological responses seen later in adolescence and in adult life.

The Influence of Latency on Society

The periods of calm, pliability, and educability that dominate the daily rounds of children capable of entering into the state of latency provide an arena for the maturation of the products of the symbolizing function of the ego. The symbolizing function and its handmaiden, the mythopoetic function, become an important pathway for communication between the drives and the outside world. The structure of latency, which defends directly against the appearance in consciousness of incestuous fantasies, consists of symbolization and preliminary forms of sublimation. This group of defenses prepares the way for the acquisition of the myths of mankind, those patterned guides that establish the working templates for participation in mass cultural phenomena. As latency gives way to adolescence, fantasy is used less for the discharge of drives and becomes more the pathway for participation in the group. Freud, in the "Outline of Psychoanalysis" (1940a) states that ". . . such an early attempt at damming up the sexual instinct, so decided a partnership by the young ego in favor of the external as opposed to the internal world, brought about by the prohibition of infantile sexuality, cannot be without its effect on the individual's later readiness for culture. The instinctual demands forced away from direct satisfaction are compelled to enter new paths leading to substitute satisfactions . . ." (p. 201). One such path is through symbolization and participation in group phenomena through sharing in myths. Two tasks are solved in this way. Indirect symbolized satisfactions fulfill the content needs of latent wishes while object-seeking needs are gratified by acceptance in new groups containing persons who can be differentiated from the primary objects. How this takes place is our subject now.

Through the medium of symbols, drives can find expression with representations of objects which so hide the true identity of latent objects that other aspects of the relationships with these objects remain undisturbed. In this regard, a peer can represent a parent. Not only may real people be used as symbols representing others; ideational elements and characters in stories and fantasies can take the place of latent objects. This is especially true in the case of latency age children, whose fantasy play takes up so much of their energies. Internalized conflicts provide the general pattern for the fantasy through which drives will be discharged. Life situations provide specific objects in fantasy. Some of the fantasy material that is produced is unique to the individual. As social influences become greater, group impact on the content of the fantasies and myths in which the child participates intensifies.[1] From the contents of the myths (group truths) provided to the latency child are drawn many of the contents of fantasy play, as well as elements and values that guide the child in assimilating into his society.

The relationship between personal fantasy and myths (group truths) may be described as follows: cultural sanction guides the elaboration of a core fantasy into a myth. Personal fantasies are creative products used in the discharge of drives. Myths serve the everyday man by providing fantasies through which the individual can discharge his drives passively and with social approval. The mythopoetic function establishes the rules within a culture by which objects can be utilized for drive gratification (see Sarnoff, 1969, p. 19).

The degree to which symbols are used by the child directs the degree of participation in the culture. The quality of the symbols of which the child is capable controls the quality of the fantasy in which he can participate. The more mature the style of symbolization, the more subtle the culture elements that the child can acquire. Humans are born without the cognitive capacity to form symbols. The symbolizing capacity matures with elaboration of the skill from simple representation to complex defense-oriented psychoanalytic symbol formation.

From birth to eighteen months, the perceptual apparatus responds to external stimuli and organ discomforts without distortion. Should these perceptions become uncomfortable, withdrawal of the organism or crying for help becomes the technique of defense. After sixteen months, the capacity to perceive abstract relations between perceptions and between perceptions and memories has developed. In the play of children one can see the use of play objects to represent other objects. This augmentation of mental skills enhances creativity. The active use of one object to represent another in creative play can be used as a means of discharging tension.

However, either through association or accidential confrontation, certain external objects with abstract relationships to memory elements with high degrees of valence for attracting affect may be introduced into the psychic moment of the child, producing anxiety. The introduction of the capacity of the child to perceive more than one meaning in a thought element or external object itself provides potential sources of anxiety. Eventually there is developed a conceptual affect unit consisting of a memory element, the affect associated with it, and an external perception which, representing the memory element, becomes associated psychically with the affect of the memory element. When such a representational triad (representer, represented, and shared affect) is associated with an uncomfortable affect, terror states and phobic avoidance reactions become characteristic responses in the child.

From our standpoint, the important element at this stage is that chance stimuli can serve as the external representations which mobilize anxiety. Thus, without warning, the strong affects of a representational triad can be activated, creating states of discomfort for the child. Conversely, the child can achieve mastery of disquieting memories and experiences by using representing objects to play or work them through under his own control. At the age of twenty-six months, a more mature form of symbolic expression becomes available. This is manifested in the ability to exclude from conscious awareness the abstract connection between what represents and what is represented. When this happens, the signifying symbol is called a psychoanalytic symbol. The representational triad continues to be viable, though in situations in which psychoanalytic symbols are formed, its existence is no longer consciously recognized by the child. Intensity of affect is controlled by the degree to which displacement is used in the selection of an external signifier as a symbol. The less easily recognizable is the representation symbol in terms of that which is represented, the less will be the valence for attracting conscious awareness to the affect associated with the triad. It is possible, from the third year of life on, actively to produce fantasy play free of anxiety. This takes place when conflicts involving primary objects are represented in highly displaced symbols. Conflicts can then be worked through using symbol-laden fantasies. These fantasies may be the product of the child's imagination. They may be relevant tales, derived from those which are characteristic of the culture. Many such tales are presented to children, and through these stories fantasy play and discharge can be achieved.

Peller (1958) points out that in the beginning of latency, "within a short time, the psychological household grows far more complicated and daydreams become an essential release. Finding his own daydream woven into a story multiplies the release—the child can enjoy his own, his personal fantasy without feelings of guilt, shame, reproach" (p. 57). Thus *passive mastery* of conflicts is produced. The role of repression in shifting the child and his memory away from primary objects and conflicts is a basic factor in producing the infantile amnesia. Active and passive participation in fantasies and themes that represent while concealing situations involving primary objects help in the dissolution of the Oedipus complex. The child with amnesia for his infantile life deals in consciousness only with the representation aspects of the representational triad. Memory for the original thought contents, and the affects associated, succumb to the amnesia. Repression proper effects the thought contents. Affects succumb to the effects of displacement as well as to a less well understood process which will be described below. As a child enters latency, society provides him with a vocabulary and schemata for comprehending his world and recalling his past with little emphasis on affect. The expression of affect and its memory are restricted within any given society to certain ritualized outlets.

A six-year-old girl was taken to see the ballet Swan Lake. When the time came that it was clear that the Prince had lost his love forever, she burst into tears at the sadness of his plight. Adults about hid their laughter. The girl had not yet learned to respond to ballet according to the schema of muted affect considered appropriate in the adult world. The major outlet for expression, including affect remnants of the representational triad, becomes speech. "Don't cry and point," says the mother. "Use words, ask for it." Direct expression of affect becomes less acceptable with the onset of latency.

Freedman (1971) emphasizes the shift to speech at the period of the onset of latency: "Both clinical and theoretical considerations indicate that [speech's] relevance becomes much greater in later [oedipal and latency] development and particularly in relation to the process of superego formation" (p. 778). If we only would try to consider how few words there are in the English language that deal with the definitions and nuances of affect, we would become more aware of the suppression of affect responses in latency and the amnesia which effects prelatency affecto-motor memory contents with the onset of latency.

Schachtel (1949) explains the amnesia for infantile events that appear with latency: "The categories (or schemata) of adult memory are not suitable receptacles for early childhood experiences and therefore not fit to preserve these experiences and enable their recall" (p. 9). The latency child must put aside full recall of the past and the chance to structure the world and respond to it as he sees it. Spontaneous memories are impaired. Interpretations of new situations are guided by stereotype-dominated patterns of memory. These are derived from the culture in which he lives. They are patterned after myths approved by the culture. Henceforth the values of the individual are dominated by the value judgments so learned. "Voluntary memory recalls largely *schemata of experience* [italics mine] rather than experience [itself]. These schemata are mostly built along the lines of words and concepts of the culture" (p. 19). Guided memory shapes the world and its customs.

Tradition guides man's footsteps. Since language contains so few words to represent the feelings, it is customary during latency in America for the affects of early childhood to be consigned to nonverbal, organ language and psychosomatic forms of expression. The memory contents associated with infantile amnesia, which include the concept as well as the affect components of the symbolic representational triad, are not recalled. What does occupy the mind of the child in relation to these contents are conscious aspects of what is represented. These are divorced from the original affect and content. They are modified so as to minimize recognition of the content's source in the infantile sexual life. Patterns superimposed by the culture as part of the transmission of cultural elements dominate. The child is "gradually and increasingly forced into a Procrustean bed of the culturally prevalent experiences and schemata which allow for certain experiences, forbid others, and omit a great many for which the culture has either no frame of reference or only an unsuitable one" (Schachtel, p. 22).

The transmission of culturally acceptable patterns of behavior, in fact of the culture itself, is accomplished through taking advantage of the child's need to use defensive fantasy in dealing with oedipal conflicts. The child seizes upon the socially approved myths to resolve intrapsychic conflict. Simultaneously they become a means of conveying social values to the child. In this way society welds the child to the mass.

Impairment in the ability of the child to participate in this activity is seen in children with symbolizing functions and concomitant fantasizing functions which are too immature and primitive to provide a safety valve for complexes. Their spontaneous symbols are too exciting and frightening. The child is incapable of appreciating the subtleties of passively experienced stories and their morals. They are more involved in the explosiveness, action, and dash of the stories. In addition, there is failure in the child to reach a state of calm, pliability, and educability which would enrich the receptive matrix through which the myths of the culture could be acquired and set. Failure to achieve such symbolization results in failure to enter latency. The moral and the identification base of the stories cannot become incorporated into the superego imagoes as they can in the child with a healthy latency.

The child who fails to enter latency and whose personality does not negotiate the work of latency lacks imagoes that could guide the child to useful socially adaptive functions. For instance, a little girl who has scary fantasies of a "bloodyheaded ghost followed by a thousand snakes which approach her and then go on to attack her mother and smother her" has only partially been able to mature in her symbolizing function. The primary object (mother) breaks through into the manifest content of the fantasy; the affect is still strong and the representing symbol is too high in valence for attracting affect for this fantasy to be considered the product of a mature symbolizing and fantasizing function. Such a child will not be able to enter the state of latency and produce a good defensive ego structure in latency. Beating, seductions, and nudity in the home can produce such impairments and interfere with entering into latency. Unstable home conditions and overstimulation can interfere with and cause regressions in this state of adjustment during the latency time period. In either case, the pliability, educability, and calm needed for the acquisition of socially acceptable fantasies and myths is not present. Antisocial immature patterns are therefore intensified in these children and the adolescents they grow up to be. In addition, these youngsters are too close to their own latent contents to be able to modify them defensively into socially accepted patterns of myth. This leads to a failure to acquire an identification with culture elements and moral elements of the society. One of the characteristics of the structure of latency which is undermined by a failure to enter the latency state is the transmutation of private fantasies into manifest content guided by society to contain socially acceptable elements. The healthier the structure of latency the more closely does the content hew to the patterns of the culture.

An important exception to this conceptualization exists in the situation in which a leader turns the group to the mass implementation of his own primitive destructive fantasies. In this circumstance, the person with the primitive symbolizing function is able to find expression for his drives easily by assimilating the leader's fantasies, while the more mature individual must either regress till his ego can blend with the ego of the mass, rationalize that assimilating the myths of the leader serves the common good, or leave the group. In these pages I deal with constructive group fantasies but am not unmindful of the dangerous potential for thought control made possible by manipulation of passive symbolization.

In the youngster who has negotiated the state of latency in healthy fashion and is entering adolescence, response to humiliation utilizes the structure of latency. It takes the form of fantasies well tuned to the guidelines necessary for adjustment in the society. At this age the name *structure of latency* can be removed from the process and replaced by the term *realistic future planning*. For the child who has been unable to achieve an adequate structure of latency, responses to humiliations take the form of confusion, lack of goal, fear fantasies, excitements, and searches for outlets which will provide nonverbal affect-laden experiences such as drug highs. For those with an inadequate latency, these are continuations of the primitive adjustments with which they had been living without interruption since infancy.

It should be kept in mind that a child in a state of latency resolves his personal conflicts by symbolizing the elements of the conflict. Latent affect-filled fantasy wishes are gratified. The original meaning and uncomfortable affect associated with the latency fantasy are hidden. Society provides such children with culture elements and entire myths which can serve the latency child in this activity. In this regard, Friedlander (1942) states:

> One reason, therefore, for the child's love of the fairy tale is that he finds in it his own instinctual situation and meets again his own phantasies, which explains the pleasure in reading or listening to fairy stories; moreover, the fairy tales' particular solutions for these conflicts appear to be a means for alleviating anxiety in the child. . . . The pleasure thus obtained is still very near to the sexual pleasure gained from masturbation . . . (p. 129).
> [An] analytic study of the fairy tale has proved that its emotional content presents the oedipal wishes and propositions for combating these, or in other words, the unconscious content of the fairy tale tallies with the conflicts pertaining to the child's age. . . . It is not hard to recognize in them some universal fantasies and defense mechanisms which are characteristic in the child's development at the beginning of latency. (p. 135)

Friedlander recognizes the existence of a tale which "satisfies . . . reading for pleasure, and yet does not ignore requirements of education" (p. 149). Beyond their formal educational contributions there are more subtle acquisitions resulting from reading or listening to stories. These are the acquisition of culture elements including limits, expectations, and social roles.

With children's utilization of myths for drive discharge, there are acquired, for the cultural imagoes internalized within the superego content of the child, social examples and moral virtues.[2] One need think only of the fair play of athletes, the fidelity of Ulysses, the honesty of Lincoln, and the purity of Washington to understand the nature of the value judgments transmitted through myths. During early latency, the stories that appeal to children deal on an ethical level with discipline, social identity, cultural details, and control of direct gratification of sadistic and masochistic instinctual urges. During late latency (after age eight and a half), the contents of stories that appeal to children shift to patterns for dealing with and modes of behavior involved in reality testing and the shift from fantasy discharge to object discharge. It is of interest that, except in situations of direct censorship, the books and stories that children select and enjoy are not assigned by society. Rather they are chosen from among those permitted to exist because their content remains within the limits of known and accepted culture elements.

The communication of culture elements in nonliterate and preliterate cultures requires media other than the written word. Ritual and performances, religious lectures, apprenticeships become the media for transmission of culture elements (see Appendix B). The nature of latency differs with different cultural organizations and media for communication of tradition. Latency age children of hunters and food gatherers tend to run free, establishing power hierarchies and with few exceptions inhibiting sexuality. Hunting and games that imitate parents aid cultural continuity. With puberty, initiation rites and performances become the means for transmitting information about expectations for adult behavior. Shame and loss of acceptance within the group, rather than guilt, are the motivating affects for these people. Latency age children among pastoral people and sedentary farmers spend their latencies close to home, lending a hand and learning: motor skills primarily from parents, beliefs primarily from priests, and a combination of skills, beliefs, and ethics from old time tales told well. In this regard it is of interest that Frazier (1966) describes dolls used by Japanese families as media for establishing for their children caste and class differences.

The fantasies produced by the structure of latency are at first highly personal and original. They are more concerned with thinly masked representations of parents and the physical nature of the child's surroundings than with the contents of the prevailing myths of the society. In time, there are added universal elements that make it possible for the child to experience the gratification of his drives through fantasy in stories told and stories read, in television shows and the like, shared with others. Oedipal themes, rivalry themes, returns to life, and rescue themes have discharge value for these youngsters. Youngsters with the ability merely to enjoy direct expressions of drives in the form of fights and explosions may spend time with such entertainments, but they have not developed a mature symbolizing function and it is doubtful that constructive superego imagoes can be acquired by them through these activities. The youngster with the mature symbolizing and fantasizing function (the latter can be defined as the ability to synthesize symbols into coherent contexts which express latent fantasy content) is able to produce his own fantasy as well as engage in what Sachs (1942) in his "Community of Daydreams" has called "passive participation" in the creativity of others. I have mentioned above that future planning is an adolescent and adult manifestation of the structure of latency. Capacity for culture is another such residue. Adults with the capacity for culture join the "community of daydreams" and passively participate in contents of plays, paintings, films, and other media that carry myths. Through them they discharge their own drives and fantasies.

Myths becomes the social glue that helps society hold its form. They become the conduit for more than moral rules. Self-confidence, identification with classes, self-representations, preparations for wars, and control of masses of people can be accomplished through the manipulation of this aspect of human psychology with its genesis in latency.

The techniques by which this is accomplished by society are worth our study. For through the medium of myth, people can be induced to part with their individual psychology and need to survive as individuals. In the special case where one is part of an audience or a group, one can regress to the sharing of beliefs in common and be led to participate in what is otherwise forbidden and frightening. Guilt, at first lessened by being shared, finds new reasons for existing. A tendency to slip away from the group becomes a new social wrong. Thus the individual is bound more closely to the mass. In this regard Leroi-Gourhan (1965) has stated:

> The body of knowledge of the group is the fundamental element of its unity and of its personality, and the transmission of this intellectual wealth is the condition necessary for the material and social survival of the group (p. 65).
>
> Transmission [of motor skills] is carried out through a hierarchy of operational chains. These automatic operational chains correspond to a communal family memory. They are concerned with all the material and moral episodes of daily life. Their inscription in the personal memory of individuals begins in infancy, following modalities [of communication and memory], where language does not play a major role (p. 66). It is different for infrequent and exceptional customs, which . . . repose in the memories of veritable specialists: heads of families, old men, poets, and priests, who have assumed in the traditions of mankind, the vital task of maintaining group cohesion (p. 66). The registration of this wealth of knowledge of the group is tied to the development of the oral literature (p. 66; author's translation).

Agricultural societies and craftsmen, through oral traditions and apprenticeships, have achieved a preservation and transmission of secrets that have permitted the maintenance of independent group status. The knowledge that belongs to a culture defines it. In literate societies, knowledge, whether transmitted by written word or a spoken tradition, gives a man an identity as part of the group. A man who cannot obtain sufficient knowledge of his culture to permit him to function socially without embarrassment is at a disadvantage. As a result of a lack of mastery of the media for cultural transmission he fails to know the ropes. He risks thralldom to the man who does master the media. In a literate society, the man without reading skills either must depend upon another man or fail to augment his knowledge of culturally acceptable alternatives, to his detriment. Failure to achieve reading skills can come about in a number of ways: culturally dictated restriction of these skills to a single group; cognitive impairments on an organic basis; cultural deficiencies involving lack of cognitive and syntactic skills—in the mastery of the primary language of culture; and impairments interfering with the establishment of the calm, pliability, and educability required for the state of latency.

We have spoken so far of the tendency of the structure of latency and its components, the symbolizing and fantasizing function, to utilize the myths of the culture for covert discharge of immature latent fantasy content. This process is utilized by society in moving the child toward a more sociocentric orientation in preparation for participation in society during adolescence and beyond. The continuity of society requires that the transmission of culture elements through myths go on in this way. In many societies this is often an unconscious process on the part of both parties. The structure necessary to maintain the process evolved and is used without thought or reflection. However, all is not unconscious. Campbell (1971) has pointed out that some peoples have transformed the references of their myths and rites from cosmological to biographical and ethnohistorical fantasies and knew exactly what they were doing. In those societies in which techniques for maintaining power are based on the use of the transmissions of myths in latency, the situation may not have been set up, but leaders become well aware of the strength of the tool once they have it and are unwilling to part with it.

The term *myth* has many definitions but is used in this book with emphasis on a specific context. Myths can serve to entertain. They can help man discharge drive energies. They serve as touchstones and recognition signals that bind men into groups and help those so bound to identify each other. Myths are the repositories of the cultural superego; they contain and transmit elements of tradition. In subsequent pages we will be dealing primarily with myths from the standpoint of these elements of tradition.

The traditions of a society are transmittable through a number of systems of knowledge. Each system of knowledge uses characteristic signifiers (symbols) organized into syntaxes (mythic elements). In many cases the classical "myth," or story rich in verbal symbols, transmits the elements of tradition. One must not lose sight of more concrete signifiers (symbols) in the transmission of culture elements. These are means for the transmission of culture traits through learned behavior patterns. Such a situation could be exemplified by one learning how to play football or how to cook. In such activities, the participant lives out the traditional role in reality, rather than through the vicarious experience and identification that occurs with participation in storytelling and ritual. Highly organized and venerable traditions are learned in this way.

In primitive societies (see Murphy and Murphy, 1974) men hunt briefly and have time to pursue fantasy. They become involved in transmission of tradition which revolves about highly symbolized culture elements. Their culture is the culture of the symbol. Women in this culture, whose work is never done, have less time for fantasy. They are involved much more in the transmission of traditional practical skills such as lengthy food preparation. Their culture is the culture of the concrete. There is no less tradition involved in this; there is, however, less verbal symbolization. Tradition is transmitted but is accomplished through behavioral examples far more than through the precepts and concepts contained in highly elaborated and symbolized myths. The raw data required for survival is transmitted in this way even to those who are not facile in the use of symbols. More abstract concepts such as ethics, cosmology, and retribution are the domain of symbol-laden mythic tales.

The transmission of tradition through behavior patterns is easily verified and responsive to group pressures. It is subject to enforcement through shame. The transmission of tradition through ritual and myth is less easily verified. Surface participation and acquiescence can be verified, but not so easily inner acceptance and identification. These involve a more personal response which is subject to enforcement through internalized superego-motivating affects such as guilt and shame associated with remembered punishers.

The transmission of culture requires that verbal descriptions, motor patterns, and appropriate affective response (or lack of it) be communicated to the child. The latter two are available throughout life. The first, in the form of the highly symbolized narrative forms characteristic of latency, is available after three years of age.

One might well ask; If the transmission of culture elements occurs through learning myths containing the culture elements, and if the skill extends from three years of age to old age, why emphasize the importance of latency and call such cultural transmission a product of the work of latency? The answer is that first impressions are lasting, and that with the beginning of the latency years an important cognitive change provides the capacity to make impressions last. During latency, an individual experiences an intensification of involvement in fantasies that deal with elements removed from himself and his family. Usually this is the first such experience. Adjustment in the oedipal phase impels the use of masking symbols. Children are most receptive to myths at this age. In addition, the socially required substitution of verbal memory schemata for affect-laden memory leaves a gaping requirement for new concepts and verbal contents. The stage is set in early latency for a vast increase in verbal knowledge. The door is open to the introduction of verbal culture elements, and schematized ways of interpreting situations. Finally, the answer lies in the fact that the educability, calm, and quietness of latency provides the leisure to harness the maturing cognitive readiness of the child in the direction of teaching him the media for the transmission of myths and culture, or at least that medium for cultural transmission needed by the child to be able to participate in the class or level of the culture to which he is to be assigned by the rules of his society. Depending on the culture, this medium may have been Latin, the common tongue, special phrasings in poems and songs known only to the initiated, stained glass windows, writing, and reading. Reading readiness is among the cognitive maturational achievements that add to making the latency period a time when a mass of knowledge is introduced to make a lasting first impression.

One of the key cognitive steps is the development of behavioral constancy. There comes a point in human development at which the child is able to keep a constant image of expected behavior in mind, coupled with the ethical concept of where the behavior is appropriate. This is associated with the development of verbal memory skills and an internalized superego motivating affect, such as guilt. This develops as a well-organized capacity between five and seven years of age. Just as at one point in development a constant psychic representation of the object (called object constancy) permitted the child comfort to separate from the mother physically, so with the onset of the latency years the child normally develops a constant psychic representation of expected behavioral patterns and the affects associated with failure to implement these patterns in appropriate situations. Behavioral constancy, then, is defined as the capacity to retain consistent behavioral guidelines within the ego ideal. This development of behavioral constancy is associated with dependable behavior patterns in the child even in the absence of supervision. The extensive role played by behavioral constancy in socialization can be appreciated if one will compare the shift in social orientation between the prelatency and the latency child. The child must change from an environment in which he has freedom to do what he pleases to the school situation in which he has to sit still for long periods of time. In latency the child has to be able to recognize social indications that require good behavior and know how to function in a given situation. He has to learn that at recess one runs and plays; that in church one sits quietly; and that in school one listens and does not fantasize. Appropriate behavior in latency is not just a question of controlling impulses; it is a question of selecting behavior that is "right" from among alternatives.

In order to achieve this, the child must be able to retain abstract concepts of adult behavioral expectations accompanied by motivating affects, such as guilt, that will force the child to follow these expectations. In addition, he has to develop the capacity to make a choice between potential behavioral alternatives. The shift from absolute parental commands, often disobeyed in private, to ethical alternatives based on guilt-motivated choice occurs as a child progresses well into the latency state. The stories children like reflect this change. Stories for four-year-olds have very cut-and-dried characters. There is no choice involved in what they do. There are heroes and villains, and no in-betweens. The six- or seven-year-old child has matured to a level of functioning that lets him appreciate more than cut-and-dried good guys and bad guys. People who prepare children's entertainments sometimes lose sight of the fact that this maturational step takes place. This explains cartoons shown on television which cater to regressed states of response in the story appreciation of children. The true classics that appeal to the matured six- and seven-year-olds depict individuals whose decisions and actions represent an awareness of a sense of choice. The story's characters are individuals who are confronted with temptations, and the opportunity to make an ethical decision. In Stevenson's *Treasure Island*, Jim Hawkins is continuously deciding between obeying orders or not. Often, his decisions get him into difficulty, but in the end his decisions win out. The decision a character makes in one of these stories represents a choice; the direction in which the choice is made conveys ethics. Information thus acquired in regard to ethical decision making contributes to the content of the superego. These internalized ethical concepts derived from cultural elements become the building blocks of the mature superego. As such they persist beyond the day of origin to serve and to guide through the years.

That ethical decisions are being made in these stories has particular appeal for the early latency child. He is in the process of acquiring alternatives for inclusion in his ego ideal, and the alternatives are associated with varying degrees of ethical acceptability. The awareness of choice predicated on right and wrong potentiates the child's appreciation of similar experiences of choice as they are depicted in the stories he reads. Ethical decisions made in these stories in turn guide his own decisions.

In this regard, the content of fairy tales told to children can be resolved into three types of ethical behaviors: (1) There is the fantasy of the character whose behavior is either purely good or purely bad. (This is typical of fantasy that appeals to children of prelatency.) (2) There is the fantasy in which the individual has choice but always chooses to do that which is within the limits of the culturally acceptable ethical patterns. (3) There is the story that contains breaks with patterns of socially acceptable behavior in the form of picaresque manifestations. The situations in the last type often contain magic solutions permitting reorganizations of society which enable the hero of the fairy tale or story to overcome adversity. In these situations, the character tricks others, including authorities, in order to gain his end. Yet even in the context of this last type of story, the behavior, the achievements, and the goals of the individual are not foreign to the culture. Til Eulenspiegel, for instance, performs merry pranks that are understandable to his social group. They are not overly sadistic or outside the common ken of his society. Thus even variations and limitations in ethical digression from established norms of behavior are conveyed through identifications with mythic heroes acquired during the process of passive mastery.

During latency, the acquisition of content augmenting the superego is, in part, effected during this process of passive mastery. Myths and stories serve as the source of new data on potential experiences and expected responses in the grown-up world. It is striking to see how children who have had no prior knowledge of a given field of endeavor quickly assume the point of view of their teacher and make adherence to that point of view the sine qua non of identification with the group, and indeed, a sign of membership in the group. Watch a little girl, for example, with no prior experience at the dance, learning in ballet class the technique for making a dance step. The child turns to children who have been trained differently in other schools and insists that their way of doing it is wrong. Such a course of events is not far removed from one in which the acquisition of a given culture myth becomes the basis for a national identity, which in turn can produce a tableau in which two men, who have more in common with each other than they have with their generals or leaders, stand eye to eye over borders with rifles in their hands.

The need in early latency to resolve oedipal conflicts by working them through in the form of masked representations adds to the attractiveness of the myth during this period. Leaders do not ignore this attribute. The utilization of myths and tales told from on high in guiding masses is based on taking advantage of personality skills perfected during latency. This aspect of mass psychology clearly does not stop when latency stops. Leaders use "the big lie" and tales with supernatural sources to shape the will of the masses to carry forth their programs and to serve their own interests. Edey (1974) noted the dependence of masses of men on the myths provided by their leaders in ancient Carthage: "In a harsh faith, interpreted to fearful people only by priests, the priestly power was obviously very great" (p. 107). Rosenblum (1965) has described in detail the modifications that took place in French painting during the years of unrest that followed the Revolution. Each change in official mood called forth the utilization of new classical themes in paintings to instruct the viewer in the direction of the belief expected of the common man. Rosenblum sums up the concept well: "Like the martyr icons of the French Revolution, the pictorial recording of Napoleonic history was an attempt to create the image of a new savior. From the ruins of the classical and Christian traditions great themes of benevolence and heroism, both natural and supernatural, were translated into secularized experience of the modern world" (p. 95). Once the myth has been changed, the world has been changed. It is in latency that the myth schemata of a culture are introduced.

Campbell (1968) has noted the tendency of man, en masse, to set aside logical structures and assume the psychological set "by which the world can be transformed from banality to magic in a trice" (p. 34). Indeed, individuals who are otherwise quite logical and capable of independent thinking can be seen to march a well-worn path when the proper myth has been introduced through a medium of communication that has been learned as an automatic source of truth during the impressionable years of latency. Campbell (p. 34) notes that "man, apparently, cannot maintain himself in the universe without belief in some arrangement of the inheritance of myth. In fact the fullness of his life would even seem to stand in a direct ratio to the depth and range, not of his rational thoughts, but of his local mythology" (p. 20).

What is rational is what is seen. What is mythical is what is felt. The oedipal child in search of a resolution to his conflicts turns to myths. In turn, myths contribute to the child guidance in his life through identifications with mythological heroes whose characteristics, once internalized by the child, will help him in fitting into his culture. The depth and range of life relate to mythic contents that indicate a man's potential, position, skills, and the assignments and expectations the world holds for him. We have already seen that these myths make their heaviest impact during latency. The shift to a sociocentric orientation in selecting fantasy objects, and the shift in memory elements from association through affects and proprioceptive memories to association through verbal concepts opens the mind to a flood of elements and contexts (myths) that will guide opinions and life choices infinitely in time and in detail.

Within a given society, not all men learn the same myths. In fact, not all men learn the same media for the transmission of culture. One of the uses that a structured society makes of the pliability, calm, and educability that characterize latency is to differentiate the media for communication that children are taught. In this way, there is established a cultural differentiation of people into classes. Sometimes, this differentiation occurs as the result of excited settings, such as deprived city environments which do not permit children the calm needed to develop symbols with low affective valence. In other circumstances, standing customs limit education for large segments of the population. If in latency, language skills and other media for expanding concepts are withheld, two classes of society can be created. The first would be those (the leaders) with the sources of knowledge and the unlimited capacity to gain more through a rich medium for acquiring knowledge. The second would be the followers whose limited knowledge makes them dependent on the first group for guidance in the ways of the world. As Cassirer (1923) has noted, "All theoretical cognition takes its departure from a world already preformed by language." Man lives with objects only as language presents them (p. 28).

A man may therefore be fixed in latency to a view of himself, an occupation or a belief, by the nature of the symbols his society has provided for him as the socially accepted expression of his occult and personal pregenital fantasy life. King or subject, student or athlete, hunter or food gatherer, priest or peasant, master or slave may be fixed in their life's lot by the nature of the myths and symbols assigned to them in latency, and by the limits placed on their skills in the media that could be used to gain knowledge that would let them traverse to expression of intrapsychic conflict through new patterns. A description of limitations placed on the media for expanding awareness in the service of the maintenance of a caste system is

to be found in Grier and Cobbs' (1968) description of the maintenance of
slavery in antebellum America: "it was forbidden to teach slaves to read
and write. They were to learn only the practical language of the field, and
that from the lips of their masters and overseers. As a result, the slaves
learned English as a series of garbled, half-understood mispronounced
words shared mainly by the few slaves on the same plantation. . . . The
slaves were even taught to speak by their masters" (p. 12).

The relationship between peoples who share the same land but are different in their identities and aspirations can be categorized into certain
groupings according to the media for communication acquired in latency
for the transmission and understanding of the myths that guide destiny.

The groupings are briefly described below.

Parallel diverse cultures.

This refers to cultures which, though occupying the same territory,
have little more than trading contact with each other. There is no
language in common. Often one group does not have a written language. Such parallel culture situations existed in South America involving Spanish-speaking residents of Peru and Equador and nonliterate indigenous populations of hunters and food gatherers (Yaguas
and Jivaros).

Parallel convergent cultures

These cultures share the same territory and have similar means of
gaining a livelihood but have differing myths and identity criteria.
During latency, different myths and awareness of available career
choices are conveyed. Skills in learning to read and pursue knowledge
are of parallel quality: Jewish populations set in predominantly
Christian nations are an example of this culture pattern.

Parasitic cultures

These cultures share the same territory. One has full access to myths
which convey awareness of available career choices and skills required for carrying them through effectively. In the other the latency
work is so interfered with that skills, meaningful occupations, and
future planning are deficient to the point that the dominating culture
must divert some of its product for the support of the dependent culture, which cannot provide for itself. Such cultural relationships as

the parasitic drug culture (see p. 150) or the welfare culture in the United States are an example of this.

Multiple-class culture

This refers to the subdivision of the peoples of the culture into classes made up of leaders, workers, farmers, and soldiers. Membership in each group is hereditary. During latency, the myths that guide career choices and responsibilities are differentiated for each group. The leader group is usually provided with skills in the acquisition of cultural elements which the others lack. Therefore, the others are at their mercy in seeking guidance for the handling of new situations and in dealing with enemies. Western society and the society of Medieval Europe have these characteristics.

Where parallel cultures consist of an advanced and an aboriginal culture, there is a tendency of the advanced culture to try to absorb the primitive culture in order to add them to the work force of the advanced culture. This often may be accomplished through education (that is, by providing the "native" with the media for transmission of culture of the advanced society).

Conversely, resistance to cultural change resulting from education is implemented by primitive groups as a means of maintaining their traditions and status as an inherently complete parallel society. There is interference with the internalization of newly acquired media for the transmission of culture, such as abilities and knowledge which are foreign to the culture from which the child comes. These skills succumb to group pressures and the sense of shame. They remain in limbo. As a result the person, though changed in his total awareness of life potential, remains unchanged in the operational, everyday dimensions of his existence. With exposure to shame and condemnation of newly acquired skills, the skills are excluded from the self-image in the area of operational potentials. Murphy and Murphy (1974) describe the influence of the Mandurucu society on girls who have spent as long as five years living and studying in mission schools, and have learned to understand and speak Portuguese:

". . . practically no women have a knowledge of more than a few trade words. . . . An almost deliberate effort is made to erase from their memories everything they have learned . . . [and] though they understand more Portuguese than they would acknowledge, [they are] almost mute when called upon to speak the language. Their amnesia for reading and arithmetic was even more striking. . . . The school however, left its imprint, for though its products were hardly Brazilians, neither were they fully Mundurucu. There was always about them a sense of alienation and removal, a lack of certainty and assuredness, which was most manifest in the virtual withdrawal from all interaction of youngsters newly returned to their villages. "They are ashamed," the older Mundurucu would say; the shame lasts for years (p. 41).

A conflict of cultural identities is introduced, achieving the same result as though there had been no state of latency to help establish a basic cultural identification. One is reminded of the social anomie, described by Boyer and Boyer (1970), in those whose cultural identification was interfered with by a failure to achieve a culturally appropriate transmission of traditions—a failure such as occurs with an interference with latency.

The effect of shame and of the social group on the ego ideal is made possible through the mechanism of *externalization of identity content for influence* that occurs in persons not in the state of latency, the primitive society member, or the person living in a small town. Externalization of identity content for influence is a specific entity. It is an ongoing possibility in all human beings, which is taken advantage of by the group to influence and to keep members in line. Murphy and Murphy (1974) have given an anthropological example of the use of shame by the social group to influence individual role behavior and identity content in the Mundurucu Indians of the Amazon.

There is on the other hand, strong public pressure to work, and the laggard, either female or male, finds herself or himself in the unhappy position of being the object of scorn and ridicule . . . in a society in which almost everyone knows everybody else, or at least knows about them, this can be a powerful incentive. It is a kind of immediate and total social control, relying on face-to-face relationships and the threat of loss of the esteem of others and therefore, self-esteem. This is the mechanism of "shame" said so often to be a characteristic of self-regulation in primitive societies as opposed to the "guilt" feelings of modern man. Actually the threat of self-defacement is found in complex societies, as well, and in exactly the same sort of small scale social settings of the village or the intimate group that are char-

acteristic of the way of life of primitives. In any event, the superego
twitches produced by self-accusation do not have the same power as
the attacks on the ego that can come from loss of public status.
(p. 66)

Cultural factors are involved in the modification of superego content
during the state of latency. A primary conduit influencing such modification is the process of passive mastery (identification with mythological and
story elements that have been introduced primarily as a means of discharge, in a verbal context, of the contents of the infantile amnesia).

Throughout life there are, in addition, ego mechanisms available for
modification of the content of the superego. From the point that a child is
aware of the outside world and can conceptualize it, the process of modification of the self to adjust to the impact of the world begins. Prior to this
point, there have been paradigms in the form of modifications of reflex
schemata (Piaget) in response to outside influences. This has influenced
primarily perceptual-motor and affect memory contents. With the acquisition of verbal memory of sufficient amount and subtlety (at about
eighteen months) cultural influences related to verbalization can be
brought to bear. Verbal communications can be used to change and convert motor patterns as well as to inhibit them. These are early elements of
superego. They become part of the self-image and the representation of
the self in the mind of the child. Verbal contents are not the only influencing factors. Tone of voice, threats of disapproval, and a fear of loss of
love also play a part.

During this phase the child is constantly changing his perception of
things. He learns of the people around him and their ways of living. They
go away and his perception turns toward himself. Having seen a bit of the
world, he changes his view of himself in keeping with that which he has
seen. Alterations of awareness of reality as well as the actual comings and
goings of people govern this continuous shift of attention from inside to
outside, with its attendant modifications of the child's view of himself and
what he is expected to be, based on the experiencing of people and the
demands of society. Often, the images of self so acquired remain for a lifetime, along with internalized partial objects and parental imagoes to
which a person in times of difficulty turns for comfort or for guidelines for
behavior. No matter how old a person grows, the capacity to expose these
inner concepts to the influence of people in the environment remains,
coupled with the ability to internalize the modified identifications. Psy-

chotherapy, social pressure, brainwashing, and peer group pressure are all examples of environmental influences that utilize this psychic mechanism to effect modifications of behavior. In superego terms, that which has been internalized and has patterned the person's behavior is projected, returning it to its original status as an influence outside of the self. It is thus exposed to change through comparison and modification under the pressure of that which the social group approves of or disapproves of. In such group situations, shame and potential depression over loss of group membership are the motivating factors in the resulting modification of superego content.

The state of latency with its passive mastery of drive energies through fantasy provides an opportunity for projection-introjection-related modifications of internalized superego contents, based on ethical concepts derived from culturally sanctioned tales. In those who have not experienced a state of latency, a shame-oriented, primitive, street-gang morality is acquired rather than the more subtle moralities that are gained through the latency state. Latency state moralities prepare the child for decision-making and the exercise of judgment in later life, providing for freedom from conflict with authorities and subtly regulated interactions in social situations.

Passive mastery and the structure of latency provide the opportunity for reshaping the internalized superego to meet the needs of society through introjection of identifications with ethical contents derived from school and myths, a subtle process which is not available to the child who seeks discharge primarily through action-oriented group phenomena.

Those who live in gang orientations during the latency years, or have found objects in reality for the discharge of drives, have strengthened the possibility of the establishment in adolescence and adulthood of a shame superego. This is primarily a group superego, with primitive potentials and limited opportunity for reflection and individualized responses. Such superegoes are primarily found in societies of hunters and food gatherers and disturbed adolescents in our own society.

In those who are shame influenced (nonlatency state children, primitive social groups, mobs), the influence to change is derived from pressure from the social group and results from the demand for cohesion without which the group could not survive.

The media for the communication of culture are learned in latency. Through the acquisition of cultural patterns, the state of latency becomes the key to the control and organization of social groups.

The means by which the media for cultural communication are manipulated during latency are important in understanding the role of latency in the continuity of society. During the Middle Ages, the specific tool for the transmission of culture for the leader group was the ability to read Latin. The word of God and the content of the Gospels became the property of those who had this power. The written word which could be challenged, reviewed, and subjected to commentary belonged to them alone. The common people served those in power out of fear and the lack of reading skills which would permit them to challenge what was told them. The media for the communication of culture were the stained-glass window and songs of minstrels. In neither medium was there the certainty of meaning or the potential for evaluation of meaning at leisure that can be found in books. Stained glass was subject to the interpretation of those who had access to the Gospels. Meanings could be changed to suit the needs of the leaders at the time. Even the songs of the minstrels and the sagas, which were transmitted in verbal form, had secret meanings.

In societies in which education in reading becomes available to all, such as our own, techniques persist for conveying caste from one generation to the next—this although reading is the great equalizer which provides the child with the opportunity to challenge old patterns, open the door to hitherto undreamed-of possibilities, and to gather in moments the experiences of lifetimes. Through this exposure patterns of injustice and patterns of constructive action can be understood and evaluated at a glance. The domination of man by myth wielded in the service of other men should be able to be extinguished in a society where all can read. This does not happen. Individual psychology and the techniques of the leader caste interfere. In some cases, this is the result of the failure of the individual to be able to give up the need to use the symbols in the myths for the passive expression of intrapsychic conflict. The leader-father must be followed and not challenged. In some cases, the adaptive orientation of the family requires myths for drive discharge.

Leader groups have techniques for maintaining a situation in which the people have a minimum of independent capacity, by which the leaders' word is preserved as the basis of all truth. By establishing for their children special schools and curricula, leaders provide themselves with broad knowledge not available to the other groups. This is important, but most important of all in differentiating the leader from the follower class is the degree of stringency required of the child in latency as he learns to read.

To learn to read for a test or for superficial meaning falls far short of the requirements of the leader class. The child being schooled for membership in this class must attain a high degree of comprehension of current events and meanings in stories as well as high levels of coherence and detail in memory function as a learned skill. The key in creating a member of the leader class is not just to know how to read, but how to understand and use what is learned in reading. Once so much subtlety is learned, the individual can take his place as leader, because of the skill so well described by St. Thomas Aquinas: "For if one of two men perceives a thing with his intellect with greater subtlety, the one whose intellect is of a higher degree, understands many things which the other is altogether unable to grasp" (p. 171).

The events of the latency state contribute to the integration of an individual into his culture. Skills in the use of the media for conveying myths from generation to generation are acquired. These may consist of reading, picture interpretation, storytelling, and memory skills. Stratification of society may be accomplished through the differential teaching of these skills. Additionally, in order to participate in group myths, the defense organizations characteristic of the psychology of the latency individual (symbolization, fantasy formation, mythopoesis, passive participation in the symbols and myths of others, passive mastery) become operative as group ego functions. The regressed ego organizations, characteristic of the workings of mass psychology, develop out of the ego organizations of latency. In mass phenomena, as in the latency state, sanction for the gratification of infantile fantasy elements is provided. In mass phenomena, sanction comes from the sharing of fantasy. In latency states, sanction comes from the masking of meaning provided by the action of the symbolizing function during the formation of fantasies. In large part, the content of these fantasies is influenced by the myths that dominate society. The child, in becoming attached to a mythic element which serves him, acquires culturally influenced imagoes which become a part of his identifications. This moves the child toward acculturation, and places some of his energies at the service of his society. This capacity for acculturation is the product of the work of latency.

Notes

1. For our purpose, a group may be defined as any combination of individuals who have functioned together for a sufficient period of time, to hold that what they believe in common is the only truth.

2. In this regard, see also Whitehead (1927) p. 112, Wellek and Warren (1942) p. 180, Bruner (1960) p. 282, and Arlow (1961) p. 388.

Chapter 6

PSYCHOTHERAPEUTIC STRATEGIES FOR CLINICAL PROBLEMS OF LATENCY AGE CHILDREN

*You who sit there in utter misery, look up
And show your friend your face. There is no darkness bears
A cloak so black as could conceal your suffering.
Why wave your hand to warn me of the taint of blood?
For fear your words pollute me? I am not afraid
To share your deep affliction with you. . . .*

—*Euripides*

Diagnoses and therapeutic interventions appropriate for the latency age child must of necessity take into account the cognitive, dynamic, and structural aspects of the latency age and the state of latency. Developmental considerations must be kept continually in mind.

Pathological states by and large are defined in terms of the inability of the child to produce at appropriate times the pliability, calm, and educability expected in the latency age child. This characteristic of the state of latency is of central importance in evaluating a latency age child in the educated sections of Western culture. However, evaluation of the ability to produce calm, pliability, and educability is only half the story. One must also evaluate the capacity to maintain the state of latency during situations of stress. The ability to demonstrate the acquisition of appropriate superego concepts and the presence of maturational steps pointing toward an adequate transition into adolescence and adulthood must be considered.

The psychiatric evaluation of the latency age child requires more than a search for symptoms and characteristics to be used in identifying an appropriate diagnostic category for statistical purposes. One must have specific information about the degree to which the child has been able to attain and sustain the state of latency. From this, one acquires the data to formulate a strategy for a psychotherapeutic approach. Weaknesses in superego, cognition, and ego strength with ominous potential for adolescent and adult adjustment can be reflected in dysfunctions of the latency state. Early detection and treatment in latency can be of value, often in situations in which the latency adjustment is not seriously impaired.

A child revealing inadequate symbol formation resulting in an interruption of latency must be approached with a different therapeutic strategy (see case 1 below) than a child with cognitive superego deficiencies, or a child with a mature symbolic function, strong structure of latency, and a rich fantasy life who has neurotic symptoms. The child who has a weak symbolizing function requires therapeutic strategies which help that function to mature, while the child who has a competent symbolizing function requires a strategy using play therapy, the working through of conflicts, and the interpretation of fantasy.

Specific Strategies

CASE 1. DEALING WITH INADEQUATE SYMBOL FORMATION

Josie was seven years old, and was four days into the second year of school at the time that we first hear of her. Her mother and father had noticed anxiety during back-to-school activities. They had experienced this the prior year with rapid resolution of anxiety. The situation was different this time. The child had become more and more anxious. She insisted upon telling everything that happened in school to the parents. This included the minutest detail. If they did not have time to listen, she became overwhelmed with anxiety. Her sense of urgency struck the parents as strange. Stranger yet was the behavior during preparation for school. She sometimes awakened her parents at four in the morning on a Saturday to go over the preparations for dressing for Monday morning. The parents became angry and yelled at the child. They felt that something was very wrong. Six weeks into the school year, the problem had become so severe that they brought her for therapy.

The father was an executive in a Texas-based engineering corporation. He was unaccustomed to psychological conceptualizations. "How can anything with so many individual variables in a single or intersecting set of fields be understood, let alone influenced and controlled?" thought he aloud during one of my sessions with him. The mother was a commercial artist.

In my interview with the parents, it became clear that Josie had always been a nagging child. She could not occupy herself when there was no structure. There was a continuous need for attention from the parents. She demanded that she be entertained. The parents could not recall a single spontaneous fantasy of the child. She had a sister, age four, who in contrast produced many. Josie had often been left in the care of her maternal aunt who was reported to give in to all demands of the child. In a store, whatever the child requested was bought. The little girl was known to scream if she didn't get what she wanted; the aunt never let her scream. The child was supplied with money, food, and toys on demand; she had no capacity to delay when it came to her desires. She did adequate school work, keeping up to grade level. This was, however, low for her potential.

A close relative described the parents' attitude toward the child as follows: "They are inconsistent. They give in or they go to extremes in not giving in. There is no happy medium. The father shouts in a frenzy. He doesn't seem to know how to talk. He can only shout. Josie copies his screaming and shouting."

The parents responded: "After a while, she gets on your nerves—you shout. It's self-defense."

Finally Josie was seen. She was an attractive blond child, appearing her stated age. She reported to me that she had to tell her parents what happens in school, because the voice of a lady told her to. She didn't know who the voice was. She was clearly without access to spontaneous play. She presented no fantasies. In sessions, she waited in expectation of my speaking; she said nothing spontaneously; she could draw nothing spontaneously. She drew stick figures representing herself when asked to draw a person. She was well oriented. There were no evidences of general cognitive impairment. There was an obvious maturational lag manifested in the absence of superficial evidences of a repression-oriented symbolizing function used in the service of latency fantasy discharge. She could remember no dreams save those which repeated recent traumatic experiences or frightening television movies. She enjoyed watching television but could recall only exciting events, never full stories or story lines. Explosions, fights, isolated episodes of magic on *I Dream of Jeannie* were all that held her interest. She had a fear of robbers. She provoked the attacks of peers. Her capacity to pay attention in school in support of learning was the product of an identification with academically oriented parents, a harsh teacher who accepted no rebellion in the children, and adequate latency ego mechanisms of restraint.

As I worked with the child, it became clear that her teacher yelled at her pupils. This recreated the home situation for Josie and stirred great anger in her. She feared to show it to the teacher, containing her anger until she returned to her home. She dealt with her acute distress by insisting upon parental attention to a reliving of the trauma of the school day. She punished them for yelling, a trait they shared in common with the teacher. She sought reassurance that future school activities would be well prepared for in advance. This was meant to head off attacks by the teacher. The amount of aggression leveled at the parents was so great that she dealt with her motivation regressively, assigning the cause of her behavior to a voice rather than to herself.

Josie was a wanted child with a normal birth, who walked at nine months and talked at one year. Her weaning was delayed. She had separation anxiety from the last half of the first year to beyond two years. Toilet training was responded to with much defiance. Bowel training was completed at two years, nine months. She never could be pushed. She became anxious when she couldn't handle things. At the age of four, she experienced a period of anxiety if her parents did not agree with or approve of each thing that she did. She was incapable of dismantling the memory of traumatic events and reorganizing and synthesizing them into highly symbolized and displaced stories. She therefore approached stresses bereft of skills through which she could gain succor or revenge without threatening the situation in which she wished to continue to function well (school). She did not have available the structure of latency that could permit this.

The diagnosis is then best seen as acute disorganization in an individual who had developed an inadequate latency because of inadequate symbol formation. Although some calm had been achieved in school, the absence of the structure of latency made it impossible for the child to remain calm in the face of ordinary stresses, where structure was minimal. If the child were to be helped at all, psychotherapy had to aim at creating a symbolizing function which she could use as a safety valve to deal with stress.

The Theoretical Basis for the Treatment

Before one can design a therapeutic strategy, a theoretical model must be conceptualized. This then serves as a guide for the therapist's role. The problem is an unimaginative child with no apparent psychoanalytic symbols.

Where do imaginative ideas come from? How is a symbol formed? How does it happen that an ugly experience can be transmuted into an unrelated idea to be used in working through the ugliness? What should happen is this. The traumatic event falls from consciousness. It is stripped of its outer garments (words) and is hidden in the mind only as the idea of what it had meant to the person who experienced the event. There are no words in the part of the mind to which I refer. There are only ideas of things. We call this part of the mind the *system unconscious*. It is a characteristic of this part of the mind that events which carry much meaning become linked to memories from the past which are related (i.e., the overwhelming yelling of the teacher and the yelling of the child's parents). The recent event and the past events in combination increase each other's momentum in seeking a conscious representation which will provide an opportunity for reliving, working through, and putting to rest the trauma. As such they are a source of discomfort. The more discomfort, the more does the complex of ideas of things acquire the quality that will attract consciousness.

The organ which opens the door to consciousness we call the *percept consciousness*. Eventually, the disquieting event and its comrades in arms knock at the door of consciousness and demand entrance. How can they be admitted? This is a land of protocol. Only thoughts that are dressed as words may enter here. Fortunately, there is an anteroom near the door to consciousness. We call it the *system preconscious*. Here there are garments in the shape of words and nonverbal visual symbols which hide the private parts of the ideas of things while cloaking them in styles and forms which are admissible into polite society. Once so attired, the concepts and ideas enter into the area of awareness which we call the *system consciousness*.

Does this happen to all events that occur in human life? The answer is for the most part no. Only when an event has an aspect which has an uncomfortable meaning to an individual (trauma) is that part of the event relegated to the system unconscious. During the latency years, the use of symbols, fantasies, and masking is a primary adjustment technique in working through such events. This was not so with Josie. A trauma remained with her, and she remained conscious of it. She could not deal with it through symbols and substitutes. These skills she had to acquire. Her way of dealing with trauma reflected a failure in development in relation to consciousness. At least three distinct stages in the development of consciousness were described by Freud: the *primal system consciousness*, the *abstract system consciousness*, and the *mature system consciousness* (see Appendix A). A child fixated at an immature stage will show inadequate symbol response to environmental stimuli. It is my impression that this course of events produced Josie's symptoms.

Josie's weakness of ego functions in the area of psychoanalytic symbol formation afforded her scant access to a mature system consciousness. She reacted to difficult situations with direct manifestations (that is, unmodified representations of the original anxiety-causing situations in her relationships with her parents). This inability to blunt affect in recalling difficult situations is characteristic of a fixation in the abstract system consciousness. There is some evidence that her fixation lay in the area between the abstract system consciousness and the mature system consciousness. She had rudiments of psychoanalytic symbol formation. She could participate passively in the psychoanalytic symbols of others (passive symbolization). She could take over the stories of others to fill her nightmares. She was able to express her affects through the excitements of television programs.

What could be done about this? A psychotherapeutic technique had to be devised to provide her with garments for the anteroom—the preconscious. An attempt had to be made to strengthen her repression and move her into the adult system consciousness through providing her with a calm, quiet, nonsadomasochistic situation in which she would be encouraged to work through traumatic situations in the form of displaced symbol-oriented fantasies. In this way she would be enabled to enter latency.

How could this be done? Her ability for passive symbolization was a resource for the therapist. Needed strengthening of the ego might be possible through conversion of passive psychoanalytic symbols to psychoanalytic symbols which are actively used. The therapist attempted this strategy in the treatment.

From the beginning, Josie sat anxiously and silently in my playroom. When I spoke to her of her problems, she answered politely, but never spoke more than a few words in direct answer to questions. I began to ask her about home, friends, her sister, and school. She described her need to talk about school to her parents. I pursued this, encouraging her to talk to me about school. I noticed that there were times when she would cut short her answers to my questions. This occurred especially when I asked her about her feelings and thoughts about her teacher? "You stopped talking in the middle of a sentence; did your thoughts stop?" "No," she said, "I know them; I can't say them."

Here was a manifestation of anxiety in response to a specific event.

I stepped over to my dollhouse and obtained a toy table, two toy chairs, a girl doll, and an older man doll. I set them up on the table at which we sat in an arrangement which duplicated our own seating arrangement. "The man," I said, "is Dr. Sarnoff. What's the girl's name?" "Lisa," said Josie. I was a little surprised. "Do you know anyone named Lisa?" I asked. "No," said Josie, "I made it up." She looked a bit shy and uncertain. An event had happened in the therapeutic situation to which a therapist should have been alerted by the theory. She had created a substitute masked form of an original representation. She had actively produced a masking symbol. I said to Josie, "Lisa, what happens in your school on a typical day?" Josie began to answer for Lisa, recounting her own experiences. When we arrived at the point where I asked her feelings when with the teacher, she fell into silence. But I was ready. She could live her fantasies passively through the stories of television characters. I would provide her with characters through whom she could tell her own story. I reached for the dollhouse and brought out several child dolls and two adult women dolls, plus some doll furniture. Josie caught the idea of the play, and using the substitute objects I had provided, played out the following story.

> In a classroom, a child makes a simple request. (I am to speak for the child; she speaks for the teacher. I do not speak except when given specific words to say by Josie.) The teacher refuses the request. When the child complains, the teacher begins to yell. At first all the children are frightened. Then they all rise up, advance upon her, and kill her.

In many guises, she repeated the same story in the months that followed. During this time, the parents noted an improvement in her behavior. The nagging stopped. The voice of the lady was heard no more. Tension occurred only on Sundays preceding school. One day in the playroom, she noticed a tiny sarcophagus containing a tiny mummy. It was made of dried clay. It was a remnant of a long-ago analysis of a child who made her own dolls to relate her fantasies. I told her this. She asked me to get some clay. I produced it from a nearby cabinet and handed it to her. She mushed it and rolled it and squashed it and then put it aside to play the game of the school situation.

In the next session, I began to mold the clay in my hand. Josie's therapeutic gain had reached the point that she could use dolls set in a context by me to tell a story that was so close to the original that the meaning was hardly masked. This is not a true structure of latency. She was only part of the way to the real symbol formation which is an integral part of the mature system consciousness. Now she must produce her own symbols. I held the shapeless piece of clay in my hand so that she could see it clearly. Then I asked, "What am I making? See how quickly you can guess it." She peered at the clay and said, "a man." So I made it into a man. The next piece of clay she saw as a dinosaur. Dinosaur it became. Then she tried her hand, producing another dinosaur. She had made the jump from the use of ready-made symbols to express fantasies to creating her own symbols. Now could she use these for working through her problems? The answer came quickly. She put a blue piece of paper and some paper trees into a small box and then arranged the figures in the box. "Write down a story about it," said I. "Okay," said she, and she did. Figure 5 is the diorama which she made. The story follows:

> Once upon a time, there was this jungle in South America and there were dinosaurs and all sorts of animals. Then one day this man came to see the jungle. He didn't know that a jungle is a dangerous place. Then all of a sudden, a dinosaur came in back of him and killed him. The man was seventy-two years old. The end.

Once again the theme of death and killing, but this one assigned away so far in time and space that a little girl need have no guilt that this is her story and these are her feelings. Other dioramas followed. Her second diorama represented the following story:

> Once there was an Indian village in India. It was a very quiet and peaceful village. There were elephants and tigers and animals. Then

FIGURE 5

all of a sudden came a bad man and he wanted to steal all the things in the village. So then a man came and shot the bad man and they all were happy.

Her third diorama represented the story of "The Happy Day":

Once upon a time there were two monsters. One monster was Harry and the other one was Sue. They lived in Africa but they didn't like it there so they moved here (Texas). They moved to a little town and the people who lived there were scared when they saw them. But there was one brave man who shot Harry. So the people were happy. They didn't kill Sue, because she was nice. And Sue didn't like Harry anyway. So they lived happily ever after.

Her fourth diorama represented the following story:

Once there were some men exploring the jungle in Africa. Then all of a sudden two lions, a lady and a man lion, came running after them. But luckily one of the men had a gun so he shot the lions and that is how it ended.

She also began to draw pictures which told stories not only of fear, but of rescue.

Story 1: "The Money Tree."

There once was a boy seven years old and his name was Tom. But nobody liked him because his mind was full of make-believes that he thought were true. So one day, he planted some money and watered it every day. Then one day he went back to see if it grew up to be a money tree and it did. So now everybody liked him because he let them use all the money on the tree and everyone was rich.

Story 2:

Once upon a time there were two girls named Sally and Jane. They were fooling around with their boat and all of a sudden it left with them in it. And then a big storm came and they almost drowned. But then Superman came and saved them. They kept on kissing him and they lived happily ever after.

It took one year to help the child to develop personality structures which could maintain a system consciousness whose contents would be sufficiently free of anxiety-causing elements for her to be able to function with sustained calm in the face of stress. Now with the fantasies available at sufficient distance that they could be discussed without disorganization, it was time to begin to work through her repetition compulsions, core fantasies, and other fantasy components which could contribute to neurotic behavior.

At home, she was much improved in behavior. Her maternal aunt described it thus: "There is a vast improvement all around. She is not fearful and does not act up. She is quite mature for her age, and it isn't at all difficult to reason with her. When she comes home from school she does her homework immediately, and then she lets off steam."

Her aunt was describing a child who is in the state of latency.

Strategies Utilizing the Potential of the Structure of Latency

One of the primary aspects of the latency state emphasized in this book has been the specific groupings of mechanisms of defense called the structure of latency. The structure of latency is definable as the group of defenses involved in the repression, fragmentation, displacement, symbolization, and organization into manifest fantasies of psychopathogenetically overcathected latent fantasy elements. This last refers to those fantasies which, when activated by sympathetic or seductive stimulation of motivating drives, set in motion psychological events which disorganize and interfere with the workings of the mechanisms of restraint which produce the calm, pliability, and educability which characterize the latency state.

In brief review (an extensive study of this appears in chapter 2), the following are the psychological events that occur in the latency age child when confronted with chronic or acute stresses which activate the motivating drives. Concurrent with the arousal of drives there is the activation of fantasies. These usually are fantasies having to do with loss of love, compensatory grandiose feelings in response to feelings of humiliation, tender feelings in relation to the mother, oedipal fantasies, sexual feelings in relation to the mother, aggressive feelings in relation to the parent of the opposite sex. Latency age children are physiologically ill-equipped to implement these fantasies in action. Defensive psychological responses therefore become necessary.

Typically, the latency age child's primary psychological response to the mobilization of libidinal drive (manifested in the activation of these fantasies) is through regression to the anal-sadistic drive organization. This is manifested clinically in tendencies to smear, to tease, to provoke, to mess, to refuse, and to be stubborn. These reactions are typical of the regressed or poorly defended latency age child's characteristic pattern of response under stress. In well-defended children, a group of defenses, the latency mechanisms of restraint, consisting of symbolization, sublimation, and obsessive-compulsive defenses (for example, collecting shells and coins) combine to produce a state of calm, pliability, and educability in response to superego demands. In societies which do not require such restraint for education other patterns are permitted or superimposed.

Calm behavior patterns appear in well-defended children in circumstances in which the expected social behavior is one of control and pliability. Regressed behavior is permitted during school recess, at parties, and in nonstructured social situations including play situations. In poorly defended children, such behavior can occur in any situation. Such poor potential for adjustment arises in a child under a number of circumstances. The parents may have failed to impart appropriate social demands for incorporation in the superego of the child. The child may not have developed sufficient cognitive skills to be able to maintain superego demands on an internalized psychological level. The mechanisms of restraint (ego mechanisms implementing superego demands) may be insufficiently competent. The structure of latency may be inadequately developed, as in the situation of an immature symbolizing function. The more stress faced by the child, the more likely is the poorly defended child to manifest anal-sadistic derivatives.

Let us return to the clinical characteristics of the structure of latency in psychotherapy. It is an important element in the psychological process which effects the mastery of oedipal fantasies during early latency. Essentially it is an organization of ego mechanisms, the purpose of which is to convert latent fantasy, which by dint of physiological unreadiness cannot guide drives to discharge with reality objects, into distortion-filled manifest fantasies. The manifest fantasies so produced in themselves serve as the pathway for drive discharge. They become a medium for vicarious problem solving. Through fantasy, conflicts can be played out in thought rather than reality. This spares the individual conflict or frustration with real objects in the environment and diminishes the impact of drives. Regressive responses are circumvented. In youngsters with an effective structure of latency, the latent fantasy that might have been responded to with regression to anal sadism is, instead, responded to through the activation of the structure of latency. The child is able to maintain pliability and calm in structured and nonstructured situations by the creation and utilization of manifest distortion fantasy as a pathway for discharge of the drives.

Fantasy formation assumes the character of a mechanism of defense during latency. A latency age child usually resolves a conflict or latent fantasy stirred up during the school day through playing out the conflict in manifest distorted form with friends after school. He is thereby able to protect the state of latency. This is the normal situation. The capacity to delay discharge through fantasy play is an important aspect of latency state adjustment. Delay is also associated with the mechanisms of restraint. Through them, the child can control responses until he finds himself in a more permissive setting. Delay is impaired when there is increased intensity of drive activity. Very intense stimulation such as yelling on the part of a teacher, or the introduction of sexual topics, can result in disorganized excited behavior in the child (failure of the mechanisms of restraint) or in the development of intense fantasy resulting in distraction from the work of the day (failure of delay).

In the latter case the limitation of fantasy to thought produces a superficial appearance of calm, pliability, and educability in children who are so distracted by fantasy that they cannot gainfully attend to the school situation. Often this good behavior causes the child's difficulty to be missed. Poor marks in an otherwise competent child should suggest this difficulty. In certain circumstances, the intensity of the drive stimulus is so great that fantasy and motor activity are activated together. Highly cathected fantasies are produced. The child acts on them in nonplay situations. Challenges of a teacher in the classroom or stealing from a friend or a store become expressions of fantasies of power or thievery. The structure of latency in this clinical situation becomes the source and molder of pathological behavior instead of a safety valve and guarantee of socially acceptable behavior (see chapter 2, case 3).

Through the latency age period, the structure of latency can be expected to contribute important elements to the psychological appearance of the child. Since overt fantasies are directly related to the sensitive latent fantasies of the child and closely related to his conflicts, they become, like the dreams of adults, royal roads to the unconscious. Techniques of using fantasy for psychotherapeutic purposes have great importance as a strategy in dealing with a latency age child.

With this in mind, the following case vignettes are presented with annotations explaining the use of psychotherapeutic interventions involving fantasy organization (the structure of latency).

CASE 2: REGRESSED SYMBOLIZING FUNCTION
(FAILURE TO ENTER LATENCY)

Carl, a seven-year-old boy, had been brought for treatment because of messiness, an inability to dress himself, thumb-sucking, crying at home and at school, and being confronted repeatedly by boys in his class who, he claimed, picked on him. He had clearly failed to enter latency.

During therapy sessions the youngster would often draw close to the therapist and attempt to touch the therapist's genitals or press against the therapist with his own genitals. Soon after such attempts the patient would try to punch the therapist. Apparently he mobilized aggressive and sadistic urges in defense against passive oedipal wishes in relation to the therapist. This is an example of regression to the anal-sadistic drive organization in response to uncomfortable oedipal urges. The same pattern was repeated with his friends in school. He made physical contact with them, and then, becoming fearful of the feelings engendered, progressively mobilized anal-sadistic urges. He usually manifested these by antagonizing the other children until they would hit him. Then, denying that he himself was angry, he was able to point out that the other children were the angry ones. His anger was thereby externalized and actualized in the behavior of others.

This was demonstrated to him in his sessions. He refused to leave at the end of sessions on days when he felt anger. He tried to actualize and externalize the anger by attempting to provoke aggressive behavior in me. At one time, he actually said, "What does it take to make you angry?" I pointed out to him the need that he had to make someone angry when he was afraid to accept his own anger. After this explanation, he minimized this behavior at the end of the sessions. Concurrently, he began to talk about his angry feelings during the session itself. He had great difficulty in putting these feelings into words. He had failed to enter latency, and his symbolizing function was immature. He was overly stimulated by passively experienced symbols met with on television. He experienced his affects (anger) in terms of the reactions of others. There was no lack of capacity to symbolize in the reports of dreams and occasional stories told to the parents. Massive amounts of overt aggression had been mobilized by at least three factors: regression to anal-sadistic drive organization in the face of negative oedipal (passive feminine) wishes, hitting and yelling on the part of parents, inadequate utilization of verbally oriented fantasy (structure of latency) for discharge. The regression had been dealt with through interpretation, and parental aggression had been dealt with through parental counseling. The development of fantasy was encouraged during the sessions. Special emphasis was put on the creation of symbolic fantasy elements, which were so well displaced from the latent signified elements that the associated affect would be bearable for the child.

Carl was encouraged to express his feelings through displaced fantasy play. The therapy room contained nonstructured play material—clay, pens, rope, pencils, paper, tape, glue, family dolls, toy furniture, and guns. Whenever he began to balk at talking about a feeling or something that had happened, I encouraged him to draw it. With this encouragement, he began to play out fantasies in the sessions. He first introduced a fantasy in which he was the king of all the world. Everyone was his slave. He insisted that the therapist play the part of the slave. He was unaware at the beginning of the treatment that he had such a fantasy since he had expressed the fantasy primarily through his family, teachers, and other children. He lived the fantasy out with them. He became extremely angry when anyone did not do what he wanted him to do. As he began to play the fantasy out through fantasy characters in the session, he himself became increasingly aware of his wish to be the ruler of the world and to make a slave of it.

The content of this fantasy was interpreted to him in the following way. The therapist assumed the role of slave, but only with the proviso that he would not say or do anything that he had not been told to do or say by the patient. Thus, it would remain the patient's fantasy alone. In this way, as he began to play out the story, he was able to see clearly what his latent motivations were.

The therapist turned to the patient from time to time and said that he wanted to talk to the king. He asked him how he felt when people did not obey him. At that point the patient described the anger and the fury that the king had, even though he was not able to describe his own anger directly. Through discussions of the reactions of the king the youngster was able to come to terms with aggressive feelings.

The child later pursued the fantasy of a robbery. It was rather specific and played out repeatedly. An elderly man would totter into a bank and ask to open up a bank account. At the point that cash drawers were opened, he pulled out a gun and made the bank teller his prisoner. The bank teller then was forced into becoming a robber himself. Often this was followed by questions relating to whether or not one could be sent to jail for robbing, what the electric chair was, and what capital punishment meant. At times the patient would take the role of the bank teller and at times the role of the old man. This related to whether he felt guilt on a particular day in response to something he had done.

In the practice of child therapy, fantasy has a number of uses. It can be encouraged so as to strengthen the state of latency by enriching the structure of latency. In addition, fantasy itself can be used as a source of information about the latent fantasy life of the child, the relationship of a child to his affects, and recent troubling specific events in the everyday life of the child. Once fantasy play has been established, it can be used as a means for working through conflicts and complexes. It is frequently wise for a therapist to approach a fantasy in terms of its affects. Often a child who cannot otherwise express his feelings can talk of them when speaking for a third person. There is an organizing and focusing effect that results from the experience of talking about a fantasy and affect in organized fashion with a therapist.

Specific events of the day can be brought into focus through an appreciation of the effect of the structure of latency on a child's latent fantasies. For instance this youngster continued to have, though in milder form, a need to produce anal-sadistic regressions upon achieving feelings of warmth toward a male figure. He was very much impressed by a woman teacher in his school whom he referred to as "Cokey." Cokey often would seek out a child, tell him he was very nice, and be gentle with him, sometimes stroking his face. The gentleness would be suddenly interrupted by a burst of rage in which she told the child to leave the room and put blame for negative behavioral attitudes on the child. She was fired eventually. The patient had witnessed this behavior. He did not speak of it in sessions. However, he came into his session one day and made a series of drawings about a character named Bokey. Bokey had a big moustache, a strange-looking car, and a strange-looking house. He robbed banks. Eventually he was attacked by the police and the army. His car-drawn trailer was located by them. The trailer turned out to be a helicopter which was able to pull the car up into the air and fly Bokey to safety. This was a complex robber fantasy ending in an escape. Guilt was not expressed.

The therapist asked about the absence of punishment. The child told of Cokey and her behavior which paralleled his own. Both defended against sexualized approaches with hostile withdrawal. He had related to recall of her pattern by mobilizing a robber fantasy. He had produced similar fantasies to express the guilt that he felt in relation to his own behavior. Recall of Cokey's behavior stirred up in him fear that he would lose control as Cokey had. Loss of control had always frightened him. To master this fear, he developed fantasies in which individuals steal and force other people into becoming robbers. The persons forced into crime could not be held responsible. These story elements paralleled his projection of responsibility for anger onto others.

Cokey had taught the child a year before the manifest Bokey fantasy was produced. This was not the proximate factor in activating the Bokey fantasies. The distant episode had been evoked to control affects relating to a more recent event. An uncle had lost control of his temper shortly before the Bokey fantasies began. The uncle, who was usually a calm and quiet person, was under stress in business. He had screamed at the youngster because the child had failed to take a package to a neighbor a few blocks away. The child did not appear to be overwhelmed. He was described by his parents as very well under control. In the session that followed, he began to master his reactions to the episode by the invocation of fantasies based on Cokey. This case has illustrated the way in which fantasy represents affects, events, and memories related to recent events. The technique for working through these relationships follows.

CASE 3: RESPECT FOR EGO DISTANCE AND RELATING A FANTASY TO STRESSFUL EVENTS OF THE DAY.

Paul was a constantly sad youngster who was brought to treatment at the age of six. His mother and father had separated when he was three years old. He had to travel a great distance to visit his father, whom he missed very much. Immediately following the separation from the father there had been a period of encopresis.

The youngster repeatedly played out a fantasy in which he ran make-believe vehicles—sometimes a car, sometimes a bus—over long highways. The highways could be anything from a game board that he brought to the office with him, to a set of books lined up on the floor. One time he was running a car on a particularly long road. The therapist said to him, "You miss your father and you're showing me how you would like to drive along the road to get to your father's house." This action-construction on the part of the therapist gave no leeway for ego distance. The phrase should more properly have been said in the following way: "The driver of the car is going to visit someone. Who is it?" Since the boy was directly confronted with his feelings about separation from the father and the long way he had to go to see him, the youngster lost control, regressing to anal-sadistic destructive behavior, throwing objects around the room, and hitting the ceiling with play furniture. He was out of control for the rest of the session.

It is unwise as a therapeutic technique to interpret directly the angry feelings of a child who is involved in fantasy. Often the fantasy structure that the child is creating is a defense against anger that cannot be dealt with in any other way. Once the defenses are removed, the child becomes directly and overtly angry and quite out of control. It is better, therefore, to work with the fantasies and to try to understand the child through the fantasies rather than through the removal of them.

In a subsequent session the child took a bus that was in the playroom and began to move it around as though he were taking it somewhere. The therapist asked the youngster who was in the bus. The child responded that there was a boy in the bus but there was no driver, and then asked the therapist, "Can a train run without an engineer?" The therapist then asked whether he could talk to the boy in the bus. He asked the boy in the bus how he felt about being on a bus that had no driver. The boy described the loneliness that he felt. The therapist remained silent to observe what effects the therapeutic intervention would have on the child's fantasy. There was a modification in the fantasy. A doll figure was used by the youngster to represent the boy on the bus. The boy on the bus began hitting other dolls on the head.

The therapist responded with a construction describing both the affect and the action that the doll figure was pursuing. He said to the doll figure, "You feel you want to hurt the other dolls." The child, responding for the doll, said, "Yes." The therapist then turned directly to the patient and made a reconstruction in question form. "Did anyone make *you* feel that way today?" The boy then talked about his school recess, when other boys with whom he had wanted to play had told him that they had already made plans. He was left alone. This activated in him feelings about being at home without his father. The patient had had a number of choices for manifesting these feelings. He could produce a regression; loss of bowel control would be an example. He could have begun provoking and teasing the children in the classroom. This time he chose neither of these; instead, through the structure of latency, he developed a fantasy of a bus with no driver carrying a lonely boy. After the child was able to discuss how lonely he felt, and had become more comfortable with the affects involved, the therapist returned to the fantasy of the bus with no driver. The therapist said, "Isn't that like a family without a father? I wonder if the feelings that the boy had aren't the feelings that you have." He got a calm positive response and could ask the boy more about his feelings.

The therapeutic strategy required coming to terms with the separation from the father. A latency age child often has great difficulty in handling such problems if there are intense feelings of anger and rage and a sense of being deserted. Though the structure of latency helps to stabilize the behavior of the child, a sense of loneliness is ever ready to be evoked in response to slights and minor desertions by peers. With such youngsters, the initial strategy for approaching the underlying problem is through identifying the affects associated with the fantasies. Then one must work in terms of defining the child's unwillingness to experience the affects. With this accomplished, the child's life stresses can be discussed free of the interpretations of fantasy. Eventually, this youngster was enabled to separate his distortions of the father's motivation from the father's true motivation. The child could see himself less as a passive deserted person than as a person who had in his power the capacity to maintain better contact with a father who was eager to spend much time with him.

CASE 4: DEALING WITH THE STRESSFUL EVENTS OF THE DAY

At times the influence of a day's event is so strong that the event itself becomes the basis for the content of the therapy session. An example of this would be the following:

A girl who had been in analysis for two years, and who had been an excellent patient from the standpoint of cooperation and the ability to work introspectively with fantasy, entered into the session in silence and told the therapist that he was contaminated and she would not talk to him.

Such a specific attitude directed toward the therapist signifies a shift into the treatment of a humiliating event which had occurred during the day. A child who hits the therapist must suggest to the therapist the possibility that the child has been hit herself. The child who treats the therapist with silence must at least be considered to have been treated with silence during the day.

The therapist therefore asked the patient, "Did someone do this to you today?" She said, "Yes. Someone came to visit my sister and they both said, 'She's contaminated; don't talk to her,' and now you're contaminated." The therapist pointed out to the child that she was doing to him that which had been done to her. The mechanism involved is identification with the aggressor.

CASE 5: IDENTIFYING AND
WORKING THROUGH A LATENT COMPLEX

Latency fantasies during therapy sessions most often are influenced by events of the day to which the patient is sensitive. Pursuing a child's fantasy leads one to the day's events which are provocative, revealing sensitive areas in the child. The therapist must study the day's events, seeking those which provoke similar fantasies. One must attempt to delineate the elements that these events have in common in order to understand the latent fantasy that has sensitized the child and triggered the reaction.

Janet was a ten-year-old girl who had recently moved to a Texas border town from a farm in Oklahoma. She developed night fears soon after the move. Her parents were divorced, and she and her mother had recently moved in search of improved working conditions. Unquestionably, the children in her new school were far more sophisticated sexually than she. In therapy session she told repeated variations of a fantasy about a child who was kidnapped and brutalized by intruders. She played at the fantasy for great lengths of time. She insisted that the therapist not interrupt while she was playing out the fantasy. However, after a few minutes of playing the fantasy out, she always asked the therapist to take one of the fantasy roles. This was varied from day to day. The therapist capitalized on his position as a character in the fantasy. To explore the fantasy he asked what he should do, why he should do it, and how he was supposed to feel.

In one session the patient turned out all but one light in the office and told the therapist that he should play the frightened child. She told him to lie down. She put on all kinds of scary masks and approached him. "What should I say? How do you want me to feel?" said the therapist. The child said, "Don't say anything, because you're very very scared." The therapist then asked, "Scared like what?" The child said, "Scared like when a boy pushes you on the bus." "Did anything like that happen to you today?"

asked the therapist. "Yes," said the child, who then began to describe the feelings of being ten years old and unable to defend herself against a twelve-year-old boy who had taken her books and teased her. With great reservation she told of a time when the boy had fallen on top of her. The night-fear fantasies had been mobilized in varied form as an active mastery of a number of seemingly unrelated situations occurring during the day. Other typical provocative events were overhearing older girls talking about sex, seeing a copy of a men's magazine which showed a nude woman, and seeing a pregnant woman.

The therapist, recognizing that all of the events that provoked this fantasy shared in common sexuality with emphasis on body forms and body contact, watched the content of the therapy session for any reference to the body of the child. Prepubescent bodily changes were the source of the child's preoccupations. Therefore the emergence of this topic was not long in coming. The child talked about a girl in the class who was sexually developed. The therapist asked the patient how she thought the other girl felt. The child answered that it's exciting and bewildering. "You don't know what you're going to look like, and you get feelings in your stomach and you get pains and you don't know whether you're sick and should stay home from school or whether that's growing pains and growing up." She then referred to the pains that she experienced in her chest and body and began to draw a picture of what her hips looked like to her, and to describe the reaction to the nipping in of her waist. She was soon able to discuss her sexual development with the therapist and organize in her mind the process that she was going through. Through this activity she corrected misapprehensions about her physical sensations. She was less apt to complain of illness, for she could accept her development as sexual development without feeling embarrassed.

Psychotherapy does not progress as much from the analysis of fantasies as it does from the analysis and synthesis of verbal associations. Topics having to do with sexuality and body form were introduced into the therapy sessions by way of her fear fantasies. She was able to clarify for herself the complex events of early puberty to the extent that she was able to gain control of her symptoms.

Working with Parents

The state of latency, which is the essential topic of this book, is the product of internal factors within the child. As such, ego, superego, id, and cognitive factors have been given primary emphasis, if only from the standpoint that the special organizations that characterize them during latency have for so long been neglected. By way of contrast, the role of parents in latency has been much emphasized in the literature. Wherever the terms society, culture, social inhibition, seduction, or guidance are used, somewhere in the chain of human involvement parents will be found. The role of parents is inseparable from the process of child development.

Even in so apparent an internally based process as Piaget's description of the development of thought in the child, one must wonder how much assimilation and accommodation could take place in the absence of parents to provide patterns for the modification of schemata and contacts with the world.

A definition of latency from the standpoint of the child therapist might be the following: Latency is the time period running from six years of age until the child is capable of working with the therapist without the help of the parents. For all practical purposes the latency age child and his parents are two parts of one unit.

The latency age child has immature ego functioning which does not provide for an adequate adjustment without the presence of the parent. The need for the child to repress recent experiences in order to cope with drive stimulation associated with those experiences results in an inadequacy of recall which interferes markedly with any attempts at psychotherapeutic work. Therefore it is necessary to have the parent provide information on events that have happened in the child's life. This includes stories that the child has told the parent that may have undergone repression by the time the child gets to the therapist's office, and future events with which the child is unfamiliar or which he does not sufficiently cathect because they are not understood to be important by the child. Examples of this would be an upcoming party, the expected birth of a cousin, or a vacation. Ordinarily, for latency age children a future event does not begin to have dynamic importance until two weeks before the occurrence. It is therefore possible for a child to be told that he's going to be doing something by the parent at a time sufficiently removed from the contact with the therapist that the idea will have lost its interest for the child. It will not be until about two weeks before the event that the child will begin to bring into the session dynamic manifestations that can be related to the future event. Often this is not enough time for the therapist to prepare the child for the event or to deal with it effectively.

Children often will remember to tell their parents dreams but are unable to tell the dreams to the therapist because of repressive processes that intrude between the dreaming and the time of the therapeutic session. At the very minimum, the child and therapist as a team work under a deficit. There is a great deal of information that would be available in the psychotherapy of adults and adolescents that does not become available in work with the latency age child. The parent is therefore necessary as a kind of alter ego to complete the total picture of the child for the therapist.

When a child enters adolescence he begins to have relationships with others that the parent can know nothing about and, in fact, should not know anything about. At this time the parent is of much less value to the therapist. During latency, because of a knowledge of the child that exceeds the child's own knowledge of himself, parents are particularly useful as sources of information. Thoughtful, intensive, and regular contact with the parents completes the therapist's ongoing knowledge of the child.

A specific therapy technique known as the child guidance technique requires that the parents be seen at least once a week and the child be seen once or twice a week. The child is seen in psychotherapy with therapeutic strategies appropriate for the child. The parent is approached with a variety of techniques. The approach to the parent takes three forms: the parent becomes a source of information; direct guidance is given to the parent; psychotherapeutic techniques are used in working with the parent.

A helpful specific strategem used in work with parents is the turning of the parent's comments about the child into a source of information about the parent's own early life. If the child misbehaves and punishment is meted out, the parent could be asked how her parents handled her in similar circumstances. Understanding of the connection between the parent's upbringing and the technique of bringing up the child can be clarified for the parent. An interest in and exploration of the parent's own problems can be introduced in this way. It is often necessary to prepare the parent for more intensive psychotherapy. At times this is the primary therapeutic activity. The latency child is in his formative years. Modifications in the parent can result in relief of the child's surface symptoms.

Concurrent individual treatment of parent and child by the same therapist with intensive treatment for both parent and child has been reported to be quite useful in those situations in which internalized conflicts result in symptomatology in both parent and child. A more common approach is for the parent to be sent to another therapist when intensive psychotherapy is indicated. Family therapy involving parent and child can be quite useful. In the circumstance in which facts brought up by the parent and denied by the child take the form of a confrontation, the therapist should be extremely careful. In such situations of exposure, it is common for a child to feel betrayed. Family therapy is most useful in situations in which internalization of conflict is not the source of difficulty. The ideal family therapy situation is one in which there has been failure of the family to achieve a modus operandi for resolving conflicts arising out of individual differences.

CASE 6: KEEPING THE IMAGE OF THE THERAPIST DISTINCT FROM THE IMAGE OF THE PARENT

It is unwise to see the parent at the same time that the child is in the waiting room. The tension created in the child often results in interference with the child's ability to communicate. Open rage at both parent and therapist can occur during the interview. When the parent and the therapist are separate in the child's mind, the child patient becomes less and less aware of the impact of the parent-therapist meetings. This permits the development of transference phenomena and the unguarded revealing through the transference of many of the child's inner secrets and urges. Ideas are conveyed which he would not reveal to the parent or to someone closely allied in his mind with the parent. The following clinical vignette is a case in point.

The patient was a nine-year-old girl who had been fascinated with a low one-story dollhouse in her therapist's playroom. She like the fact that it permitted access to each room without the risk of knocking over furniture near the front of the room as occurs with two- and three-story dollhouses. She told her father about the dollhouse and was somewhat troubled by the fact that he did not make it for her. When he eventually bought the wood to make the dollhouse, the dimensions of the house that he built were identical with those of the house in the therapist's office. This was purely fortuitous; however the child interpreted this to mean that the parent had come into my office and had entered the playroom which she had considered her private sanctum. This resulted in intense rage. Analysis of the rage revealed that the father's entering my office interfered with my function as a transference symbol. I no longer could be considered so far removed from the father that displacement of feelings from the father to me could result in a diminution in the valence which I as a symbol had for attracting affect. She therefore became intensely anxious about transference feelings she had in relation to me. The mechanism of defense, displacement to a symbol, had been interfered with. She defended against the anxiety so mobilized by the mobilization of aggression.

Situations in which parent-child interactions require intervention are multitudinous. The particular one to be dealt with in a given session is dictated by the specific problem brought by the parent to the individual parent session. Only a few can be covered in this section. Some of the developmental circumstances involving the psychological processes related to the state of latency are the following:

Overstimulation during latency

The most intense source of pressure to override the effect of the mechanisms of restraint and the structure of latency in their work of implementing superego demands for calm, pliability, and educability is seductive behavior on the part of parents. Sado-masochistic interactions, beatings, nudity, taking the child into bed at night or in the morning, sexually seductive talk, and stimulating sexual lectures places additional burdens on the ego during the latency time period. There are realistic limitations on the physical outlets and the physical equipment of the latency age child. Sympathetic stimulation and direct activation of the sexual and aggressive drives stir up intense fantasy activity. This can produce regression in the structure of latency with resulting neurotic acting out and/or regressions to prelatency behavior with disorganized aggressive activities. When such regressions are detected in the parent-child interaction during latency, it is necessary to direct the parent to cease activities which can be linked causally to such responses. Many parents will point to the fact that there are families in which such activities occur without apparent ill effect. It is necessary to point out to these parents that their child seems to be especially sensitive to such pressures and that it is he alone with whom you are working. Parents usually respond positively to an approach which individualizes their child and his needs.

Superego development in middle latency

During the middle years of latency, seven through nine years of age, there is a marked increase in dependability, reality testing, size, and strength of children. More and more, parents permit children to do things that they were not permitted to do before. One example would be crossing the street alone. Within the context of increased permissiveness the child begins to explore his newfound freedom. He tests it out in other areas such as stealing money, taking other people's things, lying, and playing with words. If this exploration meets with success, characterological leniencies are established that can cause great harm to the child in later years. Lying and cheating can become characteristic behavior patterns. It is, therefore, necessary to advise the parent to react very strongly to any attempt to establish freer patterns than are permitted within the home. Examples such as stealing of money and crossing the street without permission are easily understood. Of more subtle nature are lying and playing with words. As part of the developmental shift to the use of words as things sufficient unto themselves, there is a tendency, in latency age children, to use words to manipulate rather than to express or represent actual situations and events. The following case is given by way of illustration.

CASE 7: DEALING WITH PARENTS OF CHILDREN WHO MANIPULATE THROUGH THE USE OF WORDS

An eight-year-old became furious with his parents when he was told that he would have to go to school in spite of his statement that he was very sick. His mother demonstrated to him that he had no fever and no symptoms of illness. He stated that she couldn't see what he felt and that he felt very sick. She sent him to school anyway. His anger mounted and mounted. The situation was explored with him in a psychotherapy session. He complained that the day before the entire family had planned to go to a movie and to dinner with his uncle and the uncle's family. Shortly before the time to leave on that Sunday afternoon, the uncle called and said he had a cold. The mother accepted this information as true and canceled the plans. The child was unable to see that the mother had related to the situation that the uncle described rather than to the words. He chose to use his own words as a means of manipulating a cancellation of a scheduled event that he himself wished to avoid. Sending him to school was appropriate. Unless such behavior is interfered with, it can become the basis for difficulty in later life.

This is not the only area in which latency age children explore ethical alternatives. With the shift of cathexes to reality and peer objects, peer group influences make their appearance. The children begin to describe tastes and preferences that differ from those of the parents. It is necessary for parents to continue to make clear their own standards and ethics if the child is to be expected to function comfortably as an adult in society. At the age of twenty-six there is usually a return to a pattern of behavior which resembles parental superego dictates. Unless information about these dictates is given by parents and stressed, though not necessarily accompanied by threats, the child will be bereft of source information for patterning his life when he chooses to assume adult responsibilities and roles.

It is well for parents to appreciate that children learn superego content by example as well as by precept. The way that parents behave will convey more to the child than will an occasional admonition. In working with superego development more than in any other area in dealing with latency age children, one must constantly work in terms of the future. The implications for adolescence and adulthood of the competency of the child's ability to manifest superego-motivating affects are central. It is important that a child's superego contents be consonant with behavioral patterns required for comfortable adjustment in his society. It is equally important that the ego mechanisms of restraint and the structure of latency be sufficiently well established and strong to establish an adult ego, which will be effective in the implementation of superego demands vis a vis the seductions of society and the id.

Piaget's differentiation of the development of the morality of restraint and the morality of cooperation is of importance in working with parents. During the early latency time period there is a transition from the stern superego context of the morality of restraint to the less harsh morality of cooperation. The morality of restraint was described by Flavell (1963) as "unilateral relations between child as inferior and adult as superior" (p. 295). The morality of restraint results in the child's regarding the demands of the parents as moral absolutes. With the development of the morality of cooperation the child sees his superego contents as "formed out of the reciprocal relationships among status peers and based on mutual, rather than unilateral respect" (p. 296). This results in the child's seeking for alternatives and being able to accept digressions from parental demands in suitable situations without the mobilization of internalized superego affects such as guilt. In effect, the child becomes more of an adult with the development of the morality of cooperation. He becomes involved in give-and-take in situations in which moral judgment plays a part in decision making.

Children who are unable to make this transition and parents who are unable to take advantage of it run into trouble. Parents should be ready to replace commands, at least at times, with the ability to say to the child that they face problems similar to those the child faces, and that they are willing to share ways in which problems are solved. Mature parental behavior in latency is characterized by sharing strength with the child rather than using strength to dominate. Should a parent insist on maintaining the morality of restraint, the parents and child will soon be at loggerheads. The parent will exercise the power to control and dominate and force the child into established patterns of behavior. A child can generate great personal guilt with the act of rejecting internalized parental imagoes in favor of a growing awareness that there is a possibility of making alternative decisions. This results in a very ambivalent situation. What the child wants to do conflicts with what he ought to do. The child wishes to please the parents, but at the same time wishes to do away with psychic representations of them. The affects engendered are those of guilt, depression, internal sadness, and "crying inside." These are often accompanied by psychosomatic symptoms such as vomiting, acute episodes of diarrhea, swelling, hives, and headaches.

Encouraging sublimations and motor discharge skills

In chapter 5 the latency age child is characterized as a physiologically impotent dwarf-warrior. The child is poorly equipped to deal with sexual and aggressive drives in terms of their articulation with the external world of real objects and therefore must find substitutes.

Parental help is necessary in establishing these substitutes since they often require materials and equipment which are not readily available to the child. Parents therefore must be encouraged to overcome their own inhibitions, disinterest, social paralysis, and lack of cathexis of activities in which the child might show an interest in order to provide transportation or the equipment and material needed to perform the indicated tasks. They can join in some activities, such as model building. Stamp collecting, coin collecting, collecting of stones and shells should be encouraged. Motor discharge skills in the form of athletics and sports activities should also be encouraged. The more of these activities that the child is able to deal with, the more will the energies formerly utilized in pathological behavior be channeled into useful patterns. Fantasy activities are to be encouraged as well as literature which carries the content of the superego expected in the culture. It is worthwhile to encourage a child to harness his capacity for fantasy to future planning of activities within the child's scope.

The parent should not only be encouraged to limit stimulation and infantilization, but positively encouraged to help the child toward adult functioning by sharing the planning of activities. The child can help with the planning of trips, for instance. He can be called upon to suggest places to go on family outings. The more deeply involved the child is in these activities the greater will be the cushion between himself and pathological responses. It is wise to give to the youngster as much in the way of responsibilities as is deemed plausible.

Infantilization

Interferences with latency can result when parental overinfantilization produces vulnerabilities in the area of narcissism and oral fixation. A latency child may be infantilized in the following ways: (1) The child may be babied, responsibilities withheld; the child may be considered to be inadequate for problem solving and carrying out tasks; (2) the child may be infantilized through pressure to break down mature defenses. For instance, when a child has been confronted with frustration of a wish, he will plan alternatives aimed at getting around the frustration. This can be interdicted by a parent who responds by beating the child or yelling at him. As a result, the child is reduced to a more primitive level of intellectual functioning. This results in total disorganization and failure to experience a maturing exploration of the positive and negative aspects of the alternative that he had been developing.

CASE 8: ILLUSTRATING A STUNTING OF
PERSONALITY GROWTH THROUGH INFANTILIZATION

A six-year-old boy saw his sister throw a coin into a toll machine while driving on a major state turnpike. He insisted that he be permitted to throw the next coin. His father was concerned that he would miss the coin receptacle and refused the child permission to throw the coin. Out of fairness, the sister was also refused. The child seemed to agree. Secretly, he had a plan. At the last moment, as the parents were approaching another toll station, the child revealed his true intentions. He made a grab for the coin at the last minute. His attempt was interdicted by screaming on the part of the parents. This resulted in a regression to a level of rage and tears with disorganized motor activity in the child. The regressed state continued as a period of silence which caused the parents to say that they hadn't had so much peace in a long time. They were delighted at the outcome of their strategem. In actuality, they had caused a severe regression in the child which became apparent to them when they discovered with the beginning of silence that he had begun thumb-sucking again. He had not been involved in this activity for over two years.

A similar pattern can sometimes be seen in parent-child interaction when the child is much older. A mother may sometimes involve her daughter in battles at the time that dates come to pick the girl up, lessening the chance for the girl to leave home and marry. This is a mechanism sometimes used by parents for interfering with removal. Intense battles can occur between parent and child during late latency, puberty, and early adolescence which will result in a failure of removal because of the intensity of the cathexis involved in the battle between the parent and child. When such situations occur it is necessary to point out to the parents that they are actively involved in an inhibition of the forward progress of the child's development.

Infantilization is the product of parental actions. It is also the product of parental attitudes, and certain attitudes must be dealt with if detected during therapist-parent contacts. For instance, parents sometimes see the difficulties of their child in terms of the projection of their own guilt. An example would be deMause's (1974) description of Cotton Mather's child falling into the flaming hearth. The child was saved from the fire by a passerby. Mather himself had observed the near tragedy but did nothing. He was busy trying to figure out what sin of his had given rise to the punishment being visited upon his child by the Lord. "What have I done to deserve this?" is often heard from parents. This may be an expression of the thought that the child's difficulties are actually related to the sins of the parents rather than to the parents' interaction with the child. Such ideas detract from parental cooperation in a psychodynamic approach to the child's behavior.

Any attitude which deals with the child as an insensate object infantilizes the child. There is failure to recognize the child as a creature with mature potential. Such attitudes result in controlling the child through manipulation instead of dealing with the child as a sentient, thinking, and emotionally responding human being. The latency age child is capable of emotional responses and is aware of the potential in all people of an ability to select between alternatives in handling a problem. In his desire to divest himself of a very passive position in relation to the parents, even the well-defended child may become angry at a parent's arbitrary behavior. As the child grows toward adolescence, the ability to achieve independence results in the child's seeking peer sanction for his wishes in defiance of the parents. Action taken during latency can soften this tendency during adolescence. What is required is that parents become aware of the child as a thinking, emotionally responding human being. Such a parent would avoid such action as handing the therapist a note about the child's behavior over the child's head as he entered the session. Instead, the parent would discuss the problem with the child at the point that the therapist comes into the waiting room. Children who are dealt with as though the potential for maturity is not present become angry and respond with negativism.

Modification of the Technique of Psychotherapy Required by the Latency State Ego and Latency Phase Cognitive Growth

The ego structure of the latency state and the processes of cognitive development that take place during the latency period alter the nature of the psychotherapeutic and psychoanalytic situation from that ordinarily experienced when working with adults. Thus special developmental knowledge and technical skills must be acquired for the professional psychotherapeutic approach to a child. The body of knowledge involved is so vast that an entire volume could be devoted to its definition and elaboration. Here we must limit ourselves to discrete topics of primary importance. Early in this chapter, we discussed strategies for dealing with pathological functioning of the structure of latency. The children described in the following sections of this chapter manifest regressions and distortions of psychic function against a background of the normal structure of latency. Psychotherapy within the framework of the normal structure of latency requires special techniques. The techniques described below deal with problems of initiating, motivating, and terminating psychotherapy with children in the latency state.

Starting Psychotherapy with a Child in the Latency State

Most adults and many adolescents seek psychotherapeutic help for themselves out of an inner sense of need. In contrast, most children are brought for psychotherapeutic help as a result of a need felt by the parent.

Rarely does the latency age child initiate a request for treatment. When the rare child does seek the therapist the child's complaint is usually limited to the presence of current discomfort. He has little concern about the future influence of his surface problem or the underlying psychopathology that it represents. Even the child who seeks treatment has a short-term goal. Usually this is relief from immediate discomfort. Most parents have a more sophisticated approach. Though they seek help for their children for immediate problems, they are often concerned about the lasting potential of the child's current state of discomfort. The latency age child does not think this way; his time sense limits his vision to nearby things. Therefore, once the child who has sought therapy is freed of immediate discomfort, the motivation for treatment diminishes markedly. The cooperation and support of parents who see beyond the child's limited vision are required if therapy is to continue.

A girl of ten had entered therapy for treatment of a sustained paranoid state. She avoided school out of fear that she would be kidnapped. She became restive in treatment after the underlying motives had been made conscious and her presenting symptoms cleared. During psychotherapy, it had been determined that she had been excited by early pubertal growth. This intensified a longing to win the approval of her father, to whom she was strongly attracted. Through her anxieties and fears she was able to draw her father, a busy executive, close to her. He delighted in his ability to calm the child in the face of his wife's inability to do so. He drove her home from school, comforted her in bed, and potentiated the sexually stimulating situation at the same time that he soothed her. The kidnappers symbolized the mother's hostility, the child's guilt, and a desire to run away with an unknown man (a symbol of the father).

Working through of this material produced resolution of the intense acute symptoms. She became calmer, attended school, and made friends. However, she lapsed into periods of depressed mood and irritability when angered, and she experienced episodes of a few days' duration in which the potential for the use of projection was clearly manifest (e.g., interpreting comments of teachers and friends as attacks). These episodes interrupted the periods of comfort and calm during which the child had seen little need for therapy. Only during these episodes could interpretations of their portent for future difficulties be used to mobilize her energies for further investigation of her problems. During the intervening times, she came to treatment because of her parents' wishes. Her parents had been warned by the therapist of the possibility of such an attitudinal change and were prepared to deal with it.

Because the latency age child's world view is not the long view, the configuration of motivation that the patient presents differs markedly from the motivation the adult patient presents. It more closely resembles the presentation of the adolescent whose delinquent behavior masks depression. Both are creatures of "now" who express gratitude for quick and unsubtle solutions.

Before considering psychotherapy for latency age children, the motivation of the child should be evaluated and in this evaluation both the present and the future must be taken into consideration. Of primary concern is the present state of emotional discomfort and the degree to which it creates so much difficulty for the child that some psychotherapeutic intervention is necessary. When this circumstance is present, the child will cooperate in the treatment. Evaluation of the child must include two other areas: (1) a prediction of whether or not the anxiety will persist on into the future after developmental processes and natural resolutions have worked their way and (2) consideration of whether the current anxiety represents an underlying psychopathological state which will reassert itself in later years in a manner that will cause either acute or chronic discomfort or an undermining of the psychological adjustment of the adult that the child shall grow to be. When these areas come into consideration, alliance with the parent is necessary.

Most parents who seek psychotherapy for their child are aware of the potential for future discomforts that present discomforts portend for children. Though they come into the psychotherapeutic consultation emphasizing the present symptom, this is rarely the only concern. Parental interest quickly turns to whether the symptoms will have far-reaching implications for the child in later life. Where this concern does not exist, it should be made clear that this is a possibility so that an educated decision can be made by the parent. Not infrequently a sophisticated mother is accompanied by a doubting father who agrees to bring the child for consultation only because he is sure that the therapist will agree with him that the child's problems are only transient ones. Should potentially impaired long-range functioning come into consideration—as with severe cognitive lags, poor symbolizing function, excessive narcissism, poor peer relationships, extreme passivity, or internalized disordered relationships to the derivatives of sexual and aggressive drives—both parents should be briefed on the situation before therapeutic recommendations are made so that the trio of parents and therapist can work in concert from the beginning.

There are several indications of the need for psychotherapy which are agreed upon by parent and child: frequent teasing, beatings, and penalization by peers which the child provokes in an uncontrolled (unconscious) manner; preoccupations with thoughts about death; pathological mourning; and poor school performance without reasonable explanation. Phobias, fear fantasies, and obsessions would seem to fit into this group. However, the child often hides these symptoms or deals with them by assuming that they will go away just as colds will go away. The child's approach to psychotherapy and emotional discomforts is guided by his own limited previous experiences with illness. In addition, the phobic or obsessional child often views the therapist as an intruder. The discovery of, or reemergence of, such symptoms often galvanizes parents to seek help. They use adult criteria in evaluating psychopathology. The diagnostician must counter this tendency and place in perspective a host of impressions, doubts, motivations, and anxieties so that he may lead the family to the appropriate approach to the treatment. For instance, phobias and obsessional symptoms can be transient in latency age children. The presence of other pathological signs is needed before therapy is recommended. For instance, a nine-year-old girl insisted that her room be searched, a light be on in the hall, and all closets in her room be closed before she could go to sleep. Therapy was recommended for her. This was not on the basis of the presenting symptoms alone, which served the diagnostician only as guides to chronic underlying pathology. These symptoms were transient in the child. The chief complaints vanished after the first interview. Of more lasting concern was her long-standing inability to go anywhere alone. In the movies or watching television the child needed a companion with whom to validate consensually any ambiguous event on the screen. Otherwise, she thought of the "worst" (scary things).

When visiting relatives in Alabama she appeared to be able to travel without a substitute object. The distance between her relatives' home and her home in Arizona was great; she had to leave her stuffed animals at home. Here looks deceived. She was not really able to give up her objects with such ease wherever she went. She located smooth cloth objects which she could convert into a comforting substitute for her substitute objects. Being without a companion produced in her fear of terrible thoughts and things (unnamed) happening. Her ability to shift from one substitute object to another hid the intensity of her need for her childhood fetish. In this child, transient fears were not the reason for recommending therapy. The sustained apprehension and sense of dread that was stilled by manipulating companions and substitute objects was the reason for recommending treatment.

At times a parent brings a child for treatment because of misinterpretations of the child's behavior which are based on the parent's own emotional problems. One should look for this possibility. A most striking example that illustrates this parental misinterpretation is provided by the case of a nubile thirteen-year-old girl who had recently returned to live with her widowed mother after six years in a convent school. Though the child was naive in sexual matters as a result of a relatively secluded childhood, her mother was convinced that the girl was in need of psychiatric treatment because of the youngster's "promiscuity." The mother had already obtained three electroconvulsive treatments for her daughter and had come to a city hospital emergency room seeking more shock treatments at a lower price. The examining residents could identify no psychopathology in the child, who had not been out of the convent for a long enough period to establish a definable behavior pattern. The child was virginal. An interview with the mother revealed that the mother had had recent weight loss, depression on arising, disturbed sleep, and restless agitation. A diagnosis of involutional depression-paranoid type was made. The "promiscuity" for which the child had been treated was a delusion of the mother; it was part of her major psychosis. When this possibility was suggested to the mother, she took her daughter and ran from the emergency room.

Notwithstanding the fact that it may be a parent's distorting pathology that brings a child to a psychiatrist, the possibility of pathology in such a child cannot be ignored. Contact with an emotionally troubled parent places a child at risk for emotional problems of his own. The following case bears witness to this. A divorced woman in her early forties brought her eleven-year-old son for evaluation because he was "paranoid" about her handling of him. She was aware of being irritable a good deal of the time. This caused her to shout at him and punish him in response to minor provocation. His older brother was a passive, quiet sort; he was far less rambunctious than the patient. He therefore did not attract his mother's ire or draw down her wrath as did her younger son. The difference in punishment and privilege became great at times. This gap did not elude the sharp eye of the younger brother, who accused his mother of treating him differently and unfairly. Such were the roots of his "paranoia." The nondelusional nature of his allegations was quickly clarified during the evaluation. The child was not free of emotional problems. In addition to her irritability, the mother had difficulty coping with her own drives and feelings. Social situations that evoked sexual responses activated withdrawal and feelings of estrangement from the group. These defensive patterns in the mother were replicated in the child's own relationship to his peers. Although he had friends, did well in sports, and was well accepted in team activities, he felt out of place when his friends told sexual jokes or talked about their sexual fantasies. He described the situation that created these feelings in the following words:

A lot of kids on my block use bad language and "make fingers." They have all kinds of funny ideas, like they want to have babies with girls. You can die from that. A girl in California busted her rib cage with a baby—it's all right if you are older or are married—at our age it's dirty—that's what they talk about and everything.

Fantasies of injury and damage related to sex, coupled with the view of the whole thing as dirty, are not unusual at this age. They reflect a stage to be resolved. The boy's move toward disengagement from his peers and his dawning asceticism in the face of his distortions required psychotherapeutic work to help him to understand himself, sexuality, and his feelings and turn him toward solving the problems of adolescence. Most important of all in indicating a need for therapy was the youngster's expressed wish, told during the initial interview, that he be permitted to return to talk about things and clear up the ideas that bothered him.

In evaluating a child for the long-range implications of personality pathology, the key phenomenon seen in childhood which portends future troubles is interference with function or object relations by internalized personality structures (both fantasy structures and ego structures). The term *internalized* is used to describe psychological phenomena which influence behavior without regard to immediate environmental or social factors. No matter what the circumstance, setting, or clime, the child responds according to preset internalized patterns. Although these patterns may have been learned as the result of past interactions with parents, changes in present-day behavior in the parent alone do not lead to changes in the internalized patterns which influence the child's behavior. Internalized behavior patterns are the precipitates of past interactions. Their form is a matter closed to influence from current relationships. This includes relationships which involve the individuals who took part in the situation in which the internalized patterns were acquired. Because of the internal nature of these patterns, ordinary counseling aimed at improving the parent-child relationship through modifying parental behavior avails little in stopping the behavior. It can, however, result in the cessation of parental activity that supports continuation of the internalized behavior. Psychotherapy is indicated for the child if internalized psychological structures and fantasies control the child's behavior. The pattern has to be demonstrated to the child, analyzed, and worked through for the child to be relieved of this markedly disabling psychological characteristic. Some structured patterns undergo a spontaneous resolution. Resolution of symptoms accompanies this.

One point should be made clear: the fact that a psychic phenomenon involves internalized elements does not necessarily imply a pathological state. The superego which is motivated by guilt is necessary for normal functioning. There is, by definition, a strong element of internalization involved. The contents of the superego are acquired through the internalization of demands gathered in large part through interactions with parents, peers, and society.

A pathological state is considered present when internalized patterns produce predictable and repeated responses resulting in discomfort for the patient and others, or symptoms. In such circumstances, especially when the structured pattern is rarely known to undergo spontaneous resolution, the future impact of the child's structural impairment can best be alleviated through a psychotherapeutic approach involving direct work with the child. A good knowledge of developmental trends is important in determining the situations in which there is hope for spontaneous developmental resolution. A number of factors influencing spontaneous resolution are described in this book. For instance, in chapter 3 I describe a shift in manifest fantasy content in boys from homosexual objects to heterosexual objects associated with the first ejaculation, and resolution of conflicts over sexual identification in girls at menarche. In chapter 4 there is described the increased cathexis of reality and the future that occurs with late latency. In chapter 8 I examine the vicissitudes of the defense mechanism of projection during late latency and early adolescence, a process resulting in an alleviation of the routinely disquieting manifestations of projection that occur during the latency years. The effects of these developmental trends on the resolution of the pathology must be taken into account when evaluating the outcome of psychotherapy in late latency-early adolescence. These trends may produce results independent of therapy. On the other hand, one of the outcomes of a therapy which provides insight and discharge through fantasy is to provide a period of calm which will permit the child to negotiate these natural developmental stages of late childhood without emotional encumbrances.

In establishing a diagnosis, it is a generally accepted policy in child psychiatry to avoid classifying the behavior patterns of children as established disorders of character until after fifteen years of age. This reflects the clinical fact that internalized patterns do not assume unremitting control over social and emotional behavior until that age. For instance, the sado-masochistic personality would not be manifested continuously prior to this. Alternations occur between states of latency and periods of disordered activity during the latency period and late latency-early adolescence. These alternations relate to the intermittent appearance of the ego structure of latency in most youngsters during this developmental period. At some times the child directs sadistic aggression at peers or parents and shows many of the signs of sadomasochistic character formation. However, quiet patterns of behavior become dominant during the times when the structure of latency is active. Therefore the consistency of behavior required for the diagnosis of a neurotic character disorder is not sufficiently established.

Maturational vicissitudes in the defenses which make up the ego (see chapter 8 for the vicissitudes of projection) make the prediction of future behavioral patterns unreliable if such prediction is based upon relatively brief periods of observation and interview during the latency age. By the age of fifteen most of this maturational surge has passed. Then final adult character patterns remain. These are the product of the final developmental forms of internalized structures and established dominating organizations of defenses. We must therefore not look for clinical indications for psychotherapy in the child in terms of the fixed character patterns that represent pathology in the late adolescent and adult. Instead, indications for psychotherapy in the latency age child consist of immediate discomforts (e.g., phobias), imminent impairment to progress (fears associated with school, learning disabilities), states of disorder that will impede natural developmental trends (parental overstimulation, hyperexcited states, anxiety states), and the presence of internalized structures which would presage problems in later life, should they persist.

The two types of internalized structures which most tend to create emotional discomfort during the latency age period are fantasy structures and ego structures. Internalized fantasy structures refer to latent fantasies with representations in the system unconscious. The form with which such a fantasy is articulated with the world is far removed from its latent content. This is the result of the masking action of the symbolizing function. Often even the original situation which induced the latent fantasy is obscured by this process. By their nature, internalized fantasies persist and unremittingly influence the actions, reactions, expectations, and fears of the child, as well as those of the adult he will become. The multiplicity of manifest faces that a latent fantasy presents sometimes makes it difficult to recognize the many places in which it appears and the influences it has.

In providing examples to demonstrate the persistence of fantasy structures I will start with a behavior-influencing fantasy structure that showed little change over a period of twenty years. A boy was first brought to psychiatric attention at the age of eight. His mother had left to join his father who was in the service overseas. He had been left with an aunt, whom he knew little. She was appalled at his rejection by the neighborhood boys and at the cause of this rejection—the child's repeated play activity of cleansing and diapering dolls. His mother had offered no resistance to this behavior as well as no encouragement toward more assertive and masculine pursuits. The behavior persisted in spite of his aunt's attempts to intrude by throwing away the dolls and introducing a football, clay, and a baseball bat. He returned to his mother after four months. No psychotherapy was provided. At the age of twenty-two, he himself sought psychiatric consultation for a sexual problem. He was quite neat, soft-spoken, in no way effeminate. He was capable of fantasies about girls. However, his manifest sexual life was restricted to occasional homosexual contacts in which he achieved orgasm through passive anal penetration accompanied by a fantasy of being diapered after a bowel movement. His masturbation fantasy contained only the idea of being diapered by a woman.

The inherently pathological circumstance in persistent fantasy structures which influence behavior has two facets. From the point of view of the first facet, there is an ego configuration (pattern) which permits fantasy control over the motor sphere. In effect, the fantasy has executive power over the motor apparatus. This is a regressive pattern for an adult. In a latency state child this pattern typifies the ego structure of latency. The persistence into adult life of this pattern, which is normal for the latency state, is an attribute of one of the borderline psychotic clinical states of adulthood: narcissistic hypercathexis of fantasy. In deciding on the need for psychotherapy, the existence of an exaggeration of this state in a latency age child, that is, a state of omnipotentiality, should determine one's decision in favor of therapy. In making this decision, one should keep in mind that there is a normal phase of such hypercathexis of fantasy (fantasy gaining access to motility) which occurs in early adolescence (see chapter 3). This state is manifested in perversely tinged sexual acting out at that time.

An example of a state of omnipotentiality during the latency age period follows.

A ten-year-old boy appeared unable to function in the classroom setting in which he had been placed. Early in his academic career, he was found to be unable to progress at the rate expected; psychological testing had shown him to have above normal intelligence. An evaluation to detect cognitive defects was done. A mild defect in auditory discrimination and sequencing was found. A therapeutic regimen was undertaken aimed at remedying these defects, and progress was made in this area. However, as part of her report the special education teacher who had worked with the boy had indicated that progress had been slowed by the clowning behavior of the child, which took up much time. For instance, during one session the child slipped himself into the fireplace in the waiting area of the teacher's home/office. He insisted that he could not extricate himself and whined to be saved. All the while precious remediation time was being lost. The teacher removed the fire screen by way of demonstrating that there was no entrapment. Foiled, and much besooted but far from subdued, the youngster emerged to begin his truncated session. Once parents and teachers had been alerted to this behavior, his provocative teasing was seen to be everywhere in evidence. The child could pay little attention to studies as his mind wandered to fantasied or actual teasing of his peers. If he walked the classroom aisle, books fell. Other pupils repeatedly found themselves lightly punctured by his passing pencil. School, the reality, had no place in his scheme of things. The eagerness to help of teachers, parents, and peers was not developed into fulcrums toward success. Rather offers of aid became portals, joyously perceived in his excitement, for the issuing forth of his urge to tease and provoke. He was little aware of what he was doing. He cried repeatedly, "Why don't people like me!" When asked what he thought were the reactions of others to his behavior, he responded that they were entertained. He believed that they shared his enjoyment of the discharge of his excitement. In effect, school was not a place to learn but a theater in which his fantasies were played out. Center stage was wherever he stood.

Clearly there is a difference between the phenomena that dominate this child's life and the occasional playing out of fantasy that marks the state of latency. The state of omnipotence manifested in hypercathexis of fantasy at the expense of reality, which is illustrated here, is a pathological state that requires treatment not only for the present but for the future. Such exaggerated access to the motor apparatus will not be obliterated by the average expectable developmental trends. A state of omnipotence which puts fantasy ahead of reality in the child's scheme of things is a pathological state during the latency phase. Emphasis on fantasy as the means of relating to real events in all situations regardless of suitability is a pathological state. This state should be differentiated from fantasy's access to motility during play, a normal component of the structure of latency. After all, latency age play is appropriate only in certain situations. School is not one of those situations. Omnipotentiality interferes with the establishment of behavioral constancy. As such, hypercathexis of fantasy should be looked for in clinical situations in which behavioral constancy is impaired. Fantasy structures dominate when ego structures are organized to give the former sway over the motor apparatus. In this way fantasy influences behavior.

The second facet of the influence of internalized fantasy structures on behavior relates to the content of persistent internalized fantasies. Such fantasies impart a permanent coloration to the structure of the personal myth that shapes the events of a lifetime. The fantasy of being diapered, with its oral dependent and passive anal components, contributed elements of dependence and passivity to the character of the twenty-two-year-old patient described above.

Not all internalized fantasies are considered pathological. Were a child to play out internalized fantasies shaped from elements which are culturally defined as more mature, such as the desire to marry, have a baby, or succeed in adult competition, and should such a fantasy gain executive access to the motor sphere in adulthood, no imputations of pathology are considered.

Now we turn from internalized fantasy structures to the internalized mechanisms of defense which must be taken into consideration in evaluating a child for psychotherapy. These were referred to above as *ego structures*, a generic term used to refer to the psychic mechanisms that mediate the demands of the instincts (id), internalized social demands (superego), and the external world. Obviously, as in the case of internalized fantasy structures, internalization is not in itself a pathological characteristic for a defense. In fact, the opposite is the case. Failure to achieve typical, stabilized, and characteristic personality responses is a clinical indication of failure of internalization, which reflects a pathological state. It is only when an established personality structure guides the child to a trouble-associated obligatory response in a given situation that a pathological state exists. By way of example, the structure of latency, which consists of a group of defenses (repression, displacement, fragmentation, symbolization, and so on), provides a healthy safety valve for the latency age child. It makes it possible for the mechanisms of restraint (sublimation, obsessive-compulsive activities, doing and undoing, reaction-formations, and repression) to produce a psychological state of calm, pliability, and educability. This helps the child to adapt to a world that requires social compliance and periods of calm in which knowledge can be acquired. In addition, these mechanisms serve to channel the child's drives. The latency age child is too small physically to express his aggressive drive effectively in his relationships with adult caretakers. Latency age children are, with few exceptions, maturationally incapable of achieving orgasm or ejaculation and are therefore physically incapable of expressing sexual drives effectively through the direct use of a primary orgasm and physiological apparatus for discharge. Regression (see chapter 2) and the defenses described serve as the primary technique for coping with the sexual drives during the latency period. Fantasy, reaction-formation, and carefully monitored socially accepted behavior patterns (such as school recess and athletics) become the primary outlets for the drives. The latency age child who has been able to achieve a satisfactory emotional equilibrium through the use of these mechanisms of defense is using internalized ego structures and is said to be functioning well.

An eight-year-old girl, for example, was thrown into a social situation in which an acceptable play period involving male peer playmates became part of the routine. Specifically, her parents took her for co-ed riding lessons each Saturday. The lesson ended earlier than any of the parents could return for the children. The children, including two boys and the one girl, were directed to play together until the parents came to pick them up. Excited games such as tag and hide-and-seek stimulated the girl. She confided to her mother that one of the boys was her boyfriend. Sexual excitement during and after the game overrode the child's capacity to cope consciously. It was the child's unconscious internal pattern of response to process the incoming sexual stimulation by mobilizing aggressive feelings. No amount of advice could change this. The response occurred quickly, and the child was both unaware of it and had no conscious control of it. This was truly a pattern of response based on an internal psychic mechanism. Because of the strength of her structure of latency, this internalized pattern of response did not interfere with her adjustment or her ability to function in school. She deflected the sexual and aggressive excitement from her everyday practical life into her play life. She produced a fantasy in which boys and girls playing by the side of a swimming pool pushed each other into the pool. Thus she was able to experience, through fantasy, heterosexual excitement modified by the addition of a sadistic play element. Ordinarily peers of the same sex are chosen as playmates during the latency age in order to minimize the possibility of just such stirring of sexual feelings. When this pattern was interfered with, a distancing mechanism using masking symbols was activated so that the child could continue to enjoy the relationship while hiding its true meaning.

Should the level of stimulation exceed the ability of the ego to mask through fantasy, the structure of latency can fail. The result of this failure is action which reflects the internalized fantasy structures of the child. In such cases, psychotherapy is necessary to resolve the fantasy structures, strengthen the ego structures, and modify the reality stresses.

The structure of latency is universally present in children who can attain a state of latency. Failure to attain or maintain this state indicates pathology. A psychotherapeutic approach is indicated at the time trouble occurs. Such failure is manifested in distortion and acting out of latent fantasies and regressions. This relates to regression in both content (e.g., the appearance of oral devouring fantasies) and actions (eating and getting fat, for example, or stealing, if a robber fantasy has been part of the child's play). Deterioration of the state of latency often brings to the surface internal patterns of defense mechanisms that will contribute to the defense patterns of adult life. As such, behavior produced by a deteriorated state of latency should be evaluated for therapeutic indications, even if this state is the apparent result of correctable environmental pressures.

By way of example, consider the case of a ten-year-old boy who had been in psychotherapy for over a year because of daydreaming and distractibility while in the classroom. This had interfered with his schoolwork. He had made good progress as a result of playing out his fantasies in the therapy sessions and understanding their role in his reaction to home and school situations. All at once, he was reported to be involved in fights in the schoolyard. He blamed the fights on the other boys, who said he provoked them. At about this time, he had begun to spill watercolor paint on the therapist "by accident." In the sessions he tried to anger the therapist. Two factors were involved in the production of this behavior. First, there was a reality stress. An uncle had moved into his home for a stay of a few months' duration. This uncle shared his room. Investigation revealed that the uncle often teased the child. Second, there was an influence from his internal ego structures. In response to the stress situation, the mechanisms of the structure of latency had failed. The child regressed to the use of a mechanism of defense, actualization, to deal with his feelings. Removing the uncle could remove the cause for the reaction but not the potential for using actualization. The dynamics of actualization in this child must be understood before we can pursue this problem further. In essence, the child, in being teased and displaced by the uncle, had had reawakened within him feelings of loss and anger that he had felt both with the birth of a sibling and in the oedipal situation in which he had been displaced by his father. Aggression associated with these situations distorted the intensity of the aggression that he felt realistically in response to the teasing of the uncle. This child had great difficulty in becoming aware of, accepting, and dealing with angry feelings within himself. From the time he was four years old he feared intruders when it was dark. The aggression of the intruders was not his aggression, as he saw it. He clung to this view in spite of the fact that there was no other source for the affects by which he expressed his feeling that there was aggression in the air. As he grew older and more reality oriented with the approach of late latency, he shifted his assignment of aggression to real people. Except for the uncle, there was no one who truly behaved in a manner that could be considered aggressive. There were many, however, who could be induced to do so in response to some provocation. The child proceeded to work on these people by way of making actual the affective experience that he had that someone was angry. In this way he justified his feelings of hurt while bypassing the necessity to accept and deal with his own anger.

Should a child be brought for evaluation and such a process be identified as part of the internalized structure of the child's personality, it is incumbent on the examiner to recommend a psychotherapeutic approach that will help the child become aware of his anger and gain more positive mechanisms for dealing with it throughout life, as well as to counsel the parents about the influence of external stressful events on the child's behavior.

With the above example we complete our brief comment on the diagnostic process in the initiation of a psychotherapeutic approach in the latency age child and turn to the problems of motivation for therapy during the initial period of psychotherapy.

Problems of Motivation in Psychotherapy in the Latency State

A majority of children entering psychotherapy have no real idea of why they are there. Except for their interest in relief of symptoms, children are little concerned with the psychotherapeutic goals of the therapist. This is a most unusual circumstance in a psychotherapy. For instance, with the psychotherapy of adults it is customary to believe that one can only help someone who wants help in dealing with the roots of his problems. We call such a therapeutic orientation "psychological mindedness." This is ill applied to children who mainly seek relief of symptoms and a lessening of pressure from parents. Children are far from being psychologically minded. All things taken into account, therapeutic contacts with children continue only for as long as the parent is motivated to have them continue. This is one of the primary reasons that the therapist's contact with parents in a parallel therapeutic or consultatory capacity is required with latency age children if treatment is to progress to a successful conclusion.

The need to work through problems does not provide sustained motivation in children. Symptom discomfort itself can be vitiated by the defensive use of fantasy, which distracts the child's attention. It is necessary to bring the reason for therapy repeatedly into the focus of the therapeutic situation. This may be done either through questioning at the beginning of sessions or through interpreting the relationship of the child's play fantasies to the problems that have brought the child to treatment. One of the most therapeutically influential activities of the therapist who works with children who are capable of producing a state of latency consists of countermanding the structure of latency. Both conflicts and memories associated with high charges of affect find masked expression in the manifest fantasies of the state of latency. It is in these fantasies that they hide. Through a process utilizing symbols which have other meanings, their import is masked to such an extent that the affects of anxiety, guilt, humiliation, and shame which motivate therapy are lost to consciousness. This dilution of motivating affects by the production of fantasy is not without impact on the therapeutic situation. Through this process the possibility of working through, recognizing, and modifying affect-laden misconceptions inherent in the latent fantasy content is lost. The correcting and validating effects of verbal communication cannot be brought to bear. Latency play, though quite informative in psychotherapeutic situations, becomes counterproductive once its living through and discharge functions have been served. Technically it is necessary to work back from the fantasy to the words of the original conflict and then to work that through psychotherapeutically. The more a child has achieved a shift from the structure of latency toward verbalization and self-appreciation, the greater will be the possibility of spending greater amounts of session time in conceptually oriented discussions rather than in the defensive world of latency state play, which dilutes therapeutic productiveness.

The purpose of fantasy produced by the structure of latency is to give the child relief from the problems that he faces. When the child is encouraged to fantasize and play during the therapy session, he is in effect being encouraged to reduce the pressure, the worry, and the anxiety that could become motivating factors in bringing uncomfortable fantasies and conflicts into the session. Thus, while discharging drives, he avoids dealing with underlying problems and recalling stresses of the day. This role for fantasies, coupled with the support derived from the relationship with the therapist, often produces rather rapid movements without insight in children in psychotherapy. These improvements usually last only as long as the treatment lasts. On the basis of these transient improvements, premature discharge from therapy is often considered. This should be avoided. Parents should be warned of the possibility of rapid movement followed by return to the old symptomatology soon after leaving treatment. If any lasting result is to be achieved it is essential that parent and therapist discuss the nature of the underlying psychopathology and focus upon its resolution as a therapeutic endpoint rather than as a symptom cure.

A clinical example of just such a premature discharge follows. An eleven-year-old boy repeatedly broke windows in his school. When scolded by a teacher he became very angry. He could contain the anger but could not discharge it in fantasy. Instead, seemingly at the suggestion of another youngster, he broke windows. Dynamically speaking, he had great difficulty in accepting his anger as his own. He was able to externalize the source of his bad behavior by blaming it on another child. With this arrangement he permitted himself to act out his anger and break windows. The child was able to achieve transient control of this behavior during his first therapy sessions through the use of play. He played out scenes with the therapist in which he experienced his anger as an affect belonging to the therapist. He presumed that the therapist was angry with him after he had tried to provoke anger in the therapist. He actualized his anger in the therapeutic situation, and during the course of the treatment he used this technique to discharge anger. Such activities as breaking windows became unnecessary. The improvement in his functioning produced a decision to terminate treatment.

No understanding of the underlying dynamic was provided to the youngster during the treatment. There was therefore no structural change at the time that he left therapy. Parent and therapist had determined the date of termination on the basis of the fact that the child hadn't broken any windows for six months and that the end of the school year was approaching. The boy had to return to therapy within two weeks after termination when he started breaking windows again. The child was unaware of the internal structural defects that permitted him to destroy property seemingly without provocation. For this reason he did not object when his discharge was planned on the basis of symptom relief rather than a more far-reaching resolution.

At times, the therapist does not even have symptom discomfort as a thin base for cooperation in the patient. A child sometimes comes into therapy apparently oblivious to the reason that he is there. In some way, he may know, but he chooses to avoid confronting the anxiety and shame associated with the manifest problem. Such children find no reason to cooperate in the treatment. Many complain bitterly. Others nonchalantly lose themselves in the toys of the playroom and, with the help of the structure of latency, distance themselves from the core of their problems as far and as fast as fantasy can carry them. Both types of response are examples of resistance to therapy, whether on the surface patients present themselves as overdefiant or as overcompliant.

The overdefiant child points to the many other important things that he has on his schedule which are interfered with by the psychotherapy. The overcompliant child looks forward to the sessions as a place for relief of tension, instead of as a place to seek insight. Rarely do overcompliant children permit interruptions of their fantasy play to allow for discussion of problems.

The overdefiant child in therapy is usually involved at home in angry power struggles with parents which revolve around control of activity and freedom of movement for the child. The parents define the child's demands as pathological. The child sees the situation only in terms of deprivation of his needs on the part of the parents. In such a case, the child will surely not define the difficulty as his own in the initial contacts with the therapist. There is therefore small hope of reaching the child's role in the power struggle directly. Since the origins of the problem are in the internal workings of the personality structure of the child, a way is provided out of this seemingly insoluble psychotherapeutic situation. A problem needing psychotherapy which has internalized structural roots can be expected to surface in the behavior of the child in the psychotherapeutic situation. Verbalization is not necessary at first. This being the case, what the therapist need do is wait until the child begins to bring demands into the therapy sessions and starts to lose control of his anger with the therapist. When this happens, the similarity of the situation to the problem with the parent should be interpreted and the problem for which therapy is being sought defined for the child. The undeniable fact that the reaction is occurring during the session gives support to the interpretation. Once the problem has been defined in the session, the degree of cooperation does not immediately improve. The child usually continues to duck the issue. However, the reason for treatment has been mutually experienced and verbalized. No matter what happens henceforth, there is a tacit mutual awareness of the reason for treatment. Even in those children who have a desire to cooperate, great difficulty in free associating and approaching problems directly continues. This can be overcome by harnessing the active symbolizing function of the latency state child to the elaboration of the problem. Children can circumvent their difficulty in free associating by using the ability to fantasize. Through fantasy a multitude of symptoms and symbolic elements can be brought into the treatment. In order to encourage this with the overdefiant child whose basic problems have been exposed in therapy, I choose to say to the child, "Do you have any make-believes about that?" Hopefully this encourages the child in the production of fantasy. At best, overdefiant children remain ambivalent about working in treatment for months on end. Progress is possible because the therapist can learn a certain amount from the child's fantasy play and complaints about having to come to treatment. What follows is a description of ongoing sessions with an overdefiant youngster who uses fantasy. The techniques of focusing the fantasy material in terms of the child's conflicts and problems are illustrated.

Peter was a nine-year-old boy who was brought to treatment by his mother for "shiftiness and dishonesty." As his mother put it, she could not leave him alone. This was not because of fear that he was in danger, but because of her fear of what he might do to the house or its contents. He had already sold treasured family heirlooms to passing junk dealers. The sessions presented here took place under the shadow of a recent blowup in the home. The mother had noticed that a five-dollar bill was missing from her purse. When she asked her son about this and threatened to search him, he replied, "I was only testing to see if you would notice. I would have given the money back no matter what." The incident had been discussed in the previous session.

The child entered the therapy room flipping a coin. He looked at me and said, "Heads I talk; tails I play." He flipped the coin. It came up heads. He scrutinized the coin carefully, checking, as he said, "to be sure that there was a tail." He then decided to flip again. The coin, freely flipped, came up heads five times in a row. At first he was bewildered. Then a smile crossed his face. He began flipping the coin ostensibly to determine whether he would become "chief, president, king, Pope, emperor, god, god of heaven, god of hell, god of everything." Heads would win for him. With each flip, the coin came up tails until it came up heads on the last flip. As "king of the world," he stopped flipping and sat down. He put his feet on my desk, and said, "You can go to hell. I hope you drown. Tell my mother to take me home. Tell her I'm all better. She'll believe you." He looked down and noting that his pants were unzipped proceeded to zip them up. He then adjusted his belt exposing his underwear. He then announced that he was going to order the president of the United States and the premier of Russia to force the world to make peace. I pointed out his efforts to control the treatment through flipping the coin and ordering me to lie to his mother. I ended with the comment, "When it's not me you are trying to control, whom would you like to control?" "My parents," he muttered, "my mother and my father when they tell me to do my homework." "And you feel that way with me when you feel I'm insisting that you work in the session," added I. He fell into silence. "Any make-believes?" I asked. He ordered me to give him some toy guns. I remained where I was. "You're a pain," said he as he moved to the table where the toy guns lay. "Okay, here comes a show," said he. "Do you write this stuff down after?" "Sometimes," I said. "Why?" he asked. "So I can compare them," I remarked. Keeping in mind that when he asked a question he was willing to listen to the answer, I added some interpretive material to my answer so as to focus his activities in the session on his problems. "For instance," said I, "sometimes you tell stories about an unconscious girl and sometimes you're the one who is unconscious." He responded, "I often wonder what it would be like to be an unconscious girl. I want to tell my story now." He unfolded a fantasy of a thief, "the makeup master," who could change all his features and slip into places to rob undetected. While stealing, the makeup master is caught and, as had happened in many tellings of the tale before, is beaten unconscious. After a few moments without moving, he returns to life and patches his wound with scotch tape. He then draws a gun and shoots his attackers. He retrieves the stolen money and, concealing it in his clothes, leaves the locale of the robbery. As the makeup master walks through the streets to his home, a passing pickpocket takes the loot from his pocket leaving him no richer for all his efforts. The session ended.

In the next session, he began by telling me a joke. "What is the definition of a hypocrite?" he asked. He waited for my answer. When none came, he gave the definition, "It's someone who smiles going to school." "What does that mean to you?" I asked. "That's what my mother would like me to be," he responded. I pointed out the struggle he had with her over his actions. He didn't respond directly to me, exclaiming, "I didn't hear all that you said! I don't want to talk anymore. I want to make up a story now." (Note the switch into a defensive fantasy in response to a direct approach to his differences with his parents.) He pulled half a dozen balloons from his pocket and announced, "I'm the balloon master." He blew up balloons. He burst them or let them fly about under their own power. As this activity proceeded he called the balloons cars and rocket ships and wove gangster stories about their movements. In his mounting excitement, he took one balloon to the playroom sink. He filled it with water. Then he carried it to the center of the playroom floor and threatened to drop it on the rug if I did not tell his mother immediately that the analysis was over. I pointed out to him his use of teasing as a way of controlling others. He dropped the balloon in the sink saying, "The balloon man's gone crazy." I interpreted the frightening feeling that he has when he gets angry and feels that he is going out of control. Thus the session ended.

He began the next session by pulling a dozen balloons from his pocket. He filled some with air and rubbed them to produce some static electricity. When this was achieved, he stuck them high on the wall. He jumped repeatedly to see if he could flip them to a higher position. As he played, he announced that he planned to skip school the following Friday. I pointed out that he chose to play instead of going to school, just as here he plays instead of dealing with his problems directly. "So what?" said he, "School isn't everything. If I work hard at what I'm doing I can be the biggest man with balloons in the world." "You want to be big, grown-up?" I asked. "Yeah, without waiting," said he. (Notice that the distraction of playing at jumping high contained an element of his own wishes. He wanted to be tall and grown-up. Communication on a verbal plane brought these feelings into an area of conscious awareness that was shared by both patient and therapist.) "Why?" I asked. "What does being grown-up mean to you?" "Grown-ups get married," he quickly rejoined, "a grown-up can have a girl friend and kiss her at night and never be alone." (The fantasy of being grown-up was a way of dealing with a feeling of loneliness.) I asked if he could tell me more of his lonely feelings with thoughts about grown-ups being together at night. "I don't have any of those feelings anymore," he said, "I have lots of friends to call." His words denied his true feelings. However, the true depth of his affective reaction was disclosed by the fact of mobilization of one of the latency mechanisms of restraint—the obsessional mechanisms. He took out a coin and began to flip it endlessly in search of an impossible series of flips that could come up nine heads in a row. In this way he distracted himself from and controlled his affects. Once this coin-flipping had taken on a ritual-like quality, I interpreted the resistance involved in flipping in the context of its dynamic purpose. I pointed out that ideas of magic power over the turn of a coin came up when he felt alone, little, and weak. His defiance of his mother was interpreted as an attempt to master such weak feelings in response to her strong demands. He responded, "You're right, completely right." He hardly held to the thought for a moment before he turned to telling a story he had read of a man who was so perverse that he turned into a black cat. He then played out a game in which he cut himself with a make-believe knife. Following this he turned to breaking balloons. He fantasied that as the balloons exploded, buildings were exploding. I pursued his feeling of anger and noted how he hurt himself when he felt weak and small. He listened, but then turned to the balloons again. This time in exploding the balloon, he said that he was blowing up the world and himself. There the session ended, but not the treatment. Though insights that penetrated beyond his resistances were uncovered for him, the pain of awareness did not permit him to gaze too long upon his conflicts and his inner needs. Defenses and resistances were reasserted. In spite of this, such repeated intrusion into the innermost castle-keep of his emotions would in time permit exploration and working through of his reactions to his mother, to situations of weakness and smallness, and to oedipal situations in which he felt himself to be the lonely, left-out one. With this approach, eventually he would be able to understand himself and no longer need defenses which, while quelling intrusions from past experiences, interfered with his pursuit of the present.

Not infrequently one is confronted with the challenge that treatment of so resistant a child is a waste of time or the criticism that the child who rejects therapy so strongly has a right to be left alone. There is even the question of the degree of forbearance to be expected of the therapist. The answer to these criticisms was provided by this child who, during termination of his treatment, once stopped near the door to my office at session's end and said, "I don't know how many times I've walked through this door. I know that many of the times as I did I cursed you, threw things, and said I'd never come back. Still, no matter how many times I said bad things, you always knew that inside here I was saying 'Please help me.' Thanks for that." He pointed to his heart as he walked away.

Now we turn our attention to the child who is overcompliant in his presentation of fantasies. Only too willingly does the overcompliant child spin out his fantasies by the ream. The session becomes the place to discharge tension. Insights for the therapist and ideas tumble forth as a result of a multitude of stories told and played out by the child. As the stories go on, often latent content replaces the comfortable and familiar early manifest contents of the fantasy. So much effort often results in little therapeutic gain. The child in his rush to fantasy has no time to spend in understanding.

For instance, a seven-year-old child had been excluded from his school because of his preoccupation with fires and fire setting. He stole matches from his home and, when that became impossible, from the kitchens of neighbors. Once he had entered the playroom, he immediately embarked on a rich unfolding of fantasies. He seized upon doll figures which represented comic strip heroes and began to tell a story, repeated with variations each day of a boy hero who fought for good things only to find himself thrown off a balcony. He was not killed. Rather, he caught onto a rope just in time and was held suspended next to a wall with his legs almost touching the ground. The youngster then ran a toy car up to the boy hero. The door of the car was opened. Then it was closed on the leg of the hero. This activity could all be explained as the result of a putting together of toys that were available. On the other hand, a castration fear could be postulated to lie behind the actively produced fantasy. The latter seemed more to the point when the content of the fantasy was changed from the closing of the door of a conveniently available toy car on the hero's foot to the biting off of the foot by a crocodile. The therapist directly associated this information with the child's preoccupation with fire. The child's castration fear was defended against by a counterphobic attempt at mastery of fire. This is a nice theory. However, it is of little value without some confirmatory material derived from elaborations of the original fantasy by the child. In order to focus the fantasy-bound child on this topic, an interpretation is necessary. I have come across a remarkable variety of formats recommended for interpretive comments to be used in bringing such a conclusion to a child's attention. Some practitioners recommend a rather direct and deep approach such as "You put that in the story because you are afraid your penis will be cut off." This approach is not aimed at eliciting a confirmatory response. The therapist expects only to be able better to observe further derivatives of the castration fear fantasy after saying this. The derivatives serve as confirmatory signs. Another less formidable approach entails suggesting to the child that he is concerned with injury. Whatever may be said when the therapist interprets or relates fantasies to a child's problems in a way that interrupts the fantasy flow, the overcompliant child reveals his state of resistance either by ignoring the therapist or by stopping to say, "I don't want to talk about that now." This may result in a cessation of fantasy and the loss of fantasy as a defense. There may be activation of aggression toward the therapist or his playroom.

Whatever style of approach one uses in interpreting fantasy, it is well to keep in mind the realization that fantasy is a defense. A child escapes meaning by plunging into fantasy. When a child cannot talk about a problem directly and is encouraged to fantasize, all of the defensive potential of the structure of latency is mobilized. As a result, though the therapist gains access to conflicts, they are not seen so clearly by the child. Symbols proclaim all and hide all, all at once. Because of this, should the uninterrupted elaboration of fantasies be desired, there is value in entering the fantasy in such a way that the flow is not interfered with. One way of doing this has been illustrated above (see p. 200). It consists of asking a character in the story to tell more about what is going on, including his feelings and thoughts. Those given to more rugged interpretations at the beginning of treatment with a child often decry such an approach as timid.

It is. However, there is method in this restraint-oriented tack. It encourages the elaboration of the fantasies without risking interruptions or aggressive outbursts. The child who unknowingly discloses the conflicts hidden in his fantasy is often stunned into silence or overt aggression by an interpretation that is deep, accurate, and overly revealing. The alternative to overcompliant fantasy as a resistance in a latency age child is not always verbal insight seeking. It can be silence. In initiating play therapy, I prefer to explore the child's responses to interpretation with care. One should start with the least intrusive approaches. The idea is to increase information without blocking a vital communicative pathway open to children—fantasy.

Fantasy play per se as a means of communication harbors resistance to therapeutic insight. Culturally positive aspects of the development and use of fantasies in latency age children have negative implications for psychotherapy, for they can become the basis of resistance. For instance, the transmission of culture during the latency period is strongly tinged with passive symbolizations. The child is provided with ready-made fantasies (culture elements) into which he can tuck his conflicts (personal elements) with hardly a seam to show. The culture elements in the fantasies a child tells in psychotherapy sessions can dominate the personal elements to the point that the personal elements are submerged and become inaccessible. A child with a preoccupation with the "family romance" can retell the story of Superman's arrival from the planet Krypton and adoption here on earth repeatedly without change or cease. The child's private fantasy of being the son of royalty who has been adopted by his mother and father stands tantalizingly before the therapist, yet out of reach. The fantasy spins on, endlessly turning, conveying all, yielding nothing. It is necessary to intrude into the fantasy function of the child to the extent that elements of the child's own creation can become part of the fantasy play of the sessions. In this way responsibility for content may be assigned to the wishes, often unconscious, of the child. The uniform and universal mask of culture is thus gently eased away revealing the many faces of fear. How is this to be done? Fantasy elements based on such culture elements as superheroes and movie characters which produce a repetitive return to the same tale can be deemphasized by stressing any element that the child seems to have introduced on his own. Such spontaneous variations usually appear after a few weeks. For instance, when the fire-preoccupied child modified his story to introduce leg-biting crocodiles, the therapist did not let the new elements pass quickly from sight. He asked about them. He encouraged the child to draw a picture of them. He then cut out the figures the child had drawn and glued them to a piece of board. The board was then equipped with a little tab so that it could stand. In this way the culture-locked child was encouraged to use his own imagined figures transmuted into concrete form as the basis for storytelling and fantasy elaboration. Dream reporting can also be encouraged in a child in this way.

Even when the child is involved with fantasy production which seems related to the conflict areas, the therapist is continually confronted with resistance related to the defensive potential of manifest fantasy. The therapist must be ever on the alert to the possibility that the latency state child may move his fantasies away from the problem area toward quiet pastures and a more comfortable zone of existence. It is necessary, therefore, to find ways to bring the child's fantasies back to the problem area. This is most conveniently done by commenting on a conflict-related element in the child's personal fantasy or by formulating a question which will unobtrusively bring the child back to a pursuit of an understanding of his problems. As the underlying conflicts become more apparent, the phrasing of the questions can be more direct. In this way interpretations in depth are achieved. Lack of immediate response to these comments is no indication of failure to hear or be influenced by the comments. Changes in the activity of the child are the results for which one should be on the alert. It is wise to watch the fantasy production of the child and to study the dynamics of the changes in fantasies which are produced as a result of therapeutic interventions. Subtle changes reflective of transference, school problems, and pressures from home may also be detected through careful attention to variations in details as fantasies are repeated.

The influence of interpretation of transference, of home, and of school on the content of fantasy is illustrated by the following series of sessions involving an eight-year-old girl's emotional response to the arrival of a new maid in her home. She had been telling of her fear of the coming of the maid for about a week, but she evidenced delight at the help the new maid would offer. She was especially delighted that the maid would be expected to take over some of the household cleaning chores that were ordinarily hers. In the session before, she had reported a dream in which she presented her preoccupation with the decreased availability of parents when there is a maid in the house. In the dream, the maid escorted her to my office instead of her mother. Then she dreamed that her father had died and as a result she couldn't continue with her therapist. The thought of the arrival of a new caretaker activated dreams which disclosed her easily roused fears of loss of or desertion by close supporting family members and the therapist.

On the day the fantasy we will focus on began, the maid had arrived. She was described by the child as nice. However, her heavily accented English made her difficult for the child to relate to at first and intensified the girl's uncertainties. "I can't really tell," she said, "how she'll turn out. The thing to look for in a good maid is if when your parents go out you can stay up later and watch TV. It's also good if she cleans for you so you don't have to make your own bed." She recalled that she had told me a dream in the session before, but could not remember the content. She tried to recall it for a moment and then went over to her coat and pulled a lion cub puppet named Jimmy from her pocket. Jimmy as she used him had a distinct personality. He talked baby talk, pouted, and repeatedly went into rages at an adult character who was also played in the fantasy by the little girl. In one sequence which ended in pouting, the puppet played with a half-inflated blue balloon. For no apparent reason, he suddenly insisted that the blue balloon be replaced by another. The exaggerated rages of the puppet were similar to behavior the patient herself had shown. She became angry and started to pout over insubstantial slights when she felt insecure in new situations. She became so involved with the puppet fantasy that she had little energy for reflection. The therapist interpreted the child's feelings of insecurity and her fears of the untrustworthiness of her loved objects, which were reflected in the puppet's demands to control and replace toys at will. The similarity of the puppet's behavior to her own behavior was pointed out. Provocative attempts to dominate by using irrelevant demands such as the demand for a different-colored balloon were interpreted to her in the following words: "Jimmy makes up demands for fake changs just like you used to do when you felt out of control of adults." Note that her current problem related to doubt about the role of the new maid in her life. The child's response to the interpretation was, "Only with my parents it didn't work." She immediately changed the stance of the adult in the fantasy. Instead of depriving Jimmy the lion cub, she granted him of all of his wishes. The therapist pointed out, "That's the way you would have liked it for yourself. If you could get whatever you wanted you took that as a sign you were loved." She readily agreed and turned the half-inflated balloon so that the nipple-like projection at its end went into the mouth of the puppet. "He likes it!" she yelled. "He looks just like a baby being fed." She alternated feeding the puppet and having the puppet yell for a new balloon. In the middle of her excitement, she stopped and began to complain that she felt a hair in her mouth. The therapist immediately pointed out to her that this feeling was her own wish to suck, a wish which she had given the puppet and that now had returned to her. It was explained that the demanding and the anger were her reactions to disappointment in her parents. The wish to suck to comfort herself was another way of dealing with this disappointment. She then reported to the therapist that she still sucked her thumb, though her mother didn't know. "Sometimes, I bite it, too," she said, "at night when I'm alone. I've done it as long as I can remember." She described no fantasies while sucking, only a sense of comfort.

In the next session she brought in the puppet again. She had almost forgotten to bring him. She began to feed Jimmy the cub, and he continued to talk baby talk, to threaten, cajole, and to yell. No matter what balloon was offered, he demanded another one from the adult, who was acted by the patient. In this session the adult was called "the teacher." Once the balloon was hidden by the teacher. The puppet threatened to "tell Mommy" how mean the teacher was being. From that point on, any demand was filled by the teacher, even to the making of a make-believe tree of balloons. The therapist said, "That's the way you want to be treated when you feel let down and alone." The child responded by explaining that this is ordinary behavior in nursery school. The therapist was preparing to ask about memories of lonely feelings in the nursery school when the child abruptly modified the content of the fantasy play to convey just these feelings of aloneness. Jimmy began to cry " 'cause he's alone and has no friends.' I know what that fantasy is about," she said. "Yesterday we were talking about going to visit relatives for Easter. My sister said she's afraid she'll be lonely 'cause there won't be anyone her age there. I said that I'm not bothered by not having someone my age." She had said this to appear strong and thus show up her sister and win her parents' approval. However, one of her most heralded personality problems was that she had few friends. Her sister cut her to the quick and reinforced her distrust of loved ones when she said, "You're used to it." This was then manifested in the session by a modification of the fantasy. Though the characters, the action, and the situation remained the same, a new, teasing meanness on the part of the adult provided an element of subtle difference. The action of the sister intensified the latent fear fantasy of disappointment by loved ones and tinged with cruelty the derivative manifest fantasy that was produced by the structure of latency.

The child was apparently able to move the stress of the sister's cruelty from a position of central importance by discussing it as she did. In the next session, her thoughts returned to her preoccupation with her need for reassurance in the form of love and services. Jimmy became once more a crying and demanding cub. Then the fantasy changed. Verbal demands ceased. A subtle acting in of demanding behavior began. The cub, and gradually the patient as herself, began to make small messes all around the playroom. The messes were left for "someone else to clean up." The therapist mentioned "someone to clean up for you" as one of her signs of a good maid. She responded that "It's good to have someone clean up after you." The therapist pointed out the fact that the messes were being left for him to clean up and wondered at her need to test his loyalty by this technique, just as she tested her parents or sought reassurance that the maid did not present a danger to her.

As can be seen from this vignette, repetition of the same fantasy can be useful in the psychotherapeutic approach to children if subtle changes in manifest content are recognized to be surface indications of vaster underlying variations in latent content resulting from interpretation, transference, or life events.

The sessions above were part of a psychoanalytic treatment rather than a psychotherapy. Because of the high frequency of sessions—four in one week—it was possible to study in detail the influences of interpretations, transference, and reality events on a latent fantasy. Were the four sessions to have been spread over a period of a month, the rapid changes from one primary fantasy to another from week to week that typifies the fantasy life of the latency age child would have dominated the clinical picture. Instead, greater frequency in this case allowed observation of the subtle changes that occur within one fantasy during the course of a single week. Subtle changes in fantasy from day to day characterize the phenomena which a child presents during child analysis. Child analytic technique has been developed in response to this characteristic. Much more concentrated evidences of transference, social influences, and latent fantasy become available to the child and the analyst. In the analytically derived psychotherapies, less frequent sessions require that therapeutic attention be brought to bear on the effect of the child's inner reactions to his stories within a single session. The effect of the therapist's interpretations of fantasy content on the subsequent content of manifest fantasies in the session is also a prime object of the therapist's attention. The effect of an interpretation on the content of the next session is apt to be diluted by the passage of many days and the introduction of other latent fantasies in response to unforeseeable reality events. Though frequency of sessions dictates the degree to which the transformations of fantasy during the latency state can be used psychotherapeutically, the therapeutic use of other aspects of fantasy play can always contribute something of value.

The hiding places for conflict provided by the structure of latency can be unlocked if one only remembers that fantasy is a fine creative instrument. It is capable of sinuous and subtle variations on oft-presented themes. The therapist who learns the nature of this creativity acquires a therapeutic skill of value. Unfortunately, application of this skill is not without its pitfalls. For instance, as I have mentioned above, the child can shift into fantasy as a defensive form of overcompliance. This can lead to therapeutic stagnation as a product of encouraging fantasy play.

LULLING

Another major problem in the use of fantasy and play in the psychotherapy of children is the phenomenon which I like to call "lulling." Rare is the child psychiatrist to whom I mention this phenomenon who doesn't smile and tell about how he or she has overcome it. Lulling refers to the process of altered attention that can occur in a therapist when a child plays out similar fantasies repetitively. Therapists are always adults. As such they are used to variety in the acted-out fantasies of others with which they come into contact. These consist of plays and movies or television performances. Their own repeated fantasies such as dreams and daydreams go into repression with great rapidity and so are not contributory aspects of their life experience. In addition, the adult therapist is not used to communication through play. By definition the products of the structure of latency are constructed to hide and obscure meanings through the use of psychoanalytic symbolization. The psychotherapeutically trained adult is more comfortable interpreting verbalizations than active play. The understanding of verbal memory and thought is the natural milieu of the therapist. Supervision through which one learns about psychotherapy usually is restricted to the presentation of words to a supervisor. There is rarely direct observation of the words, actions, and excitements of the therapist-child interaction. Much is missed, for meaning conveyed through play fantasies is too diffused and too close to affect to be approached and understood totally on a verbal level. An adult who attempts to interact with a child on a fantasy level must experience a regression to a level of affecto-motor functioning that can be disquieting. This regressive pull is often responded to by a defensive reaction on the part of "the ego" of the therapist. There develops a kind of distracted inattention, of which the therapist is usually not aware. Certain aspects of the therapeutic stance are lost. Although the therapist's mind may not actually wander, there is a loss of ability to react and interpret at the right moment. For example, a child who had great difficulties in dealing with being alone was playing out repeatedly a story of an attack by an army on a desert fort. Over a period of six sessions the same story was told many times each session. Finally a small change was made in the story. One of the soldiers in the attacking army was left alone to watch the camp while the others went to fight. At this point in the session, the breakthrough of a formerly de-emphasized element in the child's conflict area caused the child to stop the story abruptly and become involved in rhythmic playing with a coin. This change in content of the session was observed but not responded to with an appropriate intervention by the therapist. The therapist's attention had not strayed from the story; it had strayed from his role and stance as a therapist. He had been lulled by repeated listening to the story into a state of inattention to his interpretive role. He was therefore not ready to talk when the time for intervention arrived. I've often thought of the problem of attention in the therapist who does play therapy as similar to that of the center fielder in a baseball game. The ball may come to him once or twice in a game. Yet he must be paying attention every moment for he cannot know when his active skills will be needed. While in a lulled state, the therapist continues to watch the fantasy. He can describe what's going on and even report it verbally to his supervisor. Often the therapist is very much involved in the fantasy, sometimes sharing in it as a defense to cover and modify his own personal versions of the underlying conflicts that a child's fantasy represents in transmuted form. In a state of lulling the therapist is geared for reflection and comprehension of what the child is doing but is not geared for interpretive action. He is more like an observer of a theatrical performance than a therapist. When the child makes a comment within the play which changes the play situation in such a way that a psychotherapeutic intervention is indicated, the therapist is just not ready and misses the interpretation, or he makes it a few minutes after the proper time for the interpretation has passed.

The proper way to deal with lulling is to analyze in oneself the conflicts which are held in common with the child which result in sharing the defensive use of fantasy. In addition, one must be constantly conceptualizing interpretations of the fantasy. Otherwise the therapist will slip into passive participation in the function of the child's structure of latency—into passive mastery of his own problems through the child's fantasy, to the detriment of the therapy.

Lulling can take many forms. The most common form is passive lulling in which the therapist sits quietly watching the child play. Active involvement as a form of lulling is not rare. As an example of active involvement in a child's fantasy, take the case of a therapist who worked with a youngster who was quite gifted in art. The child began to draw comic strips whose hero was a character who was similar in story and physical characteristics to an obscure mythological figure. The mythic figure was well known to the therapist. The therapist was quite a narcissistic fellow who enjoyed letting other people know of his extensive knowledge. He used the patient's comic strips as a basis for showing off his competence in the area of mythology. He brought the drawings with him everywhere to show his colleagues and his supervisor. Attempts at understanding the underlying content of the patient's drawings were not made because their similarity to myth occupied the therapist. The therapist was distracted from working on problems of narcissism in the child, and the child's narcissism was served by the therapist's reaction. By concentrating his attention on the manifest content of the fantasy, the therapist joined in obscuring the latent conflicts and fantasies of the child.

A more subtle manifestation of active lulling consists of writing, doodling, or other motor activity on the part of the therapist during the therapy session. The writing down of children's dreams is an interesting variant of this form of distraction. Some children recognize the distraction of attention from themselves that such writing represents and complain. Others join in the resistance and elaborate the dream content endlessly. Thus children's dreams during the latency period seem to be extensive. It's unwise to begin to write dreams that a child tells during the session because, as often as not, it will take the entire session to write the dream out, leaving little time for interpretation or fantasy associations to the dream. The effect is the same as the effect of lulling. The situation is helpful in understanding the process of lulling.

Encouraging fantasy and play is a good technique in the therapy of the child who has difficulty in verbalizing his problems. However, the most effective means of dealing psychotherapeutically with the child is to be able to discuss directly with the child the problems in words. Relatively speaking, working through with fantasies is slower and less efficient. Fantasy is a two-edged sword combining both the elements of resistance and revelation of the unconscious of the child patient. Because of this characteristic, it is a slower modality of psychotherapeutic approach than insight-motivated verbalization. One of the characteristics of the latency age child is the frequent invocation of the structure of latency as a defense. This means that fantasy formation can be expected to dominate therapy sessions. Therefore the ability to analyze fantasy is a requirement if one is to be a competent child therapist.

There are certain characteristics which define a competent therapist. He has mastered lulling. His therapy can progress through the use of the verbalizations which lulling defends against. He has skills in dealing with certain vicissitudes of fantasy formation in childhood. The most important of these skills is the ability to detect changes in a story which is repeated from session to session and the ability to recognize switches in the identification of the patient with the story characters from one moment to the next. In discussing the initiation of psychotherapy in a latency age child we have first noted the characteristics required of the child. These include such elements as internalization of conflict. It is well to reflect on the fact that these characteristics in the child will yield little if the child is not matched in his therapeutic work by a therapist who is equipped to take him through the initiation phases of therapy. This includes encouraging fantasy. More than this, the therapist must be trained to understand and deal with latency age fantasy if the treatment is to yield insight rather than the mere communication of fantasy contents.

Some aspects of the working through of fantasy beyond the stage of initiation of treatment have been described in the sections of this chapter that deal with the relating of manifest fantasies to events of the day and underlying conflicts. We now turn to problems of termination of psychotherapy in latency age children engendered by the presence of the latency state ego.

Terminating Psychotherapy with a Child in the Latency State

As in other aspects of psychotherapy with the latency state child, termination of psychotherapy has characteristics contributed by the structure of latency. There is a propensity for the use of fantasy as an escape from, and expression of, problems. Fantasies can express termination reactions which could have entered treatment through acting out, verbalization, or description of inner experiences and sensations.

In the latency age child, fantasy formation often takes precedence over verbalization. It can serve as a conduit through which otherwise unobtainable material relating to termination enters the therapeutic situation. At times the defensive masking aspect of such fantasy formation will override its communicative aspect and interfere with the working through of termination. Fortunately, there are certain characteristic fantasies which occur in latency state children during periods of termination which represent termination reactions. Familiarity with the nature of these fantasies equips the therapist to recognize them as such. Thus termination reactions can be dealt with more quickly and effectively. Such knowledge is vital early in child therapy.

Children have less control over terminations than adults in psychotherapy, and there are more frequent separations during child therapy. The nature of childhood dependence on parents for such things as mobility, place of domicile, and payment for treatment creates more possibilities for separations, interruptions, and terminations in the psychotherapy of children than there are during psychotherapeutic approaches to adult emotional problems. Adults are much more in control of their lives than are children. The lives of children are passively shaped by the movements, emotional reactions, and decisions of adults. Parents have to move for occupational reasons. Parents lose interest in therapy. Parents feel physically overwhelmed by the task of bringing a child to therapy. Parental vacations necessitate interruptions of treatment. Parents develop negative transferences that cannot be worked through. These elements create a multitude of interruptions of psychotherapy which the child cannot control and which produce psychological responses in him. In addition, there are interruptions of therapy which relate to other conditions of childhood life:

childhood illnesses, departures for summer camp, and special school trips and school holidays. Interruptions and miniterminations such as those experienced with summer camp, vacations and parental travel stir separation feelings in therapy situations long before the actual termination phase of the psychotherapy. This occurs to a far greater extent than is seen in psychotherapies with adults. Furthermore, children can predict interruptions of therapy on the basis of parental behavior long before the separation has been announced by the parent to the therapist. A child's play may contain the first clue for the therapist of an upcoming interruption of treatment.

latency age children parallel the classical termination phenomena seen during the termination phases of adult psychotherapy. Their specific manifest forms are often influenced by the ego structure of latency. Therefore they must be searched for in the fantasy life of the child as well as in overt emotional reactions and behavior. In separation situations in the psychotherapies of childhood there are two interwoven areas of reaction: reactions to object loss, and reactions to the unmasking of strong libidinal feelings as a response to expectation of separation.

Reactions to object loss include fantasy activity which can reflect all of the following: mobilization of aggression, feelings of rejection, incorporation of the therapist or symbols of the therapist, identifications with the therapist. In addition, in the actual life of the child a process of object replacement occurs.

Object replacement here refers to the seeking of new friends at the termination of treatment. Ties to these friends replace the object tie to the soon-to-be-lost therapist. Such object replacement is a common indication of a strong, often positive, relationship between therapist and patient. A study of the nature of the new objects sought can be used as an indication of the outcome of the therapy to an even greater degree than is possible in adult therapies.

In adult psychotherapies object replacement usually takes the form of an intensification and modification of ties to individuals with whom the patient is already involved in a relationship of intimacy. Changes in friends and love objects as treatment progresses are usually seen in the young or in those who began treatment with limited capacities for object ties. As a rule, a child has greater freedom in the acquisition of close new friends than has an adult.

In the evaluation of the new relationships that the child establishes during the termination phase, the detection of specific characteristics can be useful in evaluating the effectiveness of the psychotherapy. The nature of the new people who are sought out by the child and who accept the child as a friend is an indicator of the nature of the child himself. Take the example of a child of ten whose few friends, in pretreatment history, valued school performance little and were continually involved in classroom disruptions. At the end of treatment, the youngster was much concerned with his own school performance. He related to youngsters who were similarly involved with achievement. As therapy neared termination he developed a close friendship with a mature achievement-oriented peer. His presenting symptoms related to classroom disruptions. Termination had been determined on the basis of a cessation of these activities. Such a result could have been the product of manipulation of the environment or the opportunity to discharge his tensions through fantasy play sessions. The fact that his personality had restructured on a deeper level was reflected in the level of insight which had been reached in therapy and confirmed by the objective nature of the group which accepted him as a peer in maturity.

Reactions to the unmasking of strong libidinal feelings as a response to expectation of separation are manifested in uncomfortable feelings and overt rejection of associated ideas more often than they are expressed in fantasy. These reactions are most commonly seen in children who have concern about passivity and problems of sexual identity. Often these children respond to such feelings with panic reactions. In essence, the child who fears that he is homosexual becomes acutely uncomfortable when he perceives love and warm feelings for a person of the same sex. It is necessary to point out to such a child that the feelings he has for the departing therapist are the expected products of working comfortably with another person over a prolonged period of time. The feelings of love can be likened to that between father and son. As such, the homoerotic implications of the feelings can be defused. However, such a strong reaction predisposes the child to stress in similar situations which could arise subsequent to the end of therapy. The child is not ready for termination in the presence of such a reaction. His overwhelming reactions to homoerotic feelings should be worked through. In children, such reactions are tied to fear of subjection and situations of passivity. Cognates to these reactions on a deeper level consist of fear of castration and fusion.

Since the nature of childhood emphasizes a passive subjugated role in society, such relationships and the response of the child to them should be the subject of some of the therapy of every child. Strikingly, the children who are most in need of such intervention are those least capable of cooperating in treatment. They are less able to talk about and investigate their reactions than to feel them and act on them. Phobic children and children with persecutory fantasies are most prominent among those who have such underlying complexes. This important aspect of the psychology of the latency age child (especially in late latency) is often brought into focus by termination techniques which permit the child to join in the decision to terminate and in the selection of the date of termination. The child's reactions and manipulations in the actual termination situation can be brought to his attention and discussed.

Most separations during the course of therapy occur either as the result of decisions by the therapist or the parents. Rarely does the child have any role in the decision-making process. Termination of treatment is the one area in which the child and psychic processes within him are primary in determining the timing of a separation. It is worthwhile to harness this reality. The inner events of his psychic life contribute more to the decision-making process when it comes to termination than do the child's wishes. In the termination situation, it is possible for the child to learn to differentiate between the act of bowing to the will of another and the act of planning based on the limits set by reality. In this situation the reality involved relates to his own progress.

One evaluates a multitude of elements in a child's progress toward termination. For an accurate appraisal, parents, teachers, siblings, and the therapist as well as the child should be sources of data. The requirements for termination in child therapy are:

The presenting problem has been resolved.

Access of fantasy to motor activity and action is within acceptable bounds.

The child's academic and social activities reflect success.

Verbal or abstract conceptual thinking is being used in the processing and solution of stressful inputs to the extent that the child can understand his responses in terms of genetic antecedents in the parent-child interaction.

The child's progress in developmental trends reflects a stage and rate commensurate with his peers.

The child's current friends reflect the level of adjustment that he himself appears to have attained.

Further therapeutic work will only produce progress that age-appropriate natural development could provide as well.

It should be noted that fantasy, which is a product of the structure of latency, persists as a defensive structure of the ego throughout the latency age period. Therefore fantasy as a defense can normally be expected to persist on into the termination phase in the therapy of a latency state child. The persistence of fantasy as defense is not considered to be pathological during the latency age. In evaluating a child for readiness for termination, however, the nature of the fantasies should be reviewed for pathological aberrations in the fantasizing function. For instance, excessively omnipotential fantasies manifested in hypercathexis of fantasy which produces withdrawal, or fantasy based on action outside of the play situation, are unacceptable. The presence of phantasmagoric symbols or symbols which are highly charged for the child (e.g., persecutory fantasies; see chapters 4 and 8) are likewise evidences of a pathological symbolizing function during the latency age period. This is especially true when there occurs a failure to achieve a shift to fantasies based on symbols derived from the environment and contacts in reality. When this failure occurs, the expected developmental trend toward the establishing of future planning suffers. A fantasizing function with impaired characteristics is an indication for continued treatment.

Once it has been determined through conference between the parents and the therapist that the goals originally set are fulfilled or near fulfillment and the requirements for termination mentioned above have been fulfilled, it is time to think of termination. At this point the child is told that this is the case. He joins in the decision-making process. He is asked if there are still any areas or problems for which he feels he needs help. The child is not asked to give an immediate answer; he is told to think about the important question of ending therapy and to respond as soon as he can. Usually the period of self-searching lasts a few weeks. During this time the child and the therapist discuss the child's thoughts on the matter. They establish the date on which they will talk specifically about whether or not they are ready for termination. On that date, the child, in concert with the therapist, sets a termination date or decides to put off termination for a while. Often the termination date is put off repeatedly as a result of the child's heightened awareness of his problems. The fact that he is soon to lose the skilled help of his therapist adds to his diligence. One problem after another is brought into sharper focus. One youngster, who repeatedly devalued the therapist and insisted that his sports activities should be given priority over his treatment sessions, came to one of the decision-making sessions with a concerned look. He had reviewed all of his areas of progress and had found little wanting. Yet he seemed apprehensive. Said he, "I think I'm okay now. Do *you* think we have taken care of all the problems?"

The time of preparation for termination is not one of passive waiting for the therapist. An intensification of therapeutic activity marks the period. An increase of transference feelings energizes fantasies and reactions that can be usefully mined to therapeutic advantage.

Primary among the reactions that may be worked with psychotherapeutically during the termination period is the negative reaction to situations of passivity. Passivity can especially be activated as a problem when a child is involved in responding to, handling, and dealing with natural processes. A child can become frustrated when dealing with the intrinsic time sequences of natural processes. He is engulfed in a sense of passivity when his desire to control the world is frustrated. The child who has problems in dealing with passivity will often be unable to agree with any date that has been set by the therapist. No matter what date the therapist may have suggested, the child will insist on an alternative. When it is decided by the child and the therapist that a termination date should be set in earnest, any date beyond two weeks from the date of the decision can be used as a termination date. Latency age children have an emotional time awareness of about two weeks. Typically, the child with passivity problems will choose a date which differs from any first agreed upon by the therapist. For instance, one youngster, in a session in late September which was set aside for deciding on a termination date in October, suggested October 10 as the termination date. The therapist readily concurred. The child immediately changed the date to October 12. Again the therapist agreed. Again, the child changed. This time the therapist asked what was happening. The child replied, "I want to decide. I don't want you to have anything to do about it." This inability to accept guidance should be investigated with the child. If a problem in dealing with passivity is deemed to be present, then the final date of termination should be put off until the child is capable of shared decision making. The child's difficulties in this area can be interpreted to him in terms of associations and fantasies which are developed from the child's attempt to process and master the problem of accepting natural and parental influences on his behavior, plans, and decisions. (See chapter 8, p. 324 for a clinical example of a youngster involved in passivity and conflicts as well as the working through of such conflicts in the termination phase of treatment.)

Now we turn to the role of latency state fantasy formation in the evaluation and detection of conflicts associated with separations, interruptions, and terminations in latency age psychotherapy. The psychological responses of the latency state child to termination and separations can rarely be elicited by direct questioning. If one listens to the child's fantasies, however, one is often able to detect the presence of conflict-laden material. Such fantasies point to therapeutic approaches and suggest areas of conflict that might not otherwise be considered.

During any period which immediately precedes an interruption in treatment, fantasies are produced which convey information about the child's reaction to the upcoming separation. These fantasies prepare the therapist for dealing with the related intense responses of the child at the time that an actual termination date has been set and is being approached.

Fantasy as defense which is free of impairing characteristics is an acceptable ego mechanism in latency and an important precursor of mechanisms in later life that will contribute to creativity, future planning, and the enjoyment of culture. It is not the purpose of a psychotherapy to interfere with this important step in the maturation of the child's ego. A successful therapy leaves the child's fantasizing function intact; at times, it must strengthen it. Therefore much of the emotional reaction to termination in latency remains detectable through the child's fantasy productions.

The following case histories illustrate the use of fantasy and fantasy play as tools for detecting underlying emotional reactions to interruptions, separations, and terminations in latency psychotherapy.

Ellen was a nine-year-old girl who was brought to treatment because of depressed moods since the traumatic loss of her father the year before. She was able to work in school and had a few friends. Yet her days were joyless and her eyes constantly filled with tears. She was repeatedly overcome with the desire to run from the house and go in search of him. At night she would dream that he came to awaken her or that she heard his voice. She would search the house for him to no avail. She sometimes believed that he was dead and spoke of killing herself to join him. However, she never was sure of this. Her mother was an attractive woman in her late thirties. She herself was quite depressed. As she described her daughter's behavior there were no tears, but she lacked the spontaneity of a person emerging from mourning a year after suffering a personal loss. She often hit her daughter to control her behavior. When she realized that this technique had no effect, she brought the child for treatment.

The story of the father's disappearance was told in separate versions by the child and the mother. According to the child, the father had taken her and her sister on an outing one Saturday in October. Mother had stayed home to study. They had intended to visit an aunt, have lunch, and then spend an afternoon watching a puppet show in a local park. While at lunch, they met a friend of the father who was also going to the puppet show. The father turned his children over to the friend, explaining that he wanted to get home to watch a football game on TV. This was unusual for him. He usually spent his Saturdays on family outings. The child emphasized this to illustrate her closeness to her father. When she was dropped off at home, both she and her sister noticed that the parents were very quiet with one another "like after they have a fight." The following Thursday her father awakened her very early one morning by kissing her on the cheek while she slept. She did not show that she was awake because she was frightened by a strange wetness on his face. She fell back to sleep. Later in the morning she awakened to her mother's calls for her father. She kept calling his name. There was no answer. Her mother seemed upset but not surprised. The child stayed home from school and watched her mother call her father's office, relatives, friends, hangouts. Each negative answer and each passing hour tightened the noose that strangles hope. At the end of the day the mother announced to the children with a tone of certainty that their father had disappeared forever.

The mother's story paralleled that of the daughter. She added additional details which explained the certainty and final tone of her pronouncement. The father returned early from the outing, going directly home. He thought that his wife was at the library and was surprised to see her car parked near the house. When he entered the house, he went directly to their bedroom where he found her in flagrante delicto with the gardener. The interrupted couple parted hurriedly. The gardener left the house without confrontation. When she turned to her husband, he responded to everything that she said with a quiet "I understand." She waited the hours through in expectation of an outburst from him. As the days passed, she began to hope for some response, perhaps a smile or some break in the grimness. The following Thursday morning, when she awakened, he was gone. He had spent the four days liquidating his assets. When he left, the family was left without means or reserves. One friend reported to her that her husband had commented cryptically to him that he doubted that the children were his.

In the therapy, the child was encouraged to verbalize her feelings. She had had difficulty in expressing her anger in any way. This had blunted her capacity to express her feelings about her father's desertion. In fantasies of a family which she played out, she cast me in the role of the father. At times she struck out at me. She was often preoccupied with sexual fantasies and liked to tell "dirty jokes." Although her sexual preoccupations suggested that she knew of her mother's encounters, at no time did I come across any corroboration of this, direct or indirect. Her excitement was directly traceable to her mother's constant communication to the children of information couched in scientific terms related to emunctory functions and reproduction. She felt guilty about wanting to love a man other than her father or loving another male figure. In part, she used her preoccupation with her father as a way of avoiding her budding sexual feelings for boys. As she became more aware of her reasons for involving herself exclusively in the fantasies about her father, she became less tearful and more able to involve herself with peers.

With the emotional reactions that had necessitated psychotherapy resolved, it was time to introduce the idea of termination. Because a separation problem was primary here, there was an early introduction of termination. At the thought of termination, the child became emotionally brittle. She became angry in response to any comment or suggestion that broached the subject. When I asked her to set a general termination date, she suggested a date a year and a half in the future. In the next session she was sullen and silent. While in school she had heard my voice again and again, saying "There are other things." I pointed out her difficulty in letting me go. She carried me with her in fantasy. I related this to her difficulty in accepting her father's disappearance, and her difficulty in letting him go. Gradually, she began to have fantasies which were limited in content to reality possibilities. She began to fantasy that I would attend a piano recital in which she was to participate and that she would introduce me as her father. Sometimes she would see a man on a street corner and develop the fantasy that she could not be sure if it were I or her father. We spoke of the potential that a young person has to find someone new to take the place of a father as a companion. She became more content and began to tell more jokes about boys and girls. Her interest now turned to her sexual development. She was free of symptomatology when she left psychotherapy.

In this case, it is worthwhile to note that fantasies involving the therapist gave a clear picture of the motivations that dominated her response to her father's disappearance. Most of the work in depth with this child dealt with reactions of which she became aware as the result of reliving, in transference fantasy, separation reactions during the termination phase. In this case the fantasies lacked subtlety. The case was chosen for this reason. In the next case, the reaction to separation was subtly conveyed in fantasy and was unexpected. It is a prime example of a termination reaction which is solely detected through fantasy.

Arnold was seven years old and very handsome. He had dark hair and features that were strong and manly for a little boy. He was involved in disruptive behavior in the classroom. He also developed acute episodes of loss of temper and anger at his parents. This last was manifested in destructive behavior in the home; this included breaking a lamp by dropping it on the kitchen floor. The child was brought to a clinic where I was a fellow in child psychiatry. While I did not know about the nature of latency at the time, in retrospect it is possible to see that this was a youngster with a good structure of latency who had been overstimulated by a family situation. The father had given up his role of authority by default. The child was in very close contact with his mother, who overstimulated him in her search for emotional support and companionship. The father's presence interrupted the child's relationship with his mother and mobilized his aggression. It was soon seen in the therapy that the child's acting out was based on an oedipal hostility displaced from his father. Direct hostility to the father was too dangerous for him. The child played out fantasies in plenty. He established a positive relationship with me once he discovered that aggression directed toward me was not destructive. He established a nonsadomasochistic relationship with me. Very little of a psychotherapeutic nature involving insight was carried out. Most of his gains involved a balance that he was able to achieve in his relationships with men and women. Since I, in his mind's eye, provided a male object to which he could relate, the amount of object libido that he was forced to direct to his all-too-willing mother could be diminished. This lessened his guilt, his excitement, and his hostile actions.

At the end of seven months of working together, my training at that hospital was finished. Military commitments forced my relocation to another part of the country. It was necessary, therefore, for him to be assigned to a new therapist who was a year behind me in the training program. Little working through of termination was advised because a new therapist was immediately available. During our last session, which followed a meeting with the new therapist, the youngster thanked me for the help that I had given him and spoke of his hopes that his new doctor would be more comfortable to be with once he had got to know him. When I attempted to interpret this attitude as a manifestation of his anxiety at being assigned to a new therapist, he ignored my remark and placed a chair upon a low table in the playroom to which we were assigned. He placed a paper carton in front of the chair and sat as though he were driving. When I questioned him about the fantasy in which he was involved, I received no response. I noticed that from time to time he seemed to pull the imaginary steering device toward him and then push it away from him. Detecting a possibility that he was pretending to fly an airplane, I began an intervention. I asked him if he were flying an airplane. At this point he did not respond. However, he changed the content of the fantasy to include low humming airplane-like noises made with his lips and mouth. In the spirit of the game I held an imaginary microphone to my mouth and said to him, "This is the airport contacting Arnold's plane. Please answer; I want to give flight instructions." He immediately picked up his own imaginary microphone and responded, "This is Arnie, what do you want?" As so often happens in these situations, after the child responds one doesn't really know what to say to avoid possible further contamination of the child's fantasy. I asked where he was going, for want of a better question, and fortunately got an answer. He said, "I'm going to California. I'm flying there." I asked him, "Where in California? If I want to send a letter to you, how would I reach you?" He responded by radio, "That's easy. Just write to me care of the orphan's home."

The session was near an end. The explanations of the necessity for my going into military service at the end of my training had had no impact on this youngster. He saw himself as rejected and became subtly aggressive through his fantasy, in which he actively left, excluding me. I communicated information on the nature of his attitude to his next therapist. It was not possible for the new therapist to handle this material or relate to the child who rejected him. The child refused to continue treatment with this therapist and dropped out of treatment after three months. With the cessation of treatment, the child returned to his old behavior patterns. Approximately five years later, the mother contacted me. Arnold was involved in delinquent behavior. He refused to have anything to do with any "shrinks."

This case illustrates a number of points: fantasy can carry the attitudes of a latency age patient; the technique of changing therapists in training centers is fraught with difficulty; more attention should be paid to the impact of such changes on a child.

As mentioned above, children do not respond strongly to separations and terminations until about two weeks prior to actual separation. Usually a child knows that he is going to go to camp or away for summer vacation on the day that he starts treatment. This does not become a pertinent element in the treatment situation until about two weeks before the termination or separation actually occurs. This is not an irrelevant point. At times, therapists discuss termination or separation with a child from six weeks to four weeks in advance. They handle the immediate response and assume that everything has been taken care of. Even a few weeks before the separation, when the event is pressing, the child will not verbalize any difficulties. He's busy processing them into fantasies. It's only through observation of the fantasies and through heightened awareness during the two weeks before the actual event that it is possible to see through the fantasies to the fact that the child is troubled. The following case is an example of this.

Betsy was eight years old when she came to analysis because of a shyness which caused the parents great concern. She had almost no friends. She was quite explosive at home. She had difficulty in separating from her mother. As her treatment progressed, it became very clear that her mother also had difficulty in separating from her. While telling me about her phobias, the child began to dwell on recollection of a camp to which she had been sent a few summers before and to which she was to go the following summer. There was a large stand of dark trees in the camp; it was right behind her bunk. When she first came to treatment, she was sure it contained all kinds of monsters and demons which would barge in on her. As she grew older, these turned into robbers and kidnappers. At the time that the sessions presented here occurred, she was able to accept the idea of camp for the following summer more easily. In part she could consider camp because of the supportive nature of the relationship with me. She felt she could come to me if she became troubled or worried. She was convinced that I could help her to understand the reality of the situation and the inner origin of her problems. She appeared to have the camp situation well in control. Approximately a week and a half before the interruption of sessions for her summer vacation she began to tell stories of a hunter dressed in buckskin who carried a large knife and went into the woods in search of Indians. It seemed clear that she was attempting here to take an active role in fantasy and to master the fear of the fantasy people in the woods behind her bunk. I began to approach the fantasy from this aspect. She provided me with an imaginary satchel to carry and told me that I was her assistant who would help her with the hunt for the Indians. She found their camp, but no Indians were there. She was jumped on by the Indians. She fought the Indians off. Finally, she trapped an Indian and, uncharacteristically for her, told me that she was going to eat the Indian and that I should eat my own food. She then proceeded to kill the Indian and to prepare him to be cooked.

At this point I was alerted to the possible meaning of this fantasy by a previous fantasy in her treatment. I shall go back to the session in which the earlier fantasy took place, for a brief digression. In that session, the child, who had a food fad in which she refused to eat fish, had taken a wooden sculpture which had a mild resemblance to a phallic symbol and, calling it a fish that her father had caught, devoured it in fantasy. At that point I interpreted to her the confusion she had between her father (the fisherman) and fish. Her desire to devour her father made her uncomfortable about eating fish. She developed a feeling of nausea in the session. She mastered this by gobbling down the wooden figure again. She then turned to me and said that she didn't think she'd have trouble eating fish any more. Her mother reported to me that the food fad had ceased after that session. I therefore was prepared to see the devouring of the Indian as a kind of active fantasy in which she played out her cannibalistic wishes toward her father.

With this thought in mind, we now return to the preseparation session. I turned to her and asked what part of the Indian's body she was going to eat. I entertained the thought that she might be made more aware of her wishes to devour the father's penis. However, her response did not relate to any part of the body to which she had phallic associations. She said, "I would like to eat his brains." It should be noted that in the hunting fantasy I had been assigned the role of a rather dull helper. It could have been easy to rule myself out as the latent content of the Indian symbol on this superficial basis. However, the role assignment in a fantasy of a given character, whether it be therapist, patient, or parent, does not negate his role as the latent content of another character. I could have been the latent content of the Indian. Since this was a session that occurred in a preseparation period, I was especially on the alert for incorporative fantasies, such as the fantasy of incorporation and devouring that is so typical a human response to separation. I therefore asked her whether the Indian represented myself. She said that she wished that she could take some of my brains with her when she goes to camp, because she was still frightened of certain things and would have liked very much to be able to talk about these things with me when she was frightened about them.

The recognition of fantasies of devouring brains as a possible incorporative fantasy opened the way to a specific focus in our psychotherapeutic work. By making this connection, it was possible to get her to verbalize her feelings. I then asked her what she was worried about. She talked about walking to the camp bathroom at night, the dark woods, insects in the camp, and girls who might not like her. She especially feared that one of the children in the camp would begin to cry during the first days. This was especially threatening to her because of her feeling that if somebody else cried, her own wish to cry would break through. I pointed out to her that although she could not take my brains with her, it would be possible for her to discuss these problems and the origins of fears involved with them before she went away. She shifted from fantasy at that point to the direct discussion of problems that she was concerned with, although from time to time, when she became blocked in talking about what troubled her, she turned to fantasy as a means of elaborating her problems.

In this chapter, I have dealt with special technical strategies required for working with a psychotherapeutic approach to children in the latency age period. Special attention has been given to the effect of the state of latency on the ability of the child to cooperate in treatment and to special techniques for dealing with impairments in the state of latency. There is yet another clinical aspect to the age of latency. The developmental process that marks this period influences the manifestations of certain clinical phenomena. This process produces certain clinical characteristics which require special approaches and management in diagnostic and therapeutic situations. These we discuss in the next chapter.

Chapter 7

SPECIAL TECHNICAL PROBLEMS OF LATENCY AGE PSYCHOTHERAPY

The sleep of reason breeds monsters.

—Goya

During early childhood the psychic life and physiology are organized into a coordinated apparatus for carrying out life functions. Adolescence is a period devoted to the articulation of this apparatus with society. Within this schema, latency serves as a staging area. It is a time of waiting and a place of few beginnings. Usually in the latency period functions are reorganized, reequipped, and transformed as the result of cognitive growth and maturation. The state of flux produced creates unique transient clinical characteristics for some psychic phenomena in the latency age child. These require special understanding if they are to be managed well. The psychic phenomena most strikingly involved in this process are slips of the tongue, dreaming and nocturnal phenomena, and transitional objects and childhood fetishes. These areas and the techniques associated with them are discussed below.

Working with Slips of the Tongue

In the psychoanalysis of adults, slips of the tongue provide an important means for gaining insights into unconscious motivations and fantasy life. In adult therapy, slips are emphasized. In child therapy such emphasis is not made. No reference to slips of the tongue in children is to be found in the literature.

Yet slips do occur in childhood, and they are important from the standpoint of therapy and technique. The qualities and characteristics of parapraxes peculiar to childhood are presented here with an eye to establishing technical approaches for exploiting them in order to further therapeutic goals.

Four examples of slips of the tongue follow. In each case, the parapraxes in question occurred during a treatment session, and each slip illustrates a clinical context in which a parapraxis can occur. The slips are viewed in terms of their meaning in relation to the fantasy life of the patient and their meaning in relation to the context and technique of treatment. (See Sarnoff, 1969.)

Slip 1: A slip of the tongue as the confirmation of an interpretation. WRH was a girl of eleven years and four months who had come to analysis two years before because of temper tantrums, sustained transvestite behavior, and impaired learning skills.

It was Wednesday. Irritability and sullenness in her behavior had revealed her anger since the weekend before. At that time, her mother had been graduated from college. For a few brief days, the mother held the center of the stage in the family. Though my patient realized she was angry and had wondered why she was, she could not pin down the cause.

She began the session by reading to me from a letter sent to her by a maid who had just left the family employ to travel. The patient spoke of her own current difficulties. She must clean her own room. She began to sweep the rug in the playroom with a toy carpet sweeper. In her fantasy she became one of two brothers left at home by the mother to clean up the house. Instead of cleaning, they leave a mess for the mother. They do this by emptying the sweeper on the floor. One of the children writes on the board on the wall "surprize [sic]." When the mother comes home, she cleans up and then beats the children. My patient beat a bop bag which she represented as one of the children. At the height of the beating, the mother said, "You didn't know I was a surprize fighter." The mother was especially angry because the children had broken a pole used by the mother in cleaning. She threatened to beat them with it. The children were put to bed. They awakened early, and when the mother came to call them for breakfast, she was jumped upon and beaten. At this point, the therapist interpreted the child's anger at and jealousy of her mother. He related this to the preceding weekend, when college graduation brought all of the father's attention to the mother at the expense of the patient. The patient's response to the comment was to beat with more vehemence. She played a child beating a representation of the mother. Then she threw the bag over her shoulder. She began to search about the room, loudly exclaiming, "Where is that post, I mean pole you talked of?" I said to her, "You used the word 'post' for pole; what could that mean?" She smiled and told me what we both knew. The name of the college from which her mother had just been graduated was Post. She beat the bop bag with the pole. Then she let out the air and threw the mother toward the father, which role she had assigned to me for the moment.

Slip 2: A slip as a means of breakthrough of concealed historical data. The following clinical situation occurred during the treatment of the same child, WRH. The patient told of the following episode. Her sister's room was far from the center of the house. If the sister failed to make her bed, the mother could be unaware of the fact. The patient, on the other hand, had a room near the mother's room. Each transgression was quickly discovered and punished. The sister's bed was unmade. My patient reported this to the mother and thus forced the sister to make her bed. As she told me of this, she said, "Mommy comes into my bed," laughed, then changed it to "Mommy comes into my room." I asked what the slip could mean. She spoke of the formerly withheld information that she or her sister "still go into Mommy's bed on cold mornings."

Slip 3: The implications of denial of a slip of the tongue. WJB was a boy of twelve years who had come to analysis three years before because of stealing, arguments with his father, clowning, inability to progress in school, and overweight. He was the constant butt of teasing and was subjected to beatings by his peers.

The patient had begun the session by telling the therapist that he had been punished after he had told his father about losing a dollar. At the same time he had neglected to tell his father that he had got a grade of 99 on a test. Such information, he knew, would have softened his father's response. The therapist pointed out the self-punitive nature of this behavior. It was a customary pattern for the youngster to allow himself to disclose something that he felt was wrong, after telling of a punishment. It was, therefore, to be expected that he would associate to his report with the following personal fantasy. While coming by bus to the office, he was attracted to a pretty girl. He felt repulsed at the sight of the hair under her arms and he thought to himself that she might sweat during sex. He devised a plan of seduction. He would approach her and bring her to my office and use one of the rooms for sexual activity. The therapist would remain in the next room. He could describe his fantasy only in part. When he came to the description of physical contact, he left to get a glass of water. When he returned, he changed the subject. He began to talk of his father's secretary saying, "You should see my father making out with *my* secretary." The therapist said to him, "You said my, instead of his; what can this mean?" He contradicted the question saying, "I said 'his secretary'." The therapist did not press the issue but instead listened to the patient's associations. Immediately, the patient remembered and told the following dream from the night before.

It was during the German war. I am an agent for the U.S. I'm not sure which side I was on. I'm with this girl. We are supposed to kill the general. This girl is an agent from Germany who thinks I'm there to protect the general. We go to this house. We capture this guard alive. We live in the attic. It's my house. One day I told her I saw someone spying on us.from the house next door. The guard is afraid to do anything wrong. He almost slips off the roof. I try to haul him up. He falls right onto the general's table. The general thought it was another of his guards spying on him. The girl and I went back to the attic.

Once again he stopped to go to get a drink of water when speaking about entering a room with a girl. When he returned, he said,

Then I woke up. It was morning. I heard my father throw his shoes in the closet. That's what woke me up.

When the patient denied the slip ("my secretary" for "his secretary"), the next step for the therapist was to avoid controversy and to observe the productions of the patient as associations to the slip.

The slip of the tongue clearly relates to the main theme of the hour. The manifest slip conveyed the message that his father was sexually involved with his (the patient's) woman. Oedipal wishes were revealed by this slip. The secretary, the girl on the bus, and the lady spy all could represent his mother. Both the fantasy and the dream reveal inhibitions of genital sexual excitement in relation to women. Each was interrupted by a defensive oral regression at the point at which a potential or actual sexual situation was imagined. It can be inferred from the slip that the women represented a person shared with the father, desired, and forbidden as a love object (i.e., the mother). This was confirmed in a dream which occurred later in the treatment:

> I was in my living room with somebody. I don't remember who. My mother was there and right in front of me, she layed this guy, a friend of mine. Then she said it was my turn. My father came down the road. We couldn't do anything. Later he went out to a meeting. I was home alone with my mother. She was going to bathe. I said I want my chance now. She said sure. The scene changed to a camp site. I had seen it before. I set up the tents. The owner took us in a car. I had seen it before. He said let's look at the waterfall. As we went down the road we saw a place to eat.

Once again, as the manifest content of the dream approached a frankly sexual situation with a woman (directly represented as the mother), there was an abrupt switch to another location and food.

The youngster's masturbation was similarly interfered with. He suffered abrupt loss of erection when his fantasies were interrupted by the intrusion of manifest sexual thoughts about his mother.

It should be noticed that there are marked scoptophilic and primal scene elements in the contents of the association to this slip of the tongue. The patient watched his mother and his friend having intercourse in the second dream. There are reports of spying in the first dream. He placed me in the next room in the fantasy about the girl on the bus. In the slip itself, he said "see." ("You should *see* how my father makes out with my secretary.") This slip of the tongue can be seen as having an important transference determinant. Though the slip reveals his wish for a sexual situation with his mother, the act of slipping itself has a transference aspect. It can be seen as a means of manifesting a core fantasy in which a third person, in the transference, the analyst, observes a sexual situation.

Technically, in this case, the slip was handled only by pointing it out. When the patient denied that it had occurred, he was not contradicted. Emphasis was shifted to the use of the contents of the whole hour as associations to the slip.

Denial that a slip has been made is often seen in children and adolescents. Such a response has diagnostic implications. It points toward reliance on early and primitive mechanisms of defense. This slip (a break in repression) was not reversed by re-repression alone. Denial also played a part. It is the addition of denial which is the key to the pathological character of this example. It indicates that the slip is to be left alone. The patient denied the perception of the slip. He did not try to belittle or explain it away. He said it did not exist. Denial deals with withdrawal of cathexis from "reality" (that is, the external world and/or conscious psychic pain). It is present from early on and is more primitive than repression. Repression withdraws cathexis from unpleasurable items in the inner world.

Repression develops at twenty-six months when a mature symbolizing function comes into being. When a slip occurs, unconscious mental content becomes speech. At that point two things happen: (1) there is undoing of repression, and (2) a sensation (the spoken word) becomes available as a perception. Freud (1915) described a related concept (p. 175).

What happens has an analogy in the dual sensation that occurs when one touches one's own cheek. One feels a sensation in the cheek and in the touching finger too. Both the touched and the touching are felt. In a slip of the tongue, the awareness of the subject comes into contact with the content from two directions. First the content arises to consciousness from within, much as occurs in a dream. Second, the content comes into consciousness from without (the spoken word heard), much as occurs with a psychoanalytic interpretation of content. Repression serves to abrogate the slip from the standpoint of the appearance of the content from within. Denial serves to abrogate the slip from the standpoint of the awareness of the content from without (the spoken word heard). When repressed contents are perceived in words during a slip of the tongue, their memory remains in consciousness, available for use in analysis. It is viewed in totality as something outside with a source from within. It is through this that slips give us a fulcrum. We can use them as the thin edge of the wedge into the fantasy life of the patient. Whenever the perception is denied, the therapeutic fulcrum is lost. Denial of a slip by a patient indicates that there is present a fragile adjustment which cannot stand such rapid uncovering in therapy. In such cases, it is indicated clinically that the slip not be pursued directly. Rather, the patient's related productions should be observed and considered to be associations to the slip. Pursuit of the slip will only serve to uncover unconscious data and motivations which the individual is not yet ready to assimilate on a conscious level. Disorganization and pathological defenses can be expected to result from pursuit.

Slip 4: A slip of the tongue as a harbinger of repressed material soon to come into treatment. The patient, RLS, was a girl seven years, two months old who had come to treatment at six years, six months because of failure to progress in school. She presented as part of her symptomatology a maturational lag in symbol formation. Her attempts to displace her conflicts into fantasies failed to utilize sufficient displacement to shield her from the anxiety of the conflict. As a result, she was unable to achieve the latency calm required for learning. By the hundredth hour of treatment, she had reached the point at which her anxieties were no longer all-pervasive. She could learn to read and write. Her fantasy formation utilized sufficient displacement so that her fantasies could be used as a manifestation of conflict. Fantasies now both defended her from anxiety and served as a means of communication in the treatment.

One such fantasy told of conflicts between two groups over the ownership of a piece of property. She represented this by glueing small pieces of paper to a large piece of paper. The large piece of paper represented the property. The small pieces of paper represented people who wished to occupy the property. After all the small pieces of paper had been placed, strips of cloth tape were glued on top of the pieces of paper. These were described verbally as the winners. At first, small strips of tape were used. Later longer and longer strips were added. The strips of tape were called the take-all family. A father (he's the longest), a mother, two brothers, and a long friend of the father were identified. The therapist commented on the similarity of this family of long slender smothering beings to smothering snakes that appeared in a recurrent dream she had reported early in treatment. She responded by telling the therapist that she still had the dreams. "The snakes come the same and they bite," she said. As she told the dream, she wrapped the rest of the white cloth tape around her hand like a bandage. When she said "bite," the therapist pointed at the bandage and asked, "Your hand?" "Yes," she said, "they bite my hand." She moved toward the therapist quickly and began to bind his hand saying, and they bite you." "Where?" he asked. "Your penis," she said, stopping short of finishing the word as she realized what she was saying, and quickly substituting "tushie." "You said penis—what do you think of that?" asked the therapist. She took a small strip of tape and attached it to his belt, saying, "What a small penis you have—no it's big." Then she handed him the tape, saying, "I don't want to touch your penis."

She then took a long strip of tape to play tug-of-war with the therapist. She had to win. She finally cut the tape into two strips, one five feet long and the other four inches long. At first she assigned the short strip to him and the long strip to herself. Then she switched, saying, "You have a long penis." She put the short strip between her thighs, saying, "I have a little one; no, I have a vagina, I have a sissy." The therapist asked what she meant. "When I touch it," she said, "it's all mushy." She did not describe her masturbatory explorations further, for there was an abrupt change of activity. She went to the dollhouse and began to push around the furniture in the dollhouse saying, "I'm a tornado, I'll break all the furniture in the dollhouse." The therapist interpreted her anger, saying, "Now I know that when you are angry at home and you break and cut, you are really angry at your brother and want to break and cut because he has a penis and you have a sissy." She became more quiet and placed the five-foot tape and the four-inch tape in her bin. The session was near the end. Instead of leaving she told the therapist to leave. The therapist pointed out how her wish for a penis and power was expressed in the desire to change places with him.

The hours that followed confirmed her wish to castrate men and thus create a world of castrated people so that she would not need to feel deprived or dominated. The slip of the tongue was very much in the context of the direction in which her associations were going.

We may observe in slip 4 a child in the process of the development of mature ego functions in the area of symbol formation. At first the child could not substitute an emotionally uncharged word for the smothering, powerful penis. She chose snakes, which frightened her. As she developed more capacity for displacement, the number of steps between the anxiety-ridden latent content (penis) and the manifest content increased until she spoke of cloth tape strips with no anxiety at all. A complementary series had been set up. A slip of the tongue occurred when one of the displacement steps (snake-tape) was abrogated by an interpretation at a time when she was in a regressed ego state. In response to this she completed the abrogation of the displacement in its entirety and produced the affect-charged latent content in the appropriate context. This resulted in the slip of the tongue.

Ordinarily, when repression of a charged element has taken place, an uncharged element in the outside world is substituted for the highly charged repressed element through displacement. At that time, the outside element is viewed as appropriate in the context to which the repressed element really belongs. A slip of the tongue occurs when there is an undoing of the repression and the displacement and the repressed element is expressed in the appropriate context.

In the case of slip 4, the use of the long, smothering strips of tape is an example of a displacement of a concept into a representation far from the original anxiety-provoking idea, (an example of psychoanalytic symbol formation. The tape strip was a displaced representation of the dream snake. When the repressed connection between the snake and the tape strip was interpreted, a defense was removed and the way was opened for the abrogation of other related repressions. This took the form of the slip in which she revealed her wish to destroy the therapist's penis. In the transference, this referred to her rebellion against the suffocating dominance that she interpreted the treatment to be.

In the analysis of a child, sessions in which fantasies are played out represent altered ego states in which there is a shift to dominance by primary-process energies. The child is in a psychic state closer to the unconscious than the nature of the verbalizations that are presented reveal. There is then a situation of disequilibrium which predisposes to slips of the tongue. Breakthroughs of material closer to the ego state and the energic regression which is truly operative can be manifested in slips of the tongue.

On the basis of the clinical examples and the discussion, we may posit some basic suggestions for dealing with slips of the tongue in child therapy.

First, point out the slip immediately. Do not permit any time to pass, as this encourages denial. Do not let a barrier grow to recognition and acceptance of the slip on the part of the patient. This suggestion does not hold in all cases. There are some children who are diagnostically and dynamically unsuited for such an intervention. As pointed out by Ticho (1969) and Sarnoff (1968), there is a group of latency children in whom interpretations of unconscious content and slips of the tongue stir up material that is strongly defended against, resulting in increased anxiety rather than insight, and more symptoms rather than an improved adjustment. Immediate denial of a slip is a diagnostic indicator of such a state. Worse yet, these children also develop an undermining of the therapeutic alliance. Such a negative reaction indicates a fragility of the ego. Slip 3 is a case in point of such a situation.

Try to present the slip in such a way that the interpretation of it requires an active response on the part of the patient. Do not put the patient in the position of feeling that an error has been made or that there is a defect in thinking. Do not, however, expect the child to respond fully to the interpretation of the slip. Rather, follow his associations to find latent meanings.

Slips of the tongue can occur in children after the development of the mature system consciousness (see Appendix A). Only after the child has attained skill at masking latent meanings with symbols is the stage set for the latent meanings to be unmasked. When this takes the form of a sudden verbal substitution of the latent content for the displaced representation, a slip of the tongue appears.

Properly used, a slip of the tongue can serve in psychotherapy as a means of hurrying the shift from displaced derivatives to more direct representations of the latent fantasies and conflicts of the child.

The Analysis and Interpretation of Dreams

The reporting of dreams is a common phenomenon in child therapy sessions. They are potentially as rich a source of information about latent fantasy and unconscious conflicts as are the dreams of adults. Two characteristics of latency age dream psychology stand in the way. Children do not free associate to their dreams as do adults. The dreams of children are usually so long and so verbose that it is not at all unusual for a dream report which began at the middle of a session to run on till the end. Even if children were gifted at free association, it would be difficult to cover all the details. An example of such a detailed dream follows:

This is a horror dream. I dreamt that I went up skiing. I was about twenty. I went up on the throughway. I was going up alone. It was ten at night. It was a cold night. There was much snow. There was this place. An old lady ran it. I saw a shadow on the house. I saw a raven up there cawing. A dark night. I was a little scared. I walked up to the door. I saw a lady at the window rocking, a real old lady with her hair down in bangs. Real messy. I said frightfully slowly, "Have you a room?" She said, "We only have one with girls in it. Oh, wait, we do have a guest room." As I went in, it was very dark, very. There was the shadow of the trees. I saw the shadow of the raven again. All of a sudden, the raven came on my shoulder, just about to bite me. I hit it. Then it flew out. The old lady was there. She had guards all around with machetes. There were many killings. I asked for a machete. The raven came back with a teeny alligator. The guard called him a killer raven. I didn't have the machete yet. The alligator grew bigger and bigger. I got a rusty sword. Then I got a machete and chopped off the head of the alligator. The raven killed a girl. Then the machete broke on the raven's back. I killed it with my hand, strangled it. Then the old lady turned into a beautiful young girl. Then I walked over to the girl to see the bit girl. I made the girl drink antitoxin. The guards disappeared and the house turned into a beautiful building (Sarnoff, 1972, p. 83).

There are psychotherapeutic techniques for approaching children's dreams. One consists of taking the entire session as a series of associations to the dream. In this technique, the dream broadens the therapist's grasp of the patient's problems. The dream reported above revealed that masochistic trends still existed in the latent fantasy life of the boy.

The most useful technique for approaching children's dreams is to encourage the child to add to the content of the dream by including plastic and dramatic reporting as well as verbal reporting. Drawings, clay figures, and paper cutouts can be used to animate the dream. The addition of a new communicative dimension adds knowledge. Tactile and visual contact with dream elements result in added awareness of the meaning of the elements in the child. Intuitive associations occur. This expands dream content and opens the way to the disclosure of additional latent meaning. There is an example of this in chapter 3 (pp. 73-75). In that example, a child drew pictures to illustrate a dream related to a movie about menstruation. In the course of drawing the modifications in her genitals required to control menstrual flow, she created a faucet that reminded her of a penis. The association led to important insights. These would not have been reached or even hinted at if the child had merely reported the dream.

At times, the use of drawing or clay transcends an individual session and provides extensive associations to the dream. The clay dream figures can be used again in later fantasies expanding the potential for associating to dreams. The following clinical vignette illustrates this means of obtaining dream associations from children.

This material is taken from the analysis of a six-year-old girl. One of the child's presenting complaints was of repeatedly dreaming about a thousand snakes led by a bloody-headed monster. The snakes wound themselves around the mother to kill her. Another complaint was inability to eat her breakfast on school days. This stemmed from a fear that she would throw up on the way to the school. Going to school necessitated separation from her mother. The resolution of her morning anorexia was related to the appearance in the analysis of fantasy material, as follows:

> It's better to be eaten by a whale than a shark because a shark grinds you up and kills you while a whale swallows you down and you can live in there and eat the fish he swallows and when he dies he always goes to shore and then he'll vomit you out and you're okay. Once a man was swallowed by a whale and was living in the tummy. The whale swallowed a plane full of people. Something went wrong. The whale made a B.M. in the wrong direction and a pipe broke and all the duty and sissy went into the plane and they thought it was hamburger and lemonade and they ate it. Later the whale died and he went to Europe and let the people out. Then the whale went to America where he let the man out.

A death and rebirth theme is clear in this, as is the doing and undoing of oral cannibalistic fantasies.

After she was able to verbalize devouring fantasies, she began to eat breakfast in the morning more often. In fact, she ate breakfast for the first time in three years while working through these fantasies. She then developed a new symptom. She had to have her mother with her while she dressed. She related this to frightening dreams in which there was a person she feared. She feared the person in the dreams while awake, when she was dressing. She refused to tell me about the dreams. Then one day when her parents were planning to go to the city and she was going to sleep over in the house of a friend for the first time, she explained that the person who appeared in the dreams, whom she feared, was myself. As she told of the dreams she illustrated them by making clay objects. She made a long, thick, snakelike object which, she explained, was the spook and was Dr. Sarnoff. She made a large stomach that left the snake a shell from stem to stern. A large mouth, two eyes, and a control box completed the figure. She then set little pieces of clay on the table. "Watch him kill and eat people." She put the clay houses and objects into the snake's stomach.

In association to the dream she told a story using the clay snake and a small doll family. She told of the kidnapping of children who are killed and eaten by the analyst-snake-spook and return from his stomach through the mouth healthy and intact. Among the mechanisms permitting the displacements that allow these fantasies to come into consciousness are the reversal and projection of oral cannibalistic wishes toward the mother, transferred to the analyst. Doing and undoing of oral cannibalistic fantasies are clearly among the determinants of these fantasies. Fear of annihilation and of object loss were conveyed through these plastic associations, which also served as discharge fantasies associated with the structure of latency.

Differential Diagnosis of Noctural Phenomena Occurring During Sleep in Childhood

The above section discusses technical strategies for approaching children's dreams when they are presented during psychotherapy sessions. In addition to the technical handling of such productions, a differential diagnostic framework must be kept in mind in the clinical evaluation of nocturnal phenomena reported during the sleep of children. A delineation and explanation of this framework is the purpose of this section. As in other areas of the book, a developmental approach explaining the prelatency antecedents of latency dream phenomena will be used as well as reflections on the implications of these findings for adolescence and adulthood. Let us begin with a series of definitions to start us on an investigation of this area.

Dream: An event occurring during sleep which may or may not be remembered upon waking, which characteristically is visual in content.

The purpose of the dream is to provide hallucinatory wish fulfillment for the dreamer so as to preserve sleep.

Anxiety Dream: A dream in which wish fulfillment takes a form that produces anxiety during the dream.

Nightmare: An anxiety dream from which the dreamer awakes, usually with a feeling of pressure in his chest. There is recall of the nightmare the following day.

Blank Anxiety Arousal: An arousal from sleep usually occurring at twenty to twenty-six months of age in which the child awakens with great anxiety but can describe no dream content. The child is awake and can remember but can describe no thought content. Once this happens on a given night, it can be expected to repeat four or five times before morning. The condition, sometimes called tachycardia, decreases markedly or disappears during the first half of the third year of life.

Somatic Distubances: Sometimes psychosomatic conditions such as asthma begin during sleep.

Bedwetting: Refers to uncontrolled urination during sleep. It is considered pathological if it occurs beyond the age of thirty-six months in a child who is otherwise toilet trained.

Sleepwalking: A condition which recurs often within a given period of time, but usually once a night. The child leaves his bed and performs organized motor acts, responds in a confused manner to questions, and has no recall of what has happened the next morning.

Night Terror (also called *pavor nocturnus*): This is an anxiety dream from which the child cannot be awakened fully and for which the child has amnesia the next morning.

These are definitions which seem to describe more or less unrelated psychic states. They were all that was known about childhood sleep disturbances just twenty years ago. It is one of the great advances in child psychiatry that a combination of psychoanalytic and electroencephalographic researches have detected intrinsic characteristics that have resulted in a refinement of the description of these conditions and established categories of relationship between them.

From the standpoint of psychoanalytic research, the delineation of the ontogenesis of symbols has increased understanding of the dream process. When an inadequate symbol is formed, the underlying real meaning breaks through, and sleep-disturbing anxiety appears in dreams (see Sarnoff, 1972a). Freud (1916, 1917) and Jung (1946) believed that many of these symbols were universal and were inborn and inherited. Ferenczi (1913) and Jones (1916) postulated an ontogenesis of symbols, with more primitive symbolic forms appearing first. At no time did they establish a specific time sequence for use in clinical work.

Piaget, in 1951, using Jones's definition of psychoanalytic symbol but calling it "secondary symbolization," focused his work on the development of cognition and imagination in the child. Recognizing that "repression" of the association between what is represented and what represents is the key element in psychoanalytic symbol formation, he was able to search for a symbol ontogenesis useful for psychoanalytic workers (see chapter 4). Based on his work and clinical observations, the following conclusions can be drawn in regard to the timing of the ontogenesis of symbols. Quite primitive symbolic forms appear before eighteen months. These are established symbolic linkages between syncretic global apperceptions and bodily feelings or parts. Between eighteen months and twenty-six months, symbol pairs and symbolic linkages are related consciously. These are of no value to a dreamer for they fail to mask meaning. During the first half of the third year of life, symbols which mask meaning appear. These may be used to express conflicts and gratify wishes while masking the true meaning of the dream from the dreamer.

This timetable of the ontogenesis of symbols provides us with several new insights into children's dreams:

Dreams which contain psychoanalytic symbols have not been reported prior to the first half of the third year of life. Until then there is no distortion in dreams. Before twenty-six months, dreams are wish-fulfilling dreams.

Anxiety dreams occurring before this time contain direct reproductions of anxiety-causing situations met in recent daytime experience. The appearance of these events in dreams is an attempt at mastery through repetition identical to that which is seen during traumatic neuroses in latency and adulthood.

Blank anxiety arousal states represent attempts to express forbidden wishes and drives during a period when the absence of masking symbols makes the expression of such wishes through dream distortion impossible. Urges without other available representation in consciousness make themselves known through the medium of regression to the level of using somatic disturbances such as anxiety or tachycardia as a direct expression of conflict and affect. Distortion dreams that turn into anxiety dreams and nightmares represent a regression manifested in a decline in the quality of the symbols produced to representations so porous to affect that the dream distortion fails. Disturbances in behavior during the latency period related either to poor symbolizing function with weak displacements (as manifested in failure to enter latency) or to deterioration of the structure of latency are typically associated with nightmares and anxiety dreams containing such affect-porous dream symbols.

Disorders of Arousal

A term introduced by Broughton (1968), *disorders of arousal* refers to a clinical observation that there is an aberrant form of response to stimuli applied during sleeping which is manifested in failure to become fully awake. This occurs only in some children.

The phenomenon was first studied by deManaceine (1897), who found that there were some children who, when aroused from states of deep sleep, did not awaken fully. Rather they entered into a hypnopompic state which lasted five to fifteen minutes. During this state, they showed volitional motor control and one could infer an awareness of the surround. deManaceine found that if one introduced frightening thought content (e.g., the house is on fire) during these states, pavor nocturnus could be induced. Apparently a pathological altered state of consciousness had been discovered which could be entered from the state of sleep.

Still (1900), publishing in *Lancet*, described the occurrence of day terrors. These were periods of extreme anxiety occurring during the waking period of a child's day, accompanied by hallucinated threatening figures. Incidentally, such experiences were reported in adults by Macnish (1834) in the *Philosophy of Sleep* (quoted by Ernest Jones, 1931). Apparently the pathological state described above could be entered from either the sleeping or the waking state. When entered from the waking state, the condition was called "pavor diurnus." When entered from the sleeping state, the condition was called "pavor nocturnus."

There has been scant reference in the literature to pavor diurnus since Jones (1931). I suspect that this is because a break has occurred in the transmission of information from one psychiatric generation to the next, and that the condition is now being called acute hallucinosis (see Brenner, 1951).

The presence of an abnormal state of arousal in certain nocturnal anxiety states led to a loose tendency among child psychiatrists to establish in their minds a separate category of anxiety dreams. Sometimes this category was called pavor nocturnus. Others referred to all anxiety-related disturbances of sleep as pavor nocturnus. In 1958, Melitta Sperling settled the problem in the following way. She called all types of anxiety-laden sleep arousals pavor nocturnus, but then created three subgroups.

> *Type 1* contained the abnormal arousal state. It is characterized by hypermotility, psychoticlike behavior during the attack, volitional motor control, and awareness of the surround and retrograde amnesia for the behavior and thought content during the attack.

> *Type II* was the traumatic type of pavor nocturnus. This is characterized by a sudden onset of terror at night dramatically following a specific trauma. Such a dream is closely related to those occurring during the traumatic neurosis in the adult. Typical of such a dream is the one reported by Sachs (1962). In this report, a child who was frightened by the sound of a bell during the day was wakened from sleep by the same bell heard in a dream.

> *Type III* "is characterized by the occurrence of nightmares with varying contents during sleep, from which the child awakens fully, and with a vivid and often lasting memory of the contents of the dream" (p. 442).

What links all these phenomena together is the fact that there is arousal from sleep. Dreams containing anxiety that do not rouse from sleep are considered anxiety dreams and are not classified as pavor nocturnus.

Some clinical importance has been ascribed by Dr. Sperling to that classification. She felt that *persistent* pavor Type I is an indication for evaluation and treatment with the patient being considered highly at risk for schizophrenia in later life if there is no psychotherapy. It was her impression that the phenomenon occurred during arousal from deep sleep. Type III was considered by Sperling to be neurotic in nature.

In 1959, James Anthony independently reported similar conclusions in a paper in which he presented the results of a study of sixty-six children with sleep disturbances. Among Anthony's conclusions were a differentiation of sleep-wakefulness terror from nightmare identical with Sperling's differentiation. He described the sleep-wakefulness terror as occurring when predisposed individuals are roused from very deep sleep into half wakefulness.

He reported that when attempting to induce such states in predisposed sleeping children, sometimes instead of getting a pavor nocturnus Type I response, sleepwalking appeared. Thus a clinical link between sleepwalking and pavor nocturnus Type I was established. He reported too that pavor nocturnus Type I disappears spontaneously at seven to nine years of age. A statistical study of the appearance of sleepwalking and pavor nocturnus type I correlated with age resulted in the finding that pavor I predominated in the four-to-seven age range while sleepwalking predominated in the eleven-to-fourteen age range. Pavor I people did not necessarily become sleepwalkers. There was found to be a basic psychological difference between the two groups. Sleepwalkers were found to be individuals with poorly developed symbolic, visual, and verbal functions. The pavor I cases were found to be highly verbal symbolizers and visualizers. Half the children with sleep disturbances were studied electroencepholographically. Twenty percent of the cases were reported as showing high voltage slow waves in the EEG.

Electroencephalographic Findings

Electroencephalographic studies have provided a physiological contribution to the understanding of sleep disorders in children. In 1929, Berger discovered that one could record measurable electrical potentials from the brain just as one can record an EKG from the heart. A description of EEG patterns follows. During the waking states, there are two dominant patterns. One, the *beta*, has low voltage plus a frequency of 14 waves per second or greater. This pattern shows poor frequency and amplitude consistency within these ranges. This activity is associated with attention and can be brought about by any stimulus. The second, the *alpha* pattern, has moderate voltage amplitude with a frequency of 8 to 12 waves per second. The pattern shows good frequency and amplitude consistency within these ranges. This wave form indicates a mind at rest. As a person goes into states of drowsiness, the EEG changes. The wave form in drowsiness slows until waves of moderate amplitude at a frequency of 4 to 6 waves per second begin to take over. These are called *theta* waves. They dominate the EEG in light sleep. When this occurs, we say that the person is in stage 1 sleep. The deeper the sleep, the slower and higher become the wave forms until high amplitude waves at 2 to 4 per second, which are called *delta* waves, predominate. When this stage is reached, we call the sleep deep, or stage 4, sleep.

Between stages 1 and 4 there are, as one might expect, two other stages. There is stage 2, in which slow thetas are interrupted from time to time by wave bursts called sleep spindles and K complexes. As the brain wave slows more, delta waves begin to appear and the K complexes and sleep spindles disappear. This intermediate stage is called stage 3. The sleeper does not go from stages 2 to 4 and then back up to wakefulness in a single arc covering a night of sleep. Rather, there are constant shifts in the level of sleep between stage 4 and stage 2. In fact, the shift to stage 2 sleep occurs about five times per night, while a shift down as far as stage 4 sleep occurs about two times.

Within itself, stage 2 sleep has more than one psychophysiological state. Stage 4 sleep similarly is associated with a variation. Both variations are associated with dreaming. Second-stage sleep, other than the episode that occurs during the first descent into fourth-stage sleep, contains in its EEG the appearance of high voltage irregular waves of low frequency. These are caused by electrical currents induced by movement of the eyes. In children, this occurs two hours after the onset of sleep. In 1957 electroencephalographers thought that the eyes were following characters and events in the sleeping patient's dreams.

REM States. Dement (1964, 1965) described rapid eye movements as related to dreaming. Hartmann (1965) has summarized their relationship to a complex set of bodily changes including concurrent flagrant variations in respiration, heart rate and blood pressure, erections, loss of muscle tone, and dreams. These states were called D states or REM states (for rapid eye movements). The latter term has become the popular one.

Because interim wave periods during REM sleep are characterized by stage 1 patterns, one says the person ascends from stage 2 sleep into REM sleep. At first it was believed that dreams only occurred during these stages. Though REM states are almost universally accompanied by dreaming, dreams have been found to occur at any time during sleep.

Synchronized High-Voltage Slow Waves. The variations in fourth stage sleep occur during arousal from this stage. As arousal occurs, steady, high-voltage slow waves which appear all over the head occur. Gibbs (1951) first reported these waves. He noted that they were found only in children, specifically in 95 percent of children in the first year of life, and gradually diminished to zero in normal children over the age of nine (p. 96). Spitz (1970) reported that none of this activity exists on arousal from deep sleep before six months of age.

Brandt (1955) described the EEG patterns of healthy children from zero to five years of age. He described synchronized high-voltage slow wave phenomena as normal in this age group and designated it "hypnogogic hypersynchrony," for he found it to occur in drowsy states as well as states of arousal from deep sleep. Anthony found a similar wave form in the EEGs of 20 percent of children with sleeping disturbances.

Kales et al. (1966) reported on a study of the brain waves of sleepwalkers. He found that somnambulism occurs with arousal from the fourth stage of sleep. The episodes characteristically begin with the sudden onset of bursts of synchronized high-voltage slow waves. These bursts were never seen in normal children at this age (sleepwalking occurs predominantly in children older than five). Psychological immaturity and brain immaturity were implicated as a causal factor as a result of these findings. Kales (1969) subsequently reported that night terrors (pavor type I) occur only during arousal from deep stage 4 sleep. Hypnogogic hypersynchrony, through which the child does not pass into full awakening, is a constant concomitant of pavor type I. He found that bedwetting often occurs during arousal from stage 4 sleep. Ordinary nightmares which rouse one from sleep were found to be associated with REM stage sleep.

Bad dreams that awaken children fully often occur repeatedly (up to six times) throughout the night. Pavor type I and sleepwalking usually occur in the first quarter of a night's sleep. This is explained by the fact that bad dreams occur during the repeated REM states, while night terrors and sleepwalking occur during arousal from stage 4 sleep, which occurs predominantly during the first quarter of the night in children and the first tenth in adults.

The treatment recommended for the abnormal arousal triad varies. Kales (1969) feels that it will clear up with maturation. Drug therapy aimed at reducing the amount of stage 4 sleep has been suggested. Glick and Schulman (1971) have reported positive results from using Valium, which obliterates stage 4 sleep, with no untoward effects. Since exercise during the day increases stage 4 sleep, a diminution of motor activity may also be of value.

Melitta Sperling (1969) postulated a possible relationship between pavor type I in childhood and schizophrenia in adulthood. Some weight is given to this view by studies done in adults who suffer from abnormal arousal states.

Fisher et al. (1969) studied *Incubus*. This is a severe nightmare which occurs in adults. The adult awakens but is confused as to the content of his dream. This was found to occur during arousal from stage 4. Individuals subject to this condition are found to have similar but more highly symbolized dreams in REM sleep on the same night. A specific wave pattern accompanies the abnormal arousal from stage 4 sleep in these people, all of whom have histories of treatment and diagnosis involving psychotic states. Sours et al. (1963), reporting on adult sleepwalkers, states: "A study of adolescent and adult somnambulists reveals that somnambulism is frequently a symptom of pathology indicating fragmentation and profound regression" (p. 412).

The modern appreciation of sleep disorders in childhood divides them into three general categories:

1. Psychosomatic disorders occurring during sleep are not yet fully explained. Asthma (Kales, 1969) is unrelated to stage 4 sleep, but may occur at other non-REM times and during REM periods. Blank anxiety arousal is probably a form of psychosomatic disorder, being a somatic expression of a disturbing drive element occurring before the development of psychoanalytic symbol formation provides a pathway of expression through distortion dreams.

2. Wish-fulfilling dreams, distortion dreams, anxiety dreams, and children's nightmares are phenomena displaying decreasing degrees of symbolic representation of dream wishes. These occur during REM sleep. They are essentially nonpathological.

3. Persistent bedwetting, pavor type I, and sleepwalking are phenomena occurring during an abnormal arousal state involving stage 4 sleep. The latter two conditions can be treated with Valium. The occurrence of these conditions indicates in the minds of some clinicians a potential for pathology in adult life. This is based on clinical observations. Psychiatric evaluation to rule out the possibility of serious pathology potentials is indicated in children with persistent pavor nocturnus or sleepwalking during latency.

The Fetishes and Transitional Objects of Childhood

Latency, both as an ego state and as a developmental time period, is unique among psychiatry's subjects of inquiry. The developmental events and psychopathology of early childhood, of adolescence, and of adulthood: each has its champions and researchers devoted to the minute exploration of these phenomena. Conversely, the events of latency more often than not are approached with preconceived notions based upon experience with other phases. Latency, that seething caldron of developmental events, is viewed as though it were a wasteland whose features are no more than patterns of shadows cast from the zones of development with which the viewer is familiar.

This leads to much confusion. A person familiar with adult psychiatry applies adult criteria to the diagnosis of psychosis in the child. Paranoid regressions in the structure of latency are not differentiated from schizophrenia of early onset (see chapter 8).

The implications of a given clinical symptom or syndrome may be undervalued by a student of infant development who knows of the symptom as a normal step in maturation for a much younger child. Because the clinical symptoms and events of latency tend to be judged by values and laws that apply to other stages, there is a danger that the troubled child will be ill served, or the healthy child subjected to unnecessary procedures. To counter these possibilities, it is necessary in child psychiatry to use certain principles in dealing with a developmental clinical manifestation. Each such phenomenon should be approached and understood in terms of its four possible and often distinct faces. These are the emergent, the persistent, the regressive, and the progressive faces of the phenomenon.

The emergent face of a clinical phenomenon consists of its characteristics when it first comes into being. The appearance of any new phenomenon is a milestone indicating a developmental gain associated with the addition of new functions to the capacities of the ego. The seaweed phobia of little Jan (chapter 3, p. 94) was undoubtedly a pathological symptom since it was associated with anxiety and discomfort for the child. At the same time it was a sign of the appearance of a developing ego function, in this case, the function that produces psychoanalytic symbols. In spite of the similarity of clinical form between these earliest phobias and those that occur after the age of five, intrinsic differences exist because of the emergent nature of the former. One of the characteristics of the infantile phobia is the ease with which the repression of the associative link between signifier and signified can be interrupted by interpretation. A less strong form of repression is operative in the emergent face of phobias than is usually found in phobias which appear in later life. On the other hand, phobias at any stage of life signify the existence of sufficient differentiation of self and object world to permit the projection of impulses within the subject onto a thing conceived of as separate from oneself.

The persistent face of a clinical phenomenon refers to a symptom that persists beyond the time of the first appearance of the ego functions that made its manifest form possible. Its clinical characteristics change in concert with maturational gains made by the underlying ego functions. For example, at five years of age children respond to interpretations of the underlying meanings of phobic symptoms with evidences of a stronger form of repression. As a broad generality, all clinical phenomena should be carefully delineated in terms of their emergent characteristics and those characteristics acquired by the persistence of such types of symptoms (e.g., true phobias, transitional phenomena) into those phases of life in which their constituent ego underpinnings have undergone maturational changes. The nature of symptoms change as ego functions mature. In keeping with this, it is possible for an emergent phenomenon which revealed underlying growth in the years of early childhood to persist into latency where, at the same moment, it signifies and conceals underlying states of interpersonal and intrapsychic disorder.

The persistent face of clinical phenomena is manifested in three ways: (1) the symptom that has never been given up (bedwetting, fear of dogs, security blanket); (2) the symptom that appears during states of regression (fears of monsters in the dark in latency age children); and (3) sublimations reflecting involvement of the phenomenon in ongoing maturational processes (e.g., the ability to utilize, instead of phobia, displacement and psychoanalytic symbol formation for social communication through storytelling and listening).

Manifest psychic activity produced during regressive and progressive ego states are the clinical manifestations of the regressive face and the progressive face of clinical phenomena. If these faces are not considered at the same time during a discussion and the discussants choose to champion different faces, discord emerges. Typical of such discord is the evaluation of the clinical symptom variously called the infantile fetish, the transitional phenomenon, or the transitional object. These names have been applied to such phenomena of the latency age period as security blankets, toy animals, and good luck charms. The typical disagreement pits experts who insist that such objects represent a continuation of a normal stage of development against experts who point to the symptom as evidence of a current ego defect or of ongoing inadequate mothering. In addition, often undetected, such phenomena slip over into the world of sublimative activity.

These phenomena may appear to be clinically identical through similarity of clinical appearances. But a good case could be made for assigning them to separate categories on the basis of distinct and different characteristics related to the distinct and different dynamics that produce them. Since the differential characteristics relate to age and developmental phases, the concept of the four faces of a developmentally engaged clinical phenomenon may serve to differentiate similar psychic events on the basis of intrinsic characteristics.

THE EMERGENT FACE OF
THE TRANSITIONAL OBJECT/PHENOMENON

Transitional objects at any age are interpreted as normal by people whose experience has been with young children who were in the process of developing these clinical signs for the first time. Conversely, true phobias and paranoid symptomatology at any age are often seen by those without training in child psychiatry in terms of their implications when they are found in adults. The preponderant weight given to early developmental experience with transitional objects/phenomena is due to the work of D. W. Winnicott (1953, 1958, 1966). He sought the moment in human development when the child is capable of differentiating self from object and of distorting the "first not me possession" (p. 239) so that in the psychic reality of the child it could serve to gratify an instinctual need. Winnicott (1958) postulated that "at some theoretical point early in the development of every human individual, an infant . . . is capable of conceiving of the idea of something which would meet the growing need which arises out of instinctual tension" (p. 239). Such a capacity he called primary creativity (see chapter 3, p. 43). The realization of a moment in development at which object distortion becomes possible is Winnicott's contribution. Object distortion in the service of fantasy and drive fulfillment or discharge is a philosophical idea with an ancient heritage. In 1511, Erasmus, the Dutch humanist, in *The Praise of Folly* noted that "the mind of man is so constructed that it is taken far more with disguises than with realities" (p. 63). Kant emphasized distortion in his "Critique of Pure Reason." More recently Cassirer (1923), while pursuing the question of distortion of perception in the acquisition of concepts, asked, "But what are concepts save formulations and creations of thought, which instead of giving us the true forms of objects, show us rather the forms of thought itself?" (p. 7) He goes on to speak of "forces": ". . . myth, art, language and science appear as symbols; not in the sense of mere figures which refer to some given reality . . . but in the sense of forces each of which produces and posits a world of its own" (p. 8).

In 1940 Heinz Werner described as "physiognomic thinking" the interpretation of things as " 'animate,' even though actually lifeless" (p. 69) by children in the second year of life. Piaget (1945) published an extended study of a phenomenon he calls "imitation." This denotes the impact of past learned patterns and experiences on the interpretation of a newly perceived object. In Piaget's work ample attention is given to the origins and onset of this skill. In the world of psychoanalytic research, the fact of distortion was well known in the late 1890s. By 1905, Freud had identified the sexual aspects of thumb-sucking, pursuing the observations of a predecessor, Lindner, who wrote on the subject in 1876. Freud traced this phenomenon to antecedents in the anaclitic relation of sexual gratification to the physiological function of nursing. Abraham (1924) sought the paradigm for such distortions in the use by the infant of a real object ("[the child's] *earliest piece of private property*, i.e., the contents of his body, his faeces" [p. 426])•that could be distorted in the psychic imagery of the child for use as a thing for expression of infantile sexual drives. Winnicott's studies caused him to identify the appearance of distortion skills within the four to twelve month age zone in which the growing psyche becomes aware of the differentiation of self and object. The end of this time span, which involves acquisition of awareness that the mothering object can be lost, is indicated to the clinical observer, according to Winnicott (1953), by an intense cathexis of an object such as "teddy, a doll or soft toy, or . . . a hard toy" (p. 229). The zone of experience which has its paradigm in the events of this time span he considers to be the third part of the life of a human being, lying between the purely subjective and the purely objective. He calls this the "intermediate area of experiencing" (p. 239). This is the arena in which primary creativity functions, that is, the ability to conceive of the idea of something which would meet the needs which arise from instinctual tensions. Primary creativity influences the experiencing of reality objects, turning the real "first not me possession" into a need-gratifying object called by Winnicott a transitional object. Experiences characteristic of the intermediate area are referred to as transitional phenomena. The intermediate area becomes a source of instinctual gratification when in reality need-gratifying elements are not available.

The clinical evidences of the effective negotiation of this developmental stage are such transitional phenomena as the baby's own babbling and transitional objects such as a teddy bear. The dynamic nature of the transitional object during the moments of transition to the perception of the mother as a differentiated object have been reconstructed by Winnicott (1966).

> In fact, the object is a symbol of the union of the baby and the mother. This symbol can be located. It is at the place in space and time where and when the mother is in transition from being (in the baby's mind) merged in with the infant and is being experienced as an object to be ceived rather than conceived of. The use of an object symbolizes the union of two now separate things, baby and mother, *at the point of the initiation of the state of separateness*. (p. 369; italics in the original)

That such an object is the indication that self-object differentiation is taking place makes the emergent form of the transitional object an indicator of the beginnings of a healthy maturational step in early childhood. There is no reason to insist that such a step cannot take place in the absence of one of its surface manifestations. On the other hand, the presence of a transitional object provides no assurance that the development of self-object differentiation will be completed successfully. Impairments in this process can result from innate defects in ego structure or poor mothering. It is impossible at the time of the emergence of the transitional object to know if the symptom is pathological or not. At the time that it occurs it is a sign of progress in cognitive maturation as well as evidence that the mother's attendance on the child falls short of his exorbitant needs. The latter is associated with the first awareness of reality limitations and denotes the beginnings of the impingements of the outside world that initiate the development of the adaptive function of the ego. As such, the presence of an emergent transitional object denotes normal developmental underpinnings to the manifest signs of childhood growth.

The natural fate of the transitional object is that it be lost in an ever-increasing crowd of objects cathected in the ever-extending range of interest of the child (see Winnicott, 1958, p. 232). In situations of pathology, patterns of transitional objects and transitional phenomena may persist on into latency, "so that the original soft object continues to be absolutely necessary at bedtime or at time of loneliness or when a depressed mood threatens" (p. 232). This introduces us to the subject of the persistent face of the transitional object/phenomenon.

THE PERSISTENT FACE OF THE TRANSITIONAL OBJECT

The persistent face of the transitional object/phenomenon refers to its characteristics when it continues to be used long after the moment of its transition from a potential to its first moment of being has passed. These are the familiar objects used by latency age children. The character of Linus in the cartoon *Peanuts* has a blanket. Some children persist in sucking their thumbs, and where that is forbidden they suck their tongues, gums, or chew gum. A nine-year-old boy refused to sleep away from home without his unremitting bed partner, Tom-Tom, a brown plush squirrel all dressed up like an Indian girl. A ten-year-old girl willingly travels with her family only if she is permitted to take her special cushion with her. If it is lost she must have a new one selected to her specifications. These are the uncomplicated persistent transitional objects/phenomena. Other forms of persistent transitional objects are seen in situations of severe ego regressions (the regressive face) or persist in the felicitous circumstance in which they serve both to comfort in times of distress and at the same time are socially adaptive, having become linked up with the process of fantasy and sublimation. The characteristics of these latter two forms of substitute objects will be discussed in separate sections. Juvenile fetishes are used here to illustrate uncomplicated persistent transitional objects. Psychoanalysts who have studied these phenomena recognize that they represent a state of pathology. Clinically they are characterized by their persistent presence and a sustained need for them on the part of the child. Actually there is little difference between an uncomplicated persistent transitional object/phenomenon, both clinically and dynamically, and a regressive one. What difference there is is mainly one of degree of regression and ego pathology involved.

Winnicott has described a direct connection between the transitional object and the adult fetish. "The transitional object may eventually develop into a fetish object and so persist as a characteristic of the adult sexual life" (see Yaholom, 1967, p. 380). Greenacre (1960) in describing the relationship of a fetish to the transitional object states that "The fetish of the adult has something in common with the transitional object of infancy. . . . the persistence of the fetish into adult life indicating the need for so prolonged a bridge bespeaks the chronic fault in the somatopsychic structure." A dynamic description of the persistent transitional object here introduces the concept of an intrinsic defect in the "somatopsychic structure" that forms the underpinnings of the ego. Melitta Sperling (1963) has added a psychological dimension to the dynamic description of the persistent transitional object, which she refers to as a childhood fetish. From intensive and prolonged therapeutic work with youngsters manifesting this symptom she has reached the conclusion that the childhood fetish represents a pathological defense in dealing with separation from the mother in situations of pathological mothering.

Whether the interpretation of the nature of the persistent transitional object is based on future potential of the symptom or on psychological or constitutional factors, the opinion of those quoted is the same: Persistence of a transitional object phenomenon into or through latency is a manifestation of a pathological situation. Ergo, the presence of a transitional object in early childhood, though an indicator of maturational progress, is no guarantee of emotional health during the latency age and beyond.

THE REGRESSIVE FACE OF
THE TRANSITIONAL OBJECT/PHENOMENON

The regressive face refers to the characteristics of objects sought during periods of anxiety or breaks with reality (when exposed to darkness or when falling off to sleep, for instance). (Regressive objects, because they continue after the usual years of occurrence of such symptoms, must be considered to be persistent as well, with all of the implications that the presence of a persistent transitional object carries.) Winnicott (1958) at one point noted that "a need for a specific object or a behavior pattern that started at a very early date may reappear at a later age when deprivation threatens (p. 232).

The following case history illustrates one type of regressive transitional object, the psychotic fetish. The youngster turned to the persistent transitional object to the exclusion of other interests and objects including his mother as a stereotyped regressive response to a situation of stress. The characteristics of the regressive face are here illustrated.

CASE 1

A four-year-old boy diagnosed as an autistic child was brought to the clinic by his mother because she felt that his comprehension was better than he had been given credit for by other doctors and by teachers who had seen him. She explained that her nonverbal child always knew the day of the week that *TV Guide* came out, always led her to the place that it was sold on that day, and was never without that magazine. In the interview the child sat near the mother. A *TV Guide* was placed on a table across the room. I began to play with toy soldiers on a table somewhat removed from the child. All during the play, I attempted to make eye contact with the child. The child left the mother and began to move toward the soldiers. I made a move offering a soldier to the child. The child seemed to jump in place and quickly withdrew to the table with the *TV Guide*, picked it up and fumbled it in his hands. The mother was ignored. The child appeared calm. Considerable time passed before he returned his attention to the examiner. He never returned to my table and was eventually led from the room by his mother.

Two dynamic formulations are possible in describing this phenomenon: a response to poor maternal care or a constitutional deficit. Neither explanation would lead one to conclude that the condition reflects a normal developmental state. In the natural course of development, self-object differentiation provides the first non-me object in the form of the differentiated primary object (the mother). If, once object differentiation has been achieved, it is found that gratification is not possible or separations are difficult to bear, the child may turn to comforting schemata such as rocking, sucking, rubbing, or to stroking a transitional object in order to gratify libidinal needs. In such cases the appearance of the transitional object could be a sign of pathological mother-child interaction similar in magnitude to fecal play and rocking (see Spitz, 1949). Sources of the difficulty in achieving satisfaction from the mother-child relationship could be defective ego development in the child (Mahler, 1955) or actual pathology in the object relationship between the mother and the child. Mahler places the responsibility for the defect on intrinsic and innate characteristics. In symbiotic childhood psychosis, she found that "integration of the good and bad mother images, as well as clear differentiation of representations of the part objects in the inside versus the part images of the self, has been defective . . ." (p. 208). When such children are confronted with overwhelming stresses, they experience the activation of primitive organizations of drives and objects: ". . . the real mother ceases to exist as a separate entity. . . . introjected split objects dominate the psychotic child's world" (p. 208). "Very often the introjected objects gain symbolic personification by means of exclusive preoccupation with a piece of cardboard, . . . an adored extremity, a toy animal and the like . . ." (p. 298). "[When] no object image in the outside world can be depended upon . . . then the break with reality and withdrawal into an inner world serve the function of survival" (p. 211). Such a distrust could also be the residue of early experiences according to the theory that persistent and regressive transitional objects/phenomena are rooted in pathological mother-child interactions (see M. Sperling, 1963).

The first truly non-I object cathected is animate. It is the differentiating mother. As a natural progression the child seeks other animate objects. If frustration, threat, or overwhelming affect is met with in approaching these, the child returns his cathexes to himself or the mother. If the mother is not receptive, the child shifts his attention to a substitute inanimate object which can be maintained constantly at hand, can accept the expressions of the drives without complaint, and can, in the psychic reality of the child, be forced to live out the child's desires. Such an object is sought in future situations involving frustration at the hands of reality.

This theory is implicit in the approach to the transitional object of Gaddini (1970), who studied the phenomena in children going to sleep. She expanded the concept to include activities as well as objects. In describing the regressive face of transitional objects, she stated, "At times, it is not any particular object which is especially valued, but rather certain activities which always occur at moments of stress or at bedtime, like rocking or other rhythmic activities. By this means, the child can reestablish his union with the mother after separation. This is in fact the principle which underlies transitional objects and phenomena: *the basis must always be a symbol of union—union after separation*—with the mother" (p. 348; italics in original).

THE PROGRESSIVE FACE OF
THE TRANSITIONAL OBJECT/PHENOMENON

When transitional phenomena persist and are modified in keeping with the ego maturation appropriate to age and stage, yet another face is shown. There are developmental changes in sublimatory and creative potentials in the intermediate area of experiencing. These produce phase-appropriate enrichments and changes in the nature of transitional phenomena. Transitional phenomena are not the only pathway to creativity. Rhythmic movements as a means of reestablishing contact, in psychic reality, with the mother, which exist alone as well as in concert with transitional objects (e.g., rubbing of a blanket) are the experiences of the preliminary developmental stages of creativity. Winnicott (1958), after describing a series of rhythmic activities (babbling, mouthing, plucking, sucking), commented: "One may suppose that thinking or fantasizing gets linked up with these functional experiences" (p. 232).

A theoretical basis for understanding the linkup between rhythmic experiences used in the service of drive discharge and fantasy may be derived from the observations of Piaget. The explanation lies in a theory which solves a minor related mystery for us. If the handling of the transitional object is an expression of an oral wish, then why is it so often manifested in the form of rubbing the thumb and fingers over smooth objects, as in the case of the velvet-fringed blanket? The explanation lies in Piaget's description of the coordination of schemata before the time that the child has awareness of objects (see Woodward, 1965). As is well known, infants touch and rub items such as the mother's clothing or hair between finger and hand while nursing. During the first month of life this is an example of the exercise of reflexes during the stage of reflex schemata. From one to four and a half months there is further exercise of reflexes with reciprocal assimilation. This refers to a coordination of individual reflex schemata into patterns of schemata. Permanent association of patterns are acquired at this time. This development is called a primary circular reaction. One such primary circular reaction is the development of coordinated simultaneous activity of the grasping and sucking reflex ("reciprocal assimilation between grasping and sucking" [p. 62]). The sexual drive energies described in Freud's autoerotic concept as finding gratification through sucking now find gratification in both activities. When sucking is withdrawn at weaning, the other part of the reciprocal assimilation, rubbing with the hand, continues as an available schema through which sexual energies are discharged onto objects. One may theorize that when a child begins to have the capacity to conceptualize at the end of the first year, words and conscious fantasy formations are added to these activities forming a triad of activities available for drive discharge. This triad (sucking, rubbing, and fantasy formation) becomes the outlet through which the child's capacity for psychic distortion bends objects and the world into instruments for the expression of drive energies.

Acts of rubbing and sucking associated with transitional objects are not the only motor patterns (schemata) that are associated with the initiation of fantasy and artistic creativity as a means of drive gratification. At the point in development that conceptual thinking becomes possible, any autoerotic motor schema (e.g., rocking or genital masturbation) can be coordinated with fantasy patterns. *Ideas* become the objects sought or a template for selection of real objects. Though fantasy may become linked with them, transitional phenomena are not the exclusive consorts of fantasy. The following clinical cases are offered as examples of individuals who remained fixed in the developmental stage in which rhythmic activity and fantasy were coordinated in the discharge of drive energies but did not progress to the point appropriate to the child of four when fantasy may be pursued for drive gratification unaccompanied by rhythmic movements.

CASE 2

A ten-year-old girl was brought for treatment for failure to achieve in school. She had a striking, though seemingly unrelated, symptom. She sought out soap wrappers which she would rub until the ink was smeared. Then she would sniff the ink. From the time that she was weaned, she was known to grab rhythmically at the clothing of people who came near her. During the course of her treatment it became clear that during periods of excitement or in states of stress she would turn to rubbing and sniffing. Only at those times could she comfort herself with grandiose fantasies of being a dancing star. Involvement in these activities in school impeded her attention and her ability to learn.

CASE 3

A fourteen-year-old girl was brought to treatment for extended conflict with school authorities which culminated in an episode of stowing away on a California-bound airliner. In sessions, it became clear that she had had great difficulty in controlling restlessness in school since puberty. In order to leave the classroom to smoke, she would engage in such disruptive activities as sticking pins in her face and loud singing. She was well behaved at home. She controlled unrest there by going to her bedroom and bouncing up and down vigorously in a sitting position on her bed. She had been doing this for as long as her parents could remember. She reported that this was the only way she could indulge in a rich wish-fulfilling fantasy life which took her to Hollywood and stardom. Wherever she was, when she was not talking, she rocked slightly but perceptibly in her seat.

If we view this clinical material as representing fixation to an earlier time in the child's life, we can reconstruct a developmental stage in which there is established reciprocal assimilation of schemata involving rubbing, sniffing, and fantasy as a means of expressing drives. In the second year of life newly developed capacities for fantasy formation, coordinated with motor activities produce a new mode for sexual expression. The motor activity may consist of stereotyped motion which involves body contents, body parts, the entire body, or a transitional object. A persistent transitional object may be transformed from a concrete to a verbal psychic event. The object may be replaced by words contained in contexts consisting of fantasies which serve for drive discharge. This process is not at the developmental root of all fantasies but only fantasies that are manifestations of the progressive outcome that affects some forms of persistent transitional objects. Because of their origins, such fantasies can serve as transitional phenomena. As with all fantasy in the latency age, fantasies which have the characteristics of transitional phenomena are involved in the vast unfolding roles for fantasy that are described extensively in chapters 3, 4, and 5. There are some identifying characteristics to the words and fantasies and fantasy-modified situations that serve as transitional objects. These can be seen most easily in situations in which words themselves and fantasies serve as substitutes and comforts in responding to the loss of objects. Kligerman (1970) reports on a repeated dream experienced by Dickens in response to the loss of his "adored young sister-in-law": ". . . he fell into protracted mourning in which he secretly dreamed of her every night for nine months" (p. 799). Dickens included such dreams in his writings. Lost love objects are often experienced as returning in such fantasies. Sometimes they are experienced as hallucinations. Among the Kiowa Apaches such returns are expected and feared. The phenomenon is actually organized into a culture element called "ghost sickness."

Goethe, in his novel *Werther*, resolved his conflicts, at the loss to another of a girl he loved, through putting them on paper and sharing them with a multitude. Perhaps the most direct representation in literature of dependency needs and a hankering back to a lost object, the relationship to which is reawakened and relived through words, are the lines quoted by Frazier (1966) from the British poet John Betjeman, who describes his relationship to a toy bear named Archibald Ormsby Gore:

> Archibald my safe old bear
> Whose woollen eyes looked sad or glad at me.
> Whose ample forehead I could wet with tears
> Whose half-moon ears received my confidence
> Who made me laugh, who never let me down. (p. 11)

Creative artists can use their artistic products to replace lost objects. Adults who read when lonely use fantasy as companion. Many welcome novels of great length or multiple volumes because of the sadness incurred in closing a book and parting from a beloved character-friend forever. Some, especially those of later years who are bereft of company and people to love, turn directly to manifestly sexual content in books as a pathway to drive gratification often accompanied by masturbation. Words serve.

Sometimes entire art forms and audiences become the object of the libido of an individual deprived of other objects. Opera may become the personal life of such a person. Barnes (1973) describes such individuals as ". . . using the lyric theatre not only for its immediate pleasures and insights, but also as a very important way of maintaining their past as a specifically enriching factor in their present" (p. 16). He tells of an old man named Julius, "in many ways unattractive." A refugee scholar, unable to speak English, he could not work as a university professor. "As a result . . . he had to become a factory worker. His entire real life was spent at the Royal Opera House. . . . He seemed very lonely." When asked what kind of life he led, he replied: " 'I lead a very happy life. I find my family in opera' " (p. 16).

Phobias, transitional objects, juvenile fetishes, and paranoid states are not the only symptoms which appear during the latency period. These symptoms and others of the period have been explained and categorized at one time or other on the basis of experiences with other age groups. It is time that the symptoms of the latency age child are viewed from the standpoint of investigations done in clinical situations with these children. The dynamics of the early emergent phases of the development of symptomatologies or far advanced progressive phases should not be emphasized in explaining the phenomena of the latency age at the expense of direct observation during the latency period. I find it useful to keep the differentiating concept of the four faces of the symptoms of latency in mind. If this is done, perhaps more will be learned about latency. Perhaps such endeavors will produce insights which will permit the tables to be turned and provide information (such as case 2 in this section) through which intrapsychic events of other periods can be reconstructed or explained when direct sources of data are inadequate to the task.

Chapter 8

PROJECTION AND PARANOIA

"Never land . . . when you play at it by day with the chairs and table cloth, it is not in the least alarming, but in the two minutes before you go to sleep, it becomes very nearly real. That is why there are night lights."

—*J. M. Barrie*

It is sometimes difficult in the diagnostic process to distinguish between the symptoms of paranoid psychotic states during the late latency period and certain of the fantasy products of the structure of latency. This chapter is intended as an investigation of the different dynamic origins of these clinically similar phenomena. Most psychiatrists are trained first in the diagnosis of adult psychopathology. As a result, they evaluate the degree of involvement of a patient's thinking in persecutory fantasy as a criterion in diagnosing paranoid psychosis. Since persecutory fantasy is a characteristic of certain manifestations of the state of latency, problems can arise when a person trained in adult psychiatric diagnosis first approaches the diagnostic process and attempts to categorize a latency age child who produces this type of fantasy.

When the use of projection is manifest in the fantasy preoccupations of an otherwise apparently well-functioning child, psychosis enters into the differential diagnosis. For instance, a girl of ten with a school phobia reported to me that she avoided school because she was frightened that she would be harmed by the dinosaurs whose chewing she could hear outside the classroom window. This child had friends, was well behaved at home, and did well in her school work. School phobia was obviously an inadequate description of her condition. School avoidance is a situational manifestation of a multitude of different psychodynamic configurations that result from ego impairments. Paranoid reactions, phobic reactions, or symbiotic reactions are a few of the states which can result in school avoidance. The possibility of a childhood schizophrenic process was considered by a clinic group that had studied this child. However, good object relations and the history of fear fantasies during early latency militated against this diagnosis. She was placed in psychotherapy and is now a well-functioning adolescent. By the end of her treatment, she was not considered by anyone to have been a psychotic child. To understand the differential diagnosis in this case, it is necessary to understand the characteristics of some of the more frequent psychotic processes whose manifestations intrude on the latency period. In order to do this, these conditions (psychoses of early childhood, early infantile autism, affect-starvation psychoses, symbiotic psychoses, prepubescent schizophrenia, and paranoid schizophrenia with early onset) should be distinguished from the relatively normal processes which produce persecutory fantasies during the latency age (see below). The term *relatively normal* is used because of the fluidity of the sense of reality of a child in the state of latency.

Psychotic process is defined psychologically in terms of pathological ego functioning. The ego of the latency state would be pathological in an adult, but is normal for a latency age child. The unique characteristics of the latency ego, its structural organization, expected level of development at each age, and the degree of use of individual defenses all have to be taken into consideration as background when making a diagnosis or formulating a prognosis in a latency age youngster. A latency age child who is locked into a fantasy world or preoccupied with persecutors is less a candidate for the diagnosis of psychosis than an adult of thirty with the same mental content.

Benign Persecutory States during the Latency Period

We turn now to a study of the relatively normal processes which produce persecutory fantasies during the latency age. Fantasy preoccupations

which involve persecutors are rarely reported in the literature of child psychiatry (see Harrison et al., 1963). This would give the impression that they
are rare in clinical practice. This is not so, they occur frequently. Projection is one of the most commonly used mechanisms during the latency age
period, though it is not one of the characteristic defenses of the group of
mechanisms of restraint; nor is it usually the focal defense in the structure
of latency.

There are states of ego weakness, however, which occur in darkness,
following illness, and while dreaming, during which the symbolizing function involved in the structure of latency may undergo a regression. There
are even times of great stress when latency fears, which are usually deni-
zens of darkness, invade the day. One ten-year-old boy became fearful that
a lady was following him. For him she carried a threat of doom as punishment for not having done his homework. A girl who at night continually
feared robbers and required a night light became preoccupied with the
fear that the cab driver who brought her regularly to the sessions in my office would kidnap her. She wanted to break off treatment for this reason.
Typically these are children for whom the structure of latency or the latency mechanisms of restraint (especially the intensified obsessive-compulsive
mechanisms described by Silverman, 1972) have begun to fail (see chapter 4).

While a child is in one of these regressed ego states, the symbols used in
his fantasies become porous to the affects they are meant to hide. This is
the result of a shift to the use of a less effective masking signifier as a symbol for dangerous latent fantasy objects. Concurrently, there appears to be
an increase in the use of the mechanism of projection by the child.

Projection is not always a pathological mechanism of defense during
latency. The process of projection is an integral part of any symbol formation which involves denial or repression, plus a signifier derived from
sources outside the boundary of the self. As will be described at greater
length below, projection is a complex mechanism of defense consisting of a
variety of simple defenses.

Projection is operative when responsibility for an affect or thought is
denied or repressed and displaced to an external person or force. Paranoid
ideation is present when the affect or thought, usually unpleasant, is felt to
be directed toward the self from the external person or force. Such an uncomfortable outcome can be avoided through further symbolization. Normally, through the mechanisms of displacement and symbolization, the

nature of the affect, thought, external person, or force in the latent content can be so modified that the original nature of the complex cannot be recognized—that is, it is repressed. In such a state, a pleasant play fantasy is produced. A child's wish assigned to a fantasy character and denied in himself is an example of the usual process of projection involved in fantasy formation. This is a mechanism of the normal process of drive discharge through fantasy symbols that occurs during the latency state. Such strong symbolization characterizes the healthy structure of latency. Weak symbolization undermining the structure of latency results in fear-provoking fantasies. This occurs when symbols are produced that are porous to the affects they should mask. During such regressive states, which produce fear fantasies, the healthy process of projection that is involved in the production of ordinary latency play fantasies is unmasked. When affects are bound by symbols, projection is not so apparent.

When regression transmutes the imputed wish of the fantasy object into an expectation of an action directed at the subject, thus producing fear, the projective process involved in forming the fantasies resembles that involved in persecutory delusions. This impression is strengthened when maturation turns fantasy content from thoughts about fantasy objects to thoughts about real ones. The persecutory object is then a real person. For the diagnostician to whom the mechanism of projection is considered to be pathological only, the surfacing of this mechanism of defense suggests severe psychological impairment.

During the age of latency, pathology should be defined in terms of the porosity of symbolization and the nature of the symbolic signifiers rather than the presence of the mechanism of projection. When the signifiers chosen to be symbols are commonly found objects such as a horse or a dog the pathological states is called a "phobia." When the signifiers are amorphous in form and derived from the child's imagination, they are called "fears"—most often night fears, because they occur during darkness. At times this is referred to as the normal neurosis of latency. One such experience left a child in utter fear for hours when confronted by what he felt was a monster. In reality he had feared his clothes, thrown over a chair and giving the impression of a monster to him. This is typical of an early latency child. After eight to nine years of age, human forms begin to dominate the fear fantasies of children. When the signifiers derived from the child's own imagination begin to take on human form, and the fears and the context in which they appear contain elements of influence, control, and harm to the child, the diagnostician enters the borderland in differentiating psychosis from a structure of latency with transient regressions in the symbolizing function.

It is important to emphasize that the clinical shift to imaginative fantasy objects with human features (e.g., robbers, kidnappers) coincides with the cognitive shift of the object for gratification of the drives from thoughts of fantasy objects to thoughts of reality objects. This shift is characteristic of mid- to late latency. During the latency state, projection's dominant role is to guide latent objects and affects into binding in symbols derived from the world of ideas and verbal signifiers. In early adolescence reality objects replace thoughts as conduits for drive discharge. This shift to involvement with the world as a source of objects opens the way for the mechanism of projection to become involved increasingly with distortion of the world of real things. The shifts here described form part of a normal cognitive developmental series related to drive objects. The nature of objects changes as the child progresses through the developmental stages involved in the latency age period.

The usual progression calls for children to use one of a developmentally predictable series of objects for drive discharge. This has been described in chapter 3 and is briefly summarized in the following paragraphs.

In the years preceding the latency period, from three to six years, children normally derive direct gratification from parents and indirect gratification from poorly symbolized fantasies about the parents. Normally during early latency, from six to eight and one-half years, the use of parents as manifest fantasy objects is minimized. Most gratification is obtained indirectly through the use of well-symbolized fantasies. These provide discharge while masking meaning. During the bulk of the latency period, children normally involve their drive organizations in such a use of fantasy activity for discharge. The appearance of these phenomena is an indicator that the structure of latency is operative.

The mechanisms involved in the production of latency state fantasies may include projections of introjects for use as fantasy content. This process, projection of introjects, is a frequent and normal component of fantasy formation throughout the latency period. Night fears of early latency provide a typical example. The feared elements are projected introjects transformed into highly symbolized fantasy objects. During the period of late latency-early adolescence, from nine and one-half to twelve years, a transition normally occurs in the nature of objects used in fantasy thoughts. Thoughts about fantasy objects are gradually replaced by fantasy thoughts built about objects in reality other than the parents. The feared latent elements in persecutory fantasies come to be represented in the manifest fantasy by real people. With the transition from fearful thoughts about fantasy objects to fearful thoughts about real objects during late latency, the fear fantasies produced become indistinguishable from paranoid delusions involving human persecutors. The isolated presence of such a fear fantasy in late latency-early adolescence cannot be used as a diagnostic indicator of psychosis. This is so in spite of the fact that, as Otto Sperling (1954) has pointed out in describing a related projected introject of childhood, the imaginary companion, "the splitting off either of the prestages of the superego [parental introjects] or of different id drives is in no way different from the projection of the paranoic" (p. 256).

The shift to representation through real people is accompanied during the latter part of late latency-early adolescence by the maturation of the physical apparatus for the discharge of the sexual drive. In addition, there are improvements in cognition in the area of reality testing. Objects for the discharge of drives begin to be sought in reality instead of in fantasy and thought. Projection of introjects onto objects continues to occur during this process. This provides the underpinnings for persecutory ideas involving real objects unless, as normally occurs, the concepts accompanying the introject so projected undergo *more* modification as a result of comparison with reality than the concept of the object undergoes in the psychic reality of the subject.

A note of caution should be introduced about the use of the word benign in describing regressions in the structure of latency which are accompanied by persecutory fantasies. These conditions are benign in that they are usually transient and not associated with thinking disorders and impaired capacity to relate to peers. Although many of these states are transient, in some children the presence of unremitting narcissistic hypercathexis of the fantasies and the subsequent failure to negotiate the vicissitudes of projection promote clinical residua in the form of paranoid and borderline personality states. Psychotherapy is indicated for the latter group of children. It is not life itself that is threatened by such states. Rather it is the quality of life that is impaired.

Regressions in the structure of latency which are accompanied by persecutory fantasy may precede, but are not necessarily antecedent to, paranoid schizophrenia of early onset.

Persecutory States of Pathological Significance During the Latency Period

There is a gamut of possible experiences in relation to fear fantasies among late latency age children. Some youngsters rarely experience such phenomena. For some children fear fantasies are to a greater or lesser degree indicative of transient regressions in adjustment. This condition is relatively benign. It should be differentiated diagnostically from sustained fantasies contained in regressed structures of latency, from prepubescent schizophrenia, and from sustained episodes of what Stutte and Dauner (1967) described as a "delusional system of a kind observed in schizophrenic adults" (p. 418). The keys to prognosis lie in the evaluation of the degree to which there is pathologically increased narcissistic cathexis of fantasy and the success with which the mechanism of projection has undergone the vicissitudes characteristic of the developmental trends expected in late latency-early adolescence (see below). Severe cases involving pathologically increased narcissism and failure to negotiate the vicissitudes of projection are rare. At least two clinical factors appear to be involved when such clinical phenomena accompany persecutory fantasies in late latency-early adolescence. There is a reactive factor which responds to psychotherapy and an endogenous factor which appears to be a developmental phase in a lifelong schizophrenic process.

Nosological terms, such as prepubescent schizophrenia and adult form (paranoid) schizophrenia of early onset, are not applied in the child psychiatry literature consistently. Direct study of late latency age children with persecutory states of pathological significance produces three distinct entities: (1) There are primary regressions in the structure of latency; these have been discussed above. (2) There is a late appearing form of childhood schizophrenia. It has the poorest prognosis of all the childhood schizophrenias. I prefer to limit the use of the term prepubescent schizophrenia to this condition. (3) There are early appearing forms of schizophrenia with characteristics of the paranoid syndrome as it is seen in adults. Prognosis and treatment results indicate that there are reactive and endogenous forms. I prefer to use the term paranoid schizophrenia of early onset to describe these syndromes. Prepubescent schizophrenia tends to occur in late latency. Paranoid schizophrenia of early onset tends to occur in early adolescence. The time of onset may be helpful in making a differential diagnosis but it is not a consistent differentiating factor. Nor are peer relationships during the latency age.

During the premorbid state of functioning in children who develop sustained paranoid states, there is usually a poor social adjustment in school and with peers. They are often grating in their behavior toward others. This results in their having few friends. There is a tendency to use obsessive-compulsive mechanisms and evidence of great difficulty in achieving an individuation from the mother, either in reality or in the form of the struggle to disentangle themselves from internalized imagoes and superego content representing strong parental domination. Preoccupations with changes in the body are striking. Stutte (1971) reported concern in a youngster that his "limbs kept getting larger and smaller" (p. 417).

In understanding and differentiating the many persecutory delusional states during late latency-early adolescence, familiarity with the characteristics of psychoses which intrude during the latency period is necessary background. Psychoses of early childhood leave scarring in the form of cognitive, verbal, and affective impairments which are carried forward into the latency period (see Goldfarb, 1961 and Bender, 1947).

There appear in some children, early in the latency period, psychotic regressions in the face of the separations involved when children first attend school. These are usually manifestations of a symbiotic mother-child tie first brought to light in response to this stress (see Jordan and Prugh, 1971, and Mahler, 1969). These conditions are not difficult to diagnose or differentiate from other psychotic states during latency. Specific cognitive and behavioral components (e.g., intense anxiety in situations of separation from the mother) announce the diagnosis when the child is first seen (see Szurek and Berlin, 1973).

In general the clinical characteristics of childhood schizophrenia differentiate it from early appearing adult forms of the syndrome. In this regard, Bender's comparison between schizophrenia in childhood and in adulthood from the standpoint of hallucinations and persecutory objects is of value. She stated, "In childhood we look for introjection instead of projection" (p. 50). Introjects representing the "good and/or bad mother" (p. 51) become the subjects of the preoccupations of schizophrenic children. These internalized objects are normally conceived of as concrete images by children in the early infantile period. "In childhood schizophrenia, they can be demonstrated and usually persist *until near puberty* [italics mine]. They have considerable influence on the child; in adults they are treated as hallucinations or persecutory objects" (p. 51). During prepuberty, "introjected superegos tend to become projected" (p. 55).

PREPUBESCENT SCHIZOPHRENIA

Prepubescent schizophrenia is a rare, late appearing form of childhood schizophrenia. Many of the characteristics of chronic childhood schizophrenia (e.g., poor relatedness, poor peer relations, persecutory introjects) are present throughout the childhood of prepubescent schizophrenia youngsters. The efflorescence of a clinical state produces the sudden appearance of schizophrenia in late latency.

Bender (1947) described the ages of ten to eleven and a half years as a common time of onset for schizophrenia in childhood. She explained the appearance of persecutory ideas in this way: "With obsessive-compulsive thinking added to the problems of the schizophrenic child with his disturbance in identification and orientation, he evolves persecutory systems in which he suspects that either he or his parents are changed and that other children are against him because he cannot identify with them."

The ego organization of the child who will develop prepubescent schizophrenia is characterized by a domination of the child's apprehension of the world by fantasy and a preoccupation with persecutory introjects during early and middle latency and a projection of these introjects during late latency. Projection of persecutory introjects produces persecutory fantasies involving external persecutors during late latency. By way of contrast, evidence of the projection of persecutory introjects can be detected earlier than four years of age in normal children. Because of the age at which this occurs in prepubescent schizophrenia, reality objects are abruptly converted into persecutors as a result of projection. The concepts accompanying the introject so projected undergo far *less* modification as a result of comparison with reality, than the representation of the reality object undergoes in the psychic reality of the subject.

In prepubescent schizophrenia there is therefore interference with the usual progression in the relationship between drives, the world of fantasy, and the world of objects during the latency period and early adolescence. The child with prepubescent schizophrenia has a history of an extended relationship with internalized parental imagoes in the form of introjected persecutors. The differential diagnosis of psychoses in latency requires that relationships to fantasies and objects be investigated in clinical interviews. The phenomenon that moves the nonschizophrenic child out of latency and into adolescence is the shift to a search for real objects which are not parents or fantasies. There is a move toward an involvement of drives with realistic objects. The childhood schizophrenic is moved, during prepuberty, by similar forces. However, the shift involved is not as total. There is a shift from an involvement with introjects to an involvement with introjects which have been projected to populate the world outside. The shift of cathexes from inside to outside is a cognitive characteristic of the prepubertal period affecting both normal and schizophrenic development.

Some of the primary factors in differential diagnosis concern the nature and developmental history of the introject (internalized object) utilized in the formation of the persecutor. During the early latency age period childhood schizophrenics tend to relate to internalized objects in the form of consciously fantasized little people or objects within their body boundaries. Children in more normal states relate to parents, peers of the same sex, and external objects in fantasy which are not felt to be inside themselves. In nonpsychotic children who have internalized fantasy objects, the fantasy objects are patterned after actual experiences. They are derived from reality and external objects. Rapoport (1944), in comparing the relations of schizophrenic and normal children to internalized objects, stated: "As we turned from the psychoses and approached the neuroses, we found instead of the bizarre primitive and unrealistic fantasy objects [internalized objects] of the former, fantasy objects which were more conditioned by actual experiences and which were more related to reality and the external parents" (p. 320).

The presence of internal persecutors is not pathognomonic of childhood schizophrenia. Rapoport has demonstrated that they may be found in other psychotic states and in neuroses. However, while childhood schizophrenia is not the exclusive domain of persecutory introjects, such introjects are characteristic of the condition. By way of differentiation, the internal persecutors in childhood schizophrenia are more florid, fantastic, and personalized in nature than those found in other persecutory clinical states in late latency-early adolescence. Night fears and persecutory fantasies during early latency are rarely reported.

Prepubescent schizophrenia is in essence an intensification of a pre-existing psychotic state. It appears between nine and twelve years of age accompanied by a decline in school work, perceptual distortions, and persecutory delusions. The appearance of a manifest psychosis at this age is related to the projection of introjects (internal persecutors) which occurs in childhood schizophrenia during the late latency period, in contrast to a much earlier occurrence of this phenomenon in normal children. Hormonal changes, the disruptive pressure of obsessional symptoms which flower during this period, and the pressures of object and peer relationships intensify the cathexis of these fantasies to a delusional level as such an overt psychotic state appears. Those who are able to utilize schizoid mechanisms (e.g., withdrawal) may avoid a frank psychosis while still experiencing the projection of introjects. They avoid contacts that would activate delusional intensification of their persecutory thoughts. They continue to maintain distance through a state of social functioning in which they appear guileless, goalless, and girlless or mildly seclusive, abusive, and delusive. Some persist through life in this way, "well" schizophrenics with functioning that supports a marginal social adjustment; some become "sick" schizophrenics with the appearance of overt delusions in the late teens or early twenties. The appearance of a frank psychosis may call them to the attention of a psychiatrist who will recognize their condition to be an acute phase in a chronic lifelong condition which is sometimes referred to as process, or nuclear, schizophrenia. The initiation of projection of persecutory introjects in late latency, coupled with a fantastic elaboration of the real objects that are represented as persecutors, indicates a discrete clinical entity with a poor prognosis.

PARANOID SCHIZOPHRENIA OF EARLY ONSET

Paranoid schizophrenia of early onset is a form of the adult syndrome which starts in late latency-early adolescence.

During the premorbid period, the children may have good peer relationships. However, this is not reported consistently. Often shallow peer relations are mistaken for good ones. These children tend to have marked somatic preoccupation and are seen more often than the average by their pediatricians. Temper tantrums, intense night fears, persecutory fantasies in early latency, narcissistic hypercathexis of fantasies, and overconscientiousness are frequent premorbid findings. The vicissitudes of projection are poorly negotiated. The literature of child psychiatry—American

(Arthur and Schumann, 1970), German (Stutte and Dauner, 1971; Eggers, 1967), and Russian (Lopandin and Stoyanov, 1970)—contains recent articles relating to this state, which is variously called prepubescent schizophrenia [sic] (Eggers), paraphrenia (Lopandin), and paranoid delusions (Harrison et al., 1963). Although one case reported by Arthur and Schumann occurred at eight years and eleven months, this is exceedingly rare. An equally young case was seen by me, but the child had idiopathic premature puberty. Usually the age at which the delusional systems typical of those found in adult schizophrenia occur is eleven years.

The intensification of drives associated with the late prepuberty years can be overwhelming for these youngsters. Children with poor object relations can evade detection during the early phase of latency when fantasy is an accepted adjustment and the structure of latency is at its height. As a child grows older, and adequate object relations become more honored, fear fantasies take on more pathological implications. In these individuals with narcissistic impairments in object finding, the latency ego organization which operates through the psychoanalytic symbolization of introjects, affects, and latent objects continues to function. However, the projection involved becomes emphasized and the intensity of the sense of reality of the projections becomes still greater. Paranoid systems begin.

The shift to human objects outside the self, though still involved in fantasy, occurs to some extent in all late latency-early adolescent children. In paranoid schizophrenia of early onset this phenomenon results in the use of humans as persecutors and in associated psychotic states. At later life periods, regression to this ego organization produces similar symptomatology.

The ego structure that produces the delusion is difficult to distinguish from the early latency one that produced neurotic fear of monsters. There is, therefore, a problem in clinical differentiation between a disordered state of latency and paranoid schizophrenia of early onset. It is useful in differentiating the two and in establishing a prognosis to understand the vicissitudes of projection during late latency-early adolescence. After a brief comparison of the three conditions—regressed structure of latency with persecutory fantasies, prepubescent schizophrenia, and paranoid schizophrenia with early onset—we will make a digression to study the vicissitudes of projection, and then return to illustrative case histories in the context of a summary and guide to the differential diagnosis of these conditions.

The presence of a sustained paranoid state during late latency-early adolescence represents more than one underlying psychopathological condition. A prognostic differentiation can be made between those who feel persecuted by real people and those whose persecutors are wholly imagined. The former have a better prognosis. Thinking disorders are found in both prepubescent schizophrenia and paranoid schizophrenia of early onset. They are not found in a regressed structure of latency.

There is a split among those who have written about schizophrenic syndromes in late latency in relation to the nature and etiology of the conditions involved. Harrison et al. (1963) and Arthur (1970) give information supportive of psychosocial etiology and a good prognosis with psychotherapy. Stutte and Dauner (1971) write in terms of the patient for whom the "pathoplastic influences of his environment cannot alone account for the illness" (p. 419). Two factors appear to be involved. Psychological and biological factors clearly share a causal continuum. Undoubtedly the ego organization that can produce an unmasking of the projection involved in psychoanalytic symbol formation can also produce a benign clinical state indistinguishable from a paranoid delusional system of a kind observed in schizophrenic adults. The projection of an introject in a prepubertal schizophrenic could give a similar clinical picture. Good relatedness points to a benign condition. A history of bizarre, primitive, and unrealistic internalized fantasy objects points to prepubertal schizophrenia. Obsessional symptomatology appears in benign states, prepubescent schizophrenia, and paranoid schizophrenia of early onset. Thus its presence gives little clue to differentiate the type of condition involved. The prognosis in each condition is vitally dependent upon adequate transformation of the mechanism of projection to benign forms.

The Vicissitudes of Projection

As noted above, prognostic significance may be attached to the effectiveness with which the vicissitudes undergone by the mechanism of projection during late latency-early adolescence are accomplished. There is a normal developmental line, the presence of which indicates the availability of neutralized energy and a good prognosis. As Bender (1947) and Rapoport (1944) have reported, in the children diagnosed by them as schizophrenia with onset in prepuberty there is an intensification and prolongation of the child's infantile preoccupation with concretely perceived internalized objects. This condition persists into late latency, at which time it diminishes. In these children, the introjects then begin to be projected, producing paranoid symptomatology. In children in whom neurotic mechanisms are at work, projections of introjects, especially those related to superego contents, assume symptomatic proportions (e.g., night fears) as early as age four and a half and increase during the latency period. Persistence of these defenses during late latency-early adolescence produces a clinical picture similar to that produced by the schizophrenic child when he first begins to project internalized objects at this age. However, in the child with projection used in the context of the normally neurotic ego organization of latency, there is eventually a diminution in the fear symptomatology. This progress may be impeded by the degree of intensification of the narcissistic cathexes of self and fantasy that normally occurs during early puberty.[1] In children dominated by fear fantasies, a good prognosis is indicated if changes occur in the use of projection, when thoughts of fantasy objects are replaced by thoughts of real objects during late latency-early adolescence.

Gardner and Moriarty (1968), in their study of personality development in preadolescence, included an evaluation of projection. They studied psychological test results and related cognitive controls, and concluded that there is no change in the intrinsic nature of projection during preadolescence. Their finding did not preclude the possibility that there were changes in the style of use of projection or changes in the characteristic groupings of simple defenses which combine to produce projection.

Projection is a complex mechanism of defense. It is one of those defenses made up of a combination of simple defenses. Complex mechanisms of defense in their adult form are not givens. Their final forms are often the product of an interaction between maturational developmental events and the environment. In turn, modifications in defenses shape development. Late latency-early adolescence as a developmental stage contributes strongly to this process in the case of projection.

To understand the vicissitudes of projection, the various forms in which it appears should be defined.

Anna Freud (1936) has provided a most useful touchstone for the definition of projection as used by psychoanalysts:

The effect of the mechanism of projection is to break the connection between ideational representatives of dangerous instinctual impulses and
the ego. In this, it resembles most closely the process of repression.
Other defensive processes, such as displacement, reversal or turning
around the self, affect the instinctual process itself; repression and projection merely prevent its being perceived. In repression the objection-
able idea is thrust back into the id, while in projection, it is displaced on
to the outside world. (p. 132)

Waelder (1951) related the exclusion from perception of ideational representations of dangerous instinctual impulses, during projection, to the
mechanism of denial.

When projection takes place, (1) the verbal representation of an instinctual impulse is excluded from perception, (2) the instinctual impulse is
displaced on to some object, person, or thing outside the self, and (3) there
may be a reversal of the impulse, e.g., sexual feelings give way to aggressive feelings. Projection, as it appears in paranoid states, is a combination
of denial and displacement. Denial excludes ideational representatives of
dangerous instinctual impulses from consciousness. Displacement assigns
the dangerous instinctual impulse to persons or objects other than the self.
Hostility or sexual impulses are assigned to the persecutor. Projection as it
appears in a phobia is related to a more varied group of simple defenses.
Projection occurring during phobia formation is associated with repression, displacement, and psychoanalytic symbol formation.

A clinical classification of projection can be elaborated on the basis of
the simple defenses of which it consists. Projection associated with *denial*
and displacement is involved in paranoia. Projection associated with *repression*, displacement, and psychoanalytic symbol formation is involved
in the formation of phobia. This classification of projection, through the
differentiation of the combination of defenses of which it consists, will
help delineate the vicissitudes of projection that will be described.

Projections can also be classified according to the origins of their gross
content. There are projections of manifest drive representations, e.g., the
projection of an instinctual drive representation such as a thought that
someone wants to kill the subject. These may be called id projections.
There are projections of inhibitory urges, e.g., the projection of self-
condemnatory thought in depressives and the feeling of guilt that some
people have when they see a policeman. These may be called superego
projections.

The persecuting object (the "someone who wants to kill" the subject) is derived from parts of introjects with whom the drive representation or self-condemnatory thought is associated.

MANIFESTATIONS OF PROJECTION DURING THE LATENCY STATE

During the latency state children represent their latent fantasies through manifest fantasies which contain latent elements in symbolized form. The latency state is produced when the structure of latency is established. It permits the child to channel drive energies and latent fantasies away from primary objects and peers. Gratification is derived from manifest symbols in fantasy. In this way potentially disruptive motivations and drives are siphoned off or diminished. When the symbols used in this activity are insufficiently displaced from the signified object or affect, the symbol is developed with valence for attracting manifest affects. In these circumstances, the fantasies produced by the structure of latency take on a phobic quality. At such times the role of projection in the structure of latency becomes manifest. It can be identified as that form of this complex defense which is associated with repression, displacement, and psychoanalytic symbol formation.

Children seen in analysis through the late latency-early adolescent phase who experience fear fantasies expose the projection involved in the latency state. A study of the developmental changes in projection in these children provides information on the vicissitudes of projection during this period. I have chosen to describe one of these youngsters who, in the process of growth, developed transient persecutory fantasies. This will facilitate a comparison between neurotic children at this age and youngsters who develop the paranoid delusional systems of prepubescent schizophrenia.

R.B. was brought to treatment for poor school performance, massive temper tantrums with uncontrolled aggression which was clearly verbalized, intense fears that robbers would come into the house and kidnap or steal her, a disorganizing low self-picture, headaches and vomiting, and a disdain for being a girl. She had few friends. The patient had one older sister. The sister's progress in physical and emotional development gave my patient overstimulating advance information in regard to interesting sexual developments that were about to befall her. She had one overriding conscious wish: she wanted to be a boy.

One of her first statements was, "I want to be a boy. How can I get a penis?" Through hours of fantasy which elaborated on this theme, it became clear that this was not only a reexperiencing of feelings of awe, envy, and deprivation felt at the time that she conceived of the fact that the differences between the sexes were marked by organ differences. There was, in addition, the belief that being a boy would make her stronger than she was. Possession of a penis was seen as a sort of special symbol that would give her strength, rather as the medal made the cowardly lion brave in *The Wizard of Oz*. She lived out the latter fantasy in many ways. She insisted upon wearing boys' pants. When she had to wear a skirt, she wore boys' shorts underneath. Interpretation could interfere with the use of the fantasy of being a boy as a means of dealing with her drives. At such times, alternative fantasies of a phobic nature (fear of attack by intruders) were mobilized. In the sessions she tied a doll or gun in such a way that it dangled in front of her thighs. In her fantasies and stories she took the part of a boy. She cherished her secret boy's name, George. Her mother would have called her this had she been a boy. She told fantasies of lands in which there were no sexes so that she need not feel weak. As her associations progressed, it became clear that her wish to be a boy became most intense in situations in which she felt weak and pushed around and angry. She felt that a boy's physical endowments helped him to control his feelings. Similarly endowed she would magically also be able to control her weakness, loneliness, and anger. Separations, camp homesickness, and situations in which her mother's rules overrode her desires were most apt to intensify these fantasies, aggressive behavior, and temper tantrums. Masculine fantasies were interpreted as a defense in dealing with her anger at being overwhelmed. This resulted in a diminution of penis envy and the expression of aggression.

In spite of the personal meaning, her fantasies are typical latency robber phobias. She feared that robbers would break into the house when she was in bed and hurt or steal her. She needed a night light to protect her from this. Later, when she appeared no longer to need the night light, she confided to me that she turned off her light and then went to bed with her eyes closed so that she could not possibly see anyone who might come in. There was marked concern that the closet door be closed. There was fear of who might be in there.

The following are fantasies and dreams of the patient, revealing the predominant content of her fantasies early in treatment. They typify latency fantasy activity and are chosen because the projection involved in the structure of latency is so apparent.

In one such fantasy, a doctor is sleeping. He gets up and goes to his office to see a patient. He makes up his bills and gloats over all his money. He becomes excited about having so much money. As the excitement mounts, a robber suddenly comes in. The doctor kills the robber. The police come. He worries about the police. He hides the robber's body in the closet. He becomes very concerned lest the police find the body. By the end of treatment she revealed that the symbol of the robber was a projection of her own activities. The fantasy had occurred during a period when she had stolen from her mother.

A dream from early in analysis follows. It illustrates marked projection of impulses to a symbolized attacker. At the time the family lived in a small town in Texas.

There was this monster in my town. I don't know what it was and for some reason he seemed to stay especially around our house, and it said on the radio, when the monster comes, shut all the windows and put all the shades down because if he sees you through any window, he'll come and kill you, and he'll take you away and you won't know where he takes you. Of course, everyone was scared in the family, but I was the most scared for some reason. Since the monster was around our house, I wanted to go stay in an apartment. So Mommy, Daddy, and I went to another place. When we got there, Daddy said he didn't like the place. He wanted to go home. Everyone went home. I stayed and slept by myself. Next morning, I went home too, 'cause I missed the family. I was coming to the house. I didn't see the monster. Then I saw it. They were about to open the door and let me in. The monster was big, an animal like a dinosaur. He started climbing the screen and he climbed the shingle right up to my sister's room. I was sleeping there with her. Daddy called the police car to our backyard. They caught the monster. They tied his arms, neck, and leg. He was taken to a scientist. . . . It was some kind of old ancient animal, the kind they had when dinosaurs were around. They put a brain, body, and skin in and made it come alive. They didn't know it would come alive. They didn't want it to come alive. It got out during the night. They said it would never happen again.

Through an intensification of fear of attacks from robbers and intruders the mechanism of projection made possible this cryptic guise. Through it, intensification of aggression found expression. In this child the formation of phobic fantasies transmuted her drives. Projection afforded her protection against loss of direct control over her anger and temper. The child's own wish to hurt or steal was represented symbolically by a monster or a robber. The motives imputed to these attackers embodied the child's own urges. She characteristically instilled these phobic thoughts into her defensive manifest latency fantasies. Projection participates in the form of the structure of latency. When such phobic responses interfere with function, a disruption of latency can occur. Projection associated with repression is dominant at this time.

Let us take a closer look at her fear fantasies. She has already shifted the content of the thoughts involved in her fantasies to include realistic objects. A younger child would characteristically have included monsters or amorphous figures. The people she fears are not truly among those she meets each day, but are creations of her own imaginings. Most of their characteristics could be traced to introjects patterned on parental attitudes and behavior. The robber content related to the child's own experience of having stolen from her mother.

Oedipal fantasies and concern about attack, being killed, being hurt, being stolen are all present in this series of fantasies and dreams. In these fantasies her own overwhelming sexual and aggressive (id) urges are poorly repressed. They are displaced onto psychic representations of the outside world, which are perceived and feared as though they were external to herself. Rarely does she articulate her own urges with real beings. Rather, she fears symbols of herself, whose actions represent her own inner impulses and introjects. These are typical of the projection-dominated fear fantasies of latency. As such, they can be used as a baseline. The metamorphoses of projection that occur during late latency-early adolescence can be defined by referring to this baseline.

There are three developmental steps in the shift from latency to early adolescence in which specific vicissitudes of projection take part: (1) improvement in object relations, (2) maturation of sublimation, and (3) modifications in the superego. With regard to step 1, there is a shift from projection associated with repression and symbolization (e.g., phobias) to projection associated with denial (e.g., fear-fantasies regarding peers). Fantasies can be checked against reality. For step 2, there is a modification in the symbolizing function (which participates in projection) that permits the child to project urges without anxiety. For step 3, modification of the superego, there is a shift from id projection to the projection of superego introjects.

Vicissitude 1

As the patient R.B. approached twelve years of age, she had fewer fantasies and she involved herself more with real people in her environment. At the core of her fantasies had been a feeling of great weakness and vulnerability. To protect herself from this, she had mobilized aggression and searched for strength. She had represented this consciously through the fantasy that she had a penis and was a boy. Alternatively, she had projected the aggression. This resulted in her fantasies of attackers. As she grew older, the basic feelings of weakness did not cease. There was a change in symptomatology only. Though her phobic symptoms were resolved, her problem remained. New symptoms appeared to represent them. Instead of displacing her anger on to a robber who was linked to me, she recognized the anger as her own. Typically, she expressed it directly at me. At times of stress, the content of the analysis no longer emphasized fear of robbers or dreams and fantasies of being attacked. She now attacked me. She would claim that she was justly angry at me for not explaining things or not doing as I had been ordered. She noticed that the moment she left a session, the anger disappeared. The parents reported that such anger was not seen outside the office and that things were serene at home.

During one of these episodes, I interpreted to her that this anger was used to defend herself against her feelings of weakness, especially those feelings stirred up by wanting to talk with me about sex. Following this interpretation, she became calm and spoke of a worry she had had. Her sister had shared a bed with her on a recent trip. The sister had masturbated and had become very excited. She began making all sorts of hard breathing noises. This had bewildered my patient. She also talked of her fear that she would be forced to have intercourse as a teen-ager in order to be a part of a group to which she wished to belong. Projection—this time without symbol formation—colored her early adolescent fantasies. Her sexual and aggressive urges were now fused in masochistic fantasies in which she was forced by others to perform sexual acts. Her sexual urges were no longer represented in phobias. Now she had moved to the direct articulation of her sexual drives with peer objects. However, she could permit them access to consciousness only if she denied that the impulses were hers and could displace them onto potential sexual partners. The dominant mode of projection had shifted. An anxiety-laden part of the latent world of fantasy had been created through the use of projection associated with repression, displacement, and symbol formation. Manifestations of this in early adolescence became relatively unimportant. In its stead, anxiety haunted her potential relationships with others. The real world of peers now became the woof into which she wove the urges and impulses that she denied within herself. This reversion to a more primitive level of ego functioning is not pathological per se; it is to be expected at this age.

This regression provides a mechanism through which fantasy can be checked against reality. Drives are no longer primarily synthesized into derivatives which are totally fantasy, discharging energies into id-dominated dreamlands. The projections of late latency to early adolescence involve real people. The situation can be discussed and corrections made. This provides the child with the opportunity of testing the reality of her fantasies in a manner not available to the latency child. As a result, fantasy becomes less dominant and reality less threatening. Guarantees of the secondarily autonomous functioning of the ego in relation to the id are strengthened. The stage is set for appropriate articulation and discharge of drives involving real members of the peer group.

Vicissitude 2

Maturation of sublimation is the primary change involved here. Projection associated with repression and symbol formation remains, but it is quantitatively less dominant. Symbols are selected which mask meaning so well that they may be used without creating anxiety. This becomes the basis of sublimations which express latent fantasy. Projection, though persistent, appears in less obtrusive form. The mechanisms of the structure of latency are freed of their task of creating fantasies as the primary pathway for the discharge of the drives. The latency structure persists, however, as the basis of the formation of sublimative creativity. The socially obligatory aim-inhibited fantasies of latency become the basis for the socially encouraged facultative fantasies of society—the fantasies that serve culture by binding peoples through shared stories and experiences. In addition, old myths and traditions are refreshed through retelling in modern modes.

When R.B. was ten, she brought in the following poems. They are typical of the poems of latency.

That House is Really Haunted
That house is really haunted.
Ghosts come out at night.
Their howls and screams are scary.

My New Puppy
My puppy is very scared.
He was behind the chairs.
His mother is not with him.

These poems show displacement but no masking or dulling of the affects associated with the conflicts. They are typical of the poems she wrote at the time.

At the age of thirteen she brought in a different kind of poem. Note here the absence of direct personal involvement.

> The sun rises shedding her golden light
> over hill and dale.
> She called out man and animal.
> Birds take wing.
> A new day begins full of sunlight and
> happiness.

She also began to write plays for school. The plays were similar in context to the dreams and fantasies that had caused her so much anxiety. Yet now they were fun. Sublimation had begun in this area. In one play, Rat Fink Freddy is one of a band of robbers. He gets a woman to tell him where jewels are hidden while having sexual relations with her. The woman says, "You want money, I'll show you so much, you'll drown in it." The robbers are captured and go to prison where they are forced to exercise.

She continued to write poems. Some were hopeful; others continued the theme of attack. A hopeful example, "The Morning Sun":

> The sun rises and sheds her graceful
> rays upon the trees,

> In the distance, the rooster crows
> to let everyone know that
> the sun has opened the day.

An attack example, "They're coming":

> They're coming! The British are
> coming over hill and dale.
> They're coming! The British are
> coming to leave a trail of
> blood and death to show
> their hate.
> But no, no, we will withstand
> Each man will make his stand.
> Every man is his own sergeant when
> bloodshed is at hand.

In latency, projection contributed to the formation of fear fantasies. As R.B. approached adolescence, fantasies with similar content appeared. They differed in that she ceased to be the object of attack and the symbols were sufficiently masked that they were no longer sources of anxiety for her. The fantasies formed the basis of poems and plays. Creative activities (sublimations) became the phase-appropriate areas for the manifestation of projection associated with repression and symbol formation.

Creativity takes many forms as a child develops. The prelatency child has the greatest latitude in spontaneous creativity. He has access to poetic and original concepts of word use. Symbol use is relatively shallow. The latency child has less latitude because of learned cultural limitations and of socially dominated mythopoetic creative boundaries. There is in the latency child greater use of symbols which distort meaning as they represent. From the point of view of quality and depth of symbolization, there is greater creativity than in prelatency. Latency age drive discharge occurs predominantly through creative fantasy formation. Discharge in fantasy rather than communication through fantasy is primary. In the latency state, inhibition of the aim of physical discharge is a general characteristic of the organization of drive discharge. In adolescence, inhibition of the aim of the physical discharge or drives is a facultative phenomenon. When it does occur, it is usually associated with sublimation. True sublimation does not occur until the symbolic forms associated with the projective component of the creative process can absorb the projected contents of the creator's psyche and represent them in modified form, such that the affect associated with them is not identifiable with the personal experiences of the artist. As in other areas of development, including the transitions of late latency-early adolescence, the shift from fantasy as object to reality as object is of primary importance.

In the sublimatory creativity of adolescence, the fantasies and their verbal or plastic representations serve equally as a means of object finding and as a symbolic representation of aim-inhibited drive discharge. The latency child tends to use creativity as a means of expressing drives. Adolescent and adult sublimation has this characteristic, but in addition it is preoccupied with the intent to please (see Reinach, 1903, p. 265).

In adolescence, drive discharge through fantasy becomes a means of object seeking. Creativity manifested in fantasy, in poetry, prose, art, and song becomes a mature sublimative creativity when the intent to please and the communicative value become important characteristics of the work.

Vicissitude 3

In Vicissitude 1, we saw that the use of id projections in interpreting the motives of individuals in R.B.'s environment became dominant during late latency and early adolescence. A shift from id projections to superego projections also occurs in interpreting the motives of the individuals in the environment. This can result in a reevaluation of the superego, and changes in the superego may follow.

When the patient was thirteen she found that she could not write book reports. There was a definite work block. Investigation revealed that each time she was assigned a book report, she tried to put into action her mother's admonition to be creative. She tried to begin each report with a literary flourish with which she would dazzle the reader. The problem was that once this was written, she found that she had no way of connecting the introduction to material of a factual nature related to contents of the book. We analyzed her need to please her mother and the way she carried her mother with her in whatever she did. The therapist interpreted this to be a part of the conscience—inside and outside. She had no identity of her own in the circumstance of noncreative writing and was skewed out of a logical position by the influence of the maternal introject. Once she could see this, she became better able to write factual material spontaneously.

This was a step toward individuation from the mother. It was related temporally to talk of termination of treatment. Though no definite time limit has been set, she had begun to break from her mother and was soon to part from me. In her search for a substitute object, she became preoccupied with a science teacher. She denied her right to an ego ideal, and, instead, she projected the right to control her to the science teacher. Everything that she did, she checked in her mind with the science teacher's wishes. She would ask herself if the teacher would approve or disapprove of what she was doing. Actually, she actively projected her own ideas, giving them value by representing them as the wishes of another respected person.

Her conscience was an incorporation of and identification with her mother. She sought to undo this tie by finding someone else to take on the role of the conscience. She told of the relationship to the teacher without concern. Since the teacher was an unknowing passive participant, she did not threaten the patient's own fear of passivity. This was a satisfactory resolution for the child. However, the situation lost its satisfaction when her active strivings, manifested in projecting her ego ideal onto the teacher, were superseded by her passive-fusion strivings. This took the form of feeling obliged to say "science is a good subject" right in the middle of an unrelated conversation with friends at lunch. She felt embarrassed and became anxious over her embarrassment. When she analyzed her behavior, she recognized that this use of the teacher was a projection of her own internalized ego ideal (i.e., introjects). R.B. was able to recognize her search for someone to replace the mother-analyst guide for directing her behavior. She was able to accept her own principles and behavior as her own.

Concurrently she became very angry that a definite date for termination could not be set by herself alone. Tenderness, the need to take me with her, her sense of mourning had been worked through. Why did she have to continue? When I stood firm on the fact that termination was a natural process and that the decision could not be made unilaterally, she fell silent. In the next session she explained that she had been silent because she did not know what to say. She wanted to be certain of what she was going to say. She said, "I had to think it through first." I related this to the fact that she was uncertain of herself, just as she had been when she did not know whether she was a boy or girl. She wanted to be able to make a decision alone, to prove that she was in charge and could be whatever she wanted to be and could do whatever she wanted to do. She wanted to defy the rules of nature. She insisted that she make decisions even when they could only be made by a natural process. I pursued the example of being born a girl. She insisted that there were operations through which people can change their sexes; therefore such decision-making was possible. I said, "Even those who have already changed, can they change back?" She replied, "No, it's final." I said, "So there are some decisions that are out of our hands." She then said that she wanted to be honored by making the decision. Only in this way would she feel that she would be seen as an individual. I asked her if she had ever been this angry before about this. She recalled how her mother had called her and her sister "Resther" (a combination of Rose and Esther), obliterating the individual identity of the two children. She had become as furious then as she when she was not given the right to set the termination date. She also needed to think things through first so as to be in control of the analysis and not be forced to take my interpretations. Anger was mobilized by states of passivity which stirred the conflicts related to her fusion wishes. She had a problem in her ego boundaries and identification. She fought to be an individual. At the same time, she dreaded giving up the fusion with her mother. She compromised, as can be seen in the episode of the science teacher, by projecting her superego strivings onto someone whom she could control.

Such a projection of superego introjects onto the environment provides an important developmental potential. Teachers, older siblings, and peer groups do not always remain passive receptors. Often they provide new inputs. To the child these inputs can be indistinguishable from projected elements. Through the incorporation of these ideas, which accompanies reincorporation of the projected introjects, values foreign to the parents become part of the child's superego. Sanction may be obtained through this mechanism for the appearance in manifest behavior of formerly latent sexual and aggressive fantasy elements.

In early adolescence there may occur a strong conflict in response to intensification of wishes for fusion and passive yearnings. In rebellion against this, the parental imagoes within the superego are disavowed. They are projected onto others. Through this mechanism the child may continue unchanged, but with external controls, for example, the child who has inhibited masturbation, feeling that "someone is watching and doesn't approve." Peers and teachers are sought as substitutes to provide new ego ideals or to subserve the old ones, avoiding conflicts related to the child's need to avoid fusion with the parents. The outcome is not always positive. The child may use others as guidelines for behavior that defies the parents. This is an expression of the need to avoid sexualized passive positions in relation to the parents.

Early adolescence is a period during which there is a change in the superego. Usually this involves a reevaluation of limits or the acceptance of the rules of a subculture. Many defiant youths wear identical and identifying uniforms. They march to a different drum, but the rhythm is the same for all of them. Could this not be a manifestation of an externalization of the superego similar to that which my patient experienced? Instead of a teacher whose preferences could not be distinguished by my patient from her own, these youngsters choose a peer group.

My patient soon understood that she had projected her conscience onto the teacher. She resolved this by reevaluating her conscience. She reinternalized that which she felt was unrelated to her mother's neurosis.

Let us summarize here the vicissitudes of projection. During late latency-early adolescence there is a change in projection. There is also a definitive shift in its uses. The change in projection is seen in the shift in the nature of the simple component defenses that make it up. There is a shift from projection associated with repression toward projection associated with denial. This shift is supported by a number of phase-related developmental phenomena. The most important of these is the passing from prominence of the typical ego structure of latency. Residues of the structure of latency persist in daydreaming, future planning, and sublimations. The use of symbol and fantasy structures diminishes. Direct involvement of drives with objects instead of involvement with fantasy representations takes place. This is seen clinically in our patient's shift from fear of attack by robbers to fear of being forced into sexual acts by her peers.

There is a similarity of psychic events in the late latency-early adolescent phase to psychic events in the separation-individuation phase of infancy. In both phases there is an experience of separation from the mother, with increasing individuation manifested in the child's increasing executive functions. Problems of passivity coupled with fear and eagerness for fusion occur in both phases. Most striking is the fact that in both phases there are changes in the awareness of the body. In the adolescent there is massive growth and the development of secondary sexual characteristics. In the infant the sense of bodily change is related to the developmental-maturational growth of cognitive functions with a concomitant constantly modifying perception of body form. The parallel between the two periods sets the stage for a regression in the adolescent that permits the utilization of defenses, i.e., denial and displacement, appropriate to the earlier period.

A change in the use of projection is seen in the shift of the primary role of the defense from fantasy and symptom formation to an important role in (1) testing fantasy against reality in establishing object relations, (2) sublimation and creativity, and (3) opening up the superego to contemporary cultural influences.

There is a shift from projection of id impulses to projection of superego introjects. Through projection, the superego is externalized. The child who attributes her formerly internalized commands to a peer or teacher acquires an externalized ego ideal, with characteristics of the ego ideal of the new object. With reinternalization of the ego ideal (the projection-reinternalization is a dynamic, ongoing series of events) modifications of the superego take place. Evidence that the above-described normally expected changes in the use of projection are taking place during late latency-early adolescence indicates a positive prognosis in the presence of persecutory fantasies.

SUMMARY AND GUIDELINE FOR DIFFERENTIAL DIAGNOSIS

During late latency-early adolescence, a single clinical manifestation, persecutory fantasies with human persecutors, can serve as an indicator of the presence of any one of a number of psychopathological entities. Among these are: prepubescent (childhood) schizophrenia, paranoid schizophrenia with early onset, and transient paranoid states which are manifestations of a regressed structure of latency. Each of these states has distinct characteristics in terms of premorbid personality, clinical course, and prognosis.

Prepubescent (childhood) schizophrenia has the most distinctive characteristics of all of the possible conditions. Whereas in the other entities a shift from fantasy preoccupation with persecutory introjects to preoccupation with projected fantasies begins before the age of four, childhood schizophrenics engage in fantasies which are primarily related to persecution by introjects until they are eleven years of age. They behave as though the subjects of the fantasies were concrete and within the body. The contexts of these fantasies have bizarre content. They form an important part of the child's fantasy life. One seven-year-old described a lizard who lived in his throat and talked to him. A shift to thoughts of real people from thoughts of fantasy objects for libidinal drive discharge is characteristic of late latency. The schizophrenic child participates in this as does the normally neurotic latency child. This results in a change in the nature of the symbolization of the introject to greater emphasis on representations having humanoid forms.

A nine-year-old boy was referred for evaluation because of a tendency to start fights while waiting on the lunch line in school. His mother had died the year before, and as a result he had been sent to a child-caring institution for normal children, which in turn had assigned him to a foster home. He was a loner, with few friends. His schoolwork was only passing fair. He was conscientious and made efforts to please. Staff members liked him and took a more than usual interest in him, in spite of his obvious limitations and distance. He confided to those who were close to him that when the top was being placed on his mother's coffin, he had seen her hand move. The affect associated with the telling of this was quite bland. He did not integrate this information with any other preoccupations or delusions. One delusion of which he spoke related to the belief that a devil lived in his head. He broke his quiet demeanor to start fights when others cut in line in front of him in response to orders from the devil who lived in his head. If he failed to obey this devil, the devil shoveled coal into a furnace within his head which sent pain through ducts contained therein, which caused him to have severe headaches. He had no doubt that the devil and the duct system were present and drew a picture of the devil at work (see figure 6).

During prepuberty, childhood schizophrenics achieve fantasy formation through the use of symbols based on signifiers outside the body. Fantasies, affect, and conflicts, formerly expressed in terms of introjects, are dealt with through projection after the age of eleven. Therefore, in prepuberty, persecutory fantasies of childhood schizophrenics take on a characteristic form containing hostile motivations projected onto real or imagined people.

A twelve-year-old girl began to show an inability to control her aggression in school and at home. Although she tried to control herself and was quite well behaved for periods of time, her unpredictability made her

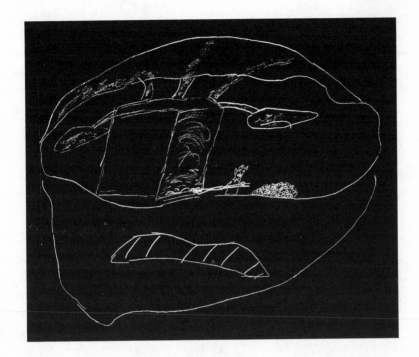

Figure 6

teachers and parents seek professional consultation. She had never had friends. There was no history of night fears or phobias. She was admitted for observation to a city-run mental hospital facility. Mercurial mood changes and poor peer relationships led to her rejection by the other children on the ward. They objected to the limitations on their activities that were placed by the staff in an effort to get the group to put pressure on the child to function well in spite of her obvious psychotic disorganization. The child complained that when she looked in the mirror her face was green. She refused to participate in individual or group psychotherapy because she feared that the FBI had placed listening devices in the office. Three months of pharmacotherapeutic and milieu therapy did not alter her condition in the least. She was transferred to a state hospital facility for children for long-term care.

The psychotic symptomatology which appears in prepuberty (usually after eleven) is characterized by persecutory fantasies, a failure to negotiate the normal vicissitudes of projection, and poor peer relations. The prognosis is poor.

Bender (1974) in her long-term follow-up study of a hundred children diagnosed as childhood schizophrenics noted that thirteen had a pubertal onset. In a previous study she concluded that "the prognosis was unfavorable especially where the onset was at puberty" (1970, p. 167). The differentiating clinical characteristic of this condition is the absence of persecutory fantasies involving projection before age eleven and the presence of preoccupation with bizarre influencing introjects before that age.

Paranoid schizophenia of adult form which may begin as early as twelve years of age and transient paranoid states which are manifestations of a regressed structure of latency are less easily differentiated, one from the other, than is prepubescent childhood schizophrenia. Both have premorbid histories of night fears and persecutory fantasies with age- and phase-appropriate fantasy objects. In both conditions neurotic mechanisms are available in latency for dealing with stresses. The structure of latency is available in both. Since in the state of latency cathexis of the idea of the word (i.e., use of fantasy for discharge) is a socially approved adjustment, no differentiation is made between those who elect this pathway and those for whom there is no alternative. Obligatory hypercathexis of fantasy (e.g., narcissistic neurosis) can not be differentiated as pathological until late latency. During the latency age for both groups of children, neurotic mechanisms and a relatively competent structure of latency produce fantasies which are responses to recent reality experiences and are colored more by them than by early introjects. During periods of stress resulting in ego regression, introjects are dealt with through the mechanism of projection associated with symbol formation, producing fear fantasies in which there are thoughts of fantastic objects in early latency and thoughts about real objects in late latency.

With the intensification of drive energies in prepuberty, concomitant intensification of fantasy distortion of external reality may appear as a transient persecutory fantasy of delusional proportions or as a sustained and organized delusional system. The case of R.B., previously described, illustrates the appearance of transient paranoid states which are manifestations of a regressive structure of latency. In such cases resolution of this symptomatology accompanies the occurrence of the expected vicissitudes of projection outlined above. Although this phenomenon is universal in children with a competent structure of latency, there are individuals, as in the case of R.B., in which the phenomenon becomes so all-encompassing as to create a distinct clinical problem. The prognosis is not assuredly positive in all cases. In such people in adult life, paranoid states may occur as the result of restitutive mobilization of the eleven-year-old ego organization in the face of disorganizing stress. There is special vulnerability in this area when the mother or father persists in manipulating the life of the child in response to inner affective responses of the parent. The degree to which the heightened narcissism of early adolescence is mastered is very important in determining if recourse to hypercathexis of fantasy will be used during situations of stress. In adult life, borderline personalities, paranoid traits, and tendencies to lose oneself in work to the exclusion of family relationships have characterized the life patterns of individuals who experienced intense use of projection in late latency-early adolescence, and retain potential for regression in the vicissitudes of projection.

By way of comparison, the following clinical presentation illustrates a case of paranoid schizophenia with early onset. The identifying clinical characteristics are persecutory fantasies of monsters in early latency, a sudden change in personality and deterioration of object relations in late latency, flat affect with ambivalence and loosening of associations during the acute clinical phase, and a total absence of the vicissitudes of projection in early adolescence. Note that in this case personality development during latency parallels that of the normal latency child.

M.J. was self-referred at age fifteen. Her chief complaint was "my mind is messed up." She was particularly concerned by the fact that while drunk, she had punched and kicked a cousin. While sitting quietly in the office, she continuously rocked. She described periods of recalcitrance, irritability, suspiciousness, and guardedness, which were interposed between brief periods of calm and good relatedness. During the periods of bad mood, she became very angry when criticized. She was aware that her characteristic attitude toward people, which she described as snotty and which her mother described as overly suspicious, varied with her mood. She was aware of doing wrong when in a bad mood; "but I still do it," she reported. She could trace her episodes of guardedness, suspiciousness, and irritability back about four years and reported that it had been more intense for the past four months.

She recalled that when she was a small child there were times when she had high fevers during which she had perceptual distortions. She would see the room as big and long and feel that she could see herself way back in the end of the room. At times, she would sense that she was upside down and would turn herself over. She had been afraid of spiders as long as she could remember, even as a small child. She had fears of monsters. In diagnostic interviews, her affect was quite flat and her associations loose. When asked how a fly and a tree are alike, she stated, "Wings and branches reach out. Trees reach out to each other and grab each other. A fly does the same thing with his wings. He reaches out." She described a condition identifiable as stoppage of thought and loss of goal-directed thinking. While talking she would suddenly become unaware of what she had been talking about. Her friends at times could not understand how she got to where she was in a conversation—because of her tendency to drift and lose goal direction. She described as her big problem that she was all mixed up. She described herself as loving and hating everybody: "I know I like it, but also I dislike it": a clear example of ambivalence. She denied hallucinations.

She is reported to have been a normal, healthy baby. She was a wanted child and the product of an uncomplicated gestation, labor, and delivery. She was weaned from the breast at four months and then bottle-fed until nine months of age. She walked at a year and a half. Between one and two she was coprophagic. She was toilet trained at thirty months. She wet the bed until she was ten years of age. She had difficulty in separating from her mother in nursery school. Her mother had to wait for her for a few weeks each time she went to a new class. She experienced repeated episodes of pavor nocturnus of undetermined type.

She had no particular problem in making friends from the first to the fifth grade, and appeared to get along well with the other children. She was considered to be even-tempered and cheerful and cooperative. Her teachers always spoke highly of her. When she was eight years old she showed an exceptional artistic ability in which she was encouraged both in school and at home. During early latency she was considered to be a well-adjusted, likable child who did well in school, usually obtaining marks in the high nineties. She was considered above average in English and history. In the fifth grade, when she was ten years of age, she began to undergo a personality change. Her handwriting especially reflected this. Whereas she wrote tiny well-formed letters, she now seemed to lose control, producing large script, at times achieving letters of two or more spaces in height. This and the cessation of bedwetting when she was ten years old were related to the onset of suspiciousness, guardedness, and uncontrolled behavior.

She began searching her room each night to see if anyone were lurking in the closet or under the bed. She insisted that her parents search with her, using a flashlight to illuminate dark places. She verbalized fear of rape and attack. She showed episodes of moodiness and began to behave in an impulsive manner. She balked at parental authority. When she was eleven, she became openly hostile. She began to wear makeup and demanded freedom of movement more appropriate for a late teen-ager. It was at this time that she began establishing lasting liaisons with boyfriends as well as short-lived sexual experiences with male friends of casual acquaintance. Menarche had occurred at age eleven. By the time she was twelve years old, she was engaging regularly in sexual intercourse through a series of casual contacts with boys.

When she was twelve, she habitually punctured her skin with pins and toothpicks, disrupting the class. She was guarded and evasive and continually concerned that new people might try to hurt her. She was especially concerned with her parents' motives and continually interpreted their behavior as intending to harm her. During psychotherapy, there was rapid remission of symptomatology with a return of diligence in school and the creation of a life plan. This was an apparent flight into health. Prognosis in these cases as in all forms of schizophrenia, according to Hawk et al. (1975), is not as negative as was formerly believed: ". . . the ability of characteristic symptoms to define an illness (schizophrenia) with a deteriorating course has been greatly overestimated in past theory and practice" (p. 347). Both schizophrenia with early onset and severe paranoid states reflecting regressions in the structure of latency should be approached psychotherapeutically.

The appearance of persecutory delusional fantasies during late latency-early adolescence presents a sustained and vexing problem for the therapist and the diagnostician. Three psychopathological entities must be considered. These are prepubescent (childhood) schizophrenia, paranoid schizophrenia with early onset, and transient reactive paranoid states which are manifestations of a regressed structure of latency. Prepubescent (childhood) schizophrenia is distinguished by poor object relatedness and a history of bizarre internalized fantasy objects during early latency. Paranoid schizophrenia and transient reactive paranoid states can be distinguished from prepubescent schizophrenia by the presence of fear fantasies involving projection during latency. The bizarre nature of the paranoid schizophrenic child's behavior, the presence of a thinking disorder, and inappropriate affect may be used to distinguish that entity from the transient reactive persecutory states of late latency. Prognosis in pre-pubertal schizophrenia is uniformly poor. A positive prognosis in the latter two conditions is inversely related to the intensity of the narcissistic cathexis of fantasy; it is directly related to the degree to which the mechanism of projection undergoes the vicissitudes that provide for modification of the impact of introjects through strengthening of reality testing, object ties, and sublimation.

Note

1. Persistence of this state is a problem of adolescence. For a description of the technical aspects of the treatment of this condition, see Sarnoff, 1973a.

Appendix A

THE ONTOGENESIS OF THE SYSTEM CONSCIOUSNESS

This appendix is included in support of the section in chapter 6 that deals with the technical handling of slips of the tongue during child therapy sessions (p. 265), Appendix B and Case 1 in chapter 6 (p. 195).[1]

Where Freud wrote of the System Cs, the major emphasis was on its use in understanding clinical events. The understanding of the intrinsic nature of the System Cs was of secondary importance. However, if we bring together Freud's references to the System Cs, a reconstruction of Freud's concepts of the intrinsic nature of the system consciousness, with emphasis on the ontogenetic steps in its development, becomes possible.

The system consciousness consists of a series of perceptual systems. These are distinguished in terms of complexity, function, and time of appearance in the developing psyche. Remnants of this development are represented in pathological phenomena. Freud (1900) introduced the developmental aspects of the System Cs as follows:

But, in order to make more delicately adjusted performances possible, it later became necessary to make the course of ideas less dependent upon the presence or absence of unpleasure. For this purpose, the Pcs system needed to have qualities of its own which could attract conscious-ness; and it seems highly probable that it obtained them by linking the preconscious processes with the mnemic system of indications of speech, a system not without quality. By means of the qualities of that system, consciousness, which had hitherto been a sense organ for perceptions alone, also became a sense organ for a portion of our thought-processes. (p. 574)

hitherto been a sense organ for perceptions alone." A developmental line is certainly to be inferred from these writings. At least three stages in the development of the System Cs can be recognized: the primal system con-sciousness, the abstract system consciousness, and the mature system con-sciousness.

The Primal System Consciousness

The earliest stage is the primal system consciousness, a "sense organ for perceptions alone." Freud (1900) delineated this stage when he spoke of the response of the "primitive apparatus [when it is] impinged upon by a perceptual stimulus which is a source of painful excitation" (p. 600):

Uncoordinated motor manifestations will follow until one of them with-draws the apparatus from the perception and at the same time from the pain. If the perception reappears, the movement will at once be repeat-ed (a movement of flight, it may be) till the perception has disappeared once more. In this case, no inclination will remain to recathect the per-ception of the source of pain, either hallucinatorily or in any other way. On the contrary, there will be an inclination in the primitive apparatus to drop the distressing mnemic image immediately, if anything happens to revive it, for the very reason that if its excitation were to overflow into perception it would provoke unpleasure (or, more precisely, would *begin* to provoke it). The avoidance of the memory, which is no more than a repetition of the previous flight from the perception, is also facilitated by the fact that the memory, unlike the perception, does not possess enough quality to excite consciousness and thus to attract fresh cathexis to itself. This effortless and regular avoidance by the psychical process of the memory of anything that had once been distressing affords us the prototype and first example of *psychical repression*. It is a familiar fact that much of this avoidance of what is distressing—this ostrich policy— is still to be seen in the normal mental life of adults. (p. 600)

The primal system consciousness itself may be divided into two stages. The earliest "primitive apparatus" (present at birth) responds to two modalities of sensation: internal visceral sensations and external sensations. These sensations are guarded against by "flight from perceptions." A more sophisticated form of the primal system consciousness comes into being with the development of memory and the addition of internal memory sensations to the stimuli available to the conscious perceptual apparatus (present from about three months on). Memory sensations in the form of presentations of objects, at first visual, later verbal, are now included in the content of the primal system consciousness. As a parallel to what has been said above, should the memory be painful, there is a mechanism of defense available for dealing with painful memories: "avoidance of . . . memory [is a] repetition of the previous flight from . . . perception" (p. 600). Only this time, the flight is directed to memory elements: "avoidance by the psychical process of the memory of anything that had once been distressing affords us the prototype and is the first example of psychical repression" (p. 600).

The Abstract System Consciousness (Present from about fifteen months)

As the ego of the growing child matures, the memories of visual and verbal percepts become organized, under the domination of experiences, into patterns. These memory patterns form the basis for the interpretation of complex new stimuli. Reflective awareness becomes possible. The thought processes which develop in this way may be included among those items that can attract consciousness. These thought processes (Freud, 1915e) deal with the abstract relationships between objects.

By being linked with words, cathexes can be provided with quality even when they represent only relations between presentations of objects and are thus unable to derive any quality from perceptions [italics mine].

Such relations, which become comprehensible only through words, form a major part of our thought-processes. (p. 202)

Quality refers to the characteristic of a "cathexis" that can attract consciousness. The developmental step which provides for the inclusion in human mental capabilities of the capacity to perceive abstract relationships between memory elements (presentation of objects) introduces an ability to achieve selective interpretation of events and decision making on the basis of memory and recognition of similarities. This provides the basis for logical thinking and judgment, and is the basis for what Freud (1900) called a "more delicately adjusted performance" (p. 574).

This ontogenetic step makes a fundamental alteration in the complexion of the potential content of the system consciousness. For heuristic reasons, I refer to this stage in the ontogenesis of the system consciousness as the "abstract system consciousness" (see also Sarnoff, 1969a, 1969b). The ability to make selective interpretations of events and to recognize similarities is a positive development. It is the primary adaptive work of the system consciousness. It also provides a pathway for the appearance in consciousness of anxiety resulting from the association of a recent perception with an uncomfortable memory. This is a potentially crippling capacity.

The Mature System Consciousness
(Present from about twenty-six months)

Fortunately, the mature system consciousness, which is the next ontogenetic step, contains an element that can neutralize this potential. The mature system consciousness has the capacity to perceive and contain all of the sensory elements of the abstract system consciousness, while excluding that which is anxiety provoking. This is done through the mechanism of repression. In fact, the mature system consciousness comes into being as a precipitate at the confluence of the abstract system consciousness and the development of repression. I have demonstrated that this occurs during the first half of the third year of life (see Sarnoff, 1970). Repression proper exists when it is possible to exclude from consciousness the link between what represents and what is represented. This results when substitute formations, which are either unrelated to the original idea of the thing or so well masked that they are unrecognizable, are cathected in the place of direct presentations of objects. When an unrelated item is cathected, we call this countercathexis. (There are other definitions for this word which do not concern us here.) When the substitute formation is related to the original idea of the thing but is well masked, we call the substitute formation a symbol.

In this presentation, when I refer to repression, I refer specifically to that mechanism which retains a rejected idea in the System Ucs through symbol formation. There are other meanings to the word *repression*. In fact Freud used the term *repression* as a generic term to describe a group of mechanisms of defense whose function "results in keeping something at a distance from consciousness" (p. 203). There are a number of defensive configurations which produce repression. Freud (1915d) refers to these as "mechanisms of repression" (p. 154).

The primitive apparatus, the primal system consciousness, could deal with discomforting perceptions by decathecting the perception, "the avoidance of the memory" (1900, p. 600), and "flight." This is related to denial or "primitive repression" (1900, p. 600). The abstract system consciousness cannot deal with the cathexis of thought processes and the awareness of the abstract relationships between perceptions by such simple means as turning away or flight, for one can fly from perception but not from awareness. Freud has pointed out (1900, p. 600) that flight and avoidance of memory perceptions are only simple precursors of repression. To avoid awareness, a psychic activity is required which permits the selecting out from access to consciousness of associational and abstract links between perceptions representing memory elements, which have high valence for attracting affect. This is accomplished through decathexis of the link and cathexis of substitute formations. The psychic activity which thus removes access to consciousness from mental events with high affective valence is called repression proper.

The result of the superimposition of repression on the abstract system consciousness is a perceptual apparatus which was described by Freud (1900, p. 574) as "a sense organ for *a portion* of our thought processes [italics mine]." This is one of the characteristics of the mature system consciousness.

Often when Freud refers to the System Cs, he has in mind this mature system consciousness. Thus he can state that "the fact of a thing's becoming conscious still does not wholly coincide with its belonging to a system, for we have learnt that it is possible to be aware of sensory mnemic images to which we cannot possibly allow a psychical location in the systems *Cs.* or *Pcpt."* (1915d, p. 232; in this paragraph Cs and Pcpt are equated). Certainly no place can be found in the mature system consciousness. However, a place could not be denied to these sensory mnemic images in the "sense organ for perceptions alone" (1900, p. 574), which is a form of the primal system consciousness and is found in adults in clinical states in which regression to more primitive forms of perceptual functioning is manifested.

The mature system consciousness, demarcated by the advent of the ego mechanism of repression (see Sarnoff, 1970, p. 570), contains a modification of the content component of the system consciousness such that thoughts and associations which have as a characteristic a potential for producing high levels of anxiety (high affective valence) are excluded. The adult system consciousness—Pcs—therefore has in its available thought component less than both primitive System Cs and the abstract system consciousness. Perceived sensory mnemic elements which cannot be assigned to the mature system consciousness are clinical manifestations of regression of the system consciousness to more primitive levels.

Note

1. The author wishes to express his gratitude to Dr. Ernst Ticho for his help in the preparation of this material. See Sarnoff (1973) and Ticho (1973).

Appendix B

THE ORIGINS OF
LATENCY IN PREHISTORY

The state of latency need not exist. It is a culture element peculiar to the lives of those who are destined to succeed in societies which require complex organizations of knowledge in adulthood. In the clinical practice of therapists whose patients are drawn from a broad spectrum of backgrounds, it is common to come upon children who experience no latency at all. This is especially to be seen in youngsters from deprived communities and primitive societies. At times the absence of a state of latency relates to the patterns of the culture. In other instances the state of latency could not be achieved because of a lack in the development of the basic ego skills required. Repeatedly, in understanding these situations, one must wonder how the state of latency evolved. What indeed were the factors that shaped brute forces to civilized pursuits and for some replaced the club with the word.

We examine here a topic that is inadequately apprehended and has rarely been pursued. Its importance lies in the relationship of the state of latency to the form, transmission, and future of civilization. It serves as background for understanding cultural evolution. In addition, a study of the origin of the state of latency in prehistory serves as a touchstone for the comprehension of psychopathological conditions during the age period six to twelve.

Psychopathological states during the latency age period can be understood at greater depth when one recognizes that the integrated group of functions that produces the latency state is a complex organization of behavior with a phylogenesis. With this knowledge, one can understand latency age regressions in personality organizations whose manifestations repeat not only the personal experience of the individual, but also reflect disorganizations of social, cognitive, and physiological processes which have become integrated into social patterns over the centuries.

Thus, physiological impairments of the symbolizing function must be considered in dealing with poor functioning of the structure of latency. Constitutional (cognitive) impediments in the way of the acquisition of contents of the superego are possible factors in poor social integration. Social influences related to a shame-society upbringing can result in misinterpretation of social cues when an individual is functioning in a guilt society. Regression to functioning typical of that prior to the development of the capacity to repress can result in states of continuous fear.

The search for the historical beginnings of latency requires tracking down a series of events separated in time. The events are related to each other in our minds only because at our moment in history the products of these events have been joined to produce the state of calm, pliability, and educability required in our society for the transmission of culture. The cultural relativism of latency as it appears in agricultural and industrial societies is supported by the late appearance of behavior typical of the latency state for which mankind has been cognitively prepared for eons.

Latency, as it is understood and presented in this book, is not the unitary phenomenon that its primary clinical characteristics (calm, pliability, and educability) would suggest. It could be likened to a beam of white light which if cast through a prism would be shattered into a myriad of colors revealing the disparate nature of its makeup and hinting at complexity in its origins. Should one attempt to seek out the beginnings of the structural components of latency in prehistory, one would be confronted with an enormous task. There is no single beginning. There are beginnings to each part and each part in turn resolves into components. There are few references in the scientific literature that have dealt with this problem. Those that do, do so by indirection and deal with individual components. Since this section is intended as a review of the literature, its limits are defined by the content of the literature. I hope, however, that the presentation of this information will encourage further exploration in the evolution of man and culture from the standpoint of the historical background of the psychological phase that arose with culture and is the mechanism for its perpetuation—latency.

The components of latency, listed below, are the functions of the personality whose interaction produces the calm, pliability, and educability of the latency state:

1. Factors involved in the acquisition and retention of superego contents. An example of acquisition of superego content would be learning the Ten Commandments.

2. The maturation of the motivating affects of the superego which cause the child to seek to implement the superego demands. For latency in our culture this specifically requires the presence of an internalized motivating affect which is called guilt.

3. Ego functions, the development of which can be used in the implementation of superego demands. These include the mechanisms of restraint as well as the structure of latency. The primary subcomponents of the structure of latency are repression and psychoanalytic symbol formation. In addition, among the required ego functions are those elements which we today consider to be innate givens and part of the ego. Among these are the ability to use words for naming, the formation of syntax, and verbal communicative skills. The last forms the basis for the child's capacity to acquire verbally subtle superego contents.

The first psychoanalyst to turn his attention to the problem of the phylogenetic origins of latency was Sandor Ferenczi, who in 1913 stated:

> Having ventured so far beyond the knowable, we have no reason to shrink before the last analogy and from bringing the great step in individual repression, the latency period, into connection with the last and greatest catastrophe that smote our primitive ancestors (at a time when there were certainly human beings on the earth) i.e., with the misery of the glacial period, which we still faithfully recapitulate in our individual life. (p. 237)

Ferenczi apparently was applying Lamarckian theories of evolution to the problem of the acquisition of the latency period by mankind. He had no way of knowing at that time that much of the early origins of human culture and latency took place during the last glacial period. His theory was at best a guess, using acceptable scientific theory for his time. Ferenczi's contribution highlights two important aspects involving the approach to the problem of human psychological evolution. The first is that at a given time in history certain theoretical approaches to observations are accepted to the degree that individuals will freely use explanations which are derived more from the generally accepted theory than they are from the facts available. The second point, which is quite important, is that as early as 1913 Ferenczi recognized that the origins of the latency period would best be approached in terms of its individual components. This can be seen in his limitation of the concept of the latency period to the representation of it as "the great step in individual repression," and then in his explanation of this component on the basis of a paradigmatic parallel in the form of the repressive hardships of the ice age. In recent years, other psychoanalytic investigators have presented general theories of the evolution of the human personality. Hartmann (1952, 1948, 1958) discussed the origin of mechanisms that inhibit drive energies. This unquestionably related to the origins of the ego mechanism of latency.

Hartmann has repeatedly stressed his belief that there are characteristic differences in ego functions through which the differences between man and his precursors can be defined:

The ego-id differentiation . . . complicates the relations between pleasure and the preservation of the individual. The id, in obvious contrast to the instincts of the animals, neglects the latter. (1952, p. 162)

Obviously many functions which are taken care of by instincts in the [lower animals] are in man functions of the ego. The characteristic plasticity of man's adaptive behavior [is] in contradistinction to the relative rigidity of that of the lower animals. . . . (1948, p. 81)

. . . the sharper differentiation of the ego and the id . . . in human adults makes for a superior more flexible relation to the external world, [concomitantly it] increases the alienation of the id from reality. In the animal, neither of these two institutions is so flexibly close to or so alienated from reality. (1958, p. 49)

Hartmann held that the differentiation between man and beast can be defined through differences in the role of the ego and the id in relation to reality. In essence, "in lower animals reality relationships provide the patterns for the aims and means of pleasure . . ." (p. 49), while in man, there is an "alienation of the id from reality" (ibid.). In 1948, he spoke of the "characteristic plasticity of man's adaptive behavior," but provided no detailed description of the intrinsic structural changes that gave rise to this plasticity. In subsequent pages, the mechanism by which this plasticity is achieved will be described. It takes the form of the burgeoning of memories of alternative technical syntaxes in *Homo erectus* and the appearance of patterns of drive discharge involving distortions of object identity which becomes possible in Cro-Magnon man when psychoanalytic symbols are available to provide substitute pathways for drive discharge. Then even the source of the energies involved may be rendered covert. The latency state contains the most florid examples of the substitution of symbolic objects and experiences in place of reality objects for the discharge of drives. Pursuit of such objects in adult life does not serve self-preservation.

Conclusions based on inference are a necessary characteristic of all approaches to the comprehension of the psychology of men long dead. This is especially so when their thinking can be approached only through incomplete groups of artifacts in the absence of individual associations. To some extent all of the conclusions presented here are hypothetical and may therefore be expected to be upheld or replaced with the discovery of new data. However, the matrix within which the conclusions are placed and the challenge presented by the concept of historical origin to latency may hopefully prove to be of lasting value.

Menaker and Menaker (1965), following Hartmann's concepts, assigned the origin of the modern ego to rudimentary beginnings: "at that point in evolution where the specificity of intellectual pattern gives way to modifiability by cortical control" (p. 82). The reduction of the dependence of sexual behavior on hormonal control is emphasized as "its phylogenetic origins" (ibid.). They speak of "nongenetic sociocultural evolution" (p. 86) which is a product of the rudimentary ego that is related to the "emergence of consciousness" (pp. 86, 236). We will pursue the important subject of consciousness and human evolution in these pages, at a somewhat greater degree of complexity.

Freud took a particular interest in the evolution of culture. We have already dealt in chapter 2 with his concept that latency had phylogenetic origins (1923, p. 35). Inheritance of acquired contents governing fantasy and social inhibitions occupied him at length. He wrote that "constitution after all is nothing but the sediment of experiences from a long line of ancestors; and why should the individual experience not be granted a share alongside the experience of ancestors?" (1911, p. 283). Freud (1923) wondered if it were wrong to assume the differentiation between ego, superego, and id in early primitive man: "Should we not honestly confess that our whole conception of the processes in the ego is of no help in understanding phylogenesis and cannot be applied to it?" (p. 38). In keeping with Freud's admonition, my discussion will use both structural and topographical concepts to facilitate the understanding of human evolution. This is of special importance during those early periods when the human ego which provides the flexibility of response had not developed and the primal system consciousness was at its highest point of development. (For a parallel to this in ontogenesis, see Spitz, 1966, p. 124.)

A multitude of prehistoric men have been discovered in times and places which are far separate from one another. They are ordered in developmental sequence by the dating of surrounding material and the hypothesis that as one goes further back in dating origins, smaller and smaller brain size can be correlated with greater primitivity. This approach will be used in this discussion. Varied popular names will be used in identifying the occupants of the ascending rungs of the ladder of human evolution. However, in order to keep reference to brain size available, each primitive man will also be identified by using a nomenclature adapted from that suggested by Andre Leroi-Gourhan (1964), a psychoanalytically oriented paleoanthropologist from France. These are in ascending order of brain size:

1. The Preanthropes (less than 600 cubic centimeters brain size)
2. the Archanthropes (600-1200 cubic centimeters brain size)
3. the Old Paleoanthropes (1200-1300 cubic centimeters brain size)
4. Neanderthals (1400-1500 cubic centimeters brain size)
5. the New Anthropes (1400-1550 cubic centimeters brain size)

The Preanthropes were tool-making creatures (*Australophithecus habilis*) who were predecessors of modern man. They had been on earth for about a million and a half years before the appearance of the Archanthropes. Archanthropes (*Homo erectus*), the first true man, emerged between one and one-half million years B.C. and spread throughout Europe, Africa, and Asia. The Old Paleanthropes were the first true representatives of *Homo sapiens*. They evolved about 200,000 years B.C. They were followed by Neanderthals. These are referred to as *Homo sapiens neanderthalensis* and appeared about 100,000 years B.C. They disappeared from all grave findings after 40,000 years B.C., apparently dying out at that time.

The New Anthropes, or *Homo sapiens sapiens*, first appeared 40,000 years ago and by 20,000 years ago were producing cave paintings and other cultural objects in Southern France and Spain. This group includes Cro-Magnon and modern man. *Homo sapiens sapiens* appear to have a brain capacity equivalent to that of Neanderthal man. This would negate the concept of a progressive developmental nomenclature based on brain size. In actuality, the similarity of volume obscures the fact that the proportions of the brain areas are different, with Neanderthal man having a larger occipital area than modern man and modern man having more of his brain volume devoted to the frontal lobes. As Freedman and Roe (1958) have pointed out, "Capacity for learning seems to be proportionate to this forebrain enlargement" (p. 459). In this regard see also Halstead (1947) and Rensch (1956).

With this framework we now proceed to reconstructions of psychological events related to the evolution of latency as theorized by various authors, including psychoanalytically oriented writers.

The Acquisition of Language, Repression, and Symbols
(Precursors of Superego Contents and the Structure of Latency)

Man's acquisition of language was important for the development of latency. It provided the groundwork for the later development of symbolism, which is an important component of the structure of latency. It also provides a basis for the acquisition of superego alternatives. Language and speech make possible the communication of subtle differences in the contents of these alternatives, increasing thereby their potential number. Thus the contents of the superego are augmented by the development of language and speech. Lerner (1968) has emphasized the role of bipedal locomotion in freeing the arms and hands to make tools and gather food. Before this development the mouth had served as the tool for gathering food. Now free of this burden, the mouth and teeth could be modified by mutation without endangering survival of the species. The way was open "for the development of human speech" (p. 65).

Leroi-Gourhan[1] (1965) has described the initial steps in this development. He considers speech to be an outgrowth of the development of motor techniques:

> Motor technique is at the same time a gesture and a tool. It is organized into a chain of motor activities through a veritable syntax. . . . The operational syntax for motor activities [is retained in memory. When called into use, it] is proposed by the memory and is introduced into the brain as well as the material environment. (p. 165)

Leroi-Gourhan postulates a parallel to this phenomenon in the sphere of language:

> One should be able in consequence of this observation, based on knowledge of motor techniques from the pebble culture [identified by smooth stones fractured to make a cutting edge, populated by Preanthropes] through the Acheulean [identified by work hand axes, populated by Archanthropes] to establish a hypothesis of the development of language in which the degree of complexity and the richness of concepts would be equivalent to that for motor techniques. Preanthropes (i.e., Zinjanthropus) with a single set of technical activities [a single worked tool] and a number of operational chains ought to be able to produce a language which . . . could be of a higher order than that of the gorilla, in that it would be possessed of vocal signals made up of symbols at his disposal and not absolutely determined. The Archanthropes [who used skillfully worked hand axes] possessed a dual set of technical activities, five or six forms of tools, and very complex operational chains. The language which should accompany such [organized syntaxes of motor skills] should be considerably more rich but still limited to concrete situations. (p. 165)

As a result of the complexities of tool use, early man developed patterned sequences of motor behavior. Once learned, these were recorded on the proprioceptive, somatic, affective, hallucinatory memory level. They could be activated in appropriate order for use in dealing with motor tasks involving the tool. The patterns were translated into action and were simultaneously represented in the interpretive cortex of the temporal lobe (see Penfield and Roberts, 1959, p. 48). The patterned chain of motor activities thus contributed to physical activities in dealing with the environment as well as being registered in the awareness of primitive man. Vocal sounds could have been part of the motor sequence patterns, especially in situations in which team work was involved.

Vocal signifiers starting from this beginning could more and more have replaced elements of motor technique within the patterned context (syntax) already established for motor activities. The greater the number of series of motor techniques and the more operating chains for the carrying out of activities that were present in a species, the greater was the requirement for these memory components. Increasing brain size provided early man with the required storage capacity for these increasingly varied forms of operating chains. Acquired skills based on a number of forms of tools entered memory. As the number of these variations increased, the number of memory elements available to conscious awareness increased, as did the number of organized syntaxes of motor skill that could both feed into patterns of motor expression and produce awareness associated with elements of vocal expression.

At this level of phylogenetic development, consciousness may be defined as awareness of sensations, in the presence of memory elements which can be used for interpretation of the familiarity of incoming stimuli as well as for the selection of responses to stimuli from among patterns and sequences of motor behavior. As vocal counterparts of motor sequences were developed, they could be used for the identification of elements of motor technique and eventually for the communication to others of new combinations of technique elements as well as for giving orders. Once vocal signals become concrete indicators of internal sensations of affect, proprioception, and patterned movement, and could be stored for retrieval with sustained definition, a primitive kind of reflective verbal consciousness such as is experienced by modern man became a potential.

Verbal signifiers at this stage (brain volume less than 750 cubic centimeters) were concretely and invariably linked to their parallels in movement or sensation. Speech was not possible from a neurophysiological standpoint; consciousness and speech concepts are neuroanatomically related at one point, the posterior temporal-parietal region of the dominant hemisphere. The articulation of speech depends on augmentation of the frontal lobe, which is not adequately developed in the Preanthrope. The sensation of interpretive awareness was possible but not speech. This condition exists in many animals. What made the Preanthropes unique

were the existence of some vocal signals at their disposal that were not absolutely determined. Their successor, *Homo erectus* (the Archanthropes),
had more than one technical skill with verbal representations at their disposal and so could choose between vocal signifiers. The adaptive advantage of the development of multiple signifiers favored mutations which increased the size of the posterior temporal-parietal region (Wernicke's
area), the area in which organization of concepts takes place. Brown
(1973), in discussing the origins of speech, points out that it is in the Archanthropes that this important step took place in the development of the
brain. The pathway for the translation into speech of the operating chains
or organized syntaxes of motor skills, which are described above, was probably through the limbic system. "Nonverbal communication—cries of
pain or pleasure, or gestures—are controlled by the limbic system deep in
the center of the brain [and bilaterally represented]" (p. 104).

The brain must reach a size of 750 cubic centimeters in order for a child
to develop the apparatus necessary for the production of articulate speech.
This apparatus develops in the cortex on the left side of the brain. It is
unilateral. It consists of a linear series of anatomical structures interposed
between sensation and response. The structures are: the angular gyrus,
which serves as a center for gathering impulses from the sensory areas of
the brain; Wernicke's area, which serves to organize the impulses that
have come into the angular gyrus according to earlier acquired conceptual-
verbal patterns for transmission through the arcuate fasciculus to Broca's
area; and Broca's area, which controls the organs of speech. It is, within
Wernicke's area that the organization of verbal syntax patterns acquired
from the motor patterns described above serve as a schema for the organization of responses to incoming sensory stimuli.

Krantz demonstrated that *Homo erectus* (Archanthrope) probably
didn't have a 750-cubic-centimeter brain size until the age of six. This is
the brain size necessary for maturation of function in the brain of the linear series of anatomical structures described above. Prior to this, *Homo
erectus* would be unable to use any speech other than simple expletives
and had to acquire, retain, and recall information primarily on an affecto-
motor level. There appears to be a general agreement of experts on this
point. Washburn and Avis (1958) comment that "oral traditions essential
for complicated human society probably were not possible with less than
700 or 800 cubic centimeters of brain, and there is no likelihood that elaborate traditions of tool making are possible at less capacities . . ." (p. 432).

They place the origin of tool making, speech, and complicated cultural tradition with the passing of Australopithecus (Preanthropes) and the appearance of *Homo erectus* (Archanthropes). Washburn (1959) has associated 900 cubic centimeters of brain capacity to hunting and well-made, finely formed tools with "cooperation within the group" (p. 26), a situation that would have placed an evolutionary premium on communicative capacities. Hulse (1963) agrees, speculating that speech appeared in Sinanthropus (Archanthrope). It should be kept in mind that though the area for the organization of verbal concepts is postulated to have developed in Archanthropes, swift verbal capacities and clear articulation are functions of the frontal portions of the brain, whose full augmentation is yet to come.

From our knowledge of human development, it can be postulated that *Homo erectus* was not able to develop the kind of speech and verbal facility which would permit him to participate in verbal memory organizations of a conceptual sort until far advanced in age. Life spans were short in those days and the chances are that the verbal capacities necessary for the acquisition and maintenance of conceptual memory, such as would be necessary for the development of subtle superego contents, were not present in the Archanthropes. It may be postulated on the basis of brain size that relatively late in their lives the Archanthropes were physiologically capable of language richer than that of the ape but limited to concrete situations.

When the Old Paleanthropes (early Paleolithic people, with a brain capacity of 1200-1300 cubic centimeters) first appeared, they were equipped with the limited concrete linguistic skills described above. With the passage of time, increase in brain size occurred. This prepared them to augment their memory contents (Leroi-Gourhan, 1965, p. 166). Increase in the quantity of memory elements was not accompanied by a change in the quality of the thinking. In the artifacts left by these people there is only evidence of concrete symbolizations similar to the initial symbolizations of the modern child during the age range of zero to eighteen months. Communication during technical activities was possible. The use of language and external objects as signifiers abstractly related to signified elements resulted from steps taken during the evolutionary tenure of Neanderthal man, Old Paleanthrope's successor.

Hockett (1959) has described an ingenious explanation for one of these steps in the evolution of man's potential for language. This step is characterized by the appearance of a new form of verbal signifier which represents an idea or a thing, the import of which lies halfway between two concrete memory contents, either sensory or motor. When this happens concrete symbolization as a form of mental function is augmented by a primitive form of abstract representation. The new verbal form has a partial similarity through sound to the old signifier, which had been viewed by the subject as an integral part of the memory it represented. In effect, a primitive form of abstract symbolization was introduced. The mechanics of the change are related by Hockett to an activity that linguists call "blending." A person who starts to say two words at once can produce a word that combines elements of both; this is blending. Psychiatrists are familiar with this activity in the thinking disorder called condensation. For example, a young woman who was condemning an act which she felt was *unethical*, in that it was contrary to the tenets of her Roman *Catholic* religion, insisted that the act was not "cethical." In the absence of pathology, a similar archaic form of slip of the tongue in which repression does not participate takes place. A mother who wanted her son to remove the mud from his boot shouted, "Take off the moot." A new word containing sounds and meanings from two old words is created. The same effect can be produced by grouping "two old signals" (Hockett, p. 37n) in order. Once the significance of such blended signifiers became generally understood, what Hocket called "the close circle" of concrete signifiers gave way to language skills that could signify the nonconcrete. The door was opened to abstraction, and what Lerner (1968) has termed *displacement*, defined as the ability to speak "of things in the past or future or of things imagined" (p. 19).

At this point in psychological evolution the idea of the word and the idea of the thing become separable entities. Hyperattention to the idea of the word or further manifestation of it can result in losing sight of the idea of the thing it represents. The inability of the word to represent the whole of the concept of the remembered thing interferes with the potential for complete recall in future memory. As memory and communication evolved to the point that they were increasingly mediated through words, it became more and more possible for memory elements to lose detail and content (amnesia), for distant and external objects to become signifiers (metaphorical symbolism), and for memory content to be hidden as a result of intensified cathexis of signifiers that have little in common with that which is signified (a primitive form of repression).

Mead (1964) has postulated the theory of a mutation that could be used to explain the expansion of the use of verbal signifiers by man. The mutation would be a prolongation of childhood through delay of menarche. coupled with a further truncation of the childbearing period through the introduction of a menopause (p. 156). The resulting evolutionary step would be a longer life span for women, who would be less exposed to the dangers of unending childbearing. Males, even with comparably delayed puberty, would continue to succumb to the dangers of warfare and hunting. With longer life spans, the possibility that women could learn speech and take advantage of the products of blending could in turn produce individuals—the wise elders—vital to the survival of the group under the laws of natural selection. Through rich years and lean years, those women could extend their knowledge of food sources and transmit this knowledge through more than one generation. Thus food-gathering techniques could become more intensely traditionalized, producing the dawn of agriculture. In addition, their newly gained effectiveness in speech would be used with small children of both sexes. Having become caretakers of children, they could introduce speech to the young, accelerating the process of evolution.

Two striking modern observations elevate Mead's theory of a mutation toward the status of fact. First, Murphy and Murphy (1974) in their "Study of a Primitive Society, Our Living Link to the Past," found that old postmenopausal women are deferred to, listened to, and respected (p. 105), and have a social position congruent with Mead's concept. Second, a prolongation of childhood ending in puberty exists in modern man.

These steps in man's evolution that lead to abstract conceptual memory were the experience of Neanderthal man. According to Leroi-Gourhan (1965), material evidence of abstract forms of symbolization may be found first at late Neanderthal sites.

Neanderthal language should not have been much different from language as it is known among living men. Essentially it continued to be linked to an expression of the concrete. It could have assured communication during the course of action, a primary function where language is directly related to the carrying out of work techniques. Language in early man could also have provided for a second function, the use of narrative as an alternative way of communicating symbols which represent actions. This second function had been emerging progressively from the time of the Archanthropes. Eventually there occurred in the course of development of Paleolithic man (Neanderthal) a third function in which language transcended the reflection of the concrete, and could express imprecise sentiments such as those involved in religiosity. (p. 165)

Technical concepts as the signified element represented by the symbols used in the speech of mankind were soon "surpassed by concepts of which we possess little knowledge" (p. 165).

Neanderthal symbolism is reflected in burials, ritual placement of cave bear skulls, ochre found at graves, and odd stones placed near graves. These indications, according to Leroi-Gourhan, "constitute the slender halo of immateriality which floats above Neanderthal man" (p. 159). There does not appear to have been a verified burial before the beginning of the last glacial period, when Neanderthals first appear. It is in Neanderthal man that the first clear evidence has been found of symbolization in which the signifier and the signified are comprehended as different. "With the Neanderthal the exteriorization of nonconcrete symbols was produced" (Leroi-Gourhan, p. 165). There is evidence, then, in findings related to the living sites of the Neanderthals that they used an early form of symbolization at the abstract level. Neanderthal man disappeared from the earth by 40,000 B.C.

Then there appeared on earth a new race of men, Cro-Magnon man (New Anthropes). These people would be difficult to distinguish from modern man physically. An evaluation of bony remnants related to vocalization and a study of the size and shape of the brain case indicate that this group could have produced the language of modern man. Metaphorical symbol formation has been inferred repeatedly from the works of art of the New Anthropes. Leroi-Gourhan (1967) illustrated this most succinctly when he stated, "it is quite possible that Paleolithic men (Cro-Magnon—New Anthropes) were [capable of] expressing something like 'spear is to penis as wound is to vulva' " (p. 173). This is the sort of simile upon which abstract metaphorical symbolism is based. The symbols used appeared to be part of a rich and far-flung culture passed down through generations. In the opinion of Leroi-Gourhan (1967), "In Western Europe . . . stable traditions over many thousands of years led to a maturing of a symbolism absolutely continuous in development from the earliest artistic manifestations [35,000 B.C.] down to the end of the Magdelenian period [10,000 B.C.] (p. 34).

There is evidence in Cro-Magnon artifacts of forms of magic used to control the environment. Leroi-Gourhan considered paintings of a wounded bison evidence of sympathetic magic, and a figure with a horn mask and a horse's tail imitative magic. Such forms of magic provide reinforcing evidence of the presence of metaphorical symbolism.

Thus far in the search for the origin of those portions of language that contribute components to the latency state of modern man, we have been able to trace the phylogenesis of language up to the point at which similes and metaphorical symbols may be postulated to have appeared. It has been postulated that up until the time that brain size reached 750 cubic centimeters, early man had been gradually acquiring a limited capacity for vocal expression of syntaxes of motor activities involving technical skills needed for survival. As brain capacity enlarged and technical syntaxes and tools increased in number, the variety of possible vocalizations increased. At 750 cubic centimeters, with the development of the brain areas necessary (Wernicke's area, arcuate fasciculus), a capacity for gross speech using verbal signifiers appeared. These signifiers were part of a concrete, syncretic thought process involved in motor acts related to survival and craft skills. This state of affairs continued, changed only by the addition of more and more complex memory patterns.

With the development of a brain capacity from 1400 to 1500 cubic centimeters, as occurred in Neanderthal man, primordial capacities for conceptualization in the abstract became possible. This is supported by the appearance of concrete signifiers in external form of things imagined, such as burials, the use of ochre, and the appearance of primitive jewelry.

Truly abstract symbolization is seen in the representation of an animal by a painting, i.e., one psychic representation (a picture) being used to signify another psychic representation (memory of an animal). Such symbol formation is necessary for the development of magical thinking and magical control of the environment. This form of symbolism does not appear until 40,000 to 20,000 B.C. with the appearance of Cro-Magnon man (New Anthropes), who painted pictures on the walls of caves. Metaphorical symbols do not quite bring us to modern man. They are still some steps away from the type of symbolization (production of psychoanalytic symbols) required for an effective structure of latency. These psychoanalytic symbols have been studied extensively by Jones (1916) and by Piaget (1951); Piaget identified them with the term "secondary symbolism" (p. 169 and following). They are characterized by the fact that the abstract connection between the signifier and the signified has been repressed. Thus the meaning of the symbol is hidden from the subject. Such symbols appear in the mental life of modern man in distortion dreams, in poetic creativity, and in the drive discharge mediating play activity of children in the latency state. The capacity to form such symbols is a potential of all modern living men. There is no evidence to the contrary. Because this symbolic form is necessary for an effective structure of latency and the transmission of culture attendant upon the related process of passive mastery, it is necessary for us to search out its origin in prehistory. Mead (1958) has placed this symbolic form in the mainstream of man's evolution: "There is good reason to believe that man's evolutionary progress depends also on his ability to dream . . ." (p. 488n). From our standpoint, the dividing line between Cro-Magnon and modern man should be made at the point at which this symbolic form appears.

Since this symbolic process is intrapsychic, it is difficult to recognize its beginnings in the signifiers themselves. To find beginnings one must differentiate between the mechanisms that produce symbols and their products. The evolution of the ego mechanisms necessary for the production of psychoanalytic symbols could have preceded their products by many generations. By definition, psychoanalytic symbols are not simple and basic unities. They are the derived products of the mechanism of repression, which acts on the abstract symbolic linkages which are in turn evidences of the activities of the symbolizing function. Concrete symbols are not affected by repression. Abstract symbols, when not affected by repression, take the form of metaphors. When repression becomes involved in symbolization, psychoanalytic symbols are formed.

Internal pressures can activate repression to produce personal symbolic responses (e.g., dreams). The time of the first appearance of such personally oriented symbols would be impossible for us to determine, for they leave no trace. The use of psychoanalytic symbols as part of the transmission of culture in a given society leaves traces in the artifacts that remain. The presence of such psychoanalytic symbols reflects not the beginning of such symbolization, but the appearance of organized and internalized social pressures. Unfortunately, proof of their presence comes too late in history. In the absence of landmarks that tell of the beginnings of psychoanalytic symbols, related products of the evolving ego must be used as the criteria for detecting the moment of differentiation of modern man from beasts and his hominid precursors.

Lerner (1968) has identified "consciousness of self" as one of the differentiating characteristics of man (p. 19). This is a useful concept. Consciousness itself has an ontogenesis which is intimately linked with the ontogenesis of symbols (Appendix A deals with this concept intensively). Briefly, it may be postulated that in the phylogenesis of man, consciousness underwent vicissitudes which parallel the phylogenesis of symbol formation. Awareness of self in a milieu with a past and future is in itself an insufficient criterion for differentiating modern men from symbol-forming hominids and even primates (see below). The development of an impairment of the capacity for total awareness of the self and the milieu as the result of repression, with attendant psychoanalytic/secondary symbol formation, which characterizes the consciousness of modern man, defines the difference between modern man and his predecessors.

There are further reasons for replacing symbol formation with the organization of consciousness, in differentiating hominids from beasts and modern man from other hominids. Recent advances in primate psychology have necessitated this approach. Formulations that man uses tools while animals do not, or that man uses symbols while animals do not, no longer bear scrutiny. Robinson (as quoted by Sullivan, 1965) has noted that the woodpecker finch of the Galapagos Islands uses a thorn to extract bugs beyond the reach of the tongue.

Goodall (1964) has demonstrated the use of tools (sticks) acquired in advance in the ant-gathering activities of chimpanzees. This has been reinforced by the findings of Kollar (1972), who has presented clear evidence of ability in chimpanzees to acquire concepts of tool use and to apply them. His findings led him to conclude that "it is the inability to communicate through the use of symbols or language that separates proto-human behavior from human behavior, not the inability to make and use tools" (p. 27).

This conclusion is in part challenged by the results of Freedman et al. (1971) who, in the study of the development of personality functions in deaf children, found that speech is not necessary for the development of human ego functions or conceptualizations. This would leave psychic concept formation with self-reflective awareness and the ability to symbolize as distinctly human characteristics. Yet even this line of demarcation has been erased, for Gardner and Gardner (1969) have demonstrated in chimpanzees the presence of complex concept formation removed in time and place from the events represented. Through the use of the American sign language of the deaf, he has helped chimps to acquire a means for symbolizing psychic concept representations through the use of physical motions. This provides a pathway for structured communication with other, even human, beings. The level of concept formation available to the chimpanzee revealed through this medium is that of conscious reflection, including self-reflective awareness. This is demonstrated in the spontaneous suggestion by a chimpanzee that she and her trainer go for a ride in an airplane. The work of Premack and Premack (1972) has confirmed these findings, using objects of varied shapes as language symbol forms.

One might question whether a sharp line of demarcation can be drawn at all between hominid and beast. A continuum involving increasing ability to use these skills with beast on one end and hominid on the other seems to be more likely. The gradual development of these skills during the phylogenetic development of man has been traced in the preceding pages through samplings based upon available products of the evolutionary tree; a sharp line of demarcation between man and beast has been effaced.

A subtle difference exists between the minds of a psychologically normal modern man and of his predecessors. We must consider that, of these predecessors, both chimpanzees and, on a more sophisticated level, Neanderthals present evidence of capacity for memory, tool use, abstract conceptualizations, the exteriorization of conceptualizations, and symbol use which can be learned. Our task at this time is not to differentiate between primate and hominid, who share much in common, but between the more sophisticated of modern man's precursors and modern man himself.

Homo erectus (Archanthropes) showed awareness through vocal signals that were immediate signifiers of concrete acts and objects. Neanderthal could externalize awareness of sensitive nonmaterial aspects of feeling. This could be expressed on the level of a repeated pattern of behavior. A concrete external item could be used to represent an inner feeling or affect. Cro-Magnon man (New Anthropes) had developed motor skills which could be used in expressing his affects and concepts in plastic form. He also had a capacity for verbalization which would permit the sharing of conceptual elements which identify a culture. Essential to the ability to communicate inner feelings through artistic representation is the ability to reflect and to choose from a variety of possible alternatives. The use of external elements such as cave paintings for the control of the environment on the part of primitive man is an indication of a capacity for self-reflection and an awareness of self in the world in terms of a multitude of possible responses rather than in terms of the syncretic relationship of animals and prehominids to the world about them. Self-awareness as a dominating feature in adjusting to the environment characterizes all of the more sophisticated hominids. A unique alteration in this awareness characterizes modern man. This idea is not new. Pardies (1678) felt that "the essential character of [human perception] is that it includes in itself a kind of reflection which it carries out upon itself, as an indivisible part of the act of thought, so that we are *conscious* that we are *conscious*. . . . Sometimes our awareness of objects, like that possessed by animals, is devoid of such reflection" (p. 171; italics mine).

Diamond (1972) has stressed the continuation of this concept in the history of philosophy through delineating the relationship between the above passage and the following one from Leibnitz (1714): "It is well to make a distinction between perception which is the internal state by which a monad represents external things and apperception which is the *consciousness* of reflexive knowledge of that internal state which is not given to all souls, nor at all times to the same souls" (p. 715; italics mine).

For our purposes the important ideas of Pardies and Leibnitz relate to the concept of apperception (i.e., consciousness of reflective knowledge) and the recognition of a unique quality in the consciousness of modern man. The unique quality is its inconsistency. Though potentially aware of more than any other being, repression removes much that is potentially conscious from the realm of consciousness. To understand this it is necessary to comprehend the ontogenesis of human consciousness and then to apply this knowledge to the evolution of consciousness. Only in this way can we find the step in development that separates modern man from his predecessors. It may be presumed that this development occurred some time between the appearance of Cro-Magnon man (New Anthropes) and modern times.

What I postulate is the theory that although the early Cro-Magnon man had a multitude of skills that separated him from his forebears, at some point in his development he experienced an evolutionary change that prepared him for the cultural organization that identifies modern man. An ability developed which permitted him to limit the degree of apperception he could bring to bear on events and memories that were associated with uncomfortable affects. In a species with a newly won awareness of danger, such an ability could limit fear and aid in hunting. Lerner (1968) has emphasized the unique awareness of his own mortality that is man's, and describes this as the basis of fear (p. 19). The exclusion of anxiety-linked memories from consciousness is one of the functions of repression. It may be achieved through the direction of attention cathexes to words or external signifiers which, though sharing similarities with that which is signified, are incapable of representing them totally. This is an ego function. It is one of the group of mental mechanisms involved in repression. When the signifier and signified, which have been dealt with in this way by repression, have been drawn away from awareness of metaphorical symbolic connections with each other, we may say that a psychoanalytic symbol has been formed. Specifically the abstract connecting link between that which represents and that which is represented has been lost to awareness either partially or totally.

In effect, at the point that this mental mechanism entered man's armamentarium of defenses, his awareness of himself and the milieu shrank. A system of fantasy structures and memories which were unable to attract consciousness or to achieve connection with their signifiers was established. Concurrently, the ability to form personal symbols associated with repression provided man with the capacity to develop neurotic symptoms as well as to utilize the structure of latency for the transmission and internalization of culture.

The wake of titans has marked the course required to solve our enigma. The conceptual threads of Pardies and Leibnitz (organization of perception, self-awareness, and consciousness as diagnostic criteria in identifying the nature of man) were continued in the work of Freud, who was able to achieve a reduction of the ontogenesis of modern human consciousness into its developmental components. A full description of the ontogenesis of consciousness may be found in Appendix A. Freud's descriptions of the system consciousness imply a differentiation between a perceptual system consciousness without verbally structured self-awareness, an abstract system consciousness with self-awareness, and an adult system consciousness with awareness blunted through the use of symbolic masks.

Perceptual consciousness (the awareness of sensations) is found in man and in beast. It may be found in chimpanzees; it may be found in *Homo erectus*; it may be found in Neanderthal man; and it appears in *Homo sapiens*. Self-reflective awareness associated with verbalization is a manifestation of the abstract system consciousness. The abstract system consciousness exists when the subject is aware of abstract relationships between things and between concepts. This ability can be demonstrated in Neanderthal man, to an extent, and in Homo Sapiens. On a nonverbal and less sophisticated level, chimpanzees can be shown to have access to this skill but not to use it in their adaptation (see Gardner above). The mature system consciousness appears at the point at which repression interferes with the capacity for full awareness of memories and the implications of events. The mature system consciousness with its concomitants (selective contents and psychoanalytic symbols) is beyond the reach of chimps and Neanderthals, but very much within the grasp of modern man. The concomitants are required for the establishment of the structure of latency. The point at which the development of these skills becomes available during the evolution of man has not been established. It undoubtedly precedes the moment in evolutionary time when artifacts which reflect symbolization associated with repression appear.

It is the link in the evolutionary chain manifested in the development of the mature system consciousness that transmutes Cro-Magnon man into modern man. When the capacities for metaphorical symbols and sublimations in the form of artistic representations of inner feelings are augmented by psychoanalytic symbols, modern man moves toward the fulfillment of his potential to be a creature with rich sublimations, extensive internalized culture elements, and symptom neuroses. When does this occur? More specifically, when and where in the artifacts of Cro-Magnon man (*Homo sapiens sapiens*) are the first evidences of repression-dominated symbolizations to be found? There is very little data on this subject. Leroi-Gourhan (1967) explains the symbolic meaning of Cro-Magnon cave paintings in terms of conscious sexual symbolism representing male and female factors as part of a magical world view. Unconscious symbolism is not specifically described by Leroi-Gourhan in the cave paintings of Europe.

Arnold Modell (1968) takes a position in regard to Paleolithic art that excludes the possibility of symbolism associated with repression: "Action upon the symbolic animal influenced the real animal creating a world that was created in accordance with omnipotent wishes" (p. 17). His conclusions would exclude even the possibility of metaphorical symbolism. In 1938, Heilbronner, a psychoanalytic investigator, presented a paper which dealt with some examples of ice age art and stated that "Man in the ice age attributed an especial significance—at first unconsciously and later consciously—to composite representations of the male and female sexual organs" (p. 439). Heilbronner's findings indicate a period of unconscious symbolization early in the span of Cro-Magnon man, which was followed by a period during which psychoanalytic symbols were less in evidence.

In 1938 Ernest Jones, commenting on Heilbronner's paper, made the interpretation that Paleolithic artists (*Homo sapiens sapiens*) of the Aurignacian (32,000-18,000 B.C.) and Magdalenian (15,000-10,000 B.C.) periods had already acquired the capacity for repression. This observation was based on the distorted female figures of the Aurignacian period. Jones drew the conclusion that unconscious motivation was involved in Paleolithic art. Pointing to the emphasis on roundness and the neglect of extremities in the Venus sculptures of the Aurignacian period, he concluded that they "point to the operation of unconscious castration fantasies" (p. 176). In later Magdalenian art, weak technique, flat, two-dimensional figures, and a predominance of male sexual organs, plus depictions interpreted as aggression led Jones to the conclusion that "the more purely libidinal motive has been displaced by others of a more conflicting order" (p. 176). In later Magdalenian art, weak technique, flat two-dimensional figures, and a predominance of male sexual organs, plus depictions interundergoing an important development" (p. 177). Jones leads us to believe that the onset of symbolization associated with repression occurred during the ice age and is reflected in such figures as the woman with shortened extremities and faceless head figures which are seen as artistic representations of the resolution of castrating wishes. An alternative explanation could be that the style of art of the period emphasized pregnancy as part of a fertility cult, and that the development of artistic conventions over the centuries tended to put less emphasis on that which was unrelated to fertility. In support of this, the heads of the figures have a phallic quality which would point away from the use of art for the mastery of unconscious castration anxiety through the representation of a figure without arms and truncated legs.

If Jones's conclusion is correct, repression affected symbols and became part of the cultural pattern during the Aurignacian period. This phenomenon receded during the Magdalenian period with a return to exclusive use of metaphorical symbols. Clear manifestations (i.e., figure distortions) in multiple artifacts that repression existed generally do not become apparent until much after Magdalenian artists ceased functioning. Approaches to the study of cave art aimed at finding evidences of the human potentials needed for the maintenance of latency produce inconclusive results. Though figure drawings of latency children have necks, depictions of humans in cave art do not show the pinching in at the base of the head that is considered characteristic. On the other hand increased self-awareness in a society is accompanied by the appearance of shadows in its art (Sarnoff, 1972a, pp. 76-77). The first appearance of molding of drawn figures through shading has been reported to occur in cave paintings in the middle Magdalenian period, 13,000-10,000 B.C. (Leroi-Gourhan, 1967, p. 211).

It is surprising that symbolic distortions in multiple artifacts which would indicate psychoanalytic symbols as a consistent and universal culture element are not seen until one observes demon figures in primitive rock pictures. Many of these may be seen in the Levant in Spain. These were painted in the first and second millenium B.C.

In describing these figures Kuhn (1956) states: "The figures are not those of ordinary men; they are those of ghosts. They are not ordinary beasts that confront us on the written rocks; they are ghostly beasts" (p. 105). The figures have necks. "Side by side with simple line drawings there are paintings in which a demonic, a spectral character is clearly visible. There is for instance . . . a four-legged figure furnished with huge crab-like claws" (p. 117). It is in these pictures that plastic representation is first given to the marked degree of distortion that provides firm evidence of psychoanalytic symbol formation. It is impossible to believe that modern man first appeared with these pictures. The people who painted them are contemporaries of the Egyptians. A review of Egyptian art gives no evidence of the distortions typical of psychoanalytical symbol formation. Yet we know from Egyptian writings of the period, such as "The Story of Sinuhe" (see Simpson, 1972), that ancient Egyptians experienced unconscious motivation. In this story, which dates from 1961 B.C., a man when confronted with a situation in which he hears of the death of a king is "impelled by some inner force he cannot explain to flee from the court . . ." (p. 57). Apparently the apparatus for the formation of psychoanalytic symbols was present, but we have no evidence of their presence as culture elements.

There is a rock painting in the Hoggar region of Africa of a distorted monster figure which is estimated to be 6,000 to 7,000 years old (p. 49, the *Concise Encyclopedia of Archaeology*). We must conclude that by the dawn of history psychoanalytic symbolism was available and widely established. Evidences of it appear in art and writings. Its origins cannot be identified in time more closely than to say that such symbolism was available early in the time of Cro-Magnon man. It is probable that even before this there appeared rudiments of the repression which turns metaphors into psychoanalytic symbols. As we have seen, these rudiments were outgrowths of "blending," an archaic form of slip of the tongue. This process results in the creation of symbolizers which obscure meaning because of their lack of congruence with that which is signified. If this is so, the precursors of the mature system consciousness are quite ancient, and Jones was probably right in describing a period of psychoanalytic symbolism during the Aurignacian culture.

There is as yet no way to determine the degree to which cave art was used for passive symbolization, or when distortion dreams first appeared. The actual use of psychoanalytic symbols as a culture element, such as that which would appear in Western art, did not occur till long after such symbols were possible. What I am postulating is a situation similar to that which involves the symbolizing function and self-awareness of the chimpanzee. These functions hardly intrude on his daily life and food-gathering habits. The introduction of sign language permits us to know that the chimp can think more complexly than his spontaneous action would allow. In like manner, psychoanalytic symbol formation became a culture element at the point that it was called into play by the needs of society. Such a situation would require the internalization of superego-motivating affects, the capacity for internal prohibitions, and a change in the philosophy of the human group. This step is close to our time.

Masking and dream symbols have been described by Mead (1958) as necessary in human evolution (see above). Whitehead (1927) has defined the role of masking symbols in maintaining the structure of society: "In the place of [social] instinct which supresses individuality, society has gained the efficacy of symbols, at once preservative of the commonweal and of the individual standpoint" (p. 113). There was a point at which dream symbols and passive symbolizations which could have existed in Aurignacian times came into the service of society. Observations of artifacts seem to place the efflorescence of this phenomenon and the dawn of latency as a social structure in the range of the fourth millenium B.C.

The literature of prehistory is not mute on this point. Reinach (1903) introduced the concept that the art of prehistoric man and modern man were intrinsically different and that the difference related to the use made of symbols: "the prehistoric sculptor was never preoccupied with the intent to please, but with the intent to evoke" (p. 265). Giedion (1962) in pursuing this phenomenon described the nature of the changes in symbolism from prehistory to historical times as follows:

> Herein lies the contrast between the function of the symbol in prehistory and in later periods.
> In prehistory, the symbol as used by a society possessed the magical power to control reality before that reality came to pass. In Greece the symbol developed a spiritual content and became an abstract concept. (p. 93)

Giedion related this change in the use of symbols to a change in the philosophical orientation of humankind. During the fourth millenium B.C. there was a change from a view of man as an animal among animals, the zoomorphic age, to a view of man as unique and separate from the animals, the anthropomorphic age (Giedion, 1962, p. 90).

By the fourth millenium B.C. gods began to take on human forms and attributes and share with man control of man's earthly fortunes (Osborn, 1975, p. 25). Individual gods became identified with individual men, their families, their progeny, and, as men and their skills proliferated, their professions. When individual men left their group, their hearth and home to wander and to trade, they left behind the influence of the public opinion of the small group. Still, they took with them as part of their identity the admonitions of their gods. When, in the absence of fellow tribesmen, they adhered to dictates that had been internalized, the stage was set for the development of myths which set the guidelines for the control of man's behavior in addition to the control of the behavior of the hunter's quarry. Drives held in check by these internal mechanisms were expressed through psychoanalytic symbols, as they had been for eons. But now the beginning of the shared worship of abstract personal gods shaped a culture in which these psychoanalytic symbols had a place. The following section is devoted to the steps mankind took while developing the internalized superego which was the instrument involved in the elevation of psychoanalytic symbols to the status of a culture element, the transmission of which is the work and the raison d'etre of the state of latency.

The Origins of Motivating Affects
of the Superego

In searching for the origins of latency in prehistory, we have delineated the origin of verbal communicative skills required for the acquisition of superego content and the origin of repression and the symbolization required for the development of the structure of latency. We have now to develop the phylogenesis of the motivating affects of the superego and the development of the brain areas necessary for value judgment.

The following is a theory of the phylogenesis of the motivating affects of the superego. It is a projection of knowledge of ontogenesis onto known events of prehistory. The motivating affects of the superego are those feelings which impel the individual to enforce superego demands. The primitive paradigm for the motivating affects is the ability to recall the danger which is associated with motor activities which in the past had resulted in some form of pain or injury. All animal species which survive have this skill to some extent. In man at his most primitive, the recall of anxiety in a potential danger situation encourages a response of flight. This happens as a result of expectation of injury. This is the protective equipment with which the earliest pre-men met their environment. An important evolutionary step took place with the maturation of self-apperception, which accompanied the addition of verbal recall to the memory for affects and motor patterns. An affect of anxiety could arise should the individual conceive of failing to work with the group. This anxiety ensured survival through group activity in situations of danger. With the development of internalized culture elements which identify the individual as a part of the group, loss of membership in the group resulted from failure to share group activities or beliefs. Loss of the survival value of group membership followed. This was accompanied by affects related to acceptance (i.e., gain or loss of love). Adherence to the rules of the group brought feelings of acceptance, elation, or happiness. The thought of breaking with the group brought fear and depression.

Hominids began to have more conscious appreciation of the value of the group at the time that the number of culture elements used for identification increased. This coincided with the enlargement of brain size, which occurred with the Old Paleoanthropes (1200-1400 cubic centimeters). Culturally disapproved behavior in the presence of group members, or when the group is in the mind's eye, results in an affect which we identify as shame. When the capacity for repression was powerful enough and the motivation to use it was strong enough, the identity of the potential punisher could be removed from consciousness. The affect developed is called guilt.

The superego-motivating affects of depression and shame are conscious. They can be augmented by the development of guilt during the occurrence of the phylogenetic phase (Neanderthal) in which early forms of repression presage the mature system consciousness. At that time the capacity to produce a primitive form of guilt would be available. The actual appearance of the internalized superego as a culture element which is important in the development of latency does not occur until mankind separates his gods from physical idols which can be avoided and replaces them with abstract concepts which cannot and which tend to become internalized. Once again, as with the development of psychoanalytic symbols, surface manifestations of the existence of these phenomena come later in history than the personality potentials that can produce them.

Hutton (1962) places this occurrence in the sixth century B.C. in stating that "we must give credit to the Ionian philosophers that they were willing to explain the visible by the invisible" (p. 66). The shift from the primitive shame culture (which has been described extensively in the work of Murphy and Murphy, 1974, and is quoted above in Chapter 5) to a culture which is regulated by guilt is assigned by Harkness (1954) to Judaic prophets during the eighth century B.C.: "The social solidarity of the people passes in the course of the Old Testament from an unreflective collective responsibility typical of primitive peoples to the reflective social sympathy of the eighth century prophets. Individual responsibility [was] affirmed by Jeremiah and Ezekiel and the redemptive world vision of Deutero-Isaiah" (p. 150).

The following passage from Jeremiah (31: 31-32) is a codification of the change in moral attitude of the time.

Not according to the covenant that I made with your fathers in the day that I took them by the hand to bring them out of the land of Egypt; which my covenant they break although I was the Lord over them, sayeth the Lord: But this shall be the covenant that I will make with the House of Israel; after these days sayeth the Lord, I will put my law in their inward parts and write it in their heart; and will be their God and they shall be my people.

During Biblical times there was destruction of idols throughout the land, a codification of the internalization of superego demands and a willingness to worship the invisible.

The Development of Brain Areas Necessary for Value Judgment

Phylogenetic increases in the size of the brain results in increased storage for the regulating concepts of the superego. This results in rapid progress in the organization within the social group. A combination of the development of superego-motivating affects and enlarged memory storage was the important new element that became at once the basis of society and its tool in establishing a concordance of beliefs for the species. Though the relative increase in volume provided space for alternatives, and a play of individual variations moved into the forefront of human response, group usage enforced certain alternatives as acceptable. "One can sense that in this evolution the Paleanthropes (brain size: 1200-1300 cubic centimeters) played a pivotal role, though through their form they belonged to a world where imperative values are the animal order and where technique in language has still not completely acquired mastery over possibilities" (Leroi-Gourhan, 1965, p. 87).

A large increase in volume provided the brain of the Paleanthrope with the ability to retain multiple alternatives, choose individual variations, and recognize values. When the number of potential individual variations made possible by expanding the capacity of the brain provided for variations in excess of those agreed upon by the elders of the group, differential group identification became possible. Concomitantly, exclusion from the group for unacceptable behavior became a potential culture element. This was the time in the evolution of man when fear of loss of love became a superego-motivating affect. This is the time when decisions of individuals took into account ethical judgments. Decisions could be made following group dictates as a means of gaining approval. Choosing an alternative unacceptable to the group could expose one to loss of love, depression, and shame. This first occurred before the mature system consciousness developed. Therefore its first appearance was not accompanied by the affect of guilt.

The specific physiological basis for the capacity to have multiple individual variations in human response is felt by Leroi-Gourhan (1965) to be related to the development of the frontal lobe: "One can see, moreover, that the expansion of the brow is rapidly followed in the history of human society by profound transformation in the relationship between man and the biological world" (p. 186). The appearance of the enlargement of the frontal lobe is linked by him to the interposition of an apparatus for instantaneous integration of emotional impulses with responses of the motor system (p. 186). Development of the prefrontal area results in the development of operational chains (p. 186). Leroi-Gourhan places the retention of operational chains of behavior in the burgeoning frontal lobes of evolving early man. Stored here are memories and patterns of behavior associated with affects related to ethical considerations. These are the behavior-guiding superego contents. Though the major expansion occurred with the Paleoanthropes, there is evidence of an increase in the number of operational chains in hominids before them. Evidence from neurophysiological research requires that slight modifications of this theory be made. The storage of patterns of activity and patterns of culture occurs in diverse parts of the brain as yet unidentified. Therefore improvement in memory function must be considered to be a product of generalized increase in brain size. This remains primarily the province of the Paleanthropes.

In attempting to identify memory areas in the brain in relation to Leroi-Gourhan's assertion that value judgments are stored in the frontal cortex, we must understand the approaches used in the identification of brain function areas by neurosurgeons. There are three ways in which identifications of function can be made.

1. By study of losses of function after loss of brain tissue resulting from injury, surgery, or neoplasm (such as loss of conscience with loss of the frontal lobes).

2. Activation of a function when an area of the brain is stimulated (such as activation of awareness when the temporal lobe is stimulated).

3. Extinguishing of a function when an area of the brain is stimulated (such as extinguishing the power of speech when Wernicke's area is stimulated).

Obviously the storage of memory, which is an ongoing process covering years, cannot be detected to have been activated or extinguished by momentary stimulation of a brain area. Studies of people who have lost brain tissue have indicated that diffuse and massive loss is necessary to effect concept storage. There is no indication that the frontal lobes are involved more specifically than other brain areas in this activity.

We may conclude that concept memory and affecto-motor memory (syntactic chains of technical procedures and affects) are stored diffusely throughout the cortex. However, there is no question that the more that brain volume is devoted to the frontal lobes, the greater is the growth of culture. Neanderthal man has a larger brain than Cro-Magnon or modern man, but the latter two have more of their brain volume devoted to the frontal lobes. The frontal lobe's importance does not lie in the storage of memory but in the interpretation of it. Culture depends on the storage, retrieval, and interpretation of memories. We have already determined that concept storage is a bilateral function of many areas of the brain. Penfield (1959) has demonstrated through electrostimulation of the living human brain that the processes of recall and recent memory are linked bilaterally to the fornix, amygdala, dorso median thalamic nucleus, the medial pulvinar nucleus and the hippocampus (p. 118), while "psychical responses come only from the temporal cortex and occasionally from the insular cortex" (p. 44). These last are the interpretive cortexes. They are the seat of conscious awareness. It is here that recurring judgments are made in regard to the familiarity and the meaning of each new experience. Comparative interpretations of new experiences and old memories are made here (pp. 47-48). This is an ability which can be demonstrated in lower animals, but which acquires a positive evolutionary aspect in light of its adaptive potential in the processing of the multiple motor and speech patterns acquired in the Paleanthropes. The interpretive cortex of the temporal lobe provides the sense of awareness. There appears to be an interpretive cortex in the frontal lobe whose specific localization is as yet unidentified. Pincus and Tucker (1974) points out that "destruction of the frontal lobe leads to poor self-control, inability to understand the consequences of actions, and an inability to orient actions to the social and ethical standards of society" (p. 103).

Superego-motivating affect and conceptual and technical alternatives in potential responses are integrated in the frontal lobes. The augmenting of the mass of the frontal area as it relates to the phylogenesis of man is important for concept storage only in that it contributes, with other portions of the brain, more storage space. Its mass is specifically important because of its function as an interpreter of value judgments and as the seat of voice control, ideational speech (Broca's area), and the superior speech cortex (Penfield and Roberts, p. 201).

In conclusion, it may be inferred that storage of concepts and syntactic chains relating to motor skills occurs in many areas of the brain not yet identified by scientists, and that the temporal interpretive cortex coordinates selection of responses to stimuli under the guidance of an interpretive area in the frontal lobe, which interprets actions in terms of superego-motivating affects. The larger the brain area available for this activity, the better was the chance that our species could set aside newly won flexibility and alternatives in individuals. This was replaced with strict conformance with the self-preservative functions of the group. In evolution, the shame-motivated superego was developed as a means of countering individuality that could have threatened the survival-ensuring potential involved in group hunting and defense. Without the group, the individual could not have survived. Each individual became a thread in the warp of mankind. Which is more important, individual or group? The eternal riddle had begun. These phenomena had origins in the Paleanthropes.

In summary, superego contents (ego ideal) are modern homologues of the syntaxes of motor movement used by early man in life support activities. Though present in very early man, superego contents do not reach a level of number and variability that makes them useful as the basis for ethical decision making until the appearance of Paleoanthropes (1200-1300 cubic centimeters of brain capacity).

The motivating affects of the superego have roots in animal anxiety reactions in the face of danger. Feelings of loss of love, associated with depression, can be mobilized by choosing a syntax of action which is unacceptable to the group. This could occur as early as the Paleoanthropes (1200-1300 cubic centimeters of brain capacity). Shame also appeared at this time as an element of superego-motivating affect. It is an affect associated with the conscious apprehension of group disapproval. It dominated culture until approximately 800 B.C. At that time internalized social demands became a culture element. Thenceforth shame would be present if the admonitions of society were disobeyed even in the absence of representatives of the social group. Admonition and punisher were both internalized. Were the identity of the internalized punisher to be repressed, and his representation symbolized by the subject, the affect in response to breaking the codes of his people would be called guilt. There is much evidence that the capacity to experience internalization of motivating affects of the superego preceded codification in Scripture.

The development of a capacity for symbolization through the externalization of affects and their representation in plastic concrete items first appears in the Neanderthal man. With Cro-Magnon man, it was organized into a cultural pattern having artistic content such as cave paintings.

The mature system consciousness is characterized by a restricted self-apprehension that is the result of the coordination of repression and symbolization. A similar pattern characterizes the function of the structure of latency. The precursors of repression may be found in the distortions of meaning produced by the process of blending. This activity occurred at the juncture of the Old Paleoanthropes (1200-1400 cubic centimeters of brain capacity) and the Neanderthal (1400-1500 cubic centimeters brain capacity). The appearance of metaphorical symbols occurs in Neanderthal man and is considerably expanded in the works of Cro-Magnon man. At any time during the period encompassing late Neanderthal and Cro-Magnon man, repression could have become associated with symbolizations of internal affects and concepts as they are expressed in external symbols. Psychoanalytic symbols could then have been produced. The only symbols of this kind that we could recognize today would be those which contained distortions. Jones and Heilbronner both felt that they were able to identify such symbols in the works of Aurignacian artists (30,000 B.C.). Acceptable proof of manifestations of psychoanalytic symbol formation later than those postulated by Jones occur at about 6,000 B.C. when demon figures reflecting distortions, projections, and symbolizations of aggressive affects appear in rupestral drawings.

All of the skills required for latency are present long before modern latency appeared during man's evolution. The actual organization of human defenses to produce latency as we know it cannot be demonstrated to occur until some time in the second millenium B.C. Although the exact date for the beginning of latency is not clear, the development of society that indicates the onset of the state of latency can be identified. It correlates with the transition from hunting and food gathering to sedentary farming, pastoral life, and industrial society. The state of latency as we

know it can be identified as beginning with the shift from the shame conscience of primitive tribes to the guilt conscience of modern man. Shame
has survival value only where there are small groups. When groups
become larger and individuals are required to act in a responsible manner
in situations in which they are not under the direct eye of their peers and
the fellow members of their culture, internalization of control mechanisms
is necessary for survival.

Latency in Primitive Societies

Latency age boys in primitive societies (hunters and gatherers) experience different organization of latency than comparable youngsters in
sedentary farming, pastoral cultures, or industrial societies. In primitive
societies there are few assigned responsibilities for boys. Latency age girls
undergo an experience like that of sedentary farmers. In more evolved
cultures children are assigned to farming or herding chores lending whatever help to the parents that they can. Traditions of the society, both technical and mythical, are conveyed to the child from close association with
parents and elders. In cultures which are literate, the children are assigned
for well-defined periods to the task of learning the media for the transmission of culture. The learning of technical skills may be delayed until late
adolescence. Typically, in present-day primitive societies children are
closely cared for during the prelatency age period and boys are permitted
to run relatively free during the latency age.

There is a distinct sexual difference in the assigned roles of latency age
children. Murphy and Murphy (1974) describe this as a classical pattern in
primitive societies (p. 173). Girls stay at home with the women and learn
from them the technical traditions of the tribe related to food raising,
handicrafts, and food preparation. Erikson (1945) describes the education
of a latency age Sioux Indian girl with emphasis on latency as a period
when inhibition of aggression and of sexuality is taught. The girls learn to
be passive, sit modestly, sleep with their thighs tied together, and remain
in the village, lest they be raped (p. 328). During latency, girls of primitive
tribes learn traditions relating to drive inhibition and the technical traditions of the tribe. Mythological traditions are not as important in their
lives as they are in the lives of men, except as they relate to menses.

Except for rare exceptions, as exemplified in the quote from Malinow-
sky on page 32 of chapter 2, inhibition of the expression of sexual drives is
demanded of both sexes. Aggression, which is inhibited in girls, is encouraged in boys. Erikson (1945), Murphy and Murphy (1974), and Read
(1965) emphasize the freedom of boys, their sadism, and the organization
of a peer group that ranges free outside the village, setting up its own hier-
archy and social pattern. The boys usually form two groups, those six and
seven and those above eight years of age. The younger group stays closer to
home. The older group is involved in independent functioning. The activities include hunting in imitation of the adults, using child-size weapons,
often, as Read (1965) described children from New Guinea (p. 57), shoot-
ing at each other. Ties to the mother are markedly diminished. At the end
of latency, the boys enter the society of men. Most of the transmission of
technical and mythological traditions awaits puberty and the acquisition
of the physical size and strength that will permit the child to participate
safely in hunting and warfare. At the time of initiation rites, the traditions
of the society needed for manhood are transmitted. The media for transmission of culture are myths, rituals, interpretation of mystical experiences, pageantry, and the explanation of symbolic pictures and patterns.

Once the patterns and traditions have been acquired, by girls in early
latency and by boys in early adolescence, adherence to social rules is enforced, with shame as the superego-motivating affect. Primitive societies
consist of small groups. If wrong is done in the eye of the group, the entire
world of the culprit knows it. Early adolescents in primitive society find
themselves in a peer group that controls through shame. This is similar to
the peer groups sought by the adolescents of industrial societies in their
defiance of important adults. But in primitive societies the peer group of
adolescence is made up of mature men and women of the culture who
accept the adolescents as co-workers and peers. This is the reason that
there is so little in the way of adolescent crisis and rebellion in primitive
societies.

Symbols and Survival

Mankind did not develop speech and awareness first and then at his leisure go on to create the mythic schemata of society. The schemata of

"mythologically educated societies" were acquired during the evolution of mankind at a point in development that preceded self-awareness in a world conceived of in three dimensions and the passage of time. As such, the evolution of society contributed to the mature form of modern man. The development of alternative mythic schemata reflected man's burgeoning capacity for alternative responses to situations. Schemata became a factor in the organization of man as a social being. This increased in inverse ratio to a decrease in binding the discharge of instincts to unalterable patterns. Different groups of men developed their own identifying patterns. Man is not born with a knowledge of absolutes. Each man must be prepared for the life of his people through instruction in the patterns of his culture. In this way man has developed and survived as a group animal. Traditions and alternatives are not transmitted as instinct, but through education, and each society has techniques for this transmission. Man's survival as a species has depended upon it.

Modern man has descended from animals who traveled in packs, hordes, and eventually tribes. Instincts and the environment existed first as an articulated unit for the gratification of drives. Initially hands, claws, and fangs were the means of contact. With the maturation of the capacity for alternative hunting patterns using either hand alone or hand and tool together, alternative syntaxes of behavior were added to early man's resources. Memory storage of these alternative syntaxes of behavior made primitive conscious selection between alternatives a fact of proto-human life. This step was an early stage in the development of the adaptive function of the ego. As alternatives grew in number, certain patterns provided greater survival value. Individual wishes and needs had to be sacrificed if patterned group function which was necessary for survival were to be maintained. Among these survival patterns was the inhibition of aggressive and sexual drives within the immediate group. This reinforced group survival, since murder was minimized. Patterns of sexual inhibition, especially incest taboos, insured survival of the young individuals, since the wrath of older larger males was avoided.

An alternative pathway disarticulated from reality developed which provided for discharge of these drives and fulfillment for these inhibited needs in the form of noctural phenomena such as symbolization during sleep (i.e., distortion dreams). In preliterate primitive societies where conformance for boys is demanded at puberty, cooperation, calm, and the channeling of energies are achieved through the utilization of myths and rituals which are used for the transmission of survival patterns. These mythic elements contain symbolic representations which discharge drives while welding individuals to the group. Symbols thus used in maintaining the continuity of the group in the face of individual needs had from the beginning provided primitive man with positive evolutionary potentials. In Western society the burden of this work falls upon the state of latency. When society proscribed direct drive expression from ages six to twelve the dreamlike symbolic mechanisms of the structure of latency were ready to serve for discharge and to preserve calm. Epigenetically they joined in the process of the transmission of culture.

Traditions serve as survival tools for the group. The individual man is reduced to the status of an element in the organic unity of mankind. Traditions transcend individual needs, causing limitations in the expression of the instinctual aspirations of single beings. Where can individual needs find satisfaction and discharge in such a system? The psychoanalytic symbols which occur in latency myths and night dreams provide outlet. Group intactness is preserved by the presence of this safety valve. It provides an evolutionary fulcrum for the survival of the group by providing nonthreatening expressions of the drives of individuals.

The transmission of traditions has provided man with a means of maintaining the identity and integrity of the group (the smallest unit capable of survival). A man is often powerless alone where a group can survive. Concurrently, the creativity of individuals which modifies reality required limitations, for this creativity provides both an evolutionary strength and a danger. Man's evolutionary potential for adaptive survival depends on the sustained capacity for development of new alternative potentials. These form the substrata of the creative and adaptive work of the individual ego of the individual man. Adaptive changes in groups are the products of individual minds. Still, groups survive through strengths. Heightened flexibility of response and the potential for individuality that this creative capacity portends is inimical to group solidarity. Nevertheless, if the group is to survive changes in environmental stresses, creative potential must survive. Like Frederick Barbarossa it dwells in sleep till needed. Dream symbols provide a pathway for the occult exercise of the expression of individual wishes. Dream symbols therefore serve a necessary function in the evolution of man. They preserve a skill. They provide an evolutionary adjustment permitting man to maintain flexibility without interfering with mythically organized group solidarity. Sublimative creativity (art) represents a communicative aspect of dream symbolism. It is the product of this process in the context of the individual man as the measure of things, instead of the group.

Note

1. All references to and quotes from Andre Leroi-Gourhan, save for those that derive from *Treasures of Prehistoric Art* (1967), are based on my translations.

Appendix C

PATHOLOGICAL CONDITIONS IN LATENCY

Immediately below will be found an index to the varieties of psychopathology related to the latency state. This listing is based upon distinguishing characteristics of personality states in latency. These may be used in developing psychotherapeutic strategies in dealing with latency period children. The categories are followed by a descriptive paragraph or by a number which refers to pages on which a primary reference to the topic appears. Through this index, information contained in this book about conditions met in clinical practice can be found quickly.

1. Failure to enter the state of latency (pp. 10, 21, 26, 162)
    A. Failure of the development of cognitive precursors (p. 86)
        a. Failure to develop the symbolizing function (pp. 92, 162) due to impaired:
            (1) displacement (pp. 101, 270)
            (2) delay (p. 101)
            (3) repression (pp. 102, 103)
            (4) object relations (p. 101)
        b. Failure in maturation of the symbolizing function (pp. 185, 279)

    c. Impairment in the development of behavioral and object constancy (p. 108) due to:

    (1) Poor superego formation (pp. 130, 370)

    (2) Poor models (p. 23)

    (3) Poor superego formation due to failure of identifications (pp. 138, 162)

    (This category is strongly related to difficulties in the establishment of appropriate behavior patterns during adolescence.)

  B. Failure to enter latency as a result of overstimulation (pp. 22, 26, 197)

2. Regressive deterioration of the organization of the ego structure of latency in an individual who has already reached the latency state:

This refers to a decompensation of the ego structure of latency manifested in a specific ego regression which takes the following form. Fantasies of the child gain access to the motor apparatus. The child begins to act on the fantasies themselves. Tension discharge disorders of the neurotic type are classical examples of this condition. These individuals are capable of entering into a sustained state of latency. However, they are pushed into a state of fantasy-driven behavior by overstimulating events, such as seductions and beatings. (pp. 10, 25, 26, 203, 208, 227, 256 (Termination), 297, 302, 303, 312)

3. Regression to prelatency behavior:

A failure of latency-appropriate ego functioning characterizes this condition. The child becomes subject to unpatterned states of regressive messing and aggressive provocative behavior without clear evidence of a well-defined pattern of behavior. There is loss of both the mechanisms of restraint and the structure of latency itself. Tension discharge disorders of the impulse-ridden type belong to this category. Individuals with this condition are able to enter into a state of latency, but are unable to sustain it. In these children the ego functioning appropriate to latency is slow in maturing. Overstimulation, fatigue, and moderately severe illnesses bring on these manifestations. Growth and maturation minimize the number and intensity of the episodes as the child passes eight years of age. (pp. 10, 26, 208)

4. Vulnerable children

This category refers to regressions from the state of latency in individuals predisposed by inherent structural personality defects. The term "borderline" (p. 309), which is sometimes applied to such children, has little validity during the latency years because the rapid shifts in the use of mechanisms of defense, often within the course of a few hours, which are the criterion of the borderline diagnosis, can be found in normal latency states as well as in most pathological situations. This makes differential diagnosis based upon this criterion very difficult. Clinically these children may have sustained states of reliability, calm, and educability; however, they are subject to decompensations under stress. There are two categories of vulnerable children who can give the appearance of a normal latency state: (A) those with oral fixations and heightened narcissistic cathexes, and (B) those who have an inadequate symbolizing function.

A. Weakness in latency ego structure characterized by oral fixations and heightened narcissistic cathexes. These are found in patients who give evidence of the following psychological signs and symptoms:

  a. Persistence of transitional phenomena (pp. 285-298)

  b. Denial of slips of the tongue (p. 272)

  c. Excessive narcissism (pp. 129, 305)

  d. Oral regressions

    (1) Oral regressions interfering with fantasies during psychotherapy sessions (pp. 241, 267)

    (2) Repeated turning to food and associated obesity during the latency age period (These children regress from oedipal fantasies through the anal-sadistic drive organization to the drive organization of the oral level.)

  e. Fantasies involving introjects (These frequently occur in children who are vulnerable to schizophrenia.) (p. 307)

  f. Sleepwalkers and children with pavor nocturnus (associated with arousal from fourth-stage sleep) which is persistant and repeated (p. 276-285)

B. Inadequate symbol formation

A latency state is produced but is not maintained because of the immature level to which the symbolizing function has developed, and the inadequate structure of latency that is produced thereby.

The following psychopathological states reflect the existence of this category.

    a. Severe mourning reactions (p. 253)

    (Latency aged children usually respond to mourning situations with the rapid repression of affect and turning to fantasy play.)

    b. Patterns of good behavior in school coupled with poor behavior at home (pp. 185-193)

    (A child with an impaired symbolizing function finds it difficult to maintain the patterns of behavior demanded by his superego once he has left the school. He is able to maintain behavior in school through the use of the inhibitory defenses (mechanisms of restraint). Once he leaves the school he enters into the non-structured family setting in which he loses control, since he does not have the safety valve of fantasy and play provided by the structure of latency. Symbolized fantasies may be present but their contents, because of inadequate symbolization, become too terrifying to be used as a defense. Often the unacceptable fantasies produced are defended through mental symptom formation. (p. 275)

5. Neurotic Symptoms

    A. Hysterical (p. 48)

    B. Phobic (pp. 94, 217, 286, 300)

    C. Obsessional (pp. 124, 217, 307)

Neurotic symptoms are usually transient during the latency age period. Phobic symptoms are the most persistent and the most frequent. Obsessive-compulsive symptoms become more apparent from nine to twelve years of age. Neurotic symptoms with an origin in the latency time period usually do not persist into adult life. Adult symptoms usually may be followed in direct line from phobic avoidance reactions of early childhood or true neurotic symptoms appearing after the age of fourteen. Neurotic symptom formation in the latency age period usually occurs in the presence of Category 4Bb, a structure of latency equipped with a poorly developed symbolizing function or a potential for regression to this. The latent fantasies are inadequately symbolized. Anxiety is produced. Compromise formation results in the formation of neurotic symptoms. Phobic symptomatology often intensifies during periods when the child is alone and in darkness, as exemplified by night fears.

6. Depression

Typically during the latency age period, depression is less of a symptom or a syndrome than it is in adult psychopathology. Depression during the latency age tends to be more of an affect, transient in its availability to consciousness, which is defended against through the production of fantasies and symptoms (p. 216). Usually these defensive responses are successful and the depressive affect persists as an unconscious potential. In this form it may be found to underlie:

A. Persecutory states (p. 300)

B. Unsuccessful attempts to adjust to new peer groups (pp. 369, 374)

C. Psychosomatic responses (p. 211)

D. Obsessional states (p. 124)

E. Oral regressive states accompanied by overweight and overeating (p. 212)

Sustained manifest depression is seen most often during states of mourning and other reactions to object loss (pp. 200, 253). Brief periods of manifest depression occur when a child has fallen short of the demands of the superego and his introjects (p. 9).

Organized states of depression are rarely characteristic of ego states (e.g., paranoid states and the state of latency) in which projection and actualization (see p. 228) are the preferred mechanisms used to deal with angry feelings.

7. Psychotic states (pp. 32, 300-334)

BIBLIOGRAPHY

Abraham, K. (1924). A short study of the development of the libido in the light of mental disorders. *Selected Papers of Karl Abraham*. New York: Basic, 1954.

Anthony, E. J. (1959). An experimental approach to the psychopathology of childhood: sleep disturbances. *British Journal of Medical Psychology* 321: 19-37.

Aquinas, T. Summa contra gentiles. *Introduction to Contemporary Civilization in the West*, Vol. 1. New York: Columbia University Press, 1946.

Arlow, J. A. (1953). Masturbation and symptom formation. *Journal of the American Psychoanalytic Association* 1: 45-57.

_____(1961). Ego psychology and mythology. *Journal of the American Psychoanalytic Association* 9: 371-393.

Arthur, B., and Schumann, S. (1970). Family and peer relationships in children with paranoid delusions. *Child Psychiatry and Human Development* 1: 68-82.

Barnes, C. (1973). You should have seen. *New York Times*, "Arts and Leisure," Sunday, July 29, 1973, p. 16.

Barrie, J. M. (1911). *Peter Pan*. New York: Scribners, 1950.

Bender, L. (1947). Childhood schizophrenia. *Journal of the Academy of Orthopsychiatry* 17: 40-56.

_____(1970). The life course of schizophrenic children. *Biological Psychiatry* 2: 165-172.

_____(1974). The family patterns of 100 schizophrenic children observed at Bellevue 1935-1952. *Journal of Autism and Childhood Schizophrenia* 4: 279-293.

Berger, H. (1929). (EEG)—Uber das Elektroenkephalogramm des Menschen. *Arch. Psychiat. Nervenkr.* 87: 527.

Bernstein, I. (1974). Panel on Psychology of Women: Latency and Early Adolescence. Fall Meeting of the American Psychoanalytic Association, New York, December 13.

Blanchard, P. (1953). Masturbation fantasies of children and adolescents. *Bulletin of the Philadelphia Association for Psychoanalysis* 3: 25-38.

Blos, P. (1957). Preadolescent drive organization. *Journal of the American Psychoanalytic Association* 6: 47-57.

_____(1962). *On Adolescence*. New York: Macmillan.

_____(1963). Acting out and the adolescent process. *Journal of the American Academy of Child Psychiatry* 2: 118-143.

Bonaparte, M. (1949). Passivity, masochism and femininity. *Female Sexuality*. New York: Grove, 1953.

Bornstein, B. (1951). On latency. *Psychoanalytic Study of the Child* 6: 279-285. New York: International Universities Press.

_____(1953). Masturbation in the latency period. *Psychoanalytic Study of the Child* 8: 65-78. New York: International Universities Press.

Boyer, L. B., and Boyer, R. B. (1970). Effects of acculturation on the vicissitudes of the aggressive drive among the Apaches of the Mescalero Indian Reservation. Page 1 of manuscript later published in *The Psychoanalytic Study of Society*, Vol. 5, ed. W. Meunsterberger. New York: International Universities Press.

Brandt, S., and Brandt, H. (1955). The electroencephalographic patterns in young healthy children from 0-5 years of age. *ACTA Scandinavian Psychiatry and Neurology* 30: 77.

Brenner, C. (1951). A case of childhood hallucinosis. *Psychoanalytic Study of the Child* 6: 235-243. New York: International Universities Press.

Broughton, R. J. (1968). Sleep disorders: Disorders of arousal? *Science* 159: 1070-1078.

Brown, D. (1973). The gift of language. *The First Men*. New York: Time-Life.

Bruner, J. (1960). Myth and identity. *Myth and Mythmaking*, ed. H. Murray. Boston: Beacon.

Campbell, J. (1959). The masks of god, Vol. 1. *Primitive Mythology*, 2nd ed. New York: Viking, 1971.

_____(1968). The historical development of mythology. *Myths and Mythmakers*, ed. H. Murray. Boston: Beacon, 1969.

_____(1971). Letter to author, Jan. 25.

Cassirer, E. (1923). *Language and Myth*. New York: Dover, 1946.

Clower, V. (1974). Panel on Psychology of Women: Latency and Early Adolescence. Fall Meeting, American Psychoanalytic Association, New York, December 13.

Cohen, M. L. et al. (1971). The psychology of rapists. *Seminars in Psychiatry* 3: 307-327.

Concise Encyclopedia of Archeology (1960). London: Hutchinson.

Coren, H. Z., and Saldinger, J. S. (1967). Visual hallucinosis in children. *Psychoanalytic Study of the Child* 22: 344-356. New York: International Universities Press.

DeManaceine, M. (1897). *Sleep: Its Physiology, Pathology, Hygiene, and Psychology*. London: Walter Scott.

deMause, L. (1974). The evolution of childhood. *History of Childhood Quarterly* 1: 503-575.

Dement, W. C. (1964). *The Oculomotor System*, ed. M. D. Bruder. New York: Hoeber.

_____(1965). *New Directions in Psychology*, ed. T. Newcomb. New York: Holt, Rinehart and Winston.

Deutsch, H. (1944). Psychology of Women, Vol. 1. New York: Grune and Stratton.

Diamond, S. (1972). The debt of Leibnitz to Pardies. *Journal of the History of Behavioral Science* 1: 109-114.

Edey, M. (1974). *The Sea Traders*. New York: Time-Life.

Eggers, C. (1967). Prepubescent schizophrenia. *Acta Paedopsychiatrica* 34: 326-340.

Eidelberg, L. A. (1945). A contribution to the study of the masturbation fantasy. *International Journal of Psycho-Analysis* 25: 127-137.

Eissler, K. (1949). General problems of delinquency. *Searchlights on Delinquency*, ed. K. Eissler. New York: International Universities Press.

Elkind, D. (1974). Cognitive adaption. Paper presented before the McGill University Symposium "The Latency Child," Montreal, Canada, Sept. 27.

Erasmus, D. (1511). *The Praise of Folly*. Princeton: Princeton University Press, 1945.

Erikson, E. H. (1945). Childhood and tradition in two American Indian tribes. *Psychoanalytic Study of the Child* 1: 319-350. New York: International Universities Press.

Fenichel, O. (1945). *The Psychoanalytic Theory of Neurosis*. New York: Norton.

Ferenczi, S. (1911). On obscene words. *Sex in Psychoanalysis*. New York: Basic Books, 1950.

_____(1913). Stages in the development of the sense of reality. *Sex in Psychoanalysis*. New York: Basic Books, 1950.

_____(1925). Psychoanalysis of sexual habits. *Further Contributions to the Theory and Technique of Psychoanalysis*. London: Hogarth, 1953.

Fisher, C. et al. (1970). A psychophysiological study of nightmares. *Journal of the American Psychoanalytic Association* 18: 747-783.

Flavell, J. H. (1963). *The Developmental Psychology of Jean Piaget*. New York: Van Nostrand.

Fraiberg, S. (1972). Some characteristics of genital arousal and discharge in latency girls. *Psychoanalytic Study of the Child* 27: 439-475. New York: International Universities Press.

Frazer, J. (1922). *The Golden Bough*. New York: Macmillan, 1951.

Frazier, A. (1966). *A History of Toys*. London: Weidenfeld and Nicholson.

Freedman, D. et al. (1971). Speech and psychic structure: A reconsideration of their relation. *Journal of the American Psychiatric Association* 19: 765-779.

Freedman, Z., and Roe, A. (1958). Evolution and human behavior. *Behavior and Evolution*, eds. A. Roe and G. Simpson. New Haven: Yale University Press.

Freud, A. (1936). *The Ego and Mechanisms of Defense*. New York: International Universities Press, 1966.

_____(1949). Certain types and stages of social maladjustment. *Searchlights on Delinquency. New Psychoanalytic Studies*, ed. K. R. Eissler. New York: International Universities Press.

_____(1958). Adolescence. *The Psychoanalytic Study of the Child* 13: 255-268. New York: International Universities Press.

_____(1965). *Normality and Pathology in Childhood: Assessment of Development*. New York: International Universities Press.

Freud, S. (1900). Interpretation of Dreams. *Standard Ed*. 4 & 5. London: Hogarth, 1953.

_____(1905). Three essays on the theory of sexuality. *Standard Ed*. 7: 123-243. London: Hogarth, 1953.

_____(1908b). Character and anal eroticism. *Standard Ed*. 9: 167-176. London: Hogarth, 1959.

_____(1909a). Analysis of a phobia in a five-year-old boy. *Standard Ed*. 10: 3-149. London: Hogarth, 1955.

_____(1911b). Formulations on the two principles of mental functioning. *Standard Ed*. 12: 213-226. London, Hogarth, 1958.

_____(1911). "Letter to Else Voigtlander." In Freud, E., *Letters of Sigmund Freud*. New York: Basic Books, 1960.

_____(1914). On narcissism. *Standard Ed*. 14: 73-104. London: Hogarth, 1957.

_____(1915d). Repression. *Standard Ed*. 14: 146-158. London: Hogarth, 1957.

_____(1915e). The unconscious. *Standard Ed*. 14: 159-216. London: Hogarth, 1957.

_____(1916-1917). Introductory lectures on psychoanalysis. *Standard Ed*. 15 & 16. London: Hogarth, 1957.

_____(1918). The taboo of virginity. *Standard Ed*. 11: 191-208. London: Hogarth, 1957.

_____(1919e). A child is being beaten. *Standard Ed*. 17: 172-204. London: Hogarth, 1955.

_____(1922a). Group psychology and the analysis of the ego. *Standard Ed*. 18: 67-144. London: Hogarth, 1955.

_____(1923). Two encyclopaedia articles. *Standard Ed*. 18: 235-262. London: Hogarth, 1955.

_____(1923b). The ego and the id. *Standard Ed*. 19: 3-68. London: Hogarth, 1961.

_____(1924). A short account of psycho-analysis. *Standard Ed*. 17: 191-212. London: Hogarth, 1961.

_____(1924d). The dissolution of the Oedipus complex. *Standard Ed*. 19: 173-182. London: Hogarth, 1961.

_____(1925). An autobiographical study. *Standard Ed*. 20: 7-76. London: Hogarth, 1959.

_____(1926a). Inhibitions, symptoms and anxiety. *Standard Ed*. 20: 77-178. London: Hogarth, 1959.

_____(1926b). The question of lay analysis. Conversations with an impartial person. *Standard Ed*. 20: 179-258. London: Hogarth, 1959.

_____(1939a). Moses and monotheism: Three essays. *Standard Ed*. 23: 7-140. London: Hogarth, 1964.

_____ (1940a). An outline of psychoanalysis. *Standard Ed.* 23: 144-208. London: Hogarth, 1964.

_____ (1950). *The Origins of Psychoanalysis. Letters to Wilhelm Fliess, Drafts and Notes: 1887-1902,* eds. M. Bonaparte, A. Freud, and E. Kris. New York: Basic Books, 1954.

Friedlander, K. (1942). Children's books and their function in latency and prepuberty. *The American Imago* 3: 129-150.

Fries, M. (1959). Review of the literature of the latency period, with special emphasis on the so-called normal case. *Readings in Psychoanalytic Psychology,* ed. J. Levitt. New York: Appleton-Century-Crofts.

Friend, M. R. (1957). In the latency period. Samuel Kaplan, Reporter. (Scientific Proceedings—Panel Reports). *Journal of the American Psychoanalytic Association* 5: 525-538.

Fries, M. (1959). Review of the literature of the latency period, with special emphasis on the so-called normal case. *Readings in Psychoanalytic Psychology,* ed. J. Levitt. New York: Appleton-Century-Crofts.

Galenson, E. (1972). Personal communication.

Gardner, R. and Gardner, B. (1969). Teaching sign language to a chimpanzee. *Science* 165: 664-672.

Gardner, R. W. and Moriarty, A. (1968). *Personality Development in Preadolescence.* Seattle: University of Washington Press.

Geleerd, E. R. (1943). The analysis of a case of compulsive masturbation in a child. *Psychoanalytic Quarterly* 12: 520-540.

Gibbs, F. A., and Gibbs, E. L. (1951). Methodology and controls. *Atlas of EEG,* Vol. 1. Reading, Mass: Addison-Wesley.

Giedion, S. (1962). *The Beginnings of Art.* New York: Bollingen.

Glick, B. S., Schulman, D., and Turecki, S. (1971). Diazepam (Valium) treatment in childhood sleep disorders. *Diseases of the Nervous System* 32: 565-566.

Goldfarb, W. (1961). *Childhood Schizophrenia.* Boston: Harvard University Press.

Goodall, J. (1964). Tool using and aimed throwing in a community of free living chimpanzees. *Nature* 20: 1265-1267.

Grier, W. H., and Cobbs, P. M. (1968). *Black Rage.* New York: Basic Books.

Halstead, W. C. (1947). *Brain and Intelligence.* Chicago: University of Chicago Press.

Hampson, J. L., Hampson, J. G., and Money, J. (1959). The syndrome of gonadal agenesis (ovarian agenesis) and male chromosomic patterns in girls and women. *Bulletin of Johns Hopkins Hospital* 97: 207-226.

Harkness, G. (1954). *The Origins of Western Morality.* New York: Scribner's.

Harrison, S., Hess, J., and Zrull, J. P. (1963). Paranoid reactions in children. *Journal of the American Academy of Child Psychiatry* 2: 677-693.

Hart, M., and Sarnoff, C. A. (1971). The impact of the menarche. *Journal of the American Academy of Child Psychiatry* 10: 257-271.

Hartmann, E. (1965). The D state. *International Journal of Psychiatry* 2: 11-47.

Hartmann, H. (1948). Comments on the psychoanalytic theory of instinctual drives. *Essays on Ego Psychology,* ed. H. Hartmann. New York: International Universities Press, 1964.

_____ (1958). *Ego Psychology and the Problem of Adaptation.* New York: International Universities Press, 1958.

_____ (1952). The mutual influences in the development of ego and id. *Essays on Ego Psychology,* ed. H. Hartmann. New York: International Universities Press, 1964.

_____ (1958). *Ego Psychology and the Problem of Adaptation.* New York: International Universities Press, 1958.

Hawk, A. B., Carpenter, W. T., Jr., and Straus, J. S. (1975). Diagnostic criteria and five-year outcome in schizophrenia. *Archives of General Psychiatry* 32: 347-356.

Heilbronner, P. (1938). Some remarks on the treatment of the sexes in Paleolithic art. *International Journal of Psycho-Analysis* 19: 439-447.

Henderson, F. (1974). Personal communication.

Hockett, C. F. (1959). Animal "languages" and human language. *The Evolution of Man's Capacity for Culture, ar.* J. N. Spuhler. Detroit: Wayne State University Press, 1968.

Hoffman, M. L. (1970). Moral development. *Carmichael's Manual of Child Psychology,* 3rd ed., Vol. 2, ed. P. H. Mussen. New York: Wiley.

Hulse, F. S. (1963). *The Human Species*. New York: Random House.

Hutton, E. (1962). *The Origins of Science*. London: Allen and Unwin.

Jacobson, E. (1964). *The Self and the Object World*. New York: International Universities Press.

Jones, E. (1916). The theory of symbolism. *Papers on Psychoanalysis*. Baltimore: Williams and Wilkins, 1948.

_____(1931). *On the Nightmare*. New York: Grove, 1959.

_____(1938). A psychoanalytic note on Paleolithic art. *Essays in Applied Psychoanalysis*, 2: 174-177. New York: International Universities Press.

Jordan, K., and Prugh, D. (1971). Schizophreniform psychosis of late childhood. *American Journal of Psychiatry* 128: 323-329.

Jung, C. G. (1946). The fight with the shadow. *Collected Works* 10: 218-226. Bollingen, 1964.

Kales, A. (1969). *Sleep*. New York: Lipincott.

_____et al. (1966). Somnambulism: Psychophysiological correlates 1. All night EEG studies. *Archives of General Psychiatry* 14: 586-595.

Kales, J. D., Jacobson, A., and Kales, A. (1969). Sleep disorders in children. *Progress in Clinical Psychology*, Vol. 8, eds. L. E. Abt et al. New York: Grune & Stratton.

Kaplan, E. (1974). Panel on Psychology of Women: Latency and Early Adolescence. Fall Meeting American Psychoanalytic Association, December 13.

Katan, A. (1937). The role of "displacement" in agoraphobia. *International Journal of Psycho-Analysis* 32: 41-50, 1951.

Keiser, S. (1958). Disturbances in abstract thinking and body image formation. *Journal of the American Psychoanalytic Association* 6: 628-652.

Kestenberg, J. (1961). Menarche. *Adolescence*, eds. S. Lorand and H. I. Schneer. New York: Hoeber.

_____(1967). Phases of adolescence, Parts I and II. *Journal of Child Psychiatry* 6: 426-463; 6: 577-611.

_____(1968). Phases of adolescence, Part III. *Journal of Child Psychiatry* 7: 108-251.

Kinsey, A. et al. (1948). *Sexual Behavior in the Human Male*. Philadelphia: Saunders.

_____(1953). *Sexual Behavior in the Human Female*. Philadelphia: Saunders.

Kligerman, C. (1970). The dream of Charles Dickens. *Journal of the American Psychoanalytic Association* 18: 783-799.

Kollar, E. (1972). Object relations and the origin of tools. *Archives of General Psychiatry* 26: 23-27.

Krantz, G. (1968). Brain size and hunting ability in earliest man. *Current Anthropology* 9: 450-451.

Krim, M. B. (1962). Psychiatric observations on children with precocious physical development. *Journal of Child Psychiatry* 1: 397-413.

Kris, E. (1951). Some comments and observations on autoerotic activities. *Psychoanalytic Study of the Child* 6: 95-116. New York: International Universities Press.

_____(1956). The personal myth. *Journal of the American Psychoanalytic Association* 4: 653-681.

Kuhn, H. (1956). *Rock Pictures of Europe*. Fairlawn, N.J.: Essential Books.

Lampl-de Groot, J. (1950). On masturbation and its influence on general development. *Psychoanalytic Study of the Child* 5: 142-174. New York: International Universities Press.

Laufer, M. (1968). The body image, the function of masturbation, and adolescence: Problems of ownership of the body. *Psychoanalytic Study of the Child* 23: 114-123. New York: International Universities Press.

Leibnitz, G. W. (1714). Principes de la Nature et de la Grace, Fondes en Raison. *New Essays Concerning the Human Understanding*, 3rd ed., ed. A. G. Langley. LaSalle, Ill.: Open Court, 1949.

Lerner, I. M. (1968). *Heredity, Evolution, and Society*. San Francisco: W. H. Freeman.

Leroi-Gourhan, A. (1964). *Le Geste et la Parole—Technique et Langage*. Paris: Editions Albin Michel.

_____(1965). *Le Geste et la Parole—la Memoire et les Rythmes*. Paris: Editions Albin Michel.

_____(1967). *Treasures of Prehistoric Art*. New York: Abrams.

Levine, M. (1951). Pediatric observations on masturbation in children. *Psychoanalytic Study of the Child* 6: 117-127. New York: International Universities Press.

Levy, E. Z. (1971). Discussion of Jordan and Prugh. *American Journal of Psychiatry* 128: 329.

Lindner, S. (1876). "Das Saugen an den Fingerns, Lippen, etc., bei den Kindern (Ludeln): Jahrbuch Kinderheilkunde, rept. Psa P. 8: 117-138.

Lopandin, V. M., and Stoyanov, S. (1970). Paraphrenia in adolescents with remittant schizophrenia. *Korsakov Journal of Neuropsychiatry* 70: 256-260.

Macnish (1834). *Philosophy of Sleep* as quoted in Jones (1931).

Mahler, M. (1969). *On Human Symbiosis and the Vicissitudes of Individuation*. New York: International Universities Press.

_____, and Gosliner, B. J. (1955). On symbiotic child psychosis. *Psychoanalytic Study of the Child* 10: 195-214. New York: International Universities Press.

Malinowski, B. (1962). *Sex, Culture and Myth*. New York: Harcourt Brace Jovanovich.

Mead, M. (1958). Culture determinants of behavior. *Behavior and Evolution*, eds. A. Roe, and G. Simpson. New Haven: Yale University Press.

_____(1964). *Continuities in Cultural Evolution*. New Haven: Yale University Press.

Menaker, E., and Menaker, W. (1965). *Ego in Evolution*. New York: Grove Press.

Milton, J. (1644). Areopagitica; a speech of Mr. John Milton for the liberty of unlicensed printing, to the Parliament of England.

Modell, A. (1968). *Object Love and Reality*. New York: International Universities Press.

Money, J. (1972). Comment. In *The Control of the Onset of Puberty*, eds. Grumbach et al. New York: Wiley, 1974.

Murphy, Y. and Murphy, R. F. (1974). *Women of the Forest*. New York: Columbia University Press.

Osborn, C. (1975). *The Israelites*. New York: Time-Life.

Pardies, I. (1678). *Discours de la Connaisance des Bestes*, 2nd ed. Paris: p. 171.

Pearson, G. H. (1968). *A Handbook of Child Psychoanalysis*. New York: Basic Books.

Peller, L. (1958). Reading and daydreams in latency boy-girl differences. *Journal of the American Psychoanalytic Association* 6: 57-70.

Penfield, W., and Roberts, L. (1959). *Speech and Brain Mechanisms*. Princeton: Princeton University Press.

Piaget, J. (1932). *The Moral Judgment of the Child*. London: Kegan Paul.

_____(1945). *Play, Dreams and Imitation in Childhood*. New York: Dutton, 1951.

_____(1951). *Play, Dreams, and Imitation in Childhood*. New York: Dutton.

Pincus, J., and Tucker, G. (1974). *Behavioral Neurology*. New York: Oxford University Press.

Pittell, S. (1971). Personal communication.

_____(1973). The etiology of youthful drug involvement. In *Drug Use in America: Problems in Perspective. Technical Papers, Vol. I, Patterns and consequences of drug use*. Washington, D.C.: U.S. Government Printing Office.

_____et al. (1971). Developmental factors in adolescent drug abuse. *Journal of Child Psychiatry* 10: 640-660.

Premack, A. J., and Premack, D. (1972). Teaching language to an ape. *Scientific American* 227: 92-100.

Pumpian-Mindlin, E. (1965). Omnipotentiality, youth, and commitment. *Journal of the American Academy of Child Psychiatry* 4: 1-19.

Rapaport, D. (1958). The theory of ego autonomy: a generalization. *Bulletin of the Menninger Clinic* 22: 13-25.

_____(1958). The theory of ego autonomy: a generalization. *Bulletin of the Menninger Clinic* 22: 13-25.

Rapoport, J. (1944). Fantasy objects in children. *Psychoanalytic Review* 31: 316-321.

Read, K. (1965). *The High Valley*. New York: Scribner's.

Reich, A. (1951). The 1912 discussion on masturbation. *Psychoanalytic Study of the Child* 6: 80-94. New York: International Universities Press.

Reich, W. (1931). Character formation and the phobias of childhood. *International Journal of Psycho-Analysis* 12: 219-230.

Reinach, S. (1903). L'Art et La Magie, a Propos des Peintures et de Gravures du L'age du Renne. *L'Anthrop* 14: 265.

Rensch, B. (1956). Increase of learning capacity with increase of brain size. *American Naturalist* 90: 1-95.

Roffwang, H. P., Muzio, J. N., and Dement, W. K. (1966). Ontogenetic development of the human sleep-dream cycle. *Science* 152: 604-619.

Roheim, G. (1943). *The Origin and Function of Culture*. New York: Nervous and Mental Disease Monographs.

Rosenblum, R. (1965). *Transformations in Late Eighteenth Century Art*. Princeton: Princeton University Press.

Sachs, H. (1942). The community of daydreams. *The Creative Unconscious*. Cambridge, Mass.: Sci-Art.

Sachs, L. (1962). A case of castration anxiety beginning at 18 months. *Journal of the American Psychoanalytic Association* 10: 329-338.

Sarnoff, C. A. (1969a). Mythic symbols. *American Imago* 26: 3-20.

_____(1969b). Slips of the tongue in child analysis. Annual meeting of the American Psychoanalytic Association, Miami, Florida, May 3.

_____(1970). Symbols and symptoms. Phytophobia in a two-year-old girl. *Psychoanalytic Quarterly* 39: 550-562.

_____(1971a). Ego structure in latency. *The Psychoanalytic Quarterly* 40: 387-412.

_____(1971b). Prepared discussion of M. Sperling's The diagnostic and prognostic significance of children's dreams and sleep. Presented to the Psychoanalytic Association of New York, June 8, 1971.

_____(1971c). Prepubescent sexuality. *Medical Aspects of Human Sexuality* 5: 122.

_____(1972a). Symbols in shadows. *Journal of the American Psychoanalytic Association* 20: 59-91.

_____(1972b). The vicissitudes of projection during the analysis of a girl in late latency-early adolescence. *International Journal of Psycho-Analysis* 53: 515-523.

_____(1973a). Narcissism, adolescent masturbation fantasies and the search for reality. *Masturbation—From Infancy to Senescence*, eds. I. Marcus and J. J. Francis. New York: International Universities Press, 1975.

_____(1973b). The Ontogenesis of the system consciousness. Part B—regressive symbolization. Presented to the annual meeting of the American Psychoanalytic Association, May 4, 1973. Honolulu, Hawaii.

_____(1974). The metapsychology of symbol formation. Introduction to the ontogenesis of the system consciousness. Unpublished manuscript.

_____(1974a). Sonhos do Infancia—Aspectos Clinicos E Electroencefalograficos De Fenomenos Relationals Ao Sono Na Infancia Precoce. *Temas Livres of the X Congresso Latino-Americano De Psicanalise* (in Portuguese). Rio De Janiero, Brazil, July.

_____(1974b). Primary creativity, transitional phenomena and passive mastery. Presented to the Long Island Psychoanalytic Association, Oct. 6, 1975.

_____(1975). The work of latency. Presented to the Association for Psychoanalytic Medicine, New York, April 1.

Schachtel, E. (1949). On memory and childhood amnesia. *A Study of Interpersonal Relations*, ed. P. Mullahy. New York: Hermitage.

Scheinfeld, A. (1944). *Women and Men*. New York: Harcourt Brace.

Silverman, J. S. (1972). Obsessional disorders in childhood and adolescence. *American Journal of Psychotherapy* 26: 362-377.

Simpson, W. K. (1972). *The Literature of Ancient Egypt*. New Haven: Yale University Press.

Sours, J. A. et al. (1963). Somnambulism. *Archives of General Psychiatry* 9: 400-413.

Sperling, M. (1952). Animal phobias in a two-year-old child. *Psychoanalytic Study of the Child* 7: 115-125. New York: International Universities Press.

_____(1963). Fetishism in children. *Psychoanalytic Quarterly* 32: 374-392.

_____(1958). Pavor nocturnus. *Journal of the American Psychoanalytic Association* 6: 79-94.

_____(1963). Fetishism in children. *Psychoanalytic Quarterly* 32: 374-392.

ed. J. G. Howells. Edinburgh and London: Oliver and Boyd.

Sperling, O. (1954). An imaginary companion, representing a prestage of the superego. *Psychoanalytic*

Study of the Child 9: 252-258. New York: International Universities Press.

_____(1966). Metapsychology and direct infant observation. *Psychoanalysis—A General Psychology*, eds. Lowenstein et al. New York: International Universities Press.

Spitz, R. A. et al. (1970). Further prototypes of ego formation. *Psychoanalytic Study of the Child* 25: 417-441. New York: International Universities Press.

_____(1966). Metapsychology and direct infant observation. *Psychoanalysis—A General Psychology*, eds. Loewenstein et al. New York: International Universities Press.

Sterba, E. (1949). Analysis of psychogenic constipation in a two-year-old child. *The Psychoanalytic Study of the Child* 3/4: 227-252. New York: International Universities Press.

Still, F. (1900). Day terrors. *Lancet* 1: 292-294.

Stutte, H., and Dauner, I. (1971). Systematized delusions in early life schizophrenia. *Journal of Autism and Childhood Schizophrenia* 1: 411-420.

Sullivan, W. (1965). Toward man. In "The News of the Week in Review." *The New York Times*, April 11, 1965.

Switzer, J. (1963). A genetic approach to the understanding of learning problems. *Journal of Child Psychiatry* 2: 653-666.

Szurek, S. A., and Berlin, I. N. (1973). *Clinical Studies in Childhood Psychoses.* New York: Brunner/Mazel.

Ticho, E. A. (1973). Discussion of C. A. Sarnoff's The ontogenesis of the system consciousness—Part B—regressive symbolization. Presented to the American Psychoanalytic Association, May 4.

Ticho, G. (1969). Discussion of C. Sarnoff's Slips of the tongue in child analysis. Annual meeting of the American Psychoanalytic Association, May 3.

Waelder, R. (1951). The structure of paranoid ideas. *International Journal of Psycho-analysis* 32: 167-177.

Washburn, S. L. (1959). Speculations on the interrelations of the history of tools and biological evolution. *The Evolution of Man's Capacity for Culture*, ar: J. N. Spuhler. Detroit: Wayne State University Press.

_____ , and Avis V. (1958). Evolution of human behavior. *Behavior and Evolution*, eds. A. Roe and G. Simpson. New Haven: Yale University Press.

Wellek, R., and Warren, A. (1942). *Theory of Literature.* New York: Harcourt Brace.

Werner, Heinz (1940). *Comparative Psychology of Mental Development.* New York: International Universities Press.

Werner, H., and Levin S. (1967). Masturbation fantasies—their changes with growth and development. *Psychoanalytic Study of the Child* 22: 315-328. New York: International Universities Press.

Whitehead, A. N. (1927). The Uses of Symbolism. *Symbolism: Its Meaning and Effect*, ed. G. Holton. New York: Macmillan, 1958. Reprinted in *Daedalus* 87: 3: 110-123.

Winnicott, D. N. (1953). Transitional objects and transitional phenomena. *International Journal of Psycho-Analysis* 34: 89-93.

_____(1958). Transitional objects·and transitional phenomena. (A paper based on Winnicott, 1953). In *Collected Papers: Through Paediatrics to Psychoanalysis.* London: Tavistock; New York: Basic.

_____(1966). The location of cultural experience. *International Journal of Psycho-Analysis* 48: 386-392.

Woodward, M. (1965). Piaget's theory. *Modern Perspectives in Child Psychiatry*, ed. J. G. Howell. Springfield, Ill.: Thomas.

Wulff, M. W. (1928). A phobia in a child of eighteen months. *International Journal of Psycho-Analysis* 9: 354-359.

Yaholom, I. (1967). Sense, affect and image in development of the symbolic process. *International Journal of Psycho-Analysis* 48: 373-384.

INDEX

Abraham, K., 288
abstract conceptual memory organization, 87, 115, 117-120
abstract operational thinking, 116
abstract system consciousness, 189, 337
Acheuleon, 351
action construction, 200
actualization, 197
adolescence, early, 126-129
  sexual development during, 59-69
affective valence, 25, 162, 341
affecto-motor memory, 106, 160, 351, 354, 373
affects, superego motivating, 132, 139, 369, 370
agriculture, dawn of, 356
alpha waves, 282
amygdala, 373
anal regression, 31
anomie, 149, 176
Anthony, J., 120, 281, 283
anxiety dream, definition of, 277
Aquinas, T., 180

arcuate fasciculus, 353
Arlow, J., 68
Archanthropes, 349, 351, 353, 354, 357, 361
arousal, disorders of, in differential diagnosis of noctural phenomena, 279-281
  blank anxiety, definition of, 277
Arthur, B., 311, 312, 353
asthma, 277, 284
Aurignacian period, 365
Australopithecus, 349, 354
autoerotism, 40
autostrangulation, 67

Barnes, C., 298
beatings, 162
bedwetting, 277, 283, 285
behavioral constancy, in first cognitive organizing period, 108-115
Bender, L., 307, 308, 312, 330
Berger, H., 281

Berlin, I., 307
Bernstein, I., 48
beta waves, 281-282
bipedal locomotion, 350
bisexual fantasies, 76
Blanchard, P., 46, 48, 50, 53
blank anxiety arousal, 277
blending, 354, 367, 375
Blos, P., 61, 71, 76, 78
body image, changes in, during third cognitive organizing period, 127
Bonaparte, M., 79
"borderline" as a diagnosis, 30, 383
Bornstein, B., 20, 51, 55, 67, 89, 152
Boyer, L. B., 149, 150, 176
Boyer, R. B., 149, 150, 176
boys, masturbatory activity in, 51-54
brain, development of areas necessary for value judgment in, 371-376
brain size and the phylogenesis of latency, 349-354, 369, 371, 375
brainwashing, 177
Brandt, H., 283
Brandt, S., 283
Brenner, C., 280
Broca's area, 353, 374
Broughton, R. J., 279
Brown, D., 353

Campbell, J., 149, 167, 172
Cassirer, E., 174, 288
character, influence of latency on, 155-156
childhood schizophrenia. See prepubescent schizophrenia
Clower, V., 48
Cobbs, P. M., 174
cognitive development, 85-145
  first organizing period, 91-115
    behavioral constancy, 108-115
    repression, 103-106
    symbolizing function, development of, 92-103
    verbal conceptual memory organization, development of, 106-108
  second organizing period, 115-125
    abstract conceptual memory organization, 117-120
    concrete operational thinking, 116-117
    fantasy contents, shift in, 120-121

superego contents, reorganization of, 122-125
third organizing period, 126-130
  body image, changes in, 127
  fantasy, intensification of narcissistic investment in, 129-130
  object relatedness, changes in intensity and direction of, 128-129
  projection, preadolescent, 126-127
organizing periods of latency and, 86-91
psychotherapeutic technique modification required by, 214-215
and superego development, 130-144
Cohen, M. L., 150
"Community of Daydreams," 165
complexes, latent, psychotherapeutic strategies for identifying and working through, 203-204
compulsions, 104
concrete operational thinking, in second cognitive organizing period, 116-117
consciousness, 336
conservation, 113
constipation, 29-30, 100
cooperation within the group, 354
Coren, H. Z., 83
countertransference, 243-246
creative artist, 34
creativity
  evocative, 323, 368
  prelatency vs. latency, 117
  and sublimation, 320-323
Cro-Magnons, 348, 357-359, 361, 362, 373, 375
cultural evolution, 150, 344ff.
culture elements, internalized, 369
culture, transmission of, 157-180
culture, types of
  multiple-class cultures, 175
  parallel convergent cultures, 174
  parallel diverse cultures, 174
  parallel parasitic cultures, 174

Dauner, I., 306, 311, 312
delta waves, 282
DeManaceine, M., 279
deMause, L., 149, 213
Dement, W. K., 282
denial of slips of the tongue, 266
depression, 132, 386

Deutsch, H., 76, 78, 79
development. *See* cognitive development;
    sexual development
diagnostic evaluation, 218-228
Diamond, S., 362
diminution of drive theory of latency, 14,
    148
disorders of arousal, 279
displacement, 101, 355, 382
dorso median thalamic nucleus, 373
dreams
    anxiety, definition, 277
    definition, 276-277
    distortion dreams, 278
    psychotherapy, technical problems of
        analysis and interpretation in,
        273-276
    recall of, 273, 277
drug culture, 150, 175

Edey, M., 172
Eggers, C., 311
ego, 8-9
    mechanisms of restraint, 23-24, 31
    modification of psychotherapeutic tech-
        nique required by, 214-215
ego distance, 200-202
ego ideal, 133, 140, 324, 327
Eidelberg, L., 46
Eissler, K., 150
ejaculation, first, meaning of, 82-84
electroencephalographic findings, in dif-
    ferential diagnosis of nocturnal
    phenomena, 281-285
Elkind, D., 113, 114
encopresis, 22, 200
enuresis, 285
Erikson, E. H., 376, 377
eternal riddle, 374
ethical individuation, 122-125
exhibitionism, 67
externalization of identity content for in-
    fluence, 176

fairy tales, 163, 171
family therapy, 207
fantasy
    contents, shift in during second cogni-
        tive organizing period, 120-121
    hypercathexis of, 129

as masturbatory activity component,
    39-47
narcissistic investment in, intensifica-
    tion of, 129-130
prepubertal activity of, 71-75
respect for ego distance in relating to,
    200-201
fantasy objects, 309
fear of the dark, 302
Fenichel, O., 76
Ferenczi, S., 106, 108, 118, 128, 134, 135,
    278, 346
fetishes, juvenile
    emergent face, 287-290
    persistent face, 290-291
    progressive face, 294-298
    regressive face, 292-293
figure drawings, 88
Fisher, C., 284
Flavell, J., 109, 136, 210
Fliess, W., 16
fornix, 373
Fraiberg, S., 48
frame behavior, 113
Frazer, J., 79, 80, 81
Frazier, A., 164, 297
Freedman, D., 160, 360
Freedman, Z., 350
Freud, A., 20, 26, 61, 68, 76, 313
Freud, S., 15-20, 23, 27, 29, 34, 39, 40, 43,
    61, 62, 82, 84, 103, 104, 105, 109,
    132, 149, 155, 156, 157, 269, 278,
    288, 295, 336, 337, 338, 339, 340,
    341, 348, 349, 363
Friedlaender, K., 55, 58, 163, 164
Friend, M., 20
Fries, M., 149
frontal lobe, 372, 373, 374
frotteurism, 67
future planning, 34

Gaddini, R., 294
Galenson, E., 44
Gardner, B., 360
Gardner, R., 360, 364
Gardner, R. W., 313
Gibbs, E. L., 283
Gibbs, F. A., 283
Giedion, S., 368
girls, masturbatory activity in, 47-51
Glick, B. S., 284

Goldfarb, W., 307
gonadal dysgenesis, 129
Goodall, J., 360
Greenacre, P., 291
Grier, W. H., 174
guilt, 131, 139-140

hair twirling, 41, 294-295
hallucinations, 32
hallucinatory perceptual thoughts, 106
Halstead, W. C., 350
Hampson, J. G., 32
Hansel and Gretel, 112
Harrison, S., 302, 311, 312
Harkness, G., 370
Hart, M., 76, 78, 90
Hartman, E., 282
Hartmann, H., 347
Hawk, A. B., 333
Heilbronner, P., 364, 375
Henderson, F., 132
hippocampus, 373
Hockett, C., 354, 355
Hoffman, M. L., 132, 136
Homo erectus, 348, 349, 353, 354, 363
Homo sapiens, 349, 350, 363, 364
hormonal control, 129, 348
Hulse, F. S., 354
Hutton, E., 370
hypercathexis of fantasy, 129-130, 223
hypnogogic hypersynchrony, 283
hypogonadotropic males, 129
hysterical anaesthesia, 48

idiopathic isosexual puberty, 33
imaginary companion, 305
inadequate symbol formation, 185-193
incestuous fantasies, 62
incestuous feelings, 34
Incubus, 284
infancy, masturbatory activity in, motor
    and fantasy components of, 39-47
infantile amnesia, 108, 160
infantilization, 212
insular cortex, 373
intercourse, sexual, during latency years,
    69-70
internal prohibitions, 122
interpretation
    of dreams, 273-276

use of third person in, 199
interpretive cortex, 374
introjects, 122, 156, 324

Jacobson, E., 84
Jones, E., 45, 97, 99, 278, 279, 280, 358,
    365, 375
Jordan, K., 150, 307
Jung, C. G., 278

K complexes, 282
Kales, A., 283, 284
Kales, J., 283, 284
Kallmann's syndrome, 129
Kaplan, E., 49, 50
Katan, A., 62
Keiser, S., 77
Kestenberg, J., 76, 77, 78, 79
Kinsey, A., 49, 52, 55, 69, 70
Kligerman, C., 297
Kollar, E., 63
Krantz, G., 353
Krim, M. B., 32
Kris, E., 44, 46, 150
Kuhn, H., 366

Lamarckian evolution, 346, 348-349
Lampl-de Groot, J., 39, 46, 51
language acquisition, prehistoric origins
    of, 350-368
language phylogenesis, 350-368
late latency-early adolescence, 59-69, 301
latency and character, 155
latency and culture, 18, 157
latency and society, 155
Laufer, M., 60
Leibnitz, G. W., 362, 363
Lerner, I., 350, 355, 360, 362
Leroi-Gourhan, A., 166, 349, 351, 354, 356,
    357, 358, 364, 366, 371, 372
Levin, S., 67
Levine, M., 41, 44
Levy, E. Z., 150
Little Hans, 29
Lopandin, V. M., 311
lulling, of therapist, problems in motiva-
    tion in psychotherapy and, 243-246

Macnish, 279
Magdalenian period, 365
magical powers of words, 35
Mahler, M., 293, 307
Malinowski, B., 31, 38, 69
marijuana addiction, 150
mastery through symbols, 159-160
masturbatory activity
   in boys, latency age, 51-54
   in girls, latency age, 47-51
   motor and fantasy components of, from
      infancy to latency, 39-47
masturbatory content, during state of latency, 55-58
masturbation, 39, 47 (girls), 51 (boys)
   genital, 44
   masked, 50, 52, 54
   scrotal, 51
   adolescent, 63-69
masturbation fantasies
   earliest, 44ff.
   prelatency, 46
   sadistic, 46, 50, 53
   state of latency, 55ff.
   late latency-early adolescence, 59
mature sublimative creativity, 320
maturational lag, 382
mature system consciousness, 189, 273,
   339-341
Mead, M., 356, 359, 367
media for transmission of culture, 168
medial pulvinar nucleus, 373
memory organization, development of
   abstract conceptual, 117-120
   affecto-motor, 106
   verbal conceptual, 106-108
Menaker, E., 348
menarche, 76-82
   delay of, 356
   organizing function of, 79
menopause, 356
metaphors, 97
Modell, A., 364
Money, J., 128, 129
moral judgment, 110, 113
morality
   of cooperation, 110, 111
   of restraint, 110, 111
Moriarty, A., 313
motivation for displacement, 101
motivation, in psychotherapy, problems
   of, in latency state, 229-246

lulling, 243-246
motor activity and masturbation, 55-58
   syntaxes of, 211-212
mourning, 253, 384
multiple class culture, 175
Murphy, R., 80, 168, 175, 176, 356, 370,
   376, 377
Murphy, Y., 30, 168, 175, 176, 356, 370,
   376, 377
myth, 164, 167
   and culture, 167
mythic basis of identity, 167
mythopoesis, 155
myths, role in latency of, 168

narcissism
   in early adolescence, 129
narcissistic cathexis, 224-225, 384
Neanderthal man (New Paleoanthropes),
   349
neurotic symptoms, 385
New Anthropes, 349, 350
nocturnal phenomena
   arousal, disorders of, 279-280
   electroencephalographic findings, 281-
      285
   occurring during sleep in childhood,
      differential diagnosis of, 276-285
   night fears, 302-304
   nightmares, 277
   night terror, or pavor nocturnus, 277
nudity, 162

object constancy, 136
object relations, 33, 126, 301
   impaired, 308
obsessive-compulsive symptoms, 89, 124,
   217, 307, 385
Oedipus complex, 20, 138, 160
Old Paleoanthropes, 354
omnipotence, 63
omnipotentiality, 63
oral regressions, 241, 267, 384
orgasm, 153
   boys, 52-53
   girls, 48-49
overstimulation, during latency, 162, 208-
   209

paranoia, 299-312
  benign persecutory states, 301-305
  differential diagnosis, summary and
    guidelines, 327-334
  pathologically significant persecutory
    states, 306-312
paranoid schizophrenia of early onset,
  310-312
paraphrenia, 311
parapraxias, 265
parasitic cultures, 174
Pardies, I., 362, 363
parents, working with, psychotherapeutic
    strategies for, 205-214
  children who manipulate parents
    through words, 209-212
  distinguishing image of therapist from
    image of parent, 207-209
  infantilization, stunting of personality
    growth through, 213-214
passive-fusion strivings, 39
passive mastery, 159
  control of societies, 163
passive participation, 165
passive symbolization, 159-160
pathology, conditions in latency, 381-386
pavor diurnus, 280
pavor nocturnus, or night terror, 277
peer group influence, 122
Peller, L., 159
Penfield, W., 351, 373, 374
penis envy, 46, 73-75, 270, 316
percept consciousness, 337
persecutory fantasies, 120, 121, 306ff.
personality growth, stunting of, through
    infantilization, 213-214
phobias, 385
  phobic avoidance reactions, 121, 159
  phobic symptoms, 94, 120, 217, 280, 300
phylogenesis, 14, 19, 343-380
physiognomic thinking, 42, 288
phytophobia, 94
Piaget, J., 35, 40-45, 98, 99, 101, 102, 103,
    104, 105, 106, 107, 108, 109, 110,
    113, 114, 116, 118, 136, 137, 177,
    205, 210, 288, 294, 358
Pincus, J., 373
Pittell, S., 150
play therapy, 185-263
Preanthropes, 354
preconscious, 336
Premack, A. J., 361

Premack, D., 361
premature puberty, 32
prepuberty
  fantasy activity, 71-75
prepubescent schizophrenia, 308-310
primal repression, 104
primal system consciousness, 336
primary creativity, 43, 289
primitive societies, latency in, 376-377
projection, 312-327
  differential diagnosis, summary and
    guidelines, 327-334
  preadolescent, in third cognitive orga-
    nizing period, 126-127
  vicissitudes of, 312-327
  manifestations, 315-327
projection-introjection, 325
Prugh, D., 150, 307
pseudologia fantastica, 67
psychoanalytic symbols, 45, 97, 121, 159
psychosis, 300-334
psychosomatic disorders, 124
psychosomatic forms of expression, 89
psychosomatic symptoms, 101
pubertal changes, 127
Pumpian-Mindlin, E., 61, 63

Rapaport, D., 33, 312-313
Rapoport, J., 309
Read, K. E., 377
Reich, A., 59, 61
Reich, W., 156
Reinach, S., 323, 367
REM states, 282-283
Rensch, B., 350
regression, 19, 20, 31, 152, 292
  to prelatency behavior, 383
  in the structure of latency, 383
  of symbolizing function, 24
  removal, 62
representational triad, 159
repression
  in first cognitive organizing period, 103-
    106
  prehistoric origins of, 350-368
  primal, 104
  proper, 104
resistance to culture change, 175
robber fantasies, 26, 318
Roberts, L., 351, 374
Roe, A., 350

Roheim, G., 155
Rosenblum, R., 172

Sachs, H., 165
Sachs, L., 280
Schachtel, E., 108, 118, 149, 160, 161
Scheinfeld, A., 79
schemata, 40, 160
schizophrenia
    paranoid, of early onset, 310-312
    prepubescent, 308-310
school avoidance and phobia, 301
scoptophilia, 67
Schulman, D, 284
Schumann, S., 311
secondary symbolism, 99, 360
security blanket, 41, 287
seductions, 162, 383
    by adults, 70
separation-individuation, 307
sensorimotor component of masturbatory
        activity, 39-47
sexual development, 37-84
    first ejaculation, meaning of, 82-84
    first menstrual period, impact of, 76-82
    late latency-early adolescence, 59-69
    masturbatory activity during
        in boys, 51-54
        in girls, 47-51
        motor and fantasy components, 39-47
    masturbatory content during, 55-58
    prepubertal fantasy activity, 71-75
sexual intercourse during latency, 69-70
shame, 176, 369
shame superego, 134, 369
Silverman, J., 124, 302
Simpson, W. K., 366
Sinanthopus, 354
sleep spindles, 282
sleep stages, 282
sleepwalking, 277, 281
slips of the tongue, working with, psycho-
        therapeutic strategies, 265-273
    denial of, 266
social organization and latency, 173-180
society, influence of latency on, 157-181
somatic disturbances, sleep and, 377
Sours, J. A., 284
Sperling, M., 100, 280, 281, 284, 291
Sperling, O., 305
sphincter morality, 133-134, 137

Spiegel, L., 68
Spitz, R., 40, 44, 283, 293, 349
state of latency, failure to enter, 26, 382
Sterba, E., 100
Stevenson, R. L., 170
Still, F., 280
Stoyanov, S., 311
stress events
    psychotherapeutic strategies for deal-
        ing with, 202-203
    respect for ego distance in relating
        fantasy to, 200-202
structure of latency, 24, 31, 163
    regressed, 383
structured society, 173
Stutte, H., 306, 307, 311, 312
sublimations, encouraging, 211-212
    maturation of, 318
Sullivan, W., 360
superego
    cognition, 130-146
    contents, reorganization of, 122-125
    development, cognition and, 130-144
    ego functions that implement superego
        demands, 153
    guilt, 135
    middle latency development, 209
    motivating affects, 132, 369-371
        origins of, 369-371
    poor formation of, 138, 162, 383
    positive affects, 132
superior speech cortex, 374
survival, symbols and, 377-380
Switzer, J., 118, 119
symbiotic reactions, 301
symbol formation
    development of, 92-93
    inadequate, psychotherapeutic strate-
        gies for dealing with, 185-193
        theoretical basis, 188-193
    regressed (failure to enter latency),
        psychotherapeutic strategies for
        dealing with, 197-200
symbolic linkages, 102
symbolic play, 102
symbolizing function, 185
    and psychopathology, 185, 279, 382
symbols
    and abstraction, 358, 359
    affect porous, 145
    development of, 92-102

exterioration of nonconcrete signifiers, 357
metaphorical, 358, 359, 375
passive symbolization, 159-160
phylogenesis, 350, 368
prehistoric origins, 350-368
psychoanalytic, 45, 97, 121, 159
   failure in maturation of, 382
   failure to develop, 382
   survival value, 377
synchronized high-voltage slow waves, 283
syntax, 106, 351
syntaxes of motor skills, 117, 351
system consciousness, ontogenesis of, 335-341
   abstract, 338-339
   mature, 339-341
   primal, 337-339
system preconscious, 336
system unconscious, 340
Szurek, S., 307

temporal cortex, 373, 374
tension discharge disorders, 383
termination, 247-262
theta waves, 282
Ticho, E., 341
Ticho, G., 272
tool use, 349, 351, 352
topographic theory, 335, 349
transference, 233, 257, 260
transient paranoid states, 304
transitional objects/phenomena, 285-298
   emergent face, 287-289
   persistent face, 290-291

progressive face, 294-298
regressive face, 292-293
transmission of culture, 157-182
Tucker, G., 373
Turner's syndrome, 32, 33

vaginal sensations, 48
value judgment, development of brain areas necessary for, 371-376
Valium, 285
verbal conceptual memory, 106
vicissitudes of projection, 312-326
vulnerable children, 383

Waelder, R., 314
Warren, A., 181
Washburn, S. L., 353, 354
Wellek, R., 181
Werner, H., 67
Werner, Heinz, 42, 44, 45, 288
Wernicke's area, 353, 372
Whitehead, A. N., 367
Winnicott, D. W., 43, 288, 290, 291, 292, 294
Woodward, M., 35, 40, 116, 294
words, naming vs drive representation, 43
work of latency, 147-182
Wulff, M., 99, 100

Yaholom, I., 291

Zinjanthropus, 351